WOMEN, THE STATE AND REVOLUTION

When the Bolsheviks came to power in 1917, they widely believed that under socialism, the family would "wither away." They envisioned a society in which communal dining halls, daycare centers, and public laundries would replace the unpaid labor of women in the home. Freed from their domestic burden, women would achieve equality with men. Mutual affection and respect would replace legal and economic dependence as the basis for relations between the sexes. A generation of Soviet lawmakers thus crafted legislation to liberate women and encourage the "withering away" of the family. They legalized abortion in 1920 and made it available to women free of charge. Yet by 1936 social experimentation had given way to increasingly conservative solutions aimed at strengthening traditional family ties and women's reproductive role. The state outlawed abortion. Party officials denounced the revolutionary ideas of the 1920s as "petty-bourgeois anarchist propaganda." This book examines this great social reversal, focusing on the dynamic relationship between state and society in the retreat from the ideology of the revolution. It explores how women, peasants, and orphaned street children responded to Bolshevik attempts to remake the family, and how their opinions and experiences in turn were used by the state to meet its own needs.

For other titles in this series, turn to page 356.

WOMEN, THE STATE AND REVOLUTION
Soviet Family Policy and Social Life, 1917–1936

WENDY Z. GOLDMAN

Carnegie Mellon University

CAMBRIDGE
UNIVERSITY PRESS

Published by the Press Syndicate of the University of Cambridge
The Pitt Building, Trumpington Street, Cambridge CB2 1RP
40 West 20th Street, New York, NY 10011-4211, USA
10 Stamford Road, Oakleigh, Melbourne 3166, Australia

First published 1993
Reprinted 1995

Library of Congress Cataloging-in-Publication Data is available.

A catalogue record for this book is available from the British Library.

ISBN 0-521-37404-9 hardback
ISBN 0-521-45816-1 paperback

Transferred to digital printing 2004

This book is dedicated to my parents
JUDITH and LAWRENCE GOLDMAN
to their values and their ideals

Contents

Tables

Acknowledgments

Many people and institutions have helped me with this project. Fellowships from the International Research and Exchanges Board allowed me to pursue research in the United States in 1983–1984 and in the Soviet Union in 1984–1985. The Social Science Research Council provided two years of funding, and the National Endowment for the Humanities granted fellowships for the summer of 1989, and the academic year 1990–1991. The history department of Carnegie Mellon University relieved me of teaching duties for a semester. I am grateful to several publishers for their permission to reprint certain material. Portions of Chapter 6 appeared in "Working-Class Women and the 'Withering Away' of the Family: Popular Responses to Family Policy," in *Russia in the Era of NEP: Explorations in Soviet Society and Culture*, eds. Sheila Fitzpatrick, Alexander Rabinowitch, and Richard Stites (Bloomington, Indiana University Press, 1991) and in "Freedom and Its Consequences: The Debate on the Soviet Family Code of 1926," *Russian History*, Vol. 11, No. 4, 1984. Chapter 7 first appeared in "Abortion, the State and Soviet Women, 1917–1936," in *Russian Women: Accommodation, Resistance, Transformation*, eds., Barbara Clements, Barbara Engel, Christine Worobec (Berkeley, Los Angeles, University of California Press, 1991). O. I. Chistiakov, Yury Druzhnikov, Carol Leonard, Kate Lynch, Richard Pisani, Leslie Rowland, Ken Straus, Richard Stites, and Ronald Suny all deserve thanks for their help and comments at various stages of this work. Amy Stanley eagerly read and discussed, helped at every stage and in every way, and was close through the best and the worst of it. Barbara Clements took much time to make the manuscript a better book, and I am grateful for her efforts. Barbara Engel's principled criticism, advice, and willingness to share ideas and opportunities have given me a model of how women in the profession can help each other to advance a common project. At our first meeting in a gloomy dormitory room at Moscow State University, we began a discussion on women that has continued, in a variety of improbable settings, over the years. I want to thank my advisor, Alfred J. Rieber, for all his help and for reaching out at a critical time. Most of all, I want to thank my husband, Marcus Rediker. The ideas of this book have been part of a lasting political conversation, and he, more than anyone, has helped me to shape its substance, style, and direction. He has been my greatest source of encouragement, my sharpest critic, and always, my "first reader."

1

The origins of the Bolshevik vision: Love unfettered, women free

It is a curious fact that with every great revolutionary movement the question of "free love" comes into the foreground.

Frederick Engels, 1883[1]

[The family] will be sent to a museum of antiquities so that it can rest next to the spinning wheel and the bronze axe, by the horsedrawn carriage, the steam engine, and the wired telephone.

S. Ia. Vol'fson, 1929, Soviet sociologist[2]

In October 1918, barely a year after the Bolsheviks had come to power, the Central Executive Committee of the Soviet (VTsIK), the highest legislative body, ratified a complete Code on Marriage, the Family, and Guardianship. The Code captured in law a revolutionary vision of social relations based on women's equality and the "withering away" (*otmiranie*) of the family. According to Alexander Goikhbarg, the young, idealistic author of the new Family Code, it prepared the way for a time when "the fetters of husband and wife" would become "obsolete." The Code was accordingly constructed with its own obsolescence in mind. Goikhbarg wrote, "Proletarian power constructs its codes and all of its laws dialectically, so that every day of their existence undermines the need for their existence." In short, the aim of law was "to make law superfluous."[3]

Goikhbarg and his fellow revolutionaries fully expected not

---

[1] Frederick Engels, as cited in Christopher Hill, *The World Turned Upside Down. Radical Ideas during the English Revolution* (Penguin Books, New York, 1975): 306.

[2] S. Ia. Vol'fson, *Sotsiologiia braka i sem'i* (Minsk, 1929): 450.

[3] A. G. Goikhbarg, "Pervyi Kodeks Zakonov RSFSR," *Proletarskaia revoliutsiia i pravo*, 7 (1918): 4, 8, 9.

only marriage and the family to wither away, but the law and the state as well. Lenin had carefully analyzed the future of the state in his famous essay, *The State and Revolution*, completed in September 1917, merely a month before the Bolsheviks took power. Based on Marx's and Engels's widely scattered remarks on the nature of the state, the ideas in *The State and Revolution* eventually came to represent the more utopian, libertarian, and antistatist strand within the contradictory corpus of Lenin's own thought as well as subsequent Marxist theory. Arguing vigorously against reformism in the social democratic movement, Lenin held that victorious revolutionaries would have to smash the bourgeois state and create a new state in its place. Yet the new "dictatorship of the proletariat" would be for the vast majority democratic, its power mobilized solely to eliminate the old exploiters. Its aim, the suppression of a minority by the majority, would be "so easy, simple, and natural a task," that the people could "suppress the exploiters even with a very simple 'machine.'" In Lenin's words, "since the majority of the people *itself* suppresses its oppressors, a 'special force' for suppression *is no longer necessary!* In this sense the state *begins to wither away.*"[4]

The ideas in *The State and Revolution* influenced Bolshevik thinking well into the 1930s. Engels's famous remark, quoted prominently by Lenin, that the machinery of state would be placed "into the museum of antiquities, next to the spinning wheel and the bronze axe,"[5] was repeated almost verbatim in 1929 by S. Ia Vol'fson, a Soviet sociologist, in reference to the family. Jurists, social theorists, and activists provided challenging theoretical and historical analyses to support these views. In brief, the Bolsheviks believed that capitalism had created a new contradiction, felt most painfully by women, between the demands of work and the needs of family. As more and more women were forced to work for wages with the advent of industrialization, the conflict between the demands of production and reproduction resulted in high infant mortality, broken homes, neglected children, and chronic health problems. A glance through the filthy windows of any nineteenth-century Russian

---

[4] V. I. Lenin, "The State and Revolution," *Selected Works*, Vol. 2 (Progress, Moscow, 1970): 352, 353, 317.

[5] Frederick Engels, *The Origin of the Family, Private Property and the State* (International, New York, 1972): 232.

factory dormitory provided ample support for their view. Women had entered the workforce, but they were still responsible for child rearing, cooking, cleaning, sewing, mending – the mindless drudgery of housework essential to the family. Women's household responsibilities prevented them from entering the public worlds of work, politics, and creative endeavor on an equal footing with men. Capitalism, according to the Bolsheviks, would never be able to provide a systematic solution to the double burden women shouldered.

The Bolsheviks argued that only socialism could resolve the contradiction between work and family. Under socialism, household labor would be transferred to the public sphere: The tasks performed by millions of individual unpaid women in their homes would be taken over by paid workers in communal dining rooms, laundries, and childcare centers. Women would be freed to enter the public sphere on an equal basis with men, unhampered by the duties of the home. At last women would be equally educated, waged, and able to pursue their own individual goals and development. Under such circumstances, marriage would become superfluous. Men and women would come together and separate as they wished, apart from the deforming pressures of economic dependency and need. Free union would gradually replace marriage as the state ceased to interfere in the union between the sexes. Parents, regardless of their marital status, would care for their children with the help of the state; the very concept of illegitimacy would become obsolete. The family, stripped of its previous social functions, would gradually wither away, leaving in its place fully autonomous, equal individuals free to choose their partners on the basis of love and mutual respect.

Throw out the household pots

In the heady months immediately following the Revolution, many Bolshevik theorists and activists predicted a rapid transition to the new social order. At a 1918 conference of women workers, Inessa Armand, the head of the Zhenotdel (Women's Department of the Party), declared with naive fervor, "The bourgeois order is being abolished. . . . Separate households are

harmful survivals that only delay and hinder new forms of distribution. They should be abolished."[6] The policies of war communism (1918–1921) contributed to the idea that new socialist
forms would quickly supplant the old. State rationing, public
dining halls, free food for children, and wages in kind all supported the optimistic assessment that household labor would
soon vanish. P. I. Stuchka, the first People's Commissar of Justice, later noted, "The period of war communism showed us one
thing: a plan for the free family of the future when the family's
roles as a cell of production and consumption, as a juridical
entity, as a social insurer, as a bastion of inequality, and as a unit
for feeding and bringing up children would all disappear."[7]
Alexandra Kollontai, one of the few female Bolshevik leaders
and author of numerous works on women's issues, optimistically
surveyed the weakened state of the family at the end of the civil
war and proclaimed it *already* outmoded: "In the present time,
when social feeding has replaced individual consumption and
become an independent branch of the people's economy, not a
single one of the economic bonds that created stability for the
proletarian family for centuries remains." The state had already
assumed the upbringing and support of children, Kollontai explained, and once household labor was transferred to the realm
of waged labor, nothing of the family would remain except a
"psychological tie." The institution of marriage had become irrelevant because it entailed "no economic or social tasks" and no
longer needed "to be subject to the account, control, or leadership of the collective."[8]

Kollontai's enthusiasm may have been somewhat premature,
but she was not alone in her thinking. Jurists, Party members,
social planners, and women's activists, among others, widely promulgated the notion throughout the 1920s that the family would

[6] As remembered and quoted by Sophia Smidovich, "O Novom Kodekse Zakonov o Brake i Sem'e," *Kommunistka*, 1 (1926): 45.

[7] P. Stuchka, "Semeinoe Pravo," *Revoliutsiia prava*, 1 (1925): 180.

[8] A. Kollontai, "Sem'ia i Kommunizm," *Kommunistka*, 7 (1920): 17, 18.
On Kollontai and her contribution see Barbara Clements, *Bolshevik
Feminist. The Life of Aleksandra Kollontai* (Indiana University Press,
Bloomington, 1979) and "Emancipation through Communism: The
Ideology of A. M. Kollontai," *Slavic Review*, 30 (1973): 323–338; Beat-
rice Farnsworth, *Alexandra Kollontai. Socialism, Feminism, and the Bol-
shevik Revolution* (Stanford University Press, Stanford, 1980).

soon wither away. Hundreds of pamphlets, books, and articles were published for academic and popular audiences on the creation of a "new life" under socialism.[9] Discussions raged among young people. The family's sexual division of labor, legal foundation, moral credibility, and economic efficiency were all called into question. Although Party theorists shared the belief that the family would eventually wither away, they expressed numerous differences on family and social relations. The Party did not maintain a rigid orthodoxy and differences were freely expressed, especially regarding such contentious issues as sexual relations, child rearing, and the need for the family in the transition to socialism.

Given that the family was widely expected to wither away, the issue of how to organize household labor provoked extensive discussion. Lenin spoke and wrote repeatedly of the need to socialize housework, describing it as "the most unproductive, the most savage, and the most arduous work a woman can do." Sparing no harsh adjective, he wrote that "petty housework crushes" and "degrades" a woman, "chains her to the kitchen and the nursery" where "she wastes her labor on barbarously unproductive, petty, nervewracking, and stultifying drudgery." Lenin obviously despised housework. He argued that "the real emancipation of women" must include not only legal equality, but "the wholesale transformation" of household into socialized labor.[10]

Kollontai, too, argued that under socialism all household tasks would be eliminated and consumption would cease to be individual and internal to the family. The private kitchen would be replaced by the public dining hall. Sewing, cleaning, and washing, like mining, metallurgy, and machine production, would become branches of the people's economy. The family, in Kollontai's estimation, constituted an inefficient use of labor, food, and fuel. "From the point of view of the people's economy," the family was "not only useless, but harmful."[11] And Evgeny Pre-

[9] See, for example, the collection of articles gathered by Em. Iaroslavskii, *Voprosy zhizni i bor'by. Sbornik* (Molodaia Gvardiia, Leningrad, 1924.)
[10] V. I. Lenin, *The Emancipation of Women* (New York, 1934): 63, 69.
[11] A. Kollontai, "Tezisy o Kommunisticheskoi Morali v Oblasti Brachnykh Otnoshenii," *Kommunistka*, 12–13 (1921): 29.

obrazhenskii, the well-known Soviet economist, noted that the traditional division of labor in the family prevented a woman from achieving real equality by placing "a burden on her that comes before all else." The only solution, according to Preobrazhenskii, was a "great public cauldron, replacing the household pot."[12]

Unlike modern feminists, who argue for a redivision of household tasks *within the family*, increasing men's share of domestic responsibilities, Bolshevik theorists sought to transfer housework to the public sphere. Preobrazhenskii expressed this difference crisply. "Our task does not consist of striving for justice in the division of labor between the sexes," he wrote, "Our task is to free men and women from petty household labor."[13] The abolition of the family, rather than gender conflict within it, held the key to women's emancipation. The socialization of household labor would eliminate women's dependence on men and promote a new freedom in relations between the sexes. Trotsky declared that as soon as "washing [was] done by a public laundry, catering by a public restaurant, sewing by a public workshop," "the bond between husband and wife would be freed from everything external and accidental." New relationships, "compulsory for no one," would develop based on mutual feelings.[14] The Soviet marital ideal of the 1920s was a partnership of equals, a union of comrades founded on mutual affection and united by common interests.[15]

Soviet theorists recognized that a companionate union required that women become the equals of men. The writer M. Shishkevich, offering advice to a broad audience of workers and peasants, remarked, "How often quarrels and fights occur because the spouses grow apart in their views. A husband reads a little, goes to a lecture, sees how others look at life. But a wife is with the kitchen pots all the time, gossiping with the neighbors."

[12] E. Preobrazhenskii, "Put'k Raskreposhcheniiu Zhenshchiny," *Kommunistka*, 7 (1920): 19.

[13] Ibid., p. 20.

[14] Leon Trotsky, "From the Old Family to the New," *Pravda*, July 13, 1923, reprinted in his *Women and the Family* (Pathfinder Press, New York, 1970): 26.

[15] For a discussion of the changing Soviet marital ideal, see Vladimir Shlapentokh, *Love, Marriage, and Friendship in the Soviet Union. Ideals and Practices* (Praeger, New York, 1984).

If women did not participate in cultural and political life, their relations with men could not be based on mutual respect. Invoking the ideal of companionate union, Shishkevich counseled his readers: "The participation of both spouses in public life eases mutual understanding, and develops respect toward the wife as an equal, a friend and a comrade."[16] Soviet theorists foresaw relations based on "free union" or "free love." Lenin, it should be noted, strongly disliked these terms because of their association with bourgeois promiscuity. But he nonetheless held that without love, there was no basis for a relationship. "One cannot be a democrat and a socialist," he wrote, "without demanding full freedom of divorce."[17]

Yet how long were unions based on mutual feelings expected to last? For a day, a year, a lifetime? Soviet theorists differed in their answers. Some foresaw a free sexuality limited only by natural desire. Kollontai contended that morality, like the family, was historically constructed and therefore subject to change. "In nature there is neither morality nor immorality," she wrote. "The satisfaction of healthy and natural instinct only ceases to be normal when it transcends the limits established by hygiene." She explained, "The sexual act should be recognized as neither shameful nor sinful, but natural and legal, as much a manifestation of a healthy organism as the quenching of hunger or thirst." Lenin took a more conservative position, displaying his hidebound Victorian prejudices in the very metaphor of his reply: "To be sure," he wrote, "thirst has to be quenched. But would a normal person lie down in the gutter and drink from a puddle?"[18]

Semen Iakovlevich Vol'fson, a sociologist and professor of law, economy, and dialectical materialism, agreed with Kollontai, arguing that the duration of marriage would "be defined exclusively by the mutual inclination of the spouses." Affection and attraction would be the sole determinants of the duration of a relationship. Against Kautsky's prediction that the family would

---

[16] M. Shishkevich, "Sem'ia i Brak v Usloviiakh Novogo Byta," in *Sem'ia i brak v proshlom i nastoiashchem* (Moscow, 1925): 101–102.

[17] See Lenin's exchange with Inessa Armand in Lenin, *The Emancipation of Women*, pp. 36–40, 42.

[18] Kollontai, "Tezisy o Kommunisticheskoi Morali v Oblasti Brachnykh Otnoshenii," p. 31; Lenin, *The Emancipation of Women*, p. 106.

be preserved under socialism as an "ethical unit," Vol'fson snorted, "The family as an 'ethical unit,' deprived of its social and economic functions, is simply nonsense."[19]

Others were more cautious in their approach to sexuality. Shishkevich agreed that "under the conditions of new life we will achieve full freedom of sexual union," but he saw the need to limit sexual freedom during the transition period. As long as the state could not care for children and as long as sex entailed the possibility of pregnancy, men should not be freed of their responsibilities toward women. "If the question is resolved in favor of the sexual irresponsibility of men," he wrote, "then there is no doubt that in our economic conditions, women and mothers will suffer."[20] For women, fear of pregnancy was still the great stumbling block to the free expression of sexuality.

Lenin, too, stressed the social consequences of sexual relations, although he was deeply uncomfortable with speculations about sexuality in general, and considered such preoccupations idle and unproductive diversions. "I mistrust those who are always absorbed in the sex problem," he told Clara Zetkin, "the way an Indian saint is absorbed in the contemplation of his navel." Concerned about the consequences of free sexuality in a precontraceptive society, Lenin noted that an individual's personal behavior assumed a new importance for the collective when children were involved. "It takes two people to make love," he said, "but a third person, a new life, is likely to come into being. This deed has a social complexion and constitutes a duty to the community."[21]

Clearly, the fate and upbringing of children was central to any discussion of sexuality. And here too, Soviet theorists differed. All vaguely agreed that eventually all children would be cared for by the state in public nurseries, childcare centers, and schools. Zinaida Tettenborn, an expert on illegitimacy and the rights of children, confidently declared: "Upbringing will be equal, the same for all children, and not one child will be in a worse position than any other."[22] Yet Soviet theorists remained

[19] S. Ia. Vol'fson, *Sotsiologiia braka i sem'i*, p. 446.
[20] Shishkevich, p. 110.
[21] Lenin, pp. 101, 106.
[22] Zinaida Tettenborn, "Roditel'skie Prava v Pervom Kodekse Zakonov RSFSR," *Proletarskaia revoliutsiia i pravo*, 1 (1919): 26, 27.

uncertain about how to implement this principled prescription. Were parents to retain a primary role in their children's upbringing? Or was the state to assume the parental role in its entirety? Some theorists argued that parents were not fit to bring up children: Parental ignorance and family egoism stunted children's development and narrowed their outlook. The state could do a far better job of rearing healthy citizens. Others held that the state would simply help parents to combine work with child rearing through an array of supplementary services.

V. Diushen, an educator, set out a painstakingly detailed blueprint in 1921 in which he argued that the egotistical spirit of the family was incompatible with socialist ethics. The family, he wrote, "opposes its interests to society's, and assumes that only those people related by blood deserve help and care." Mothers did children more harm than good, for even "mother-pedagogues" were incapable of approaching "their children with sufficient objectivity." Diushen constructed an elaborate plan for entire children's settlements and towns, populated by 800 to 1,000 children, aged 3 to 18. Houses would be separated by age and sex, headed by specially qualified pedagogues, and governed by a soviet composed of children, teachers, and technical personnel. Diushen even planned outings in which the children in the settlements would visit families to "see the seamy side of life."[23] Diushen's grim view of the parental role was shared by Goikhbarg, author of the Family Code. Goikhbarg encouraged parents to reject "their narrow and irrational love for their children." In his view, state upbringing would "provide vastly better results than the private, individual, unscientific, and irrational approach of individually 'loving' but ignorant parents."[24] Diushen sought to create democratic, communal organizations to counter the hierarchical, authoritarian relations within the family. And both he and Goikhbarg sought to substitute science for love, the "rationality" of educators for the "irrationality" of parents.

[23] V. Diushen, "Problemy Zhenskogo Kommunisticheskogo Dvizheniia – Problemy Sotsial'nogo Vospitaniia," *Kommunistka*, 12–13 (1921): 26–27.

[24] A. G. Goikhbarg, *Brachnoe, semeinoe, i opekunskoe pravo Sovetskoi respubliki* (Moscow, 1920): 5.

Kollontai was less critical of parents, but she too foresaw a greatly expanded role for the state. In her view, the attenuation of the parent–child bond was historically inevitable. Under capitalism economic want prevented parents from spending time with children. Forced to work at a young age, children quickly gained economic independence: "The authority of the parents weakens and obedience is at an end." Alluding to Engels's depiction of the family in *The Condition of the Working Class in England*, she concluded, "Just as housework withers away, so the obligation of parents to their children withers away." Communism would complete this process. "Society will feed, bring up, and educate the child," Kollontai predicted, although parents would still preserve emotional bonds with their offspring. Women would have the opportunity to combine motherhood and work without worrying about the welfare of their children. According to Kollontai, a woman would give birth and then return "to the work she does for the large family-society." Children would grow up in the crèche or nursery, the kindergarten, the children's colony, and the school under the care of experienced nurses and teachers. And whenever a mother wanted to see her child, "She only has to say the word."[25]

Tettenborn placed more emphasis on the parent–child bond, although she too imagined a large role for the state. Public upbringing, in her view, would not "remove parents from their children" but allow them more time together. Socialized child rearing would be organized democratically. Happily anticipating the future, she wrote, "We will then be in a completely democratic society. The upbringing committee will consist of parents – men and women – and their children."[26]

Soviet theorists thus differed on how large a role parents would play in their children's upbringing, but they all agreed that the state would render substantial help and that motherhood would no longer keep women out of the workforce and public life. Most important, as the state assumed much of the burden of child rearing, the family would lose yet another social function that had historically provided its basis for existence. In the words of the jurist Iakov Brandenburgskii: "We are un-

[25] Alexandra Kollontai, "Communism and the Family," in her *Selected Writings* (W. W. Norton, New York, London, 1977): 257–258, 134.
[26] Tettenborn, pp. 26, 27.

doubtedly moving toward the social feeding of children, to compulsory free schools, to the broadest social welfare at state expense." And as "the government develops and becomes stronger, as its help becomes all the more real, the broad family group will gradually disappear."[27]

In sum, Soviet theorists held that the transition to capitalism had transformed the family by undermining its social and economic functions. Under socialism, it would wither away, and under communism, it would cease to exist entirely. In Kollontai's words, "The family – deprived of all economic tasks, not holding responsibility for a new generation, no longer providing women with the basic source of their existence – ceases to be a family. It narrows and is transformed into a union of the marital pair based on mutual contract."[28]

The Bolsheviks thus offered a seemingly straightforward solution to women's oppression. Yet their prescriptions, despite an outward simplicity, rested on complex assumptions about the sources and meaning of liberation. First, they assumed that household labor should be removed, almost in its entirety, from the home. It would not be redivided along new gender lines within the family. The Bolsheviks did not challenge men to share in "women's work," but sought simply to transfer the tasks to the public domain. Although they frequently noted that men should "help" women at home, they were not deeply concerned with remaking gender roles within the family.

Second, they assumed that women would only be free if they entered the world of wage labor. Rather than reconsider the value society attached to the tasks women performed at home, they spurned domestic labor as the mind-numbing progenitor of political backwardness. Only a separate wage could offer women economic independence and access to a wider public world. If women were to be liberated economically and psychologically, they needed to become more like men, or more specifically, more like male workers.

Third, the Bolsheviks attached little importance to the powerful emotional bonds between parents and their children. They

---

[27] Ia. N. Brandenburgskii, *Kurs semeino-brachnogo prava* (Moscow, 1928): 20.

[28] Kollontai, "Tezisy o Kommunisticheskoi Morali v Oblasti Brachnykh Otnoshenii," p. 29.

assumed that most of the necessary care for children, even infants, could be relegated to paid, public employees. They tended to slight the role of the mother–child bond in infant survival and early childhood development, although even a rudimentary acquaintance with the work of the prerevolutionary foundling homes would have revealed the shockingly low survival rates for infants in institutional settings and the obstacles to healthy child development.[29] In the views of many theorists, the problems posed by children appeared almost identical to those of housework. Their solutions therefore were roughly the same.

Fourth, the socialist vision of liberation held within it a certain tension between the individual and the collective or the state. Although the Bolsheviks advocated personal freedom for the individual and the elimination of religious and state authority in matters of sexual choice, they assumed that the state would take on the tasks of child rearing and household labor. Thus while Bolshevik ideology promoted the libertarian freedom of the individual, it also enlarged immeasurably the social role of the state by eliminating intermediary bodies like the family. Ideally, the individual and the collective stood in dialectical balance, the very freedom of the first assured by the increased care and responsibility of the second. In this sense, the vision of sexual freedom did not differ appreciably from the larger Marxian promise of individual creative fulfillment in the context of a widely socialized economy. Yet the ideal was subject to imbalance, and the tension between individual freedom and the powerful increase in state functions and control generated an increasingly savage struggle into the early 1930s.

Stripped of embellishment, the Bolshevik vision was thus based on four primary precepts: free union, women's emancipation through wage labor, the socialization of housework, and the withering away of the family. Each of these had its own distinct history, though they conjoined at different moments in time. The idea of free union developed first, surfacing in the Middle Ages, and again, in the seventeenth century, yet detached from any commitment to women's liberation. It was followed in the eighteenth century by debates on women's equality and a grow-

[29] For an excellent treatment of the prerevolutionary foundling homes, see David Ransel, *Mothers of Misery. Child Abandonment in Russia* (Princeton University Press, Princeton, N.J., 1988).

ing consciousness of women's oppression. In the nineteenth century, free union and women's emancipation were welded to demands for the socialization of household labor and the withering away of the family, all now supported by a larger emphasis on the state as the primary source of social welfare. Most of these ideas were born of and sustained by movements for a more just, communal social order. By tracing their origins and trajectories it will be possible to establish the intellectual foundations of Bolshevik thought on women and the family and to suggest what was new and original in the contribution of the generation of revolutionaries who came to power in 1917.

Free union

Throughout the Middle Ages, the church accused numerous sects of the heresies of libertinage and free union. In the twelfth century, the Brethren of the Free Spirit eagerly awaited a final stage in the world's history when men would be tutored directly by God. A hundred years later, French believers claimed that a man truly united with God was incapable of sin.[30] In the fourteenth century, the *beguines* and *beghards* of Germany, small groups who dedicated themselves to poverty and a simple communal life, were accused of promulgating the heresy of the Free Spirit, the notion that "where the spirit of the Lord is, there is liberty" and that people could practice sex without sin. This idea was given voice again by Martin Huska, a fifteenth-century Bohemian rebel who preached "Our Father who art in us" and who was burned for this heretical prayer in 1421. His most radical followers, the Adamites, were accused of imitating a false Edenite innocence by going naked, having sexual relations, and avowing their own sinlessness.[31] Many of these sects also practiced a primitive communism and preached hatred of the wealth and power of the church.[32] Yet while they often practiced collec-

[30] Walter Nigg, *The Heretics* (Knopf, New York, 1962): 226–236.

[31] Malcolm Lambert, *Medieval Heresy. Popular Movements from Bogomil to Hus* (Holmes and Meier, New York, 1977): 173–178, 322–323.

[32] Karl Kautsky sees these sects as the direct forebears of modern socialists. See his *Communism in Central Europe at the Time of the Reformation* (Russell and Russell, New York, 1959).

tivism, their ideas about free union were based on notions of sinlessness and union with God, and were not intended to transform marriage and the family or to emancipate women.

Ideas of free union emerged again in the seventeenth century, sparked by the English Revolution and what one historian has called "the first modern sexual revolution." Although here too, the idea of free union found its most vigorous promoters in the religious millenarian sects, it was accompanied by a strong critique of traditional marital patterns from both the lower and middle classes. By 1600, one-third of Britain's population had lost access to land or a craft. Migrant wageworkers, expropriated peasants, and failed tradesmen had broken free of older peasant marital customs. With little prospect of ever establishing an independent household, their marital behavior was looser, often based on self-marriage and self-divorce.[33] Drawn to millenarian sects as well as radical antinomianism, these groups attacked older forms of custom from below.

At the same time, the rising businessmen and prosperous farmers who benefited from enclosure and the new opportunities in trade and production attacked popular culture from above. Deriding peasant practices as vulgar, they rejected older custom in favor of a new emphasis on the companionate couple. In the 1640s and 1650s, these two strands – antinomianism and puritanism – reinforced each other and united in their attack on the existing order.[34]

The critiques of marriage spanned a gamut of alternatives from companionate union to free love. Puritan doctrine emphasized the idea of the companionate marriage in which the wife, still subordinate to the husband's authority, would be more a "helpmeet" and an equal. Critical of public festivities, they advocated small private weddings and briefly instituted civil marriage (1653–1660) in the hope of gaining greater control over their children's marital choices.[35] Other religious sects also rejected the marriage ceremony in favor of a simple declaration by the

---

[33] John Gillis, *For Better, For Worse. British Marriages, 1600 to the Present* (Oxford University Press, Oxford, 1985): 102, 13, 99.

[34] Lawrence Stone, *The Family, Sex, and Marriage in England 1500–1800* (Harper, New York, 1979) offers a different interpretation, noting that by 1640, allegiance to kinship networks had declined, turning inward toward the family, pp. 107, 109. Gillis, p. 102

[35] Gillis, pp. 82, 85, 55, 56, 86.

couple before the assembled congregation and practiced an analogous form of divorce. And while the Puritans sought stricter controls over marriage, other critics aimed to loosen restrictions. The poet John Milton spoke passionately in favor of the liberalization of divorce and others sought to limit the absolute patriarchal authority wielded by husbands and fathers. The Ranters, one of the most radical religious sects, went even further, preaching free love, the abolition of the family, and "casual sexual relations with a variety of partners."[36] They celebrated sexuality, and like their medieval predecessors, denied that sex was sinful. Some raised the secular notion of marriage by contract, renewable by husband and wife annually. Abiezer Coppe, a Ranter and an Oxford scholar, found an enthusiastic audience among the poor for his fiery condemnations of monogamy and the nuclear family.[37] Various sects advocated an expansion of women's rights based on their religious conviction of "fundamental natural rights." Some sects permitted women to participate in church government and even to preach. The Quakers, emphasizing each individual's privileged relationship to God, omitted from the marriage ceremony the wife's vow to obey her husband.[38]

Yet even among radicals and dissenters, the critique of the family and women's oppression remained rudimentary. Gerard Winstanley and his radical Diggers reaffirmed the man's place as head of the family and attacked the Ranters' doctrine of free love. Winstanley argued that free love did little to improve the lot of women. "The mother and child begotten in this manner," he wrote, "is like to have the worst of it, for the man will be gone and leave them . . . after he hath had his pleasure." As Christopher Hill has noted, in the absence of effective birth control, "sexual freedom tended to be freedom for men only."[39] Moreover, many of the radical sects never agreed to women's equality and even the Levellers, who argued for "natural rights," did not include women in their plans to extend the political franchise.[40]

The critiques of the family that emerged in the mid-

---

[36] Christopher Durston, *The Family in the English Revolution* (Basil Blackwell, Oxford, 1989): 12.
[37] Gillis, pp. 102–103.
[38] Hill, pp. 308, 310, 312, 315; Durston, pp. 10, 12, 15, 16, 18–19, 20.
[39] Winstanley as quoted in Hill, p. 319.
[40] Durston, pp. 25, 26, 30; Gillis, p. 103.

seventeenth century were thus quite limited. The narrow ac-
knowledgment of women's rights was rooted in the new religious
idea of each individual's unmediated relationship to God. This
idea had strong libertarian implications and it seriously challenged established church and state institutions. But it did not
reject patriarchal rule within the family. Some religious sectaries
expanded women's role within the church, but they did not offer
a critique of women's economic dependence or oppression. The
Puritan notion of companionate marriage mitigated women's
subordination, but it did not spring from an impulse to liberate
women. Justified on religious grounds ("The soul knows no difference of sex"), the idea of companionate union corresponded
to the increasing importance of middling-sized households in
which the wife served as "a junior partner" in a family-owned
and operated business.[41]

If the Puritan idea of companionate union was rooted in the
needs and aspirations of prosperous farmers and businessmen,
the ideas of the Ranters, the most extreme critics of marriage
and the family, were based on the practices of the mobile poor.
Dispossessed peasants and impoverished craftsmen, having no
property to bind them and forced to travel about to earn their
keep, frequently joined together and separated by mutual consent through "self-marriage" and "self-divorce."[42] But the practices of migrant workers did not constitute a dominant social
force in the seventeenth century. Like the Ranters' preachings,
they were more a harbinger of later radical ideas than a realistic
program for a popular movement.

After the English Revolution, the twin strands of puritanism
and antinomianism began to unravel. Puritan elites attempted to
limit marriage to the economically independent and to exclude
the poor. By the end of the eighteenth century, their emphasis
on the narrow, companionate, accumulative family unit was
widely accepted by all propertied classes regardless of religion.
The radical religious sects, who rebelled against marriage fees,
went underground. Their vision of the world as one great family
had little appeal for the rising middle classes.[43]

[41] Hill, pp. 311, 306–307.
[42] Gillis, p. 99.
[43] Ibid., pp. 101, 135, 100, 102.

Questioning women's nature

Throughout the eighteenth century, the growth of cottage or domestic industry had a significant impact on women's roles as the household economy was increasingly characterized by a combination of agriculture and manufacture.[44] The development of domestic industry undermined patriarchal authority and the gender division of labor, lowered the age of first marriage, and resulted in an increase in the birth rate. As earnings replaced property as the basis for forming a separate household, young people increasingly married for personal attraction, "without any thought to material considerations."[45] Women gained "a new economic citizenship" and greater standing in community politics.[46] In the English villages where cottage industry flourished, villagers favored simpler weddings in place of the large peasant celebrations. Radical ideas of marriage based

[44] In France, for example, fully 50 to 90 percent of the land holdings were insufficient to maintain a family in the eighteenth century. See Olwen Hufton, "Women, Work, and Marriage in Eighteenth Century France," in R. B. Outhwaite, ed., *Marriage and Society. Studies in the Social History of Marriage* (St. Martin's Press, New York, 1981): 186–203. And for England, see Bridget Hill, *Women, Work, and Sexual Politics in Eighteenth Century England* (Basil Blackwell, Oxford, 1989).

[45] Rudolf Braun, "The Impact of Cottage Industry on an Agricultural Population," in David Landes, ed., *The Rise of Capitalism* (Macmillan, New York, 1966): 58. A great deal of attention has been given to this process, known as protoindustrialization. See for example, Hans Medick, "The Protoindustrial Family Economy: The Structural Function of Household and Family during the Transition from Peasant Society to Industrial Capitalism," *Social History*, 1 (1976): 291–315; David Levine, "Proto-Industrialization and Demographic Upheaval," in Leslie Moch, ed., *Essays on the Family and Historical Change* (Texas A & M University Press, College Station, 1983): 9–34; David Levine, "Industrialization and the Proletarian Family in England," *Past and Present*, 107 (May 1985): 168–203; Wolfram Fischer, "Rural Industrialization and Population Change," *Comparative Studies in Society and History*, Vol. 15, no. 2 (March 1973): 158–170.

[46] John Bohstedt, "The Myth of the Feminine Food Riot: Women as Proto-Citizens in English Community Politics, 1790–1810," in Harriet Applewhite, Darline Levy, eds., *Women and Politics in the Age of the Democratic Revolution* (University of Michigan Press, Ann Arbor, 1990); 34, 35.

on mutual feeling rather than property had a strong appeal to rural and urban plebeian groups who were already practicing more "flexible" forms of marriage.[47]

The plebeian challenge to patriarchal authority from below was paralleled by a philosophical challenge from above as debates over women and the family engaged the free thinkers of the Enlightenment. Although the philosophes were not concerned directly with women's liberation, they framed the discussion of women's roles in a wholly new way by opening up the questions of gender difference and women's potential for equality. Unlike the religious radicals of the seventeenth century, the philosophes did not base their thinking on the individual's special relationship to God but on the role of education and the environment in shaping the potential innate in every (male) human being. The notion that education could play a critical role in creating human personality logically led many of the philosophes to question sexual differences and the "feminine character."[48]

While much of the philosophes' thinking was new, their conclusions remained generally conservative. Diderot, for example, criticized many of the institutions and customs that held women back, but he also believed that women were innately prone to hysteria, incapable of sustained mental concentration, and ultimately unable to achieve genius. D'Holbach held that women were incapable of reason, justice, or abstract thought. Most of the philosophes emphasized an exclusively domestic role for women and denied the ultimate possibility of equality.[49]

Like the Puritans, the philosophes advocated an essentially middle-class ideal of marriage based on monogamy, mutual affection, and companionship. Unlike the Puritans, however, they

---

[47] John Gillis, "Peasant, Plebeian, and Proletarian Marriage in Britain, 1600–1900," in David Levine, ed., *Proletarianization and Family History* (Academic Press, New York, 1984): 138–150.

[48] Katherine Clinton, "Femme et Philosophe: Enlightenment Origins of Feminism," *Eighteenth Century Studies*, 8 (1975).

[49] Elizabeth Gardner, "The Philosophes and Women: Sensationalism and Sentiment," and P. D. Jimack, "The Paradox of Sophie and Julie: Contemporary Responses to Rousseau's Ideal Wife and Ideal Mother," in E. Jacobs, W. Barber, J. Block, F. Leakey, E. LeBreton, eds., *Women and Society in Eighteenth Century France: Essays in Honor of John Stephenson Spink*, (Athlone Press, London, 1979): 21–24, 152–153.

placed less emphasis on women's subordination to men, although their views of marriage were still molded largely by male needs. Rousseau's ideal wife was predicated on his "rational" assessment of the ideal man's requirements, and Helvetius's reforms of marital law and sexual mores were undertaken with male interests in mind.[50] Their critique of marriage, however, was secular. And like the new plebeian practices arising among workers in cottage industry, they too, challenged a "divinely ordered patriarchy."[51]

At their most radical, the philosophes questioned the "natural" superiority of men and argued for broader educational opportunities for women. Voltaire and Diderot both challenged women's legal inequality and Montesquieu argued that the "feminine character" was not innate but the result of poor education and limited opportunity. By raising the idea of human potential, these thinkers opened the way to new conceptions of citizenship and political rights. A few argued for civil equality for all, male and female, although none seriously challenged the institutions of marriage, family, or the gender division of labor.[52] The philosophes were mainly concerned with the corruption of such female "virtues" as simplicity, frugality, and domesticity by an atmosphere of frivolity and decadence. Yet their critique, by its very nature, was confined to the "faults" of aristocratic women, the only group who had the luxury of such corruption.[53]

Although many historians agreed that the "age of light" left women in the dark, in fact, the ideas of the philosophes were more or less congruent with women's relationship to the prevailing mode of production.[54] The philosophes were incapable of deeply questioning women's roles because no large-scale eco-

---

[50] Clinton, pp. 291–295; Jimack, p. 152.

[51] Jane Rendall, *The Origins of Modern Feminism: Women in Britain, France, and the United States, 1780–1860* (Macmillan, New York, 1985): 4.

[52] For a more favorable assessment of the philosophes' attitudes toward women, see Clinton, and Sylvana Tomaselli, "The Enlightenment Debate on Women," *History Workshop Journal*, 20 (1985).

[53] See Joan Landes, *Women and the Public Sphere in the Age of Revolution* (Cornell University Press, Ithaca, N.Y., 1988) for the extension of this argument to republican ideology.

[54] Abby R. Kleinbaum, "Women in the Age of Light," in Renate Bridenthal, Claudia Koonz, eds., *Becoming Visible. Women in European History* (Houghton Mifflin, Boston, 1977): 233.

nomic disruption had occurred in the balance of production and reproduction. Despite the changes spurred by the growth of domestic industry throughout the eighteenth century, the household was still the primary unit of production, and the vast majority of women in the countryside and the towns were firmly integrated into the family economy. Women engaged in a variety of crafts as a result of market penetration in the countryside, but these tasks were still performed within the home around the traditional work of farming, child rearing, cleaning, spinning, and mending. On the eve of the French Revolution, fully 85 percent of the population were peasants, and even in the cities, few women worked apart from their husbands or families; women's work remained an extension of work within the family.[55] The ideas of the philosophes thus reflected a world in which capitalism and wage labor had yet to shatter the division of labor within the family by involving large numbers of women in paid work outside the home. The contradiction between production and reproduction remained in the future, and it was therefore not surprising that the philosophes did not address themselves to its resolution.

The limited expressions of feminism within the French Revolution demonstrated that demands for women's emancipation could not be successful as long as the household retained a primary role in production. Women simply had no economic options outside the family, for a single women could not survive on her wages alone.[56] Although Condorcet and other pamphleteers called for equal rights for women, women never organized as a separate constituency in the French Revolution to advance a self-consciously feminist program. There were a few maverick voices – several women's newspapers demanded more civil rights for women and limited participation in the political process, and Olympe de Gouges penned her famous *Declaration of the Rights of Woman and of the Citizen* – but despite their potential constituency, these feminist voices represented "a minority inter-

---

55 Elizabeth Fox-Genovese, "Women and Work," in Samia Spencer, ed., *French Women and the Age of Enlightenment* (Indiana University Press, Bloomington, 1984), and Rendall's chapter, "Work and Organization," p. 150.
56 Candice Proctor, *Women, Equality, and the French Revolution* (Greenwood Press, Westport, Conn., 1990): 70.

est." The cahiers of 1789 contained a few specifically female grievances, but these were rare, never debated nor even seriously discussed.[57]

Women in the French Revolution were active primarily on behalf of their class rather than their sex. They marched, rioted, formed women's clubs, and joined the army, but not as feminists with a clear program for women's rights. Political ferment did open new possibilities for women's participation, and for a brief period in the spring of 1792, women actively promulgated a concept of female citizenship based on their right to bear arms.[58] The women of the laboring classes gave tremendous support to the Revolution, but their activism, like their work, was still powerfully conditioned by their roles within the family. Urban women had long been responsible for supplementing their husbands' wages, and their participation in the bread riots grew directly out of their roles as foragers and providers for their families. In Olwyn Hufton's words, "The bread riot was maternal terrain."[59]

The language of natural rights and republicanism did lead to a reexamination of the political and educational limits placed on women, but the dominant voices of the revolutionary era – male and female – still conceived of republican motherhood as the greatest service a woman could render the revolution. Mary Wollstonecraft's *Vindication of the Rights of Woman*, considered by many to mark the beginning of modern feminist thought, advocated expanded opportunities for women so they could become better wives and mothers. Wollstonecraft still adhered to clearly

---

[57] Jane Abray, "Feminism in the French Revolution," *American Historical Review,* 80 (1975): 59, 47; Ruth Graham, "Loaves and Liberty," in *Becoming Visible,* p. 238–242; Darline Levy, Harriet Applewhite, "Women, Democracy, and Revolution in Paris," in Spencer, ed., *French Women and the Age of Enlightenment,* pp. 64–67.

[58] Darline Levy, Harriet Applewhite, "Women, Radicalization, and the Fall of the French Monarchy," in Applewhite and Levy, eds., p. 90; see also Dominique Godineau, "Masculine and Feminine Political Practice during the French Revolution," ibid., for argument that women did try to gain acceptance as citizens through the right to vote and bear arms.

[59] Olwyn Hufton, "Women in Revolution, 1789–1796," *Past and Present,* 53 (1971): 94. For a similar argument on women's role in food riots in the first half of the nineteenth century, see Rendall, pp. 200–203.

demarcated gender roles and a strict division of labor. In general, even the most radically feminist writers of the period were unable to "envision a convincing, liberated female character."[60] The idea of republican motherhood opened a new vista of education, but it did little to free women from their cramped domestic confines. Both conservatives and republicans emphasized domesticity for women, and women made few advances into a larger public and political realm.[61]

Ultimately, the French Revolution accomplished little for women in general and even less for the women of the poor. The government closed the independent women's clubs in 1793 and banned women's admission to popular assemblies soon after. Many of the Revolution's new legal freedoms, including simplified divorce, rights for illegitimate children, and expanded property rights for women, were swept away by Napoleon's Civil Code in 1804. At no stage had the Revolution enfranchised women politically or granted them civil rights.[62] By 1796, as the country slid from famine into mass starvation, many women who had actively participated in the Revolution began to turn against it.[63]

The French Revolution produced few concrete gains for women less because of the persistent efforts of men to exclude them than because of women's lack of organization on their own behalf. They were active but never constituted "an autonomous force." In one historian's words, "France's small-scale, home-based economy needed middle class and working class women to contribute . . . to their families. Women were not yet a large, independent group in the working class." Ordinary women did not respond to the language of feminism, for neither its "words nor actions" "made any sense."[64] Yet as capitalism began to

---

60 Katharine Rogers, *Feminism in Eighteenth Century England* (University of Illinois Press, Urbana, 1982): 183–189, 246.
61 Rendall, pp. 68, 70.
62 Roderick Phillips, "Women's Emancipation, the Family, and Social Change in Eighteenth Century France," *Journal of Social History*, 12 (1974); Adrienne Rogers, "Women and the Law," in *French Women and the Age of Enlightenment*; Mary Johnson, "Old Wine in New Bottles: Institutional Change for Women of the People during the French Revolution," in Carol Berkin, Clara Lovett, eds., *Women, War and Revolution* (Holmes and Meier, New York, London, 1980).
63 Hufton, pp. 102–103.   64 Graham, p. 252; Abray, p. 59.

transform domestic relations, and women began to enter the workforce, movements of working people were forced to wrestle with women's new roles as independent wage earners. Slowly a new vision of women's liberation began to take shape.

Socialize and communalize

By the early nineteenth century, workers in both Britain and France were increasingly resorting to the practice of self-marriage or free union. Many simply could not afford to marry, and large numbers simply postponed marriage and lived together. In France, many workers, particularly in the metal industry, refused marriage on principle. Licenses were expensive and anticlericalism rampant.[65] In England, sexual and religious nonconformity was also widespread. The early industrial centers were hotbeds of hostility toward the clergy and their marriage fees. In many cities, anticlericalism took a radical, even socialist form. Painite free thinkers, feminists, and socialists fiercely debated the institution of marriage, expressing what many workers had been practicing for several decades.[66]

Utopian schemes for alternative communities proliferated throughout Europe and America in the first half of the nineteenth century. Movements based on the ideas of St. Simon, Charles Fourier, and Robert Owen strongly appealed to workers and artisans who were already practicing less rigid forms of marriage.[67] Many of the utopians, like their millenarian predecessors, advocated ideas of free union, but for the first time these ideas were linked to plans for socializing the household and emancipating women. In France, Prosper Enfantin, a charismatic quasi-religious figure, began popularizing the work of the utopian theorist St. Simon. Although St. Simon had written almost nothing about women, Enfantin founded a group – soon "a religion" – that focused much attention on women's equality.

[65] Rendall, p. 194.   [66] Gillis, *For Better, For Worse*, p. 192.
[67] John Gillis, "Peasant, Plebeian, and Proletarian Marriage in Britain, 1600–1900," p. 150, writes "when the Owenites experimented with collective living arrangements and advocated the freedom to divorce they were not building on elite values but on well-established plebeian practices."

Enfantin himself was a strong believer in clearly defined sex roles: Man represented reflection; woman, sentiment. But he prized women's emotional contribution and argued therefore for their full participation in the public sphere. Enfantin eventually expelled the women from the leadership or "hierarchy" of his group, leaving France for Egypt on a mystical quest for the female messiah. Yet his group gave rise to a breakaway faction of women who published, for a brief time, a feminist paper advocating free love, the abolition of illegitimacy, and the socialization of child rearing. Unlike male utopians, however, whose careers prospered in the 1830s and 1840s, the feminists found it almost impossible to survive financially outside of marriage. Extreme poverty led many to reconsider their earlier ideas about free love.[68]

If Enfantin's program for women proved largely abortive, Charles Fourier's elaborate plans for alternative communities or phalanxes had somewhat greater success. Fourier's ideas drew advocates throughout Europe and America, and over forty Fourier-inspired communities appeared in America between 1840 and 1860.[69] American Associationist literature proclaimed women equal to men, yet like the St. Simonians, most Associationists affirmed traditional gender roles and division of labor. Women were "the beautifiers, spiritualizers, and sympathizers." Associationists condemned the individual household, yet did not challenge traditional relations between the sexes. In the phalanxes, household duties like cooking, laundry, and child care were socialized, but they were still performed, albeit communally, by women. Women were "equal" but still not the same as men. Fourierists assumed that women's innate character would naturally incline them toward domestic work. Thus the inequalities between men and women in society at large were reproduced in the phalanxes: Women were consigned to domestic work, were accorded little political power, and were paid less

---

[68] Claire Moses, *French Feminism in the Nineteenth Century* (State University of New York Press, Albany, 1984): 41–83. On the St. Simonians, see also Robert Carlisle, *The Proffered Crown. Saint Simonianism and the Doctrine of Hope* (Johns Hopkins University Press, Baltimore, 1987).

[69] Robert Lauer, Jeanette Lauer, *The Spirit and the Flesh: Sex in Utopian Communities* (Scarecrow Press, N.J., 1983): 37.

than men. The constitutions of some phalanxes actually stipulated that women receive only a fixed percentage of the male wage; in one case, the women's maximum was the men's minimum.[70]

In Britain, Robert Owen, a utopian theorist and organizer, built a workers' movement aimed at creating worker-owned and -managed shops. After a series of bitter strikes in 1834, Owen shied away from class-based activism and turned to the creation of utopian communities to be built according to his own blueprint. The communities eventually collapsed amid fighting, financial difficulty, and Owen's own growing antidemocratic, antiworker sentiments.[71] But despite the dismal record of the communities, the ideas of Owenism had a tremendous impact on working men and women throughout the country and abroad.

Between 1825 and 1845, Owenites lectured and wrote extensively on the position of women. Owenites promulgated the ideas of "moral" marriage, simple, nonreligious vows, and cheap, easy divorce. Although they criticized patriarchal power, like the Associationists, they rejected the family less for its gender relations than its antisocial nature. In Owen's new society, living arrangements would be fully collectivized and housework performed on a communal rotating basis. Plans included separate rooms for all adults, married or single, dormitories for children, and common rooms for dining, socializing, and group activities. The Bolsheviks would later adopt an almost identical critique of the family and blueprint for communal life. Yet the Owenites, like the Associationists, did little to overturn or reform the traditional gender division of labor. Housework and child care was to be rotated only among women, not shared by all. And by and large, Owenite women fared as poorly as their

---

[70] Carl Guarneri, *The Utopian Alternative. Fourierism in Nineteenth Century America* (Cornell University Press, Ithaca, N.Y., 1991): 130–131, 205–206, 209. Guarneri provides an insightful and detailed account of women's treatment.

[71] The following section on Owenism is based largely on the work of Barbara Taylor, *Eve and the New Jerusalem. Socialism and Feminism in the Nineteenth Century* (Pantheon, New York, 1983). See also Gillis, *For Better, For Worse*, pp. 224–228.

Associationist counterparts: communalizing individual tasks frequently created more, not less work.[72]

After 1840, Owenites began to recognize that it was impossible to change the institution of marriage without restructuring the prevailing system of property. In part, this recognition was prompted by protest from women who were becoming increasingly uncomfortable with the idea of free union or "moral marriage." The Owenite position on marriage began to splinter into a number of competing views. One Owenite editor warned that "moral Marriage" offered few protections to women. Without legal constraints men would always be tempted to desert. Owenite feminists, particularly among the poor, took a less celebratory view of unfettered sexuality than their male counterparts. Always conscious of the costs of unwanted pregnancy, they recognized the truth of one Owenite's assertion that "a moral marriage is not so much an emancipation of woman as an emancipation of man." This assertion had been noted before, by critics of the Ranters and the St. Simonian feminists, and it would be noted again, by Russian radical women in the nineteenth century and Soviet women in the 1920s and 1930s. In the 1840s, however, the debate was still largely defined by men as the church battled against Owenite sexual libertarians. Women's interests were not well served by either position. The absence of an independent female voice within Owenism ultimately aided the church in reasserting its traditional, conservative view of marriage.[73]

The idea of women's independence – economic, social, sexual – was still relatively undeveloped within utopian socialism despite its basic affirmation of equality. Yet the utopians clearly differed from both the religious communitarians and the philosophes in their emphasis on collectivity and equality. The 1830s and 1840s marked the beginning of a great change in the industrial labor force as women began entering the world of waged work outside the household. The ideas of utopian socialism took shape within a world where the family was being transformed and women were gaining a new economic independence. Workers' struggles to come to terms with female labor provided

[72] Ibid., pp. 37–40, 48–49, 247–249.   [73] Ibid., pp. 207–216.

an enormous spur to movements for women's equality as well as a socialist vision of women's liberation.

Challenging the sexual division of labor

The initial reaction of male workers to women's entrance into the labor force, in England as well as other countries, was actively hostile. Women began entering the tailoring trades in England during the Napoleonic War, diverting work from the older workshops and undermining the control male workers had won over hiring, wages, and work organization. Men rapidly began organizing to keep women out of the trades, arguing that women workers drove wages down and made it impossible for a man to support a family. They launched major strikes in 1827 and 1830 designed in part to exclude women from work. Employers used women as strikebreakers, and by the late 1830s, they had successfully broken craft control of the tailoring industry.[74]

In France, male tailors fought similar battles to exclude women. As the ready-made trade began undercutting the power of the organized crafts, both master tailors and employees organized against piecework and female labor. Men saw women's labor as a sharp "threat to domestic stability and security."[75] Flora Tristan (1803–1844), a feminist and socialist, launched an appeal on behalf of women workers, advocating equal pay and the right to enter male trades. She was met by fierce hostility from artisans and skilled workers who claimed that women would be better off at home.[76]

The new phenomenon of female labor outside the home provoked tremendous bitterness and confusion in all trades for it turned the workers' world upside down. Men and women fiercely competed for jobs as women replaced men for lower wages. Women abandoned their traditional family duties for

[74] Ibid., pp. 102–117.   [75] Rendall, pp. 163, 166, 168.
[76] Joan Moon, "Feminism and Socialism: The Utopian Synthesis of Flora Tristan," in Marilyn Boxer, Jean Quataert, eds., *Socialist Women. European Socialist Feminism in the Nineteenth and Early Twentieth Century* (Elsevier, New York, 1978).

waged work, frequently leaving an angry, unemployed husband
at home to mind the baby and stir the soup. As wages fell, even
women with working husbands were forced to find work. Men
began to organize against women and to raise the demand for a
"family wage." Their reactions, later termed "sexual Toryism" or
"proletarian antifeminism," deemed women's entrance into the
workforce "an inversion of the order of nature." And although
many women retorted that they had no choice but to work,
others supported the call for a family wage, shrinking from the
prospect of combining full-time waged work with household
labor.[77] Craft unions mounted a series of losing battles in an
attempt to turn back the clock, and demands for a family wage
could be heard throughout Europe as late as World War I.

The first challenge to the sexual division of labor, however,
did not come from liberal feminists, who were largely uncon-
cerned with the problems of workers, but from socialists, whose
constituents were coping with the vast disruptions created by
female labor. Liberal feminists, taken up with educational, civil,
and political rights, and by religion and philanthropy, did little
to question women's domestic role. Even John Stuart Mill, in his
famous *The Subjugation of Women* (1869), argued that within the
"most suitable division of labor," men earned the income and
women managed the domestic expenses. He never considered
that a large number of working-class women had no choice but
to work.[78] By and large, the liberal feminists of the nineteenth
century "identified most closely with single, educated women."

[77] Barbara Taylor calls this response by male workers "sexual Toryism." See pp. 101, 111–112. Werner Thonessen calls it "proletarian
anti-feminism" in his *The Emancipation of Women. The Rise and Decline
of the Women's Movement in German Social Democracy, 1863–1933* (Pluto
Press, Frankfurt am Main, 1973): 16. Male workers sought to increase male wages and decrease male unemployment by excluding
women from the workforce and pushing them back into traditional
domestic roles. These male demands were heard throughout the
industrializing countries in the nineteenth century and were a response to employers who increasingly substituted women for men
and paid them lower wages. The phenomenon was recognized by
Engels in *The Condition of the Working Class in England* in Karl Marx,
Frederick Engels, *Collected Works*, Vol. 4 (New York, 1975). Male
workers believed that by excluding women, they could keep wages
high enough to support a family.
[78] Rendall, p. 287.

They sought to extend "the sexual division of labor into the capitalist economy" by emphasizing women's domestic proclivities and expanding their share of the female-dominated service sector.[79]

Socialist theorists and organizers, on the other hand, were forced to confront the problems created by the female labor in the workplace and the home. Initially bewildered, they floundered for years in an attempt to devise a solution. Even Marx and Engels, who offered the most penetrating insights into the transformative power of capitalism, were initially bereft of analysis or strategy. Their period of confusion, however, was relatively brief. They quickly came to see that the extensive employment of female labor was inevitable and irreversible, and in doing so they mounted the first serious theoretical challenge to the gender division of labor. Arguing against strategies based on proletarian antifeminism, their work had enormous impact on the European labor movement and eventually provided the essential framework for Bolshevik thinking about women and the family. Although many of their ideas were similar to those of the utopian socialists, their analysis of the origins and development of women's oppression was entirely new and unprecedented.

Marxism and women

The first Marxist work to engage the subject of women and work directly was Engels' *The Condition of the Working Class of England*, written in 1844. While the book dealt at length with the effects of capitalism on the family, it lacked a genuine theoretical analysis and stood primarily as a powerful moral indictment of industrial practices. One of Engels's main themes concerned the introduction of new machinery and the increasing substitution of women and children for male workers for a fraction of men's wages. Although Engels viewed this process as "inevitable," he remained deeply concerned about its effects on women and the family. Nursing infants sickened and starved at home while their mothers' swollen breasts dripped milk at the machines. Confined to unnatural positions throughout the long working day, women

[79] Rendall, pp. 186, 183, 184.

developed a variety of grotesque occupational malformations. Pregnant women, fined for sitting down to rest, developed horrible varicosities and often worked "up to the hour of delivery" for fear they would lose their wages and be replaced. Engels noted that "the case is none too rare of their being delivered in the factory among the machinery."[80]

In his stark exposé of the lives of working women, Engels intuitively grasped the contradiction between capitalist production and family stability. He was quick to perceive the "total neglect of children" when both parents worked twelve to thirteen hours a day in the mill. "The employment of women," he noted, "at once breaks up the family." Summarizing the effect of industry on the family, Engels cited the long hours women spent at work, the neglect of housework and children, demoralization, a growing indifference to family life, men's inability to find work, the early "emancipation of children," and the reversal of gender roles. Capitalism, in his view, was destroying the family.[81]

Engels saw the process as an inevitable part of economic development, but he was unable to move beyond an angry condemnation of the exploitation of female labor. Groping for an analysis, he advanced two opposing perspectives on the dissolution of the family. On the one hand, he described the inversion of family roles – husband as dependent, wife as breadwinner – with great moral indignation. His thinking still reflected "conventional 19th century assumptions" and was quite similar to the proletarian antifeminism of male workers themselves.[82] On the other hand, he questioned his own condemnation of this gender role reversal. He noted tentatively, "If the reign of the wife over the husband as inevitably brought about by the factory system is inhuman, the pristine rule of the husband over the wife must have been inhuman too."[83] Engels thus accepted a "natural"

---

[80] Engels, *Condition of the Working Class in England*, 431, 497, 483, 452.

[81] Ibid., pp. 406, 438, 489, 497.

[82] Lise Vogel, *Marxism and the Oppression of Women* (N.J., 1983): 46. Engels's nineteenth-century assumptions about "natural" gender roles are present throughout *Condition of the Working Class in England*. Discussing the substitution of male by female labor, he wrote, "this condition which unsexes the man and takes from the woman all womanliness without being able to bestow on the man true womanliness or the woman true manliness – this condition . . . degrades in the most shameful way both sexes," p. 439.

[83] Engels. *Condition of the Working Class in England*, p. 439.

division of labor based on woman as homemaker, but he was beginning to question both the nature and the future of this division.

Within a year, Marx and Engels took a great leap in their thinking on women and the division of labor. Formulating a general theory of historical development in *The German Ideology* (1845–1846), they began to question the very idea of a "natural" division of labor. Here they first posited the production of material life and "the relation between men and women, parents and children, the family" as the basic premises of human existence. Outlining their materialist conception of history, they discussed the relationship between the basic stages of production, property, and the sexual or so-called natural division of labor. They suggested that the family was more than a set of natural or biological relations, but took a social form that corresponded to the mode of production. They insisted that the family must be treated empirically at all stages of history, not as an abstract concept. They wrote, "The production of life, both of one's own in labour and of fresh life in procreation, now appears as a two-fold relation: on the one hand as a natural, on the other as a social relation."[84]

Their idea of the family as a mutable social form corresponding to a given mode of production was an enormous advance over prevailing notions of the family as a natural entity. Yet their twofold conception of the family – as a set of both natural and social relations – created a contradiction in *The German Ideology* that Marx and Engels were as yet unable to resolve. The contradiction was most clearly expressed in their effort to formulate a theoretical and historical explanation for women's oppression. According to Marx and Engels, the social division of labor in the tribal stage was essentially "a further extension of the natural division of labor existing in the family." In this early tribal period, a natural or biological division of labor prevailed, based on the biological differences between men and women, or more specifically, on women's maternal function.

According to this early formulation, women's oppression emerged from the "slavery latent in the family" that developed gradually with "the increase in population, the growth of wants, and the extension of external intercourse." The very first form

[84] Karl Marx and Frederick Engels, *The German Ideology*, in *Collected Works*, Vol. 5, pp. 41–43.

of private property had its origin in the family: Women and children were the slaves of men. They explained, "This latent slavery in the family, though still very crude, is the first form of property, but even at this stage it corresponds perfectly to the definition of modern economists, who call it the power of disposing of the labor of others." The "natural" division of labor in the family, combined with the separation of society into distinct, opposing family units, necessarily implied an unequal distribution of labor and its products.[85] Thus Marx and Engels argued that women's oppression originated in the natural or sexual division of labor within the family. Women were the first form of private property: They were owned by men. Women's oppression was rooted in motherhood.[86]

Yet Marx and Engels were not fully satisfied with this biological explanation of women's oppression, for it contradicted their idea that family relations had a social as well as a natural content and were ultimately determined by the existing productive forces.[87] If women's oppression predated every form of production, originating in immutable biological differences, a crucial determinant of gender roles and relations transcended the productive forces.

Marx and Engels's theoretical confusion on this question resulted, in large measure, from their ignorance about the family within tribal society. While they acknowledged the existence of human history prior to the development of private property, they were unable to conceptualize a family form that differed from the male-dominated paired unit. They argued that women's oppression and the patriarchal family accompanied the earliest forms of communal property.[88] Thus the oppression of women by men existed at every stage, even in tribal society, predating even the development of private property. Biology was the only conceivable explanation. This contradiction between Marx and Engels's newly advanced social perspective on

[85] Ibid., pp. 33, 44, 46.
[86] Claude Meillasoux offers a more sophisticated argument along similar lines in *Maidens, Meal, and Money. Capitalism and the Domestic Community* (Cambridge University Press, Cambridge, 1981): 3–88. Meillasoux argues that the roots of women's oppression lie in the demographic needs of hunting and gathering bands.
[87] *German Ideology*, p. 50.   [88] Ibid., pp. 75–76.

the family and their strictly biological explanation for women's oppression within it was not resolved by Engels until forty years later, when new anthropological discoveries allowed him to argue that group marriage and matriarchy characterized many societies based on communal property.[89]

Although Marx and Engels were still stymied by the "natural" versus the "social explanation for the division of labor in the past," they quickly perceived the ramifications of capitalism's new division of labor for the future. In *The German Ideology*, they addressed the question of household labor, arguing that a communal domestic economy was a necessary prerequisite for women's liberation. Although they never defined this term, it appeared to denote the transfer of all domestic work from the individual household to the public sphere. Discarding Engels's initial blanket condemnation of female labor, they argued that capitalism was the first system to create the possibility of transferring housework from the private to the public sphere.[90]

Moreover, they maintained that the substitution of the indi-

[89] Engels's work on the origins of patriarchy has been subject to enormous debate among contemporary anthropologists, historians, and feminists. See for example, Eleanor Leacock, "Introduction" in Frederick Engels, *The Origin of the Family, Private Property, and the State*, pp. 7–67; Janet Sayers, Mary Evans, Nanneke Redclift, eds., *Engels Revisited. New Feminist Essays* (Tavistock, London, 1987). For critiques of Marxism from a feminist perspective, see Zillah Eisenstein, ed., *Capitalist Patriarchy and the Case for Socialist Feminism* (Monthly Review Press, New York, 1979); Heidi Hartmann, "The Unhappy Marriage of Marxism and Feminism: Toward a More Progressive Union," and Carol Ehrlich, "The Unhappy Marriage of Marxism and Feminism: Can It Be Saved?" in Lydia Sargent, ed., *Women and Revolution* (South End Press, Boston, 1981); Alison Jaggar, *Feminist Politics and Human Nature* (Harvester, Sussex, 1983); Batya Weinbaum, *The Curious Courtship of Women: Liberation and Socialism* (South End Press, Boston, 1978); Anja Meulenbelt, Joyce Outshoorn, Selma Sevenhuijsen, Petra DeVries, eds., *A Creative Tension. Key Issues of Socialist Feminism* (South End Press, Boston, 1984); Annette Kuhn, Ann Marie Wolpe, *Feminism and Materialism. Women and Modes of Production* (Boston, London, 1978); Sonia Kruks, Rayna Rapp, Marilyn Young, eds., *Promissory Notes. Women in the Transition to Socialism* (Monthly Review Press, New York, 1989); Alena Heitlinger, "Marxism, Feminism, and Sexual Equality," in Tova Yedlin, ed., *Women in Eastern Europe and the Soviet Union* (Praeger, New York, 1980).

[90] *German Ideology*, pp. 75–76.

vidual family economy by a communal economy would be accompanied by the abolition or "supercession" of the family itself. This positive view of the abolition of the family contrasted sharply with Engels's censorious observations of family breakdown in *The Condition of the Working Class in England*. In *The German Ideology*, Marx and Engels argued that the new proletarian family was a prototype of future social relations. Unlike the bourgeois family, based on property, the working-class family was held together by bonds of real affection.[91] This idealized notion of the proletarian family was firmly at odds with Engels's earlier descriptions. In *The German Ideology*, Marx and Engels abandoned the conventional stereotypes of proper family life in favor of a romantic vision of a union of individuals not motivated by property considerations. This idea remained essentially unchanged throughout Marx and Engels's subsequent work. It appeared in *Principles of Communism* (1847), *Draft of a Communist Confession of Faith* (1847), *Manifesto of the Communist Party* (1848), and *The Origin of the Family, Private Property, and the State* (1884). Marx and Engels repeatedly contrasted the loveless matches of the propertied bourgeoisie with the affectionate unions of the propertyless proletariat. In their view, property was the main obstacle to relations based on love, equality, and mutual respect. They never discussed the specific forms of women's oppression in the working-class family, nor did they advance beyond a rudimentary distinction between relations in the propertied versus propertyless family, although other Marxist theorists would return to this question in the future.[92]

[91] Ibid., pp. 76, 180–181.
[92] Modern feminists and women's historians are quite critical of Marx and Engels's idealized notion of the proletarian family. Vogel, for example, writes that Marx and Engels's view of the working-class household misses its significance as a social unit for reproduction, overlooks the nonpropertied but nevertheless material basis for male supremacy, and "vastly underestimates the variety of ideological and psychological factors that provide a continuing foundation for male supremacy and the working-class family," pp. 84–85. Subsequent Marxist theorists like Clara Zetkin, Alexandra Kollontai, E. O. Kabo, and others went considerably beyond these early formulations of Marx and Engels. See also Alfred Meyers's *The Feminism and Socialism of Lily Braun* (Indiana University Press, Bloomington, 1985); and Claire LaVigna on the ideas of Anna Kuliscoff in "The Marxist

Drawing upon the theoretical formulations in *The German Ideology,* Marx and Engels summed up the programmatic aspect of their thinking in *Principles of Communism* and *Manifesto of the Communist Party.* Women's emancipation depended on the abolition of private property and the creation of a communal domestic economy. Under socialism, relations between the sexes would be based on genuine affection, not property. Relations would become "a purely private affair," concerning "only the persons involved." Religious and secular authorities would have "no call to interfere."[93] This commitment to the personal and sexual freedom of the individual constituted a powerful libertarian motif in nineteenth-century socialist ideology. Strongly marked in August Bebel's work, it would become an integral tenet of early Bolshevik thought as well.

Thus as early as 1850, Marx and Engels had already formulated many of the ideas that would shape the Bolshevik vision. Unlike earlier utopian theorists, they grounded their vision of the future on a study of the modes of production and reproduction in the past. Recognizing the family as a social and not simply a natural construct, they began to challenge the gender division of labor. They acknowledged not only the inevitability of female labor, but its future role in creating a new, less oppressive family form.

Yet despite these profound insights, the socialist workers' movement throughout Europe was slow to accept female labor. In Germany, LaSalle's Workers' Association, founded in 1863, sought to exclude women from the labor force on the grounds that their presence worsened the material condition of the working class. And even many German Marxists refused to accept Marx and Engels's views. In England, the Secretary of the Trade Union Congress in 1877 was cheered as he demanded a family wage to enable women to return to their proper places in the home. In France, the workers' movement was particularly hostile to women's causes; French socialists sponsored legislation to limit women's right to work. The French Workers' Party (POF),

Ambivalence toward Women," in Boxer, Quataert, eds., *Socialist Women.*
[93] Frederick Engels, *Principles of Communism,* p. 354, and Karl Marx, Frederick Engels, *Manifesto of the Communist Party,* pp. 501–502, in *Collected Works,* Vol. 6.

founded in 1879, was the first to break with the tradition of proletarian antifeminism and to demand complete equality of the sexes in public and private life. Yet even the POF was deeply divided and made little effort to organize women despite their growing presence in the industrial labor force. In Italy, the Socialist Party, founded in 1892, shied away from women's issues for fear of alienating a conservative trade union movement. And even the first Congress of the International rejected the inevitability of female labor despite Marx and Engels's position in *The Communist Manifesto* and other writings.[94] The battle over female labor was long and bitter: It took almost another half century of struggle before the workers' movement accepted the strategic implications of women's role in the wage labor force.

August Bebel's famous work, *Women and Socialism*, first published in 1879, was an important landmark in the move away from proletarian antifeminism and toward a more unifying strategy within the workers' movement. The book quickly became the most popular offering in the libraries of German workers. It was translated into numerous languages, and reissued in more than fifty editions in Germany alone. It became the basis for subsequent social-democratic organizing efforts among women and had an enormous effect on many of the future women leaders of the international socialist movement. Clara Zetkin, a leader of the German Social Democratic Party (SPD), noted, "It was more than a book, it was an event – a great deed."[95]

The book covered the entire history of women, from primitive

---

[94] On the responses of the European labor movement to female labor, see Marilyn Boxer, "Socialism Faces Feminism: the Failure of Synthesis in France, 1987–1914," and Claire LaVigna, "The Marxist Ambivalence toward Women," in Boxer, Quataert, eds. *Socialist Women;* Taylor, *Eve and the New Jerusalem,* p. 274; Thonessen, *The Emancipation of Women,* pp. 15, 20–22.

[95] Philip Foner, ed., *Clara Zetkin. Selected Writings* (International, New York, 1984): 79. Hereafter cited as *Zetkin.* Jane Slaughter and Robert Kerr, eds., note in their introduction to *European Women on the Left* (Greenwood, Conn., 1981): 5, that Bebel's book changed the SPD's attitude toward women; and Richard Stites, *The Women's Liberation Movement in Russia. Feminism, Nihilism, and Bolshevism, 1860–1930* (Princeton University Press, Princeton, N.J., 1978): 234, called the book "the unofficial bible of the European Marxist movement."

society to the present, including material on Greek drama, Athenian wives and courtesans, Christianity, the Middle Ages, the Reformation, the eighteenth century, and industrial society. Unlike Engels in his later work *The Origin of the Family, Private Property, and the State,* Bebel offered little theoretical analysis. His critique was primarily moral, centering on the evils and hypocrisy of bourgeois society. Bebel also departed from Marx and Engels in his interest in the history of sexuality. His discussions of the antisexual nature of Christianity, the church's views toward women, and the cult of the Virgin Mary were remarkably novel, anticipating feminist discussions a full century later.[96]

Bebel extolled sexuality, writing frankly of "the natural desires implanted in every healthy adult." "Sexual impulse," he explained, "is neither moral nor immoral; it is simply natural, like hunger or thirst." He wrote movingly of the sexual unhappiness in so many modern marriages and the pernicious effect of the double standard that forced women to suppress their most powerful instincts. He saw women's subjugation most clearly through the lens of sexuality. "Nothing can prove the dependent position of women in a more emphatic and revolting way," he wrote, "than these vastly differing conceptions in regard to the satisfaction of the same natural impulse." Like Marx and Engels, he posited a free union founded on love in place of the "forced relations" created by capitalism.[97]

Surprisingly, the book devoted a scant ten pages to the subject of its title: women and socialism. Here, like Marx and Engels, Bebel predicted a new freedom of union for women. Socialism, he argued, "will merely reinstate on a higher level of civilization . . . what generally prevailed before private property." In keeping with his emphasis on sexuality, Bebel's predictions had a powerful libertarian cast. "No one is accountable to any one else and no third person has a right to interfere," he wrote; "What I eat and drink, how I sleep and dress is my private affair, and my private affair also is my intercourse with a person of the opposite sex."[98]

In 1884, soon after Marx's death, Engels published *The Origin of the Family, Private Property, and the State,* a comprehensive study

[96] August Bebel, *Women and Socialism* (New York, 1910): 76, 83.
[97] Ibid., pp. 76, 100, 104, 174.   [98] Ibid., pp. 466, 467.

of the origins of women's oppression and the development of the family. The book had a great impact on socialist thinkers, including Bebel, who quickly incorporated Engels's theoretical advances into subsequent editions of *Women and Socialism*. Engels based *The Origin* on Marx's "Ethnological Notebooks" compiled in 1880–1881. Marx's notes covered a groundbreaking study of kinship among the American Indians written by Lewis Henry Morgan in 1877. In Engels's words, the new data made it possible to go beyond "the Five Books of Moses," to develop a theory of the evolution of the family.[99]

In *The Origin*, Engels directly acknowledged the centrality of reproduction to the historical process. The social organization of any given period, he argued, was determined not only by the division of labor, but by the form of the family as well. He began his analysis of the family with a discussion of tribal relations, claiming that there was a stage when "unrestricted sexual freedom prevailed within the tribe." Over time, marriage groups were gradually formed along generational lines, and pairing no longer occurred between parents and children. Group marriage by generation was slowly superceded by a new family form as intercourse between brothers and sisters (children of the same mother) became taboo. Engels argued that this system, known as the gens, lay at the heart of the social orders of most barbarian peoples until the advent of the Greek and Roman civilizations. The early history of the family consisted of the progressive narrowing of the circle that had originally embraced the whole tribe. Finally, only the single pair remained.[100]

Yet even the single-pair system was still based on a communal household and descent through the female line. Engels argued that communal housekeeping guaranteed the supremacy of the woman in the house, while the exclusive recognition of the female parent (due to the difficulty of identifying the male) ensured that women were held in high esteem. Women lived with their gens, inviting men from other gens to live with them permanently or temporarily. Women kept the children and shared household tasks with their sisters. If a man displeased a woman, she tossed him out of the communal dwelling. According to

[99] Frederick Engels, *The Origin of the Family, Private Property, and the State*, p. 74.
[100] Ibid., pp. 71–72, 94–112.

Engels, the communal household formed "the material foundation of that supremacy of women which was general in primitive times."[101]

Engels never clearly specified the reasons for the transition from group marriage to the loosely paired couple. He suggested that the change may have been caused by increasing population density and the erosion of older communistic forms of social life. Women themselves may have brought about the change. Yet matriarchy and the communal household still prevailed despite the widening application of the incest taboo and the narrowing of the marriage circle.[102]

According to Engels, the critical change in the position of women occurred as a result of the domestication of animals and the development of agriculture. Once human labor produced a surplus over its maintenance costs, slavery arose. Men, who had always owned the instruments of production, replaced their bows and arrows with cattle and slaves. Yet a man was still unable to pass on property to his children. Upon his death, his property reverted either to his brothers and sisters or to his sisters' children. The development of private property demanded that "mother right" be overthrown. The offspring of the male now remained with his own gens, and the offspring of the female went to the father's gens. Paternity was ensured by the enforcement of women's fidelity. Monogamy for women replaced the loosely paired family. The man took command in the home and "the woman was degraded and reduced to servitude." The patriarchal family replaced the communal household of sisters. "The overthrow of mother right," Engels declared, "was the *world historic defeat of the female sex.*"[103]

Blasting the bourgeois hypocrisy that surrounded patriarchal monogamy, Engels scornfully denied that it was "the fruit of individual sex love," insisting instead on its historical origin as "the subjugation of one sex by the other." Women's oppression was rooted in the destruction of the communal household. Once household management lost its public character and became a "private service," "the wife became the head servant, excluded from all participation in social production."[104]

According to Engels, capitalism created the first real possi-

[101] Ibid., pp. 112, 113.   [102] Ibid., p. 117.   [103] Ibid., pp. 118–121.
[104] Ibid., pp. 122, 128, 137.

bility for women's liberation since the overthrow of mother right, by once again involving women in social production. Yet it simultaneously gave rise to new contradictions between women's social role and the older family form. If a woman carried out "her duties in the private sphere of her family," her ability to earn a wage was limited. And if she entered the workforce, she could hardly "carry out her family duties."[105] Engels believed that this contradiction between the older family form, based on the private domestic services of the wife, and the increasing involvement of women in production could not be resolved under capitalism. Capitalism created the preconditions for women's liberation by giving women their economic independence, but only socialism could create a new family form that properly corresponded to women's new roles.

Under socialism, private housekeeping would be transformed into social industry. The care and education of children would become a public affair. And "the economic foundations of monogamy, as they have existed hitherto will disappear." Monogamy would be replaced by "individual sex love." The only moral marriage would be one in which "love continues." And if "the intense emotion of sex love," differing in duration from person to person, came to an end, separation would be "a benefit for both partners as well as for society."[106]

In *The Origin*, Engels provided the fullest expression of Marxist thinking on women and the family, offering an analysis of women's oppression based on changing relations of production. He initiated the theoretical discussion of the contradiction between the reproductive and the productive spheres under capitalism, advancing a new imperative for the abolition of the family under socialism. He confidently predicted a new dawn for women's liberation under capitalism, premised on women's increasing involvement in the wage labor force.

The work of Engels and Bebel was crucial in combatting proletarian antifeminism in the workers' movement, but so were the practical efforts to implement their ideas. One of the key figures in popularizing and developing new strategies was Clara Zetkin (1857–1933), an immensely talented leader of the German social-democratic movement and tireless proponent of the rights

[105] Ibid., pp. 137–138.   [106] Ibid., pp. 139, 138, 145.

of working women. Zetkin first read Bebel's book while in her early twenties and it immediately changed her views of women. Although her theoretical efforts never rivaled that of Engels or Bebel, her organizational work, speeches, writing, and lifelong commitment to women workers helped chart a new direction within the European socialist movement and the Social Democratic Party of Germany in particular.[107]

Zetkin's theoretical work was closely intertwined with her organizational activities on behalf of women. Like Marx, Engels, and Bebel, she recognized that women's increasing involvement in waged work was historically inevitable, and she fought to ensure that this analysis was reflected in the practical strategies of the socialist parties. She repeatedly clashed with the more conservative members of the labor movement who sought to eliminate women from the workforce by demanding a family wage. Zetkin considered this demand to be futile. If employers insisted on female labor because it was cheaper, men and women must fight for "equal pay for equal work." The trade unions had to begin organizing women. In her speech to the founding Congress of the Second International in 1889, Zetkin spoke forcefully on behalf of women workers. She explained, "It is not women's work per se which in competition with men's work lowers wages, but rather the exploitation of female labor by the capitalists who appropriate it." She later summarized this speech in a pamphlet that became a guide for the future policies of the SPD. Zetkin not only defended women's right to work, but believed that waged work was a "quintessential prerequisite" for women's independence. Although in Zetkin's words, "the slave of the husband became the slave of the employer," she insisted that women "gained from this transformation."[108]

On a theoretical level, Zetkin enlarged upon the initial insights of Engels and Bebel. Focusing on the transition from an

[107] For two fine essays on Clara Zetkin and the SPD, see Jean Quataert, "Unequal Partners in an Uneasy Alliance: Women and the Working Class in Imperial Germany," in Boxer, Quataert, eds., *Socialist Women;* and Karen Honeycut, "Clara Zetkin: A Socialist Approach to the Problem of Women's Oppression," in *European Women on the Left.* Alfred Meyer presents a more negative view of Zetkin as an antifeminist in *The Feminism and Socialism of Lily Braun.*

[108] *Zetkin,* pp. 56, 45, 47.

agrarian to an industrial economy, Zetkin explored the change in women's roles with the expansion of commodity production. She argued that in precapitalist society, women were "an extraordinarily productive force," producing all or most of the goods needed by the family. The transition to machine production and large-scale industry rendered women's economic activity within the family superfluous, for modern industry produced needed goods cheaper and faster. As the production of goods within the home became increasingly unnecessary, women's domestic activity lost its function and its meaning. This created a new contradiction between women's need to participate in public life and their legal inability to do so. The very existence of the "woman question" was premised on this contradiction.[109]

To Zetkin, a women's movement was unthinkable in a peasant society. It could emerge only "within those classes of society who are the very children of the modern mode of production."[110] Following Engels, she argued that women's oppression resulted from the development of private property, but she added that a women's movement against such oppression could only result from the conditions of capitalist production that thrust women into the public sphere while placing numerous restrictions on their ability to function within it. Zetkin thus used a Marxist framework to explain the genesis of the nineteenth-century "woman question" itself.

Marx and Engels made no distinction between the various forms of oppression suffered by women of different classes. Zetkin was the first to situate women's oppression within a more subtle understanding of class. In essence, she posited a different "woman question" for each class in capitalist society. Upper-class women were primarily concerned with the freedom to manage their own property. Middle-class, educated women sought professional training and job opportunities, or in Zetkin's words, "untrammelled competition between men and women." Proletarian women, compelled to work to supplement their families' wages, furthered their own interests by joining with men to fight for better working conditions for both sexes.[111]

Zetkin's years of efforts on behalf of women workers received

[109] Ibid., p. 46.   [110] Ibid., p. 74.
[111] Ibid., pp. 74–76. Despite Zetkin's close experience with male hostility to female labor, she reserved her contemptuous phrase, "un-

international recognition in 1907 at the Congress of the Second International. The first International Conference of Socialist Women was held at the same time, and the International endorsed the principle of women's right to work, the creation of special women's organizations within all the socialist parties, and a position on active organizing for women's suffrage.[112] An official strategy for women's full enfranchisement – political, economic, and social – was finally in place.

Soviet theorists

By 1900, the ideas of August Bebel and Clara Zetkin were widely known in Russian social-democratic circles, for many of the social-democratic leaders had read extensively in Marxist literature abroad. The first Russian edition of Bebel's famous work was published in 1895 and others soon followed. Kollontai had been greatly influenced by Marx, Engels, and Bebel, as well as by the literature of the French Revolution and the utopian socialists. A meeting with Zetkin in 1906 convinced her of the need to begin organizing working-class women at home.[113]

The advances of European social democrats on the women question undoubtedly influenced their Russian counterparts, but progressive circles in Russia had long championed ideas of free union and women's equality. George Sand's emphasis on

trammeled competition," to describe only middle-class women's demands.

[112] Stites, pp. 237–239; Thonessen, pp. 44–45, 65.

[113] Stites, pp. 247, 250–251. Stites offers the best and most comprehensive treatment of the development of ideas about women's liberation. See also Linda Edmondson, *Feminism in Russia, 1900–1917* (Heinemann Educational Books, London, 1984) and her "Russian Feminists and the First All-Russian Congress of Women," *Russian History*, 3, part 2 (1976): 123–149; Dorothy Atkinson, Alexander Dallin, Gail Lapidus, eds., *Women in Russia* (Harvester, Sussex, 1978); G. A. Tishkin, *Zhenskii vopros v Rossii v 50–60 gg. xix v.* (Leningrad, 1984); Anne Bobroff, "The Bolsheviks and Working Women, 1905–1920," *Soviet Studies*, 26, no. 4 (1974); Barbara Clements "Bolshevik Women: The First Generation," in Yedlin, ed. *Women in Eastern Europe and the Soviet Union*; M. Donald, "Bolshevik Activity amongst the Working Women of Petrograd in 1917," *International Review of Social History*, 27, part 2 (1982).

love and the emotional imperatives of the heart found an eager audience among the Russian gentry in the 1830s, and advocates for women's education in the 1850s reiterated many of the European debates over women's potential. Moreover, Russians quickly made these ideas their own. Nikolai Chernyshevskii's famous novel, *What Is to Be Done?* converted several generations of young rebels to the causes of free union and women's emancipation. The nihilists attempted to put his ideas of communal living and working arrangements into practice in the 1860s. Such experiments were not altogether successful, but they nonetheless influenced subsequent generations of radicals who continued to reject the traditional family and to demand women's independence. The populists and terrorists of the 1870s and 1880s subordinated the woman question to a broader politics of class, but they unhesitatingly embraced the ideals of comradeship, companionate union, mutual respect, and women's equality pioneered by the nihilists. Women's unusually influential role in the leadership of these groups, especially the terrorist People's Will, was "a unique phenomenon in nineteenth century European history."[114] Bolshevik views of marriage and the family drew not only on a European tradition shaped by the work of Marx, Engels, and Bebel, but also a native revolutionary culture shared by Marxists and non-Marxists alike.

Yet Bolshevik thinking on the family went far beyond the communal experiments of Russian radical movements. In terms of its analytical categories, its historical methods, and its prescriptions for structural change, Bolshevik thinking drew heavily on the precepts of "scientific" – not "utopian" – socialism. The party's concern with the production and consumption functions of the family, its insistence on the withering away of the family as historically inevitable, and its emphasis on the link between wage labor and women's liberation, were all drawn directly from Marxist theory.

Not surprisingly, given the overwhelmingly peasant character of the country and its relatively recent experience with industrialization, Soviet theorists were particularly interested in the transformation of the family in the transition from a peasant to

[114] Stites, p. 153; See also Barbara Engel's pioneering study, *Mothers and Daughters. Women of the Intelligentsia in Nineteenth-Century Russia* (Cambridge University Press, Cambridge, 1983).

an industrialized society. Marx, Engels, and Bebel had observed that capitalism stripped the family of its most crucial functions, but they had never dealt empirically or theoretically with this transformation. Zetkin was the first to offer a Marxist analysis of the loss of the family's productive function in the move from peasant to proletarian. In examining this transition, Soviet theorists posited the idea of the waged, urban family as a unit of consumption, a novel conception that was considerably more sophisticated than the idealized proletarian family offered by Marx and Engels. Their innovative thinking permitted the discovery and exploration of deeper patterns of dependency and domination within the working-class family.

Many Soviet theorists were interested in the dwindling economic importance of the family and the gradual atrophy of its various social functions. Nikolai Bukharin, a member of the Politburo and a highly respected theoretician, provided a brief historical overview of the family in his well-known work, *Historical Materialism: A System of Sociology*. Here Bukharin distinguished between the peasant family, "a firm unit" based directly on production, and the working-class family, a weaker entity, based largely on consumption. He described the atrophy of the productive function of the family in the transition to urban life and wage labor, noting that city services, women's entrance into the labor force, and the increased mobility of labor all served to "disintegrate the family."[115]

Kollontai took Bukharin's dichotomy between production and consumption several steps further in her investigation of its effect on social traditions and sexual morality. She argued that family and marriage relations were strongest in those precapitalist economies where the family served both as a unit of production and consumption. The "withering away" of the family was the result of a long historical process that began with the elimination of the family as the primary unit of production. The

---

[115] Nikolai Bukharin, *Historical Materialism. A System of Sociology* (International Publishers, New York, 1925): 156. P. I. Stuchka, the first commissar of justice, also identified the productive function of the family with the peasantry. Like Bukharin, he argued that with the development of capitalism, the family was replaced by the factory as the primary unit of production. See his "Semeinoe Pravo," *Revoliutsiia prava*, 1 (1925): 175.

sociologist Vol'fson explained this process: "Already at the end of capitalism, the family has almost no productive labor function, its child-rearing function is strongly limited, its political function is withering away, and even its household function is circumscribed. Under socialist society, the disintegration of the family is fully achieved." Both Kollontai and Vol'fson reasoned that the loss of the productive function was another indicator of the inevitability of the family's historical demise.[116]

Unlike Vol'fson, however, some theorists were less sanguine in their predictions of the family's demise as they probed its role under capitalism more deeply. Marx and Engels had argued that little held the propertyless proletarian family together other than genuine affection, and that moreover, given its lack of property, there was "no basis for any kind of male supremacy" in the proletarian household. E. O. Kabo, a leading economist and sociologist of working-class family life in the 1920s, strenuously challenged this idea in her sophisticated theoretical and empirical work on the Soviet proletarian family of the 1920s.

Kabo pointed out important structures of gender dependency within the working-class family that had been overlooked by Marx, Engels, Bebel, and Zetkin. She argued that although the working-class family was no longer a unit of production, it remained the primary unit of organizing reproduction and consumption, providing for the care of the old, the sick, and the very young. In the absence of other social forms, mothers with young children, the old, and the disabled could not survive without the support system of the family. Without the family, the working class would be unable to reproduce itself. The family represented "the most profitable and most efficient organization of workers' consumption and the upbringing of a new generation."[117]

In Kabo's view, the family functioned as a unit of consumption by organizing the care of the nonwaged *at the expense of the wage-workers*. One of the most essential functions of the working-class family was thus to redistribute income by combining the contributions of all its members to ensure a basic living standard for

---

[116] Kollontai, "Tezisy o Kommunisticheskoi Morali v Oblast Brachnykh Otnoshenii," p. 28, and her "Sem'ia i Kommunizm," *Kommunistka*, 7 (1920): 17; Vol'fson, p. 375.

[117] E. O. Kabo, *Ocherki rabochego byta* (Moscow, 1928): 25–26.

both its paid and unpaid members. She wrote, "The construction of the working-class family is such that the standard of living of all its members is approximately the same. In this way, equality of consumption is achieved despite the extreme inequality of salary payments." The family served as a mechanism by which the burden for the reproduction of labor was shifted onto the wage-earning male. The very existence of the working-class family was based on "the voluntary exploitation of one worker by the others."[118] Thus Kabo turned Marx and Engels's analysis on its head: The central fact of family life was not that the husband exploited the wife, but that the wife, and all the non–wage-earning family members, "exploited" the wage-earning husband. Kabo used this word in its narrowest sense, of course, to signify that the non–wage-earning lived at the expense, or by the labor power, of the wage-earning.

In contrast to Marx, Engels, Bebel, and Zetkin, who variously explored the process by which capitalism undermined traditional family roles and ultimately the family itself, Kabo focused on the forces of capitalism that held the family together. She argued that women's lower levels of pay and skill and their maternal responsibilities reinforced and perpetuated their economic dependence on men. Salary differentiation according to skill supported "the dependence of one worker on another, preventing unskilled workers from leaving the family." Unlike Marx and Engels, who argued that capitalism undermined the family by involving women in waged work, Kabo saw the more subtle ways in which labor market segmentation, salary differentials, and women's reproductive role created powerful economic fetters within the family.

Perhaps most important, Kabo's observations applied with equal force to the working-class family under both capitalism and socialism. Positing an inverse relation between salary differentiation and the strength of the family, she wrote, "Low salaries, wide wage disparities among workers, low norms of social insurance, and high waves of unemployment, all ensure a stronger taproot of family life." These were precisely the factors, Kabo knew, that characterized Soviet labor relations in the 1920s. Only a reversal of these conditions – through an egalitar-

[118] Ibid.

ian wage policy, comprehensive social welfare programs, and full employment– could lead to the liberation of women, children, the old, and the disabled, "the weakest economic elements of the working-class family." Only then would the family cease to be a necessary form of social organization.[119]

Like Kabo, Kollontai was sensitive to the forces that held the propertyless working-class family together. But whereas Kabo stressed the dependence of women on men, Kollontai emphasized the mutual dependence of the sexes in the absence of the socialization of household labor. Male workers depended on women for the preparation of food, clothing, and a variety of other nonwaged but essential tasks. Despite the loss of the productive function, the proletarian family "preserved for itself a certain stability." Focusing on the contribution of domestic labor, Kollontai explained, "The less accessible the apparatus of social consumption was for the masses, the more necessary was the family."[120] For Kollontai, the family would continue to serve an indispensable function as long as household labor remained privatized.

These Soviet theorists went considerably beyond the hasty sketches offered by Marx, Engels, and Bebel of the family under socialism. Emphasizing the transition from peasantry to proletariat, they explored the loss of the productive function within the family and the continuing significance of consumption. Both Kabo and Kollontai provided new theoretical insights into the bonds that held the working-class family together under both capitalism and socialism. Moreover, their work had major strategic implications. If the state was serious about women's liberation, it had to implement policies to abolish wage differentiation, to raise wages, to establish broad social services, and to socialize household labor.

The first code on marriage, the family, and guardianship

The Bolsheviks recognized that law alone could not liberate women, but the first steps they took, naturally enough, were to

[119] Ibid.
[120] Kollontai, "Tezisy o Kommunisticheskoi Morali," pp. 28–29.

eliminate Russia's antiquated family laws and to provide a new legal framework for their own vision of social relations. Reform-minded jurists had attempted to update Russia's laws for more than a half-century prior to the October Revolution but had met with little success. In two brief decrees, published in December 1917, the Bolsheviks accomplished far more than the Ministry of Justice, progressive journalists, feminists, the Duma, and the Council of State had ever even attempted: They substituted civil for religious marriage and established divorce at the request of either spouse. A complete Code on Marriage, the Family, and Guardianship was ratified by the Central Executive Committee of the Soviet (VTsIK) a year later, in October 1918.[121] The new Code swept away centuries of patriarchal and ecclesiastical power and established a new doctrine based on individual rights and gender equality.

Prior to the Revolution, Russian law recognized the right of each religion to control marriage and divorce according to its own laws, and incorporated this right into state law. Women were accorded few rights by either the church or the state. According to state law, a wife owed complete obedience to her husband. She was compelled to live with him, take his name, and assume his social status. Up to 1914, when limited reforms permitted a woman to separate from her husband and obtain her own passport, a woman was unable to take a job, get an education, receive a passport for work or residence, or execute a bill of exchange without her husband's consent.[122] A wife was "responsible to obey her husband as head of the household," in "unlimited obedience." In return, the husband was "to live with her in harmony, to respect and protect her, forgive her insufficiencies, and ease her infirmities." He was responsible to support her according to his status and his abilities. The only mitigating factor in this bleak prescription for patriarchal power was that Russian law, unlike European law, did not establish joint property be-

[121] *1-i kodeks zakonov ob aktakh grazhdanskogo sostoianiia, brachnom, semeinom i opekunskom prave* (Moscow, 1918). The best treatment of the development of the 1918 Family Code is offered by N. A. Semiderkin, *Sozdanie Pervogo Brachno-Semeinogo Kodeksa* (Izdatel'stvo Moskovskogo Universiteta, Moscow, 1989). See also A. M. Beliakova, E. M. Vorozheikin, *Sovetskoe semeinoe pravo* (Moscow, 1974): 63–65.

[122] William Wagner, "In Pursuit of Orderly Change: Judicial Power and the Conflict over Civil Law in Late Imperial Russia," Unpublished Ph.D. dissertation, Oxford University, 1981. pp. 2–7.

tween spouses. Within this legal configuration, each spouse was permitted to own and acquire separate property. A woman's dowry, inheritance, special purchases, and gifts were recognized as her own.[123]

The power relations between husband and wife were replicated between father and children. A father held almost unconditional power over his children, not merely to the age of majority, but for life. Only children from a recognized marriage were considered legitimate; illegitimate children had no legal rights or recourse. Up to 1902, when the state enacted limited reforms, an illegitimate child could only be adopted, recognized, or subsequently legitimatized by special imperial consent, even if the father was so inclined.[124]

It was almost impossible to divorce in prerevolutionary Russia. The Orthodox Church considered marriage a holy sacrament that few circumstances could dissolve. Divorce was permissible only in cases of adultery (witnessed by at least two people), impotence, exile, or a prolonged and unexplained absence by a spouse. In cases of adultery or impotence, the responsible party was permanently forbidden to remarry. The Holy Synod granted divorce grudgingly and rarely.[125]

Progressive-minded jurists attempted to reform family law after 1869, but powerful conservative state and religious authorities blocked even the most timorous attempts. A special commission within the Ministry of Justice published a new civil code after 1900, but it was never enacted, despite the commission's elaborate precautions to avoid infringing on the prerogatives of the church. The horizon of possibility itself was clouded by the intransigence of the Holy Synod. Even the most radical critics of family law did not advocate equality between men and women, and in fact they proposed little beyond the inclusion of mutual consent as grounds for divorce and the adoption of illegitimate children at the father's request.[126]

The Soviet state's first Code on Marriage, the Family, and Guardianship highlighted the timidity of the prerevolutionary

[123] *Svod zakonov Rossiiskoi Imperii*, 10, part 1 (1914): 11–13.
[124] Wagner, pp. 5–6.
[125] N. A. Semiderkin, "Tserkovnyi Brak i Oktiabr'skaia Revoliutsiia v Rossii," *Vestnik Moskovskogo Universiteta*, 2 (1980): 30–31.
[126] Wagner, ch. 3 and 4.

attempts at reform. Goikhbarg, a former Menshevik who joined the Bolsheviks after the Revolution and became the Siberian *oblast'* commissar of justice, headed a committee to draft the Code in August 1918. Only 34 years old at the time of the Revolution, Goikhbarg had already written several commentaries on prerevolutionary civil law. A member of the *kollegiia* of the Commissariat of Justice, he also helped draft the new Civil Code and other pieces of legislation. He wrote extensively on family law, economic law, and civil procedure in the 1920s.[127] In its insistence on individual rights and gender equality, the Code constituted nothing less than the most progressive family legislation the world had ever seen.[128] It abolished the inferior legal status of women and created equality under the law. Eliminating the validity of religious marriage, it gave legal status to civil marriage only, and set up local bureaus of statistics (known as ZAGS) for the registration of marriage, divorce, birth, and death. The Code established divorce at the request of either spouse: No grounds were necessary. And it extended the same guarantees of alimony to both men and women.

The Code swept away centuries of property law and male privilege by abolishing illegitimacy and entitling all children to parental support. All children, whether they were born within or outside a registered marriage, had equal rights. The Code thus severed the concept of marriage from that of family by constructing familial obligations independent of the marriage contract. Zinaida Tettenborn, noting "the sharp delimitation of the rights of marriage and the rights of the family," wrote, "In this area, the Code breaks with the tradition of European legisla-

[127] A subdepartment of the Department of Legal Suggestions and Codification (OZPK) was responsible for editing legal plans after they were developed by the appropriate commissariats, and before their submission to Sovnarkom. The OZPK was abolished during the civil war, reestablished in 1920, and reorganized in 1921 to serve as a consultative body for the VTsIK and Sovnarkom (Council of People's Commissars). On the early history of the Commissariat of Justice, see L. I. Antonova, "Pravotvorcheskaia Deiatel'nost' Vyshikh Organov Gosudarstvennoi Vlasti Rossiiskoi Federatsii v 1917–1922," Candidate Degree, Leningrad State University, 1964, pp. 141–161; and A. A. Nelidov, *Istoriia gosudarstvennykh uchrezhdenii SSSR, 1917–1936* (Moscow, 1962).

[128] *The Marriage Laws of Soviet Russia: The Complete Text of the First Code of the RSFSR* (New York, 1921).

tion and jurisprudence which views family relations in connection with the institution of marriage."[129]

The Code forbade adoption in the belief that the state would be a better guardian for an orphan than an individual family. In a primarily agrarian society, jurists feared that adoption would allow peasants to exploit children as unpaid labor. Anticipating the time when all children would enjoy the benefits of collective upbringing, jurists and educators considered the abolition of adoption the first step in transferring child care from the family to the state.

In accordance with the prevailing idea of marriage as a union between equals, the Code sharply restricted the duties and obligations of the marital bond. Marriage did not create community of property between spouses: A woman retained full control of her earnings after marriage and neither spouse had any claim on the property of the other. Although the Code provided an unlimited term of alimony for either gender, support was limited to the disabled poor. The Code presupposed that both parties, married or divorced, would support themselves.

From a comparative perspective, the 1918 Code was remarkably ahead of its time. Similar legislation concerning gender equality, divorce, legitimacy, and property has yet to be enacted in America and many European countries.[130] Yet despite the Code's radical innovations, jurists were quick to point out "that this is not socialist legislation, but legislation of the transitional time."[131] As such the Code preserved marriage registration, alimony, child support, and other provisions related to the continuing if temporary need for the family unit.

As Marxists, the jurists were in the odd position of creating legislation that they believed would soon become irrelevant. Discussing the role of the civil registry offices (ZAGS), Goikhbarg wrote, "It will be possible, perhaps within a very short time, to

---

[129] Zinaida Tettenborn, "Vvedenie," in *Pervyi kodeks zakonov ob aktakh grazhdanskogo sostoianiia, brachnom, semeinom i opekunskom prave* (Moscow, 1918): 14.

[130] On the history of European family law, see Mary Ann Glendon, *State, Law, and Family. Family Law in Transition in the United States and Western Europe* (North Holland, Amsterdam, 1977).

[131] *Piatyi sozyv Vserossiiskogo Tsentral'nogo Ispolnitel'nogo Komiteta. Stenograficheskii otchet* (Moscow, 1919): 146. Hereafter cited as *1918 VTsIK*.

eliminate the need for certain registrations, for example, marriage registration, for the family will soon be replaced by a more reasonable, more rational differentiation based on separate individuals." Surveying the legal field from the lofty heights of revolutionary victory, Goikhbarg considered that the new Family Code, and other legislation as well, would not last very long. He firmly proclaimed, "Of course, in publishing these law codes, proletarian power, in constructing socialism, does not want to rely on these codes for very long. It does not want to create 'eternal' codes or codes which will last for centuries." The purpose of the law was *not* to strengthen the family or the state. "The new dictatorship of the proletariat," Goikhbarg noted, "does not want to imitate the bourgeoisie, aiming to strengthen its power by the help of eternal codes that would exist for centuries." Law, like the family and the state itself, would soon wither away. In its absence, society would preserve only "organizing norms" for demographic purposes, such as statistics on birth and death.[132]

Other commentators also stressed the transitional nature of the Code. Tettenborn acknowledged that provisions such as alimony were necessary as long as the state could not support its needy citizens, but that ultimately, responsibility would belong "to the state or society." Alimony, "a necessary condition of the transitional moment," was justified "only by the present inability to organize a comprehensive program of social welfare." Tettenborn advanced a similar argument on child support and parent–child relations. Although the Code made striking and important changes in the relationship between parents and children by substituting parental "rights," exercised "exclusively in the interests of the child," for parental "power," it still preserved the family as the primary unit for bringing up children. Tettenborn explained, "The new family rights stand on the border between the old world and that shining new world where all society will be one family."[133]

In Goikhbarg's opinion, the new Family Code went as far as

[132] A. G. Goikhbarg, "Pervyi Kodeks Zakonov RSFSR," *Proletarskaia revoliutsiia i pravo*, 7 (1918): 5, 3, 4.

[133] Tettenborn, "Vvedenie," p. 16, and her "Roditel'skie Prava v Pervom Kodekse Zakonov RSFSR," pp. 27, 28. See Kurskii's comments in *1918 VTsIK* for similar views, pp. 146–147.

possible given the constraints of the transitional period. It liberated women "insofar as it is possible to liberate them in this transitional time." Looking forward to the free unions of the future, Goikhbarg optimistically explained that "each day of the existence of such laws on marriage undermines (as much as possible) the idea of individual marriage, the legal fetters of husband and wife."[134]

The committee drafted the new Family Code quickly and smoothly with only a few minor disagreements.[135] Committee members debated whether spouses should be required to assume a common surname. M. A. Reisner, a representative of the Extraordinary Commission for the Suppression of Counter-revolution, Sabotage, and Speculation (Cheka) and Commissariat of Internal Affairs (NKVD) who propounded a controversial theory of competing systems of class-based law, contended that people should have the right to choose their own names, but Goikhbarg's argument that a common surname was "a strong weapon in the struggle with the church" prevailed. Reisner suggested that children, as well as adults, should have rights to manage property, but this proposal was also rejected. The jurists were extraordinarily sensitive to the language in the Code describing children born out of wedlock, and struck the term *vnebrachnye*, literally "outside marriage," from the text, replacing

[134] A. G. Goikhbarg, "Pervyi Kodeks Zakonov RSFSR," pp. 8, 9.
[135] The Code was drafted in the aftermath of an extensive organizational shakeup in the newly formed Commissariat of Justice (NKIu.) Initially, NKIu was headed by a *kollegiia* composed of three left Socialist Revolutionaries (SRs) and three Bolsheviks, and chaired by the People's Commissar of Justice, the Bolshevik P. I. Stuchka. The department of codification was chaired by the Deputy People's Commissar, the left SR A. Shreider. In March 1918, after the Brest-Litovsk Treaty, the left SRs officially withdrew from the Soviet government in protest, and Shreider resigned from his posts. After some confusion, the SR leadership ordered its members in NKIu to remain at their jobs. Shreider announced his decision to return, but Stuchka promptly declared his opposition. The Bolshevik members of the *kollegiia*, Stuchka, P. Krasikov, D. Kurskii, and M. Kozlovskii, quickly voted to expel Shreider and the other left SRs from their leadership positions, and in a miniature coup, reallocated the various departments among the remaining Bolsheviks. See TsGAOR, fond 1235, opis' 93, delo 199, pp. 1–2, and pp. 161–188 for a draft of the 1918 Code.

it with the longer, clumsier formulation, "children of parents who are not in a registered marriage." Yet the committee resolved these minor disputes amicably and quickly approved a final draft.[136]

Critics outside the Commissariat of Justice, however, were less satisfied with the final draft. Goikhbarg noted that there was "particularly sharp carping" in the discussion of the Code, especially over the provision on marriage registration. Several critics wanted to abolish marriage altogether. Quoting his opponents, Goikhbarg recounted: "They screamed at us: 'Registration of marriage, formal marriage, what kind of socialism is this?'"[137] N. A. Roslavets, a Ukrainian woman delegate to the 1918 Central Executive Committee of the Soviet (VTsIK), objected strongly to the section on marriage, noting that she could not reconcile it with her "socialist consciousness."[138] She argued that registered marriage was a step backward, away from socialism. "In the final analysis," she declared, "we are moving the population away from a basic socialist understanding, from the freedom of the individual, and from the freedom of marriage relations as one of the conditions of individual freedom." Roslavets argued that marriage was the personal and private affair of every citizen," and that the "choice of every person entering marriage should be absolutely free." She branded the Code "some kind of bourgeois survival" from a period when the state had a vested interest in the marital pair. Marriage "is very significant for the capitalist state," she charged, "but the interference of the state in the business of marriage, even in the form of registration which the Code suggests, is completely incomprehensible, not only in a socialist system, but in the transition." Roslavets, taking a strong libertarian position, contended that "the invasion of the state," sanctioned by the Code, violated "the freedom of the individual in the most intimate area," as well as

---

[136] TsGAOR, fond 1235, opis' 93, delo 199, pp. 154–160. See also N. A. Semiderkin, *Sozdanie pervogo brachno-semeinogo kodeksa*, p. 35, for information on Reisner and the committee to draft the Code.
[137] Goikhbarg, "Pervyi Kodeks Zakonov RSFSR," p. 7.
[138] Ibid. Semiderkin notes that Roslavets entered the VTsIK as a representative of a non-Party group, which included communists and noncommunists.

"the most elementary rights." Angrily, she demanded, "I cannot understand why this Code establishes compulsory monogamy." In Roslavets's opinion, the only statistic that the state needed to register was birth.

Roslavets also opposed the Code's provision on alimony, arguing that it was "nothing other than a payment for love." Marriage, she argued, should not entail any economic consequences. Bourgeois society constructed a single economic unit from the marital pair and encouraged the spouses to accumulate private property. The task of socialist society was to destroy this petty bourgeois form of family. "We should help create the possibility of more freedom," Roslavets urged, "and not encourage anyone to such a form of marriage." Alimony simply promoted "the view that girls should search for and attach themselves to a marriageable man and not develop themselves as people." Roslavets suggested that the VTsIK reject the marriage section of the Code. "Only then," she concluded, "will the state liberate the individual."[139]

Goikhbarg, the official representative of the Code in the VTsIK, attempted to rebut Roslavets's objections. He patiently explained that the Code limited alimony to the disabled poor, and that it was impossible to abolish everything at once. Without the right to alimony, a woman would be unprotected; "This will be a hypocritical phrase," Goikhbarg argued, "not equality in law." Goikhbarg's main argument, however, was that marriage registration was absolutely crucial in the struggle against the church and its control of marriage. Without civil marriage, the population would resort to religious ceremonies and the church would flourish. In his opinion, Roslavets's suggestions were "radical in words" but "reactionary in deed."[140]

Goikhbarg's arguments evidently convinced the majority of delegates, for in October 1918, one year after the Revolution, the VTsIK voted the new Code on Marriage, the Family, and Guardianship into law. The Code contained a mix of reformist and revolutionary legislation: Its provision on civil marriage brought Russia up to date with changes in other European countries, but its provisions on illegitimacy, gender equality, marital

[139] *1918 VTsIK*, pp. 150–152.
[140] Ibid., pp. 152–153; Goikhbarg, "Pervyi Kodeks Zakonov RSFSR," p. 8.

obligations, and divorce surpassed the legislation of any other country. The Code drew freely on the Marxist vision of family relations in its emphasis on freedom, independence, and equality of both spouses. More important, the jurists who drafted the Code viewed its progressive and libertarian features as but a first step toward the eventual withering away of the family and the law. According to Goikhbarg's confident prediction, "We must accept this [code] knowing that it is not a socialist measure, because socialist legislation will hardly exist. Only limited norms will remain."[141]

Conclusion

It took seven centuries for the demand for free union to evolve from the Brethren of the Free Spirit, who claimed an Edenite innocence but showed no desire to liberate Eve, to the Bolshevik vision of women's emancipation and independence. The four components of this Marxist vision – free union, women's liberation through waged labor, the socialization of housework, and the withering away of the family – did not come together until women began to enter the wage labor force in large numbers and an older gender division of labor began to crumble. At this point, a great struggle ensued between the advocates of male working-class prerogatives and the growing ranks of women workers. The ideas of Marx, Engels, Bebel, and Zetkin were worked out on this battlefield.

Historically, no individual or group – religious, philosophical, feminist, or utopian socialist – was capable of mounting an effective challenge to the gender division of labor before capitalism began undermining the family as the basic unit of production. The religious sectaries and the philosophes could not even conceive of such a challenge, the feminist voices of the French Revolution were weak and isolated, the revolutionary Jacobins scorned women's issues, and the early utopian socialists communalized but did not equalize. It was not until the rapid industrial changes of capitalism propelled massive numbers of women into the workforce and systematically undermined the social roles of

[141] *1918 VTsIK,* p. 153.

women in the family that a new vision of women's liberation arose to answer the needs of a mass audience. For despite the difficulties created by female wage labor, it was this fact, above all others, that created the preconditions for women's independence, for a rethinking of gender roles, and for a new conception of the family, in short, for a new material foundation for women's liberation.

The Bolsheviks strongly emphasized waged labor as a prerequisite for women's liberation precisely because the struggle to incorporate female labor into the working-class movement was central to working-class women's equality in the nineteenth century. Their commitment to the socialization of housework and the withering away of the family were direct responses to capitalism's assault on the family and traditional gender roles. Female waged labor and its attendant consequences provided the link between the various components of the Bolshevik vision.

If certain components of the Bolshevik vision were a response to relatively recent transformations, others were age-old. Revolutionaries had long envisioned various forms of free union and debated their implications for women. The practice of free union had repeatedly given rise to criticism that a lack of legal protection exacerbated the vulnerability of women and children. The radical religious sects of the English Revolution, the utopian socialist movement, and prerevolutionary Russian radical circles had all struggled with this problem in an attempt to put their ideals into practice. The same arguments were replicated again, with uncanny similarity, between Bebel and Engels, Kollontai and Lenin, and the Soviet libertarians and their more conservative counterparts. Like their historical forebears, Soviet proponents of unfettered sexuality met their critics in the defenders of women and children. The issues of free sexuality and women's vulnerability were to become crucial determinants in the direction of Soviet family policy.

By 1918, the Bolsheviks stood heir to a multifaceted vision of women's liberation rooted in a long revolutionary tradition. They had taken the first decisive steps toward their ideals in a new Family Code that radically broke with the laws and mores of their country's past. It remained to be seen what would happen to the revolutionary vision now that the revolutionaries actually held power.

2

The first retreat: *Besprizornost'* and socialized child rearing

In March 1921, an organizer for the Detkomissiia (Commission for the Betterment of the Life of Children), traveled south from Moscow into a famine-stricken area. Deeply shaken by what he saw, he wrote in his report:

> Our train arrived at night and stopped not far from Samara. For some reason we could not go any farther. It was one or two in the morning. It was quiet and there was frost on the beets. Our train slept, all was silent, but suddenly, I could make out a thin, weak, remote wailing. I listened – the wailing grew strong and then fell again. I went out onto the platform. In the moonlight, at a great distance, lay some kind of gray rags. As I looked I could see them turning, and from the bosom of these rags came a weak, lingering wail: "Kh-le-b-tsa-, kh-le-b-tsa." One could scarcely distinguish the separate voices, but due to their faintness, they all merged in a weak drawn-out wail. They were children, perhaps three, maybe four thousand, and at my disposal I had ten pounds of bread.[1]

By 1922 there were an estimated 7.5 million "starving and dying" children in Russia.[2] Many, having lost one or both parents, fled broken families and desolate villages, and descended on the towns in search of food. Known as the *besprizorniki* (homeless waifs), they traveled alone and in bands, illegally riding the rails from one end of the country to another. They gathered in shifting crowds in the railroad stations and marketplaces, stealing, begging, picking pockets, and prostituting themselves to survive. Sleeping in the streets, around the railroads, under

[1] TsGAOR, fond 5207, opis' 1, delo 14, p. 7.
[2] "O Bor'be s Detskoi Besprizornost'iu. Utverzhdennoe Kollegiei NKP Postanovlenie Vserossiiskogo S"ezda Zav. ONO," in S. S. Tizanov, M. S. Epshtein, eds., *Gosudarstvo i obshchestvennost' v bor'be s detskoi besprizornost'iu* (Moscow, Leningrad, 1927): 35.

bridges, and in abandoned buildings, they lived like wild creatures, beyond the socializing institutions of family, school, or community. They eyed adult authority with a mixture of fear, hostility, and suspicion, and they consistently defied the efforts of educators to settle them in children's homes and colonies. Although their numbers diminished considerably in the decade after the famine of 1921, they remained a vexing concern to the state well into the 1930s. Their numbers stood as a direct index of the disruption of social life; their treatment, a direct barometer of the state's attitude toward the family.

Children's liberation: Early ideas and policies, 1917–1921

Homeless children roamed the streets of Russian cities well before 1917, but the human losses and social disruptions of World War I, the civil war, and the famine of 1921 swelled their numbers by a staggering magnitude. One historian described the period from 1914 to 1921 as a "demographic earthquake": Sixteen million died in the war, civil war, famine, and epidemics.[3] Two and a half million men never returned from the battlefields of World War I, another million died in the civil war. Men and women who never saw battle perished from hunger, cold, and disease. Epidemics of typhus, cholera, and scarlet fever killed millions. Typhus alone left 1.5 million people dead in 1918–1919. The death rate in the cities tripled.[4]

Families broke apart under the strains of survival and hundreds of thousands of children were orphaned or abandoned. In the winter of 1916–1917, prices increased by half, but family income plummeted as women and children replaced men in the factories for a fraction of the wages. On the eve of the February revolution, *besprizorniki* were a common sight in the larger towns

[3] Moshe Lewin, "Society, State and Ideology during the First Five Year Plan," in his *The Making of the Soviet System* (Pantheon, New York, 1985): 210.

[4] Pierre Sorlin, *The Soviet People and Their Society* (Praeger, New York, 1969): 68, 78, 71, 49, 41, 46; Daniel Brower, "The City in Danger: The Civil War and the Russian Urban Population," in Diane Koenker, William Rosenberg, Ronald Suny, eds., *Party, State and Society in the Russian Civil War. Explorations in Social History* (Indiana University Press, Bloomington, 1989).

and the amount of juvenile crime had more than doubled. Although the food shortage grew steadily worse, the provisional government did little to provide any real assistance to the children.[5]

The Bolshevik seizure of power in October had no immediate effect on the deteriorating food supply, and by 1918, people in the cities were dying of hunger. The writer Viktor Shklovsky described his return to St. Petersburg in the winter of 1918: "The city had grown quiet. Like after an explosion . . . everything was wide open. And there was no regular life of any kind, only wreckage." The harvest of 1920 barely covered the most basic needs of the population. People lived on "linden leaves and vegetable greens."[6] As famine threatened in the winter of 1920–1921, thousands more children were abandoned. One of the delegates at the Congress of Child *Besprizornost'*, Defectivity, and Crime, held in 1920, noted that hunger was causing irreversible damage among the child population and that child prostitutes were roaming the streets in desperation.[7]

As the transportation system collapsed, oil and coal shipments no longer reached the cities. People stoked the old-fashioned furnaces with furniture, but eventually all fuel ran out. Shklovsky wrote: "People who lived in housing with central heating died in droves. They froze to death – whole apartments of them."[8] Factories closed and food disappeared; city dwellers fled back to their old villages. A woman delegate to the Congress for the Protection of Childhood in 1919 observed, "Our towns are literally dying out." She reported that Moscow had lost 1,200,000 people between May and October of 1918, and that the children remaining in the cities were suffering terribly. By 1921, Moscow had lost half its population; Petrograd, two-thirds. The end of the civil war brought victory to Soviet power but the country lay in ruins.[9]

The first large meeting of pedagogues and social activists took place in 1919 at the All-Russian Congress for the Protection of

[5] P. I. Liublinskii, "Okhrana Detstva i Bor'ba s Besprizornost'iu za 10 Let," *Pravo i zhizn'*, 8–9 (1927): 28.

[6] Viktor Shklovsky, *A Sentimental Journey, Memoirs 1917–1922* (Cornell University Press, Ithaca, N.Y., 1969): 133–144.

[7] TsGAOR, fond 2306, op. 13, delo 11, p. 39.   [8] Shklovsky, p. 175.

[9] TsGAOR, fond 2306, op. 13, delo 11, p. 47; Lewin, p. 211.

Childhood. Three hundred delegates met in Moscow to discuss the urgent problems of food and shelter and to formulate an overall policy on *besprizornost'*. Their speeches and discussions reflected the poignant mix of idealism and harsh reality so prevalent in the early years of Soviet power. Elizarova, a member of the Presidium of the Congress, spoke about provisioning, arguing that children above all had to be shielded from poverty and prostitution, and given first priority in the distribution of food and fuel. Extending the idea of society as one big family to encompass the *besprizorniki,* she avowed, "There must be no wretched children who don't belong to anyone. All children are the children of the state." In her discussion of juvenile crime and *besprizornost'*, Elizarova took a strong antiauthoritarian stance. "Children cannot be criminals," she declared, "they cannot be judged as adults. . . . Children should not be put in prison, they should be rehabilitated, not punished." Elizarova's position, based on a progressive, humanist tradition of pedagogy, typified the approach favored by Soviet educators in the 1920s. She suggested that the state create "family-type" institutions for needy children with a minimum of hired personnel. Applying the principle of self-management, the children themselves would "establish and maintain order." The institutions would maintain an "open-door" policy, allowing children to join or leave the community at will. The estates of the former nobility, in her opinion, could finally serve a socially useful function as sites for children's colonies.[10]

Lilina, another delegate, echoed Marx's vision in the *Communist Manifesto* as she spoke of child development in terms of "the many-sided development of the personality, where every person can be an artist, a composer in his work." Many delegates voiced great confidence in the state's ability to replace the family. Women delegates enthusiastically noted that the socialization of child rearing would contribute to the liberation of women. And one delegate happily called out, "What about children's liberation!"[11] The delegates optimistically envisioned a future in which all children, free from hunger and want, would have the

[10] TsGAOR, fond 2306, op. 13, delo 11, p. 6. Unfortunately a stenographic report of this congress is not available, and the minutes contain only selections from the speeches of the delegates.

[11] Ibid., pp. 9–14.

opportunity to realize their individual capabilities. Children would be freed from the family and empowered within their own self-managed, democratic institutions. The state would wield a gentle but effective influence on juvenile delinquents, emphasizing rehabilitation over punishment, moral suasion over discipline.

Yet despite their hopeful schemes and honorable intentions, the delegates still had to face the forbidding problems of the present. Outside the doors of the Congress, thousands of children were starving in institutions that lacked even the most basic provisions. The government had begun evacuating children from the cities to children's homes in the southeast in 1918, in the hope that it would be easier to feed them in the rural grain-producing areas. Organizers put 4,500 children on trains and sent them to children's homes in the provinces of Ufa, Perm, Viatka, and Saratov. About 200 children of workers in the Putilov factory were sent out of the city, and hundreds more sent to abandoned dachas and nobles' estates.[12] Although it made sense to move children out of the starving cities into the countryside, the practice frequently proved ineffective and even dangerous.

Il'ina, a delegate from Voronezh province, lashed out angrily against the policy: "The experiment of the past year of putting children on trains and sending them to Voronezh or Saratov province has not worked," she announced. "Practice shows that these children live much worse than those in the district of Moscow." She accused the organizers of the transport of acting with "unpardonable frivolity." "Moscow was evacuated too hastily," she declared. "It was done by just sending, and not asking where." Moreover, the services for the care of the *besprizorniki* were chaotic and unorganized. Red Army soldiers were dumping large numbers of children at the Commissariat of Social Security. The poorly trained staffs of the children's homes could barely cope with the demands for admittance. "It is possible that many pedagogues are mistaken in their vocation," Il'ina remarked bitterly; "perhaps it would be more useful if some would take up telephone installment."[13]

[12] TsGAOR, fond 2306, op. 1, delo 139, pp. 30–31.
[13] TsGAOR, fond 2306, op. 13, delo 11, pp. 47, 48. The Commissariat of Social Welfare (Narodnyi Komissariat Obshchestvennogo Prizreniia) became the Commissariat of Social Security (Narodnyi

Il'ina argued that children were being placed in "intolerable conditions." Although the original idea of using abandoned manors for children's homes seemed reasonable, after several years of civil war, looting, and destruction, many of the estates were unfit for human habitation. Reproaching her fellow delegates, she said, "You know the gentry estates are completely changed now. It is common knowledge that often the chimneys are smashed and the beams broken. There are no latrines, no beds, and the roofs leak. To put children on trains and send them to such places is a crime, and this crime has been committed for an entire year."[14] Il'ina injected a note of sober realism in the Congress by raising a question that would haunt educators and social workers throughout the twenties: How were the *besprizorniki* to be supported? The government had decided simply to send the children to the bread-rich areas. Yet "every fruitful area with bread can become an area without bread," she noted, "just send a great detachment of the requisitioning committee and the bread-rich provinces will be devastated." Cautioning the hastier delegates, she argued that all talk of abolishing the family was irrelevant as long as the state could not assume the upbringing of children. "We have forgotten that the family is not only a consumer cell," she cautioned, "but a cell of producers. . . . children are not only born and brought up in the family, but are supported by their mothers and fathers." In a dark portent of future debates, Il'ina noted that a children's home "is a society of consumers who demand prepared goods." Economically, the homes were "parasitic" because they "only consume." Il'ina regarded the family with a clearsightedness often lacking among the more utopian thinkers. In her view, it would be pointless to replace the family with children's homes "as long as the children's homes do not take on the other basic features of the family – its economic independence and its productivity."[15] And at that very moment, conditions in the homes amply justified her warning.

Komissariat Sotsial'nogo Obespecheniia) in April 1918. It was responsible for running the children's institutions under the direction of Alexandra Kollontai. In 1919, the Commissariat of Enlightenment took over the management of the institutions, although the Commissariat of Health retained control over facilities for sick and abnormal children, and the Cheka supervised special disciplinary colonies for juvenile delinquents.

[14] Ibid., p. 47.   [15] Ibid., p. 49.

After the Congress, the government made a strong effort to coordinate relief activities for children. In January 1919, Sovnarkom set up the Soviet for the Protection of Children, with representatives from the Commissariats of Enlightenment, Social Security, Health, and Food Supply. The Soviet was charged with distributing food and provisions to children. In May and June, the government authorized free food for all children under 16.[16] Throughout the year, the Soviet continued to evacuate famine-stricken children from Petrograd to the Urals.

As conditions worsened, the number of children in the homes steadily increased from 30,000 in 1917 to 75,000 in 1918; 125,000 in 1919; 400,000 in 1920, and 540,000 in 1921.[17] A. Kalinina, the wife of the president of the Central Executive Committee of the Soviet (VTsIK), described the state of the children's homes in 1920. Children were going about in rags because the state was able to distribute only 10 inches of cloth per child. There was a single spool of thread for 29 people, a pair of stockings for every 264, and only one blanket for 3,124. In the winter, the rooms were dark and freezing, for there was

[16] "Dekret o Besplatnom Detskom Pitanii," and "Postanovlenie Soveta Narodnykh Komissarov," in N. K. Krupskaia, *O bytovykh voprosakh* (Moscow, 1930): 70, 71. Free food was distributed to minors until 1921 when the rationing system was abolished.

[17] Z. Sh. Karamysheva, "Pedagogicheskie Problemy Sotsial'no-Pravovoi Okhrany Nesovershennoletnikh v RSFSR, 1917–1932," Candidate thesis, Nauchno-Issledovatel'skii Institut Obshei Pedagogiki Akademii Pedagogicheskikh Nauk SSSR (Moscow, 1976): 17, 64. N. I. Ozeretskii cites a lower figure for 1922, noting in "Nishchenstvo i Besprizornost' Nesovershennoletnikh," in E. K. Krasnushkin, G. M. Segal, Ts. M. Feinberg, eds., *Nishchenstvo i Besprizornost'* (Moscow, 1929): 140 that according to the "extremely incomplete, inaccurate" figures of the Department for the Social and Legal Protection of Minors (SPON) 444,412 children were in the receiving stations and children's homes. Although social welfare agencies such as the Commissions on the Affairs of Minors, receiving stations, and children's homes and colonies gathered statistics on homeless children, these figures were often inexact. The social service agencies were so overwhelmed by children during the famine that it was almost impossible to keep accurate records. Moreover, many *besprizorniki* passed through the agencies repeatedly, while others had no contact at all. On the problems in determining the statistical dimensions of *besprizornost'* see Jennie Stevens, "Children of the Revolution: Soviet Russia's *Besprizorniki* in the 1920s," Unpublished M.A. thesis, Georgetown University, Washington, D.C., 1985: 29–35.

no electricity and no oil. The children wore the same unwashed rags for months on end. Their bodies were covered with sores. "It was useless to think of any educational scheme in this nightmare," she wrote. "The children did absolutely nothing. The older ones played cards, smoked, and drank, and the girls of 16 and 17 abandoned themselves to prostitution."[18]

Despite the efforts of the Soviet for the Protection of Children, most of the *besprizorniki* remained without any organized shelter. Huge unorganized camps of children sprang up around the railroad stations. In the fall of 1920, 300 children were camped out in the Tikhoretskaia station, 500 in Piatagorsk. Thousands of children milled about the Rostov-on-Don station, an important crossing that joined the north with the Caucasus, the Volga region with the southeast.[19]

The Soviet had trouble coordinating its relief work in part because it lacked the power to issue orders directly and to command resources. Feliks Dzerzhinsky, the head of the Cheka, had become increasingly concerned over *besprizornost'* in his repeated encounters with beggary, juvenile crime, and prostitution. In 1920, Dzherzhinsky called Anatoly Lunacharsky, the head of the Commissariat of Enlightenment, to urge the creation of a strong, interdepartmental agency with direct power to deal with the *besprizorniki*. "I want to devote part of my personal attention, and the main attention of the Cheka to the struggle with *besprizornost'*," he told Lunacharsky. We need to create a broad commission, covering all departments and organizations that might be useful in this business. . . . We are all moving now toward the work of peaceful reconstruction, and I thought: Why not use our military apparatus to struggle with a disaster like *besprizornost'*?"[20]

In January 1921, the presidium of the VTsIK replaced the Soviet for the Protection of Children with the Commission for the Betterment of the Lives of Children, soon known as the

18 A. Kalinina's report is cited by Vladimir Zenzinov, *Deserted. The Story of the Children Abandoned in Soviet Russia* (London, 1931): 23–25.
19 N. V. Shishova, "Bor'ba Sovetskogo gosudarstva za preodolenie detskoi besprizornosti v 1920–1936," Candidate Thesis, Kubanskii Gosudarstvennyi Universitet (Krasnodar, 1982): 37.
20 L. A. Zhukova, "Deiatel'nost' Detkomissii VTsIK po Okhrane Zdorov'ia Detei (1921–1938)," *Sovetskoe zdravookhranenie*, 2 (1978): 64–65.

Detkomissiia. Headed by Dzerzhinsky, with representatives from the Cheka, the Commissariats of Provisioning, Enlightenment, and Health, and other organizations, its tasks were to ensure provisioning for the children's institutions and to care for the *besprizorniki*.

The famine

In the spring of 1921, severe drought hit the Volga region, the southern Ukraine, the Crimea, and the north Caucasus. The resulting famine affected 25 million people in 34 provinces.[21] Hunger and disease annihilated 90–95 percent of children under the age of 3 and almost one-third of those older. Thousands of surviving children – homeless, abandoned, starving – poured into the central railroad stations and overran the markets and streets of the towns.[22] A frantic telegram from a relief worker noted that the town of Bazuluk was literally "flooded by children" with "corpses freezing in the streets, lying about in disorder." More than 3,000 nursing babies had been orphaned or abandoned. The relief worker declared, "We must quickly aid 38,000 children or the town will be choked by children." In Ufa, there were 65,000 homeless children; in Orenburg, 55,000; Simbirsk, 36,000; and Cheliabinsk, 48,000. Throughout the towns, "corpses loll[ed] about, uncollected." The anguished telegram continued: "The preschool children are dying in their native villages, at the dried-up breasts of their mothers and in the exhausted arms of their fathers."[23]

The Commissariat of Enlightenment (NKPros) received grotesque reports of hunger-crazed children gnawing at each other. Mothers tied their children in separate corners of their huts in fear that they would eat each other.[24] In the fall of 1921, 60,000 children poured into the district of Kubano-Chernomorsk.

[21] TsGAOR, fond 1064, op. 5, delo 4, p. 140; Shishova, p. 33. The famine hit hardest in the provinces of Astrakhan, Viatka, Samara, Saratov, Simbirsk, Ufa, and Tsaritsyn. Other provinces were also affected, but less severely. These included Stravropol, which lost 64% of its crop, the Don, 24%, and Kubano-Chernomorsk, 17%.

[22] Zhukova, p. 65   [23] TsGAOR, fond 5207, op. 1, delo 14, pp. 5–6.

[24] V. I. Kufaev, "Pravo Narusheniia i Besprizornost' Nesovershennoletnikh v Rossii," *Pravo i zhizn'*, 1 (1922): 37.

There were 43,000 *besprizorniki* in the towns of Krasnodar and
Armavir. Stavropol province alone contained 108,000 starving
children.[25] Between 200 and 500 children showed up every day,
begging admittance to children's homes that were ill-equipped
to feed, house, or clothe them.[26] The children's homes in the
Volga region were teeming with sick and dying children, overcrowded by 300 to 500 percent.[27]

A journalist described an overcrowded receiving station with
500 children, many suffering from typhus, cholera, and tuberculosis. "Huddled on cots, they lie moaning in rows in a long
fetid room without warmth, without sheets or blankets, without
medicine of any kind, with nothing." Those who were not too
sick sat in the garden, "unmoving, unsmiling, unspeaking." The
journalist spoke with the station's doctor, who said, "We have
nothing, and so they die."[28] A telegram to the Detkomissiia
noted that there were several thousand children in the homes
"without clothes, naked, barefoot, ill, covered with eczema and
spotted fever." Epidemics swept the region; crime, beggary, and
prostitution raged.[29]

According to incomplete figures from 1921–1922, there were
6,603 children's homes holding 540,000 children under the
most makeshift conditions.[30] In the famine-stricken provinces
there were 611 institutions supporting 36,549 children.[31] One
organizer noted helplessly that conditions in the homes were
terrible and that children were dying everywhere: "They are
dying in the homes, in the streets, wherever fate throws them,
they are meeting death." Conditions in some of the homes were
so dreadful that the staff ran away: People could not be persuaded to work in them. Other homes simply closed for lack of
food. The children disappeared into the streets.[32]

Thousands of peasants tried to flee the region by train. Alexander Neveroff, a writer who as a boy had traveled throughout

25 Shishova, p. 37.
26 TsGAOR, fond 5207, op. 1, delo 14, p. 6.
27 Zhukova, p. 65.
28 Walter Duranty, *Duranty Reports Russia* (New York, 1934): 26.
29 Zhukova, p. 65.
30 Liublinskii, p. 30.
31 TsGAOR, fond 1064, op. 5, delo 4, p. 180.
32 TsGAOR, fond 5207, op. 1, delo 14, p. 6.

the famine area in search of bread, described a typical railroad station:

The fields beyond the station, the holes, the ditches, were smeared and befouled. And in the midst of this filth the people lay, stupified with misery, tortured by vermin, surrendered to sodden despair. Trains came and went. The fortunate ones got away, on the buffers, on the roofs. The unfortunate roamed the station for weeks at a time, long despairing days, fever-shaken nights. Mothers wailed over their starving babies; starving babies bit at their mothers withered, milkless breasts.[33]

The Detkomissiia organized mass evacuations: Children had been sent from the cities to the grain-producing areas two years earlier, but now starving children were put on trains and sent out of the very same areas. Between 120,000 and 150,000 children were removed from the famine-stricken provinces to already overburdened children's institutions and hastily organized shelters.[34] Eventually as many as a quarter million children were evacuated.[35] Because of poor planing and coordination, some trains received no food, which meant that many children died in the boxcars. An official from the Evacuation Department of the Commissariat of Health angrily demanded that a local evacuation committee explain the large numbers of deaths on a particular train. The official accused the local committee of evacuating the children haphazardly, without contacting the Commissariat of Food Supply about provisions.[36] Another report mentioned that the policy of evacuation "played a sad role in the children's misfortunes."[37]

The Detkomissiia sent long trains of food and medical supplies to Kazan, Samara, Ufa, Simbirsk, and Bugul'ma, towns with large refugee populations. Each train served more than 6,000 meals a day.[38] The Commissariat of Food took on responsibility for feeding 1,500,000 children and 500,000 adults.[39] By

[33] Alexander Neveroff, *City of Bread* (New York, 1927): 74.
[34] TsGAOR, fond 1064, op. 5, delo 4, p. 186. Zhukova cites the higher figure, p. 65.
[35] TsGAOR, fond 5207, op. 6, delo 10, p. 3.
[36] TsGAOR, fond 5027, op. 1, delo 104, p. 12.
[37] TsGAOR, fond 5207, op. 1, delo 14, p. 6.
[38] Zhukova, p. 65.
[39] TsGAOR, fond 5207, op. 1, delo 104, pp. 11, 24; TsGAOR, fond 5207, op. 1, delo 163, p. 33.

the spring of 1922, there were 10,588 public kitchens in the famine area, serving more than 1.5 million people. Schools closed down and reopened as kitchens for abandoned and orphaned children. Yet despite these efforts, one report stated that "only 10 percent of the child population [was] eating in public dining facilities." "And the others?" it grimly queried. "The countryside is silent on this question. But the towns, overflowing with . . . exhausted, dying children, give you an answer."[40]

Despite the massive efforts of the Detkomissiia, children suffered terribly. The Commissariat of Enlightenment received only half the rations it needed to feed the children housed in its various institutions. On the average, each province received 2,000 to 4,000 rations for every 10,000 to 20,000 children. The provinces that accepted children from the famine area did not receive extra rations.[41] The children's homes could not support the influx of new children: There was simply not enough food. In a forced retreat from the provision of the 1918 Family Code prohibiting adoption, the government began placing children with better-off peasant families in other areas. Although officials knew that the peasants regarded such children as little more than unpaid labor, there were few alternatives under the desperate pressure of mass starvation.

In 1921, starving refugees in Ivanovo-Vosnesensk plaintively sang:

> We are dying out
> The people are dropping
> The houses are closed up
> The fields are all burnt
> We remain without bread
> Who listens to our grief?
> Who hears our sadness?
> Who understands our grief?
> Are you listening?[42]

The song, a direct appeal for relief, captured the pleas of millions. Under conditions of almost complete economic collapse,

[40] TsGAOR, fond 5207, op. 1, delo 14, p. 15.
[41] M. Frumkina, "Detskie Uchrezhdeniia v Novykh Usloviiakh," *Kommunistka*, 1 (1922): 8.
[42] R. Barkina, "Pomoshch' Golodaiushchim Detiam i Moskovskaia Robotnitsa," *Kommunistka*, 1 (1922): 13. The song was reported by a working-class woman from Moscow who traveled through the famine area.

hundreds of thousands of children required immediate shelter, food, medical attention, and care. The family had not withered away gradually, it had been smashed. The brutal blows of war and famine had rapidly accomplished what Soviet theorists had envisioned for a considerably more distant future. And the new state was left, woefully unprepared, to shelter the human wreckage. As the educator P. I. Liublinskii later explained: "Government support of children appeared in the socialist plan as a more remote stage of socialist development when the economic strength of the country was significantly developed." Yet Soviet power had taken on this task "under conditions of unprecedented economic exhaustion."[43]

NEP, women, and the children's homes

The famine heightened a grave shortage of food that had already been apparent by the end of the civil war. By 1920, angry peasants throughout the south rebelled against the policy of requisitioning grain to feed the army and the cities. Their actions soon affected every sector of the economy. As state grain procurements dropped, miners and oil workers returned to the villages to scavenge for food, precipitating a fuel shortage that brought the railroads and factories to a standstill. Faced with the prospect of rural revolt and urban starvation, the Bolsheviks keenly perceived the need to repair relations with the peasantry, increase agricultural production, and restore industry. In February 1921, Lenin proposed a seemingly small remedial measure to the Politburo. The government would replace the practice of grain requisitioning with a set tax in kind and permit the peasants to market their surplus. The measure, adopted at the Tenth Party Congress in 1921, soon became known as the New Economic Policy, or NEP. The delegates accepted the proposal readily though as E. H. Carr observed, "Its full significance was scarcely realized at the time."[44]

NEP began as a simple measure to increase grain production and was not initially intended as a comprehensive economic policy. Yet the revival of the market soon had a significant impact on

[43] Liublinskii, p. 29.
[44] E. H. Carr, *The Bolshevik Revolution,* Vol. II (Macmillan, London, 1952): 281.

industry and social services. Measures affecting production, wages, employment, banking, and budgeting followed inevitably from the state's initial decision to permit the free marketing of grain. In July 1921, the government passed a decree permitting cooperatives and individuals to lease nationalized industries. A month later, cost accounting and decentralization were introduced in state-run enterprises. Food rations – a common form of wage payment during the civil war – were phased out. Managers were made responsible for paying wages, procuring their own raw materials, and selling their own finished products. The number of workers receiving state rations drastically decreased from 1.5 million in October 1921 to 500,000 by the summer of 1922.[45] In August, the government reintroduced a state budget, a practice that had been scornfully abandoned during the civil war years. In September, payment for all public services and facilities, including dining rooms, daycare, and other social services, became obligatory.[46] By the end of 1922, the transition to "commercial principles" was complete.

NEP was thus adopted piecemeal over the course of two years. Although the Party did not initially regard it as a "comprehensive turnabout," their initial decision to permit the peasants access to a free market for agricultural products had far reaching consequences.[47] Although no one opposed NEP at the Tenth Party Congress, a growing number of critics stepped forward as the full implications of the policy became apparent. Shliapnikov, a Party member and former participant in the Workers Opposition, complained at the Eleventh Party Congress in 1922, that NEP was benefiting peasants at the expense of workers. Disgruntled advocates of social welfare complained loudly of the

[45] Maurice Dobb, *Soviet Economic Development since 1917* (New York, 1948): 152.
[46] Carr, pp. 345–48, 354–55.
[47] Moshe Lewin, *Political Undercurrents in Soviet Economic Debates. From Bukharin to the Modern Reformers* (Princeton University Press, Princeton, N.J., 1974): 84; Silvana Malle, *The Economic Organization of War Communism, 1918–1921* (Cambridge University Press, Cambridge, 1985): 453. According to E. H. Carr, "It was impossible to combine private capitalist agriculture with state industry in the same economy unless the state sector accepted the principles of the market," Carr, p. 304. For Carr's treatment of the adoption of NEP, see pp. 271–332.

negative impact of NEP on women and children. Yet the policy was clearly successful in increasing grain production and reviving industry; its rapid successes offset many of the early criticisms.[48]

Among NEP's ill effects was the shriveling of services available to needy women and children. With the shift to cost accounting, numerous enterprises closed, and unemployment, especially among women, quickly increased. As the government curtailed state spending, it reduced support of the children's institutions, transferring their operating costs to the localities. In practice, however, there were few local funds to sustain the institutions. Moreover, many local executive committees preferred to allocate scarce resources to profit making enterprises, thereby closing thousands of children's institutions.[49]

The combination of closings and persistent high demand led to even more severe overcrowding in the remaining homes. During 1921–1922 the Party and the state issued a series of decrees aimed at reducing the number of children in the homes. New rules for admission were posted and large numbers of children were expelled. Only orphans and children who had lost a parent in the Red Army were now to be accepted. Children of technical or pedagogical workers, those with parents or relations, and teenagers over the age of 16 were no longer eligible for care. Red Army orphans whose parents had died at the front received first priority, followed by the children of Red Army widows, then by other orphans.[50]

In accordance with the new rules, officials sent large numbers of children to relatives, private guardians, production *artels* (co-

[48] Carr, p. 294.
[49] Primary and secondary schools were also affected badly by the transition to NEP. A report to the Detkomissiia in the spring of 1922 noted that the position of the schools in the famine-stricken *guberniias* was terrible. See TsGAOR, fond 5207, op. 1, delo 14, p. 10. Between April and October of 1921, only 307 out of 2,256 primary schools were still functioning; and the number of secondary schools dropped from 150 to 18. There were almost 40,000 fewer students. The number of preschool centers dropped from 215 to 52, although the number of children in them increased from 9,344 to 11,842. See TsGAOR, fond 5207, op. 1, delo 104, p. 42. These figures cover the provinces and districts of Simbirsk, Saratov, Serdobsk, Viatka, Malmyzh, and Iaransk.
[50] Karamysheva, pp. 63, 66.

operatives), workshops, and peasant families. The state developed plans to reorganize the homes into self-sufficient working colonies and allotted plots of land so they could feed themselves.[51] Trade schools were organized to teach industrial and agricultural skills. Joiner, metal, and sewing workshops were set up. Individual workers as well as enterprises and institutions were encouraged to take responsibility for housing and training children. In the face of scarce resources, state policy stressed the importance of learning a trade and becoming a self-supporting member of society. Children were to pay their own way as much as possible through their labor in an individual peasant family, a workshop apprenticeship, or a self-sufficient colony. It was clear that comprehensive state support was not available.

The orphanages were hit hard, but daycare centers suffered an even more drastic decrease in state funding. Many centers received no support at all and were forced to close, which created new hardships for single working mothers. A circular to Provincial and District Departments for Social Upbringing frankly admitted, "The existing grid of preschool institutions does not serve even the neediest part of the working population." According to the circular, the preschool institutions served only 1.8 percent of Russia's people.[52] As daycare centers all over the country folded, the Commissariat of Enlightenment attempted to force the provincial organs to maintain their commitments. In January of 1923, the commissariat issued a decree "categorically demand[ing] an end to further closings of the grid of preschool institutions." It ordered local officials to preserve a minimal number of centers in each province and district and to fund them from local budgets.[53] Another circular, addressed to the Provincial Departments of Peoples' Education, noted that in the transition to local funding, the curtailment of the centers had been "quite sharp with a purely spontaneous character." Local officials had decided, entirely on their own initiative, to

[51] According to Karamysheva, p. 72, the children's towns began to break up in the late twenties. In 1927–1928, there were 77 children's towns in Russia with 20,038 children. A year later, the number had dropped to 68 with 16,000 children.

[52] TsGAOR, fond 2306, op. 1, delo 2744, p. 12.

[53] TsGAOR, fond 2306, op. 1, delo 1795, pp. 4–5. The circular states that there must be no less than two types of preschool facilities in the provincial centers, and one type in the districts.

close the centers. The circular glumly summed up the results of NEP: "All the work done in the past five years in the area of preschool upbringing has come to almost nothing."[54] The head of the preschool department under the Commissariat of Enlightenment also made special mention of the disaster wrought by NEP. She unequivocally declared in a report, "The spontaneous closings of the institutions at the time ruined preschool work."[55]

The government tried to offset the economic effects of NEP through voluntary fundraising campaigns. In February 1923, the Detkomissiia, the Commissariat of Enlightenment, and the Commissariat of Health launched a campaign on behalf of sick and homeless children: Organizations would collect money in the towns and bread in the countryside. The VTsIK and the Detkomissiia acknowledged that "large material means are needed, which are not at the disposal of the state in sufficient quantity." The Detkomissiia added: "The position of our children's institutions is very painful."[56] A year later, the second Congress of the Soviets of the USSR set up a fund in Lenin's name to eradicate *besprizornost'*. The Presidium of the TsIK set aside 100 million rubles and separate local funds in every republic, region, and province. Sovnarkom allocated 20 million rubles: 10 million from the RSFSR budget and an additional 10 million to be collected from local organizations and voluntary contributions. Unfortunately, the fundraisers barely managed to collect 1 million rubles from voluntary sources and the total sum fell considerably short of original expectations.[57] The Detkomissiia continued to complain about shortages, poor conditions, and overcrowding in the children's homes.

Although the Detkomissiia struggled heroically to organize support, the voluntary contributions of an impoverished population could not maintain a network of childcare facilities, and in spite of the decrees, organizational efforts, and fundraising attempts, the children's institutions continued to close. The number of children's institutions in Russia's provincial centers contracted from 3,971 in October 1923 to 3,377 in April 1924 to 2,836 in January 1925. The number of children in the institu-

[54] Ibid., p. 7.   [55] Ibid., p. 5.
[56] TsGAOR, fond 5207, op. 1, delo 14, p. 5.
[57] TsGAOR, fond 5205, op. 1, delo 336, pp. 14–15.

tions dropped from 252,317 in 1923 to 239,776 in 1924 to 228,127 in 1925. A report of the Detkomissiia in 1926 noted that the institutions that remained still lacked shoes, sheets, clothing, other supplies, and badly needed repairs.[58]

The decrease in children's homes and daycare centers inadvertently increased the numbers of *besprizorniki* as the needs of women and the needs of children formed the tight, alternating links of a vicious circle. Without daycare, many single mothers were unable to search for work, and without work, they were unable to support their children, who in turn ran away from impoverished homes to join the *besprizorniki* on the streets. The large numbers of *besprizorniki* then forced the state to divert scarce resources from daycare centers to children's homes, increasing the hardships of both employed and unemployed mothers, and ultimately increasing the numbers of *besprizorniki*.

Equally important, the lack of child care seriously undermined any attempt to liberate women. Mothers had no opportunity to acquire job skills, to get an education, or to participate in public and political life. Married mothers, dependent on their husbands' wages, remained tied to the family. Single mothers faced an even worse situation: They were unable to supervise their children if they found work and unable to support them if they did not. One critic summed up the plight of women:

If a mother appeals to a creche or children's home at the present time, they tell her: 'Your child has a mother. We take only orphans.' They have a point: of course, we must provide for orphans first. But the mother has a point too when she thinks that deprivation, need, and birth have exhausted her, that her salary barely covers her own famished existence, and that it is impossible to work and care for a child at the same time.[59]

Besprizornost' and crime

As the children's homes closed, many children drifted back onto the streets. Efforts to place them in peasant families, workshops, and children's colonies frequently came to naught. The Depart-

[58] TsGAOR, fond 5207, op. 6, delo 10, pp. 6, 5.
[59] I. Stepanov, "Problemy Pola," in E. Iaroslavskii, ed., *Voprosy zhizni i bor'by. Sbornik* (Moscow, Leningrad, 1924): 207.

ment for Social and Legal Protection of Minors (SPON) in Ufa
revealed that fully 40 percent of the people who accepted responsibility for a child were unsatisfactory guardians.[60] Children were too often placed in homes where they were neglected,
exploited, or abused. Large numbers of children who did not
qualify for care, or were exploited by peasant families, escaped
to the streets.

The children became the scourge of the markets and the railroad stations. Begging and stealing to survive, *besprizorniki* were
responsible for at least half of all juvenile crimes. They quickly
became involved in the criminal underworld, learning the tricks
of survival from adult thieves and con artists. They joined gangs
specializing as apartment burglars, bazaar crooks, garret thieves,
railway pilferers, suitcase lifters, swindlers, cheats, and sharps.
They perfected elaborate begging ruses and pickpocketing
schemes, mimicking deformities, singing obscene ditties, and
using smaller children and baby dolls to evoke sympathy among
passersby.[61] They "knocked" or mugged people, working in
pairs to trip unsuspecting victims and seize their bags, and
moved through the markets in groups, tipping over carts and
barrows, and swooping down on the rolling produce.[62]

Their marauding depredations tried common sympathy and
eroded pity for their plight. One eyewitness wrote, "These children run wild in gangs like packs of wolves and are regarded by
the population as human lice." He described their tough, contemptuous demeanor and their "puffed-out and cunning looking faces that remind one of middle-aged roués."[63] Other people spoke with even greater dispargement and resentment. One
law-abiding citizen angrily pontificated, "I would put the whole
tribe of those sons-of-bitches in a sack and sink it in the river and
drown every last one of them. What a burden they are to the

[60] Karamysheva, p. 83.
[61] Vyacheslav Ia. Shishkov, *Children of the Street* (Strathcona, Royal Oak,
Mich., 1979): 113, 28–29. Shishkov's book, first published as a short
novel in the Soviet Union in 1930, dealt with the lives of two *besprizorniki* and their gang. Set in the early 1920s, the fictionalized story was
based on years of primary and secondary research.
[62] Rene Bosewitz, *Waifdom in the Soviet Union. Features of the Sub-culture
and Re-education* (Peter Lang, Frankfurt, 1988): 18.
[63] Lancelot Lawton, *The Russian Revolution 1917–1926* (London, 1927):
231.

government! It's just awful! There are more of them than you can count. There are as many of them in every single city as there are bedbugs in a flophouse. They catch them and send them to orphanages and what happens then? The lousy little rats run away."[64]

Although many town denizens may have regarded the *besprizorniki* as human lice and bedbugs, official policy toward juvenile crime throughout the 1920s remained compassionate and lenient. Anton Makarenko was a maverick educator who headed a labor colony for *besprizorniki* and juvenile delinquents in the 1920s and 1930s. Taking issue with the pedagogical permissiveness of the 1920s, Makarenko remarked ironically that "the generally accepted theory of those days" was "that punishment of any sort is degrading, that it is essential to give the fullest possible scope to the sacred creative impulses of the child, and that the great thing is to rely solely upon self-organization and self-discipline."[65] Although Makarenko believed these ideas unworkable without strong adult authority, a progressive, child-centered philosophy guided early Bolshevik policy toward juvenile crime.

Sovnarkom moved quickly in January 1918 to abolish court trials and prison sentences for juvenile offenders under 17 and to substitute newly formed local Commissions on the Affairs of Minors, staffed by pedagogues, judges, and doctors to hear cases, to send needy children to the appropriate institutions, and to conduct criminological research. In 1920, the commissions were transferred from the Commissariat of Social Security to the Commissariat of Enlightenment, under the department of SPON. The number of local commissions grew quickly, from 190 in 1921 to 275 in 1924. A central commission was created in 1923.[66]

Initially, criminologists saw juvenile crime as a direct conse-

[64] Shishkov, p. 100.
[65] Anton S. Makarenko, *The Road to Life. An Epic in Education* (Oriole Editions, New York, 1973): 217.
[66] The commissions were dissolved in 1935 and replaced by the Detskie Komnati Militsii, See Karamysheva, pp. 53–43. I. I. Sheiman, "Komissii po Delam Nesovershennoletnikh," in *Detskaia besprizornost' i detskii dom. Sbornik statei i materialov II Vserossiiskogo s"ezda SPON* (Moscow, 1926): 37. Hereafter cited as SPON Sbornik.

quence of homelessness and hunger. In the first half of 1920, the Commissions on the Affairs of Minors treated 12,500 minors (outside of Moscow and Leningrad) charged with "socially dangerous" activities. In the first six months of 1921, they treated 32,585 children, which represented an increase of 160%. The criminologist V. I. Kufaev summed up the problem succinctly: "The road to lawbreaking is very short. . . . . The emotions of hunger are enough."[67] Kufaev argued that the increase was directly attributable to the famine. A report from Ufa province during the famine noted "dreadful waves of child crime and *besprizornost'*."[68] In Krasnodar, where large numbers of *besprizorniki* from the Volga region gathered, the commission saw 2,596 minors, an increase of 27 percent over their caseload in 1920. In Moscow, over 9,000 children passed through the commissions in 1920, and 11,460 in 1921.[69]

A study in 1922 showed a close connection between *besprizornost'* and crime. Most of the juvenile offenders in Moscow (62.5%) had lost one or both parents, and many were living on the streets. Over 90% of the children were guilty of theft, the most frequent crime committed by the *besprizorniki*.[70] Kufaev wrote: "The minors arriving from one of the hungry areas gather in front of the stores, shops, trays, and handcarts, near the crowded provisions. And here, exhausted by hunger, they are forced by temptation to steal. Buy? There is no money. Beg alms? People rarely give. In this situation the child decides to steal, becoming in this way a lawbreaker."[71] According to Kufaev's reasoning, the children stole out of hunger and necessity. The imperatives of survival gave them no choice. The elimination of hunger and poverty would gradually result in the disappearance of *besprizornost'* and juvenile crime. The govern-

---

[67] Kufaev, p. 38.   [68] Ibid., p. 37.   [69] Ibid., p. 38.
[70] O. L. Bem, "Ekonomicheskoe Polozhenie i Perspektivy Bor'by s Detskoi Besprizornost'iu," in SPON Sbornik, p. 13. According to Bem, 22% of those engaged in juvenile crime were orphans, 32% had only a mother, and 8% only a father. Among those engaged in repeated crime, fully 25% were orphans.
[71] Kufaev, pp. 38, 39, argued that the growth of juvenile crime could be directly tied to increases in the price of bread. He noted that in Ufa, for example, bread reached 18,000 rubles per pound in 1921.

ment had to launch an attack on these underlying conditions, not on the children themselves.

Yet even after the effects of the famine began to recede, juvenile crime continued to increase. Between 1922 and 1924, the Russian commissions dealt with 145,052 cases of juvenile crime.[72] In June 1922, a new criminal code was introduced and all teenagers over 16 were transferred from the jurisdiction of the commissions to adult courts. As a result, the number of new cases before the commissions dropped by 16% between 1922 and 1923. Yet by 1924, the number of new cases had risen sharply by 25% over the previous year, and surpassed the caseload of 1922. I. I. Sheiman, a delegate to the Second All-Russian Congress of the Department for the Social and Legal Protection of Minors (SPON) in 1924, contended that the growing number of cases was directly attributable to the closing of the children's homes under NEP. The proliferation of the commissions and their increasing effectiveness were only secondary explanations for the burgeoning caseload.[73]

Statistics from the commissions showed strong ties between crime, family breakdown, and *besprizornost'*. About half of the children passing through the commissions for the first time in 1921–1922 were missing one or both parents. Among those guilty of repeated violations, the figure was 70%. One-quarter and one-third of the first-time and repeat offenders, respectively, were the children of impoverished single mothers. A first-time offender was three times more likely to have lost a father than a mother, and among repeat offenders, four times more likely.[74] In Moscow, the connection between *besprizornost'* and crime was even stronger. In 1924, 40% of the children passing through the commission were orphans; 28% had only a mother; 7% only a father. Only 24% came from homes with both parents.[75] The statistics showed not only a clear connection between *besprizornost'* and juvenile crime, but reflected the terrible plight of single mothers and their inability to care for their children in a period of high unemployment, low wages for women, and inadequate daycare.

Over 75% of the crimes committed by children were property

[72] SPON Sbornik, p. 139.   [73] Ibid., p. 139.
[74] Ibid., p. 141. These figures do not include Moscow and Leningrad.
[75] Ibid., p. 142.

violations, such as pickpocketing and theft.[76] Children stole from stores, apartments, and people on the streets, reselling the goods in street markets where peasants, former nobles, and crippled veterans hawked everything from used boots to candelabras. Children caught stealing or committing other crimes were usually arrested by the militia and sent to the Commissions. The overwhelming majority (90%) of the children passing through the commission were boys.[77] The commissions were neither courts nor punitive organs, but rather, by their own description, "medico-pedagogical institutions." At the SPON Congress, Sheiman explained that the commissions "should employ measures of social help." Although in some instances the commissions acted incorrectly as "a court for juvenile offenders" and sentenced children to forced labor, incarceration, and fines, abuses occurred mainly in district commissions that were more likely to be ignorant of the law.[78]

Unfortunately the commissions were often stymied in their efforts to "employ measures of social help." The children's homes and institutions were overcrowded and there were few alternative services. Between 1922 and 1924, the commissions took action on 145,052 cases of juvenile crime.[79] The most common measure (in about one-quarter of the cases) was a verbal rebuke. Although this method may have been useful in dealing with childish pranks or mischief, it was obviously ineffective for children who stole to survive. The gentle admonishments of a social worker or pedagogue were useless under the social conditions that created *besprizornost'*. (See Table 1.)

About 15% of the children were sent back to their parents, most often a mother, who could not provide proper care. Unemployed mothers often sent their children out to beg or steal. Others, unhinged by poverty and the difficulty of life, became alcoholics and abandoned their families. Children of single mothers passed through the commissions repeatedly, and time

---

[76] Ibid.

[77] Ibid., p. 141. It is not clear why so many of the children treated by the commissions were male, and it is difficult to determine whether this reflected the composition of the larger population of *besprizorniki*. Whereas boys resorted to theft, girls may have become involved in prostitution and been treated by different agencies.

[78] Ibid., p. 143.   [79] Ibid., p. 145.

Table 1. *Dispensation of cases by the Commissions on the Affairs
of Minors in the RSFSR, 1922–1924*

Action taken by commission	1922		1923		1924	
	N	%	N	%	N	%
Verbal rebuke/ conversation	13,270	23.8	10,418	25.5	14,640	30.1
No action taken	14,657	26.3	7,530	18.4	8,086	16.6
Remanded to parental care	6,336	11.4	5,617	13.7	7,775	16.0
Remanded to people's court	10,436	18.7	4,889	12.0	4,936	10.2
Labor colony	4,044	7.3	5,114	12.5	4,793	10.0
Placed in children's home	2,386	4.3	2,937	7.2	3,112	6.4
Remanded to care of social worker	1,829	3.3	1,839	4.5	2,349	4.8
Sent home	910	1.6	980	2.4	1,063	2.2
Sent to work	931	1.7	636	1 5	551	1.1
Placed under guardianship	291	0.5	400	1.0	434	0.9
Placed in school	389	0.7	397	1.0	604	1.2
Remanded to psychiatric clinic	201	0.4	138	0.3	234	0.5
Total cases	55,680	100.0	40,895	100.0	48,577	100.0

Source: SPON Sbornik, p. 145.

after time were sent back to impoverished homes. They eventually returned to the streets, were rearrested by the militia, and sent back to the commissions, starting the cycle all over again. In about 20% of the cases, the commissions took no action at all.

The commissions, desperately seeking solutions to the problem of repeat offenders, sent a sizable number of juveniles to adult court. The numbers varied widely from region to region, depending in part on the alternatives available. Not surprisingly, the commissions located outside the town centers sentenced more children to court. The district commissions sent almost 50% of their cases to people's court, while the provincial commissions transferred less than 6% of their cases. Yet the number of children sent to court dropped from about 19% in 1922 to 10%

in 1924 as local commissions became better informed about the proper procedures.[80]

The commissions sent about 18% of the children to labor colonies or children's homes, depending on the age of the child and the severity of the crime. Yet almost one-quarter of the children passing through the commissions were orphans, and an additional quarter had only one parent. Thus, at the very least, 25% of the children, if not more, needed full-time care, although only 18% were placed in a home or colony.

Approximately 14% of the children were placed under the supervision of a social worker, 1% were sent to work (presumably those older than 14), and an even smaller fraction were placed with a guardian. Of the remainder, about 1% were sent to school, and less than 1%, to psychiatric clinics.[81] Apart from the decrease in the number of juveniles remanded to adult court, there were few changes in the practices of the commissions between 1922 and 1924.

The figures revealed the continuing difficulties the commissions confronted in coping with juvenile crime and homelessness. They were frequently frustrated in their attempts to place needy children in a supporting institution, to find a suitable guardian, or to provide employment. The shortage of funds and overcrowding in the children's homes sharply reduced the number of available places, and most of the children were too young to live and work independently. Homeless children could not be placed in regular schools because they had no place to live and no one to support them. Urban workers were reluctant to assume the burden and expense of an extra child when apartment space and income were severely limited; moreover, many were afraid to accept a delinquent off the streets. It was pointless to send the children to people's court, where the judge faced the same narrow range of options. He could sentence them to pro-

[80] Ibid., p. 148.

[81] Data from the commission in Ufa, although not as detailed, shows a similar dispensation of cases. Between October 1924 and October 1925, the commission dealt with 238 juveniles. Of these, 102 received a reprimand, 37 were transferred to people's court, 91 were sent to children's homes, 6 remanded to parental custody, 1 to the custody of an educator, and 1 to a psychiatric clinic. See Karamysheva, p. 53.

bation, which required a guardian, or place them in a children's home, which did not have the room. Sheiman explained that the commissions resorted to verbal reprimands so frequently because there were so few alternatives.[82]

The commissions were caught in a bind. Charged with the task of eradicating juvenile crime and homelessness, they had neither sufficient punitive nor rehabilitative means at their disposal. They were also understaffed, poorly paid, and lacking in support from other social organizations. Under these circumstances, the commissions resembled a great bureaucratic revolving door, taking in thousands of *besprizorniki,* processing their vital statistics, and spewing them back onto the streets.

"Chronic *besprizornost'* ": The psychology of the streets

The placement of a child in a home or colony did not guarantee a successful outcome. The children's homes and colonies also had great difficulty coping with the *besprizorniki.* Educators were committed to the idea of rehabilitation through persuasion, self-government, and collective activity, and largely opposed to "the application of compulsary measures." According to the consensus of the SPON Congress in 1924, children were to participate voluntarily in the collective life of the institution.[83] As a result, the homes and colonies could do little with children who refused to cooperate or repeatedly ran away. Unlike officials in

[82] I. I. Sheiman, in SPON Sbornik, pp. 147–148.
[83] For a detailed account of the debates among educators and criminologists on the treatment of *besprizornost'* and juvenile crime, see Peter Juviler, "Contradictions of Revolution: Juvenile Crime and Rehabilitation," in A. Gleason, P. Kenez, R. Stites, eds., *Bolshevik Culture* (Indiana University Press, Bloomington, 1985); and Jennie Stevens, "Children of the Revolution: Soviet Russia's Homeless Children in the 1920s," *Russian History,* 9 (1982). "Rezoliutsii Vtorogo Vserossiiskogo S"ezda SPON," in SPON Sbornik, pp. 200, 201. Up to 1924, a patchwork of pedagogical approaches to *besprizornost'* and juvenile delinquency prevailed. The SPON Congress in 1924 marked the adoption of a clearer ideological line based on the more permissive approach to child rearing and rehabilitation. See Stevens, pp. 74–76.

prisons or detention centers, educators did not apply coercive measures to keep the children in the homes. Many children drifted in and out, using the homes as waystations for a meal, a bath, some clean clothes, and a pair of shoes. Sometimes they disappeared for months before showing up again, barefoot and in rags, hungry, lousy, and exhausted.

Living on the streets, shifting for themselves, the *besprizorniki* developed a distinctive psychology and subculture that became the bane of educational authorities. Kolya Voinov, a *besprizornik* who later wrote about his experiences, noted that the young army recruits who had grown up on the streets "recognized one another instantly" in 1941. He called them "the boys from 'our world'." These former waifs, "useless where discipline, punctuality, and tactical knowledge were required," were often deployed on dangerous reconaissance teams that demanded "agility and resourcefulness."[84] Many children, despite terrible deprivations, became accustomed to life on the streets. They had difficulty adjusting to authority, work, and an organized institutional environment. The material deprivations were tempered by a freedom, irresponsibility, and autonomy that they were loathe to relinquish to state authorities. The children, repelled by work, family, and stability, were strongly attracted to the criminal world. Educators and social workers, recognizing the special problems this psychology posed for the state, began to speak of the problem of "chronic *besprizornost'*." They feared that years of war and disruption had produced a generation of vagabonds who would never be capable of steady work or a settled life.

Grisha M., born in Simbirsk in 1914, was a typical example of chronic *besprizornost'*.[85] During the civil war, his parents moved to Sudugda in Vladimir province and left Grisha in Simbirsk. His father soon died of tuberculosis, and Grisha, a mere 7 years old, fled the famine-stricken town in 1921 to rejoin his mother. She rejected the little boy and drove him away from the house. Grisha remembered her with bitterness: "She was always barking at us and now I suppose she is glad she doesn't know where I

[84] Voinov, *Outlaw. The Autobiography of a Soviet Waif* (Harvill, London, 1955): 199, 205.
[85] The following three case histories are taken from T. E. Segalov's two-part article, "Det-Brodiagi," *Pravo i zhizn'*, 7–8, 9–10 (1925): 84–89, 89–95.

am." The boy was sent to the Vladimir orphanage with his older
brothers. Expelled from the orphanage for misbehavior, Grisha
was sent to a children's colony, but he ran away and returned to
Vladimir. After hanging around the railroad station, he hid in a
train bound for Moscow. There, he met some boys from Sudugda, and together, they wandered around the market and the
railroad station. Grisha survived on what he stole from the market and on the money he made in a lewd juggling act he performed in the streets. Eventually he wearied of life on the streets
and appealed to officials in the Moscow Department of People's
Education, who promptly sent him back to his mother in
Vladimir. Realizing once again that his mother did not want him,
he hopped a train to Leningrad, stayed briefly in an orphanage
there, ran away, and landed back in Moscow.

In Moscow, Grisha shuttled between the railroad station, the
market, and the streets. In desperation, he turned himself in at
the Pokrovskii receiving station for *besprizorniki* a number of
times, and each time the authorities sent him back to the orphanage in Vladimir. In seemingly endless, restless repetition,
the boy traveled back and forth between Vladimir and Moscow,
between the orphanage and the streets. Ragged, hungry, lousy,
he was in and out of various children's institutions at least ten
times.

An interviewer noted that Grisha had nothing but contempt
for the administrators of the children's homes. He was, moreover, very proud of his ability to deceive them. Possessed of a
rich supply of dirty jokes, curses, and anecdotes, he was foul-
mouthed and rude to his teachers. He showed no interest in
school, work, or family life, and had ties to neither home nor
institution. Unable to sit still for very long, he was easily dis-
tracted. Terrified of rebuff, moody, unforgiving, and hostile, he
was afraid to trust or open up to people. "I am too twisted," he
remarked with an odd pride. He was confident of his ability to
survive and had no moral scruples about thievery. "I was a thief
and remain a thief," he boasted, "There is a reason for theft."

Aleksei P., another example of "chronic *besprizornost'*", also
spent most of his childhood on the streets. He was born in
Ekaterinasburg in 1911 to a factory worker and a laundress.
After his father died in the war, his family sank deeper and
deeper into poverty. One by one, his mother sold their belong-

ings, but she soon became very ill. When she came out of the hospital, the family had no place to live; they slept in a field. Under the strain of trying to provide for her children, she collapsed again and returned to the hospital. Aleksei and his brothers and sisters were sent to an orphanage. He ran away and began hanging around the markets in town. Eventually he hopped a train to Viatka, rode to Vologda, and finally ended up in Moscow. Entering an apartment to beg, he saw some boots, stole them, and sold them in the Sukharevskii market. Bumping into some friends from Vologda, he treated the group to a hearty meal at a tavern on the proceeds from the boots. In the afterglow of the warm meal, the boys decided to work together as thieves, stealing clothing, primuses, and other household items. After much success, the militia eventually caught up with them, dragged them into the police station, beat them, and sent them over to the Commission. Aleksei said, "When the militia catches and dispatches you, they begin to beat you, and they beat you so, you are scarcely living when you leave." His head bore the scars of many beatings. He claimed that each time he was caught he had escaped from the commission.

Aleksei was finally sent to a children's colony, where he avoided the other children, refusing to go to school or to participate in the common work of the colony. "You cannot force me," he said. Although he looked back on his street life as a very painful time, he finally chose to return to the streets when the colony staff gave him the choice to leave or become part of the community.

Vasily G., a thin, childlike boy with sparkling black eyes, was also sent to a children's colony by the commission in Moscow. His family background was marked by alcoholism, poverty, and abuse. His father, an official in the post and telegraph office, was a heavy drinker who beat his wife and children, and finally abandoned his family in 1915, leaving his wife with eight children. After two years of erratic support, his father stopped helping the family entirely. In 1921, at the age of 11, Vasily went to his father to plead for help. His father told him, "I no longer consider you my son." The family lived in extreme poverty on the mother's small wages.

Dreaming of trains and travel, Vasily ran away from home repeatedly only to return, gloomy, silent, refusing to explain where he had been. Like Grisha and Aleksei, he rode the rails to various towns and cities, begging and stealing to survive. He was unhappy both at home and in the children's colony. He could not settle down anywhere: Driven by an inner misery, he was always on the run. An interviewer noted that he was a shy boy, with a sweet and even manner, but he cried all the time, seemed chronically depressed, and could not get along with other children. The smallest slight or difficulty spurred him to run away again.

These three children possessed very different personalities, but their stories reflected patterns common to thousands of other nameless *besprizorniki*. All three boys came from families headed by single women: Grisha's and Aleksei's fathers had died; Vasily's father had abandoned the family. The mothers found it extremely difficult to care for their children and the boys wandered in and out of children's homes, colonies, and receiving stations. All three children were involved in petty crimes such as beggary and theft. They came into contact with several social agencies – the receiving stations, the commissions, the Department of People's Education, and the orphanages – but none were able to keep the youngsters off the streets or stop their criminal activities. According to Aleksei's testimony, the militia, frustrated perhaps by the commissions' inability to deal with the children, followed its own "pedagogical course," routinely beating the children before sending them to the commissions. Despite educators' aversion to coercion, the actual policy toward *besprizornost'* may in fact have been a mixture of high ideals and brutal practices.

The children's stories provide a glimpse of life on the streets, of the huge, floating fraternity of waifs that spontaneously grouped, dissolved, and regrouped in different cities. As they traveled around, the children renewed old acquaintances from other towns. They had their own slang, songs, customs, and rough camaraderie.[86] Although life was difficult, many of the

---

[86] Soviet sociologists did considerable research on the life, customs, slang, and even the songs of the *besprizorniki*. For more on this subject, see V. S. Krasuskii, A. M. Khaleskii, "Sreda Besprizornykh, ee Traditsii i Navyki," in *Nishchenstvo i besprizornost'* (Moscow, 1929); B. O. Borovich, ed., *Kollectivy besprizornykh i ikh vozhaki. Sbornik statei* (Kharkov, 1926); M. I. Levitina, *Besprizornye. Sotsialogiia, byt, praktika raboty* (Moscow, 1925); V. L. Shveitser, A. M. Shabalova, eds., *Besprizornye v trudovykh kommunakh. Sbornik statei i materialov* (Moscow, 1926).

children became fond of the freedom and the mobility. One young thief asked rhetorically, "Why is it that we exist?" Disorder, turmoil, the German war, the civil war, and the Volga famine, he dutifully listed all the causes of *besprizornost'*. "And the main thing of all main things," he explained, "was that once they proclaimed freedom for the people, how could they keep children away from that freedom? For us, freedom is paradise."[87] If a socialist revolution had ironically spawned a ruined subsistence economy, the new socialist man could, analogously, have been represented as the half wild child growing up in the streets. The *besprizorniki*, in symbol and flesh, embodied the chaos, anarchy, and breakdown of the new postrevolutionary society.

T. E. Segalov, an educator, expressed this concern in an article written in 1925. In a fascinating analogy, Segalov likened the *besprizorniki* to the vagabonds and wanderers created in the violent transition from feudalism to capitalism, when large numbers of peasants were declassed, thrown off the land and forced to survive through petty crime. Unlike nomadic peoples – socially integrated groups with their own forms of governance – vagabonds refused to submit to any state system of order; they paid no taxes and rejected all forms of regulated life. According to Segalov, the *besprizorniki* were growing up like vagabonds: They had no skills, education, or proper work habits; they were capable only of begging and petty crime. Segalov expressed the fear that the *besprizorniki* would become a permanent part of a vagabond underclass that could never be integrated into society.[88]

The very term "chronic *besprizornost'*" marked an ideological departure from an earlier, largely economic view of waifdom. "Chronic *besprizornost'*" implied the development of a psychology and culture which was rootless, criminal, anti-Soviet, and perhaps most important, impervious to improvements in social conditions. The term itself suggested the necessity of a new orientation in policy. The identification of a subculture, stubbornly entrenched and inimical to the ideals of the state, required new approaches. Although the SPON Congress in 1924 was dominated by pedagogues advocating permissive, humanist methods of rehabilitation, many officials were increasingly frus-

[87] Shishkov, p. 114.
[88] T. E. Segalov, "Poniatie i Vidy Detskoi Besprizornosti," *Pravo i zhizn'*,4–5 (1925): 95–101.

trated by the ineffectuality of this approach. The fear of "chronic *besprizornost'*" was accompanied by an impatience with the intransigence, crime, and parasitical lack of productivity of the *besprizorniki*. The words of one Komsomol leader to a gang of waifs were typical of this shift in approach. Sternly, he scolded them, "You, and by you I mean the countless ranks of your whole street urchin brotherhood, are an incurable ulcer on the body of our country. . . . From you the state gets neither milk nor wool – just as if you were a counter revolutionary goat."[89]

The retreat from socialized child rearing

The fears of chronic *besprizornost'* and crime put sharp pressure on jurists, educators, and state officials to clear the children from the streets. In April 1924, the Central Commission of Land and Forest Workers (Vserabotzemles), the Commissariats of Land and Enlightenment, and the Detkomissiia sent a circular to all of their local branches, instructing them to put teenagers to work in agriculture. The local organs were instructed to set labor targets for each province, provide land plots for *artels* of orphans, and employ the "maximum number" of *besprizorniki* possible on the state farms.[90] In August, with the prospect of a poor harvest spurring fears of an increase in *besprizornost'*, Aleksei Rykov warned against a further expansion in state services for homeless children. "We are bringing up idlers who do not know how to work," he told his fellow Party members. The children's homes had to stop admitting children who had families, especially in areas where the harvest was bad. "In cases where the family is not in a position to feed the child," he explained, "it is better to help the family than to take the child and feed it in a children's home."[91]

---

[89] Shishkov, p. 128–29.

[90] "Vsem gub-i Oblzemupravleniiam Narkomzemam Avtonomnykh Respublik, Vsem Gub-, Oblotdelam Vserabotzemlesa, Vsem Obl-, Gubupolnomochennym po Uluchsheniiu Zhizni Detei, Detkomissiiam Avtonomnykh Respublik, GubONO, Narkomprosam Avtonomykh Respublik," in Tizanov, Epshtein, pp. 43–44.

[91] E. H. Carr, *Socialism in One Country, 1924–1926*, Vol. 1 (New York, 1958): 35.

A letter from the Commissariat of Enlightenment and the Central Peasant Commission for Mutual Self Help a year later clearly stated: "Our task is not to feed the *besprizorniki* but to teach them to support themselves." It recommended that children be organized into agricultural communes and repair workshops. The letter emphasized the importance of stopping *besprizornost'* before it began by providing support to widows with large families, by organizing work for teenagers, and by helping the children of poor peasants.[92]

Given the scarcity of funds, the older children in the homes were seen as obstacles to accepting additional children from the streets. A decree from the Fifth Congress of the Department of People's Education stated that its central task was to get teenagers out of the homes and into jobs. It noted: "There are now 15,000 teenagers out of the entire 220,000 inmates in the children's homes (7 percent) who are not adapted to a working life and tie up the places and means for those *besprizorniki* in the street who need state help." Yet the decree added that the teenagers were not "adapted to a working life" because there was little funding for training programs. In 1925 and 1926 only 50 percent of the teenagers received job training. Many of the children's homes, particularly those outside the towns, were scarcely able to *feed* the children they housed. The resolution confessed that when "80 percent are unclothed and barefoot, it is impossible to organize job training."[93]

Local leaders eagerly took advantage of the mood and began expelling teenagers, closing the homes, and firing staff. The children's institutions were largely supported by local funds, although they were centrally organized and held children from all over the country.[94] Local authorities, tired of supporting chil-

---

[92] "Vsem Krest'ianskim Komitetam Obshchestvennoi Vzaipomoshchi i Otdelom Narodnogo Obrazovaniia," in Tizanov, Epshtein, eds., pp. 41–43.

[93] "O Bor'be s Detskoi Besprizornost'iu," in ibid., pp. 35–40.

[94] TsGAOR, fond 5027, op. 1, delo 104, p. 4. The social origins of the children in the homes was 55% peasant, 24% workers, 15% white-collar workers and craftsmen, and 3% Red Army. Thus more than half the children came from peasant families. In terms of age, 11% were between the ages of 4 and 8, 62% were 8 to 14, 22% were 14 to 16, and 5% were older than 16. In regard to family composition,

dren from other areas, expressed their resentment in their interpretation and implementation of the decrees from the center.
Officials in the Stalingrad Provincial Department of People's Education (ONO) actually demanded that the district (*uezd*) ONO
close its children's home. One official wrote, "The Department
of People's Education is carrying out this work badly, often stall-
ing, and trying to preserve the children's homes. This must
come to an end. The policy of curtailing the children's homes
and freeing the local budget must be carried out."[95]

To counter local malfeasance, the VTsIK and Sovnarkom sent
harsh reprimands to the local TsIKs in January 1927. The letter
noted that although officials had zealously complied with the
order to transfer children out of the homes, in actuality, the
order was used as a pretext to close the homes and reduce expenses. About 26,000 children were sent out of the homes between January and September 1926, but only 9,800 were en-
rolled in their place. In the provinces of Moscow, Stalingrad,
Saratov, and Sibirsk, the North Caucasus, and the Urals, "the
discrepancy [was] particularly large." Officials emptied institutions with little regard for the future of the children; many of
those sent to factories, for example, had no place to live.[96] They
transferred large groups of children from one area to another
without permission from the center, and with no assurance that
the children would be accepted at their destinations. Children
were sent to institutions in remote areas that had no room and
no funds to support them. Many were packed off to relatives
who were unable or unwilling to care for them.[97] In some areas,
officials confined their welfare work to the *besprizorniki* born in
their region and ignored the others. Local officials were advised
to continue sending teenagers out of the homes, but were strictly

67% of the children were orphans, 30% had only one parent, and
the remaining 3% had both parents but were unable to live at home.

[95] Ia. N. Drobnis, "Itogi i Perspektivy Bor'by s Detskoi Besprizornost'iu," in Tizanov, Epshtein, eds., p. 7.
[96] "Tsentral'nym Ispolnitel'nym Komitetam Avtonomnykh Respublik
Kraevym, Oblastnym, i Gubernskim Ispolnitel'nym Komitetam," in
ibid., pp. 24–26.
[97] "Vsem Tsentral'nym Ispolnitel'nym Komitetam Avtonomnykh Respublik Vkhodiashchikh v RSFSR. Vsem Ispolnitel'nym Komitetam
Avtonomnykh Oblastei, Vsem Gub-i Oblispolnitel'nym Komitetam
RSFSR," in ibid., pp. 45–46.

warned not to close the homes, limit care to "their own" *besprizorniki,* or dispatch teenagers without adequate preparations.[98]

In January 1926 the Commissariat of Enlightenment sent an angry letter to the provincial, regional, and district executive committees: "Instead of the struggle with *besprizornost',* we have an actual increase in it, at the expense of the children sent out from the children's homes without proper care for their future life." The letter demanded that local officials stop shutting down the homes and take in 30,000 new *besprizorniki* by sending 23,000 older children to work in factories and on peasant farms, and by organizing new children's homes for the remaining 7,000. The letter acknowledged, however, that the local organs could not afford to build and staff new institutions. It raised the hope that the central budget might provide additional monies through the Lenin fund established two years before.[99]

Soon after the letter, the government decided to distribute 2,500,000 rubles to the provinces for the campaign against *besprizornost'.* The Lenin fund contributed 40 percent of the funds, another 40 percent came from the Detkomissiia, and the remaining 20 percent from Sovnarkom (RSFSR). Yet the number of children in need of support, both on the streets and in the homes, remained enormous. Table 2 shows the amount of money allotted to each province in 1926, and the number of children remaining in the homes and on the streets in April 1927. The Detkomissiia estimated in 1926 that the homes held between 225,000 and 250,000 children, and that an additional 300,000 waifs were at large.[100]

The 2,500,000 ruble allotment thus permitted an additional expenditure of 11 rubles for each child in a state institution or a mere 5 rubles for every child in need of care (including those on the streets.) The Commissariat of Enlightenment calculated that

---

[98] "Tsentral'nym Ispolnitel'nym Komitetam Avtonomnykh Respublik, Kraevym, Oblastnym, i Gubernskim Ispolnitel'nym Komitetam," ibid., pp. 24–26.

[99] "Pis'mo Narkomprosa o Bor'be s Detskoi Besprizornost'iu," ibid., pp. 33, 32.

[100] On source of funds, see TsGAOR, fond 5207, op. 1, delo 336, p. 36. TsGAOR, fond 5207, op. 6, delo 10, p. 4. N. I. Ozeretskii notes in "Nishchenstvo i besprizornost'" that according to the Detkomissiia, there were 278,398 children in the various children's institutions.

Table 2. *Effect of the 1926 expenditure:*
Besprizorniki *on the streets and in the homes, April 1927*

| | | April 1927 | | |
| | Rubles allocated in 1926 | Number of children | | |
Guberniia		On streets	In homes	Total
Astrakhan	38,530	3,400	1,257	4,657
Arkhangelsk	12,200	138	1,643	1,781
Bashkir	–	1,200	1,372	2,572
Briansk	32,530	1,000	1,923	2,923
Buriat-Mongol	–	497	368	865
Cherepovets	15,900	650	807	1,457
Chuvash	–	0	745	745
Dagestan	–	300	516	816
Far East	–	8,000	2,672	10,672
German Kommune	–	–	772	772
Ivanovo-Vosnesensk	26,900	237	1,765	2,002
Kalmuk	–	1,085	2,035	3,120
Kaluga	23,300	3,300	1,358	4,658
Karelia	–	200	918	1,118
Kazak	–	5,781	10,202	15,983
Kirgiz	–	880	–	880
Komi	–	0	299	299
Kostroma	26,800	815	1,394	2,209
Krym	–	595	2,035	2,630
Kursk	53,268	1,500	2,910	4,410
Leningrad	62,970	384	23,551	23,935
Marii	–	2,000	1,113	3,113
Moscow	–	500	23,570	24,070
Murmansk	4,500	50	100	150
Nizhegorod	39,530	3,000	4,096	7,096
Northern Caucasus	167,175	18,650	25,000	43,650
Novgorod	22,500	700	1,437	2,137
Oirat	–	0	–	–
Orlov	43,130	4,000	2,742	6,742
Orenburg	34,960	700	2,500	3,200
Penza	27,230	3,295	1,600	4,895
Pskov	39,045	0	1,372	1,372
Riazanov	40,630	2,500	2,556	5,056
Samara	71,779	2,500	2,196	4,696
Saratov	80,242	1,436	2,482	3,918
Sev. Dvinsk	14,800	404	1,357	1,761
Siberia	–	2,855	2,885	5,740

Table 2. (*cont.*)

Guberniia	Rubles Allocated in 1926	April 1927		
		Number of children		
		On streets	In homes	Total
Smolensk	52,980	650	2,700	3,350
Stalingrad	53,430	6,000	3,155	9,155
Tambov	53,010	1,500	3,914	5,414
Tatar	–	1,500	5,328	6,828
Tver	43,200	1,900	2,200	4,100
Tula	40,630	–	1,164	1,164
Ulianov	46,260	210	2,326	2,536
Ural	123,575	2,250	16,000	18,250
Viatka	42,230	–	4,088	4,088
Vladimir	30,000	1,000	2,500	3,500
Vologda	29,930	3,000	1,200	4,200
Voronezh	85,615	1,500	8,000	9,500
Votkinsk	–	3,615	1,353	4,968
Yakutsk	–	0	45	45
Yaroslavl	43,668	1,040	2,542	3,582
Totals	1,522,447	96,717	190,063	286,780

Source: The table is constructed from figures in TsGAOR, fond 5207, op. 1, delo 336, pp. 36, 40, 41.

it cost 27 rubles a year just to feed a child.[101] To feed the 550,000 *besprizorniki* on the streets and in the homes for one year – let alone to clothe, shelter, shoe, teach, and train them – would have cost at least seven times more than the entire 2.5 million ruble allotment. The allotment was clearly insufficient to make a significant difference in state care for children. Of the money, 1,522,447 rubles were sent directly to the provinces, and the remaining 977,561 rubles to the various commissariats coping with *besprizornost'*. Vast numbers of children continued to roam the streets, especially in the North Caucasus, the Far East, and the province of Stalingrad. Yet by April 1927, the number of

[101] "O Bor'be s Detskoi Besprizornost'iu," in Tizanov, Epshtein, eds., p. 37.

children on the streets dropped from 300,000 to 96,717, a decline of almost 70 percent. In the children's homes, the number fell from 225,000–250,000 to 190,063. Provincial authorities reported a total drop of 45 percent in the numbers of *besprizorniki* in the homes and on the streets. Although the allotment must have helped the provincial authorities to some degree, it was clearly not responsible for the precipitous decrease. Provincial authorities were either underreporting the number of children that remained in the homes and on the streets, or continuing their policy of unauthorized reductions through closings and expulsions.

Throughout the 1920s, the financial expenditures on *besprizornost'* occurred at the expense of other educational institutions, especially those for preschool children.[102] In the summer of 1924, the Commissariat of Enlightenment issued instructions encouraging unions, factory committees, and the Komsomol to open daycare centers at their own expense to offset the problems created by the continuing loss of state-funded preschools. In a further effort to reduce state spending the commissariat decreed that preschool institutions should charge for their services. Although members of the armed services and political staff, disabled workers and veterans, and other groups were excluded from payment, everyone else was to pay in accordance with their earnings.[103] Neither single working mothers nor poor families in which both parents worked were exempt from payment. Only unemployed workers registered with the labor exchange were eligible to use the centers, thus excluding many housewives and peasant migrants in search of work. The burden of organizing and paying for daycare was shifted from the state back to local organizations and individual families.

The same shift occurred in the state's policy toward the *besprizorniki*. The fear of chronic juvenile homelessness and crime, and of a permanent underclass of unemployables, impelled the Commissariat of Enlightenment to get the children off the streets. As unskilled teenagers were pushed out of the homes, the policy of *"vypusk v zhizn'"* (sending them into the

---

[102] The children's homes received a regular allotment of 46 million rubles or 27.5% of the RSFSR's budget for education. TsGAOR, fond 5207, op. 6, delo 10, p. 5.

[103] TsGAOR, fond 2306, op. 1, delo 2744, pp. 24, 28–29.

world) often created a new, older group of *besprizorniki*.[104] A new approach was needed to solve the problem of chronic *besprizor-nost'* and to train the children to work at the least expense to the state.

In a noteworthy reversal of earlier views, the criminologist S. S. Tizanov wrote in 1925 that families should be strongly encouraged to bring up their own children. If a family could not support a child, it was preferable for the state to pay the parents a stipend rather than to put the child in a children's home.[105] Here was tacit recognition that the family performed an essential function – bringing up children – at a minimum social cost. Given the enormous expense involved in housing large numbers of children and paying professional staff to care for them, a family could use a small ruble allotment far more efficiently than the state. Women's labor in the household cost the state nothing, while the cost of transferring this socially necessary labor from the private to the public sphere was painfully high. By the mid-1920s, the social and economic problems created by thousands of homeless children made this grim message perfectly clear. Not only was the Soviet Union unprepared to transfer children from intact families to institutions of social upbringing, the country could hardly support the orphans it already had.

In August 1925, the Commissariat of Health sent out instructions to the children's homes urging them to place infants and young children with urban, wage-earning families. The instructions stated: "In light of overcrowding in the children's homes, it is necessary, as a temporary measure, to transfer abandoned children and orphans." The sole requirements of the adoption were that the child be older than 3 months and that the adoptive family have a steady income and few children. The families would receive 15 to 30 rubles a month, and the children would arrive equipped with their own sheets and sleeping cots or baskets.[106] It was quickly apparent, however, that few urban families were interested in adoption. And although the Commissariat

[104] "Pis'mo Narkomprosa o Bor'be s Detskoi Besprizornost'iu," in Tizanov, Epshtein, eds., p. 33.
[105] S. S. Tizanov, "K Voprosu o Bor'be s Detskoi Besprizornost'iu," *Kommunistka*, 10 (1925): 59.
[106] Ia. A. Perel', A.A. Liubimova, *Bor'ba s ditskoi besprizornost'iu,* Vypusk 4 (Uchpedgiz, Moscow, Leningrad, 1932): 94

stressed that the measures were temporary, the government had, within a year, launched an even more vigorous campaign to promote adoption among the peasantry.

In April 1926, the VTsIK and Sovnarkom issued a decree reversing the prohibition against adoption in the 1918 Family Code, encouraging peasant families to adopt children in the state institutions.[107] An explanatory letter from the Commissariat of Enlightenment frankly explained that the purpose was "to relieve the state and local budgets of the financial burden of supporting children and teenagers in the internment institutions."[108] The decree had two aims, both freely and publicly admitted: to cut state expenditures on orphans and to prepare the children for future employment. By placing the older children from the homes into peasant families as agricultural workers and opening new places for the young, it fulfilled both purposes simultaneously. It assumed that adoption would be an economically attractive option for peasant families, who could use the labor of older children on the land and in the household.

According to the decree, a peasant household (*dvor*) could adopt no more than one child.[109] The terms of adoption were formalized by a written contract between the head of the household (*khoziain*) and the local Department of People's Education. The *khoziain* pledged to support the child at the same level as other members of the *dvor*, and to provide agricultural training, schooling, and material aid. The child was entitled to a free education and school supplies. The *khoziain* received a lump-sum payment – determined by the local executive committee at local expense – to provide the child with basic necessities. Payments ranged from 30 to 50 rubles.[110] The *dvor* also received an extra plot of land (*nadel*) from the commune for the child, free of agricultural taxes for three years. Additional tax incentives could be established locally, and the commune's permission was not required for adoption. If the child left the *dvor* after the con-

---

[107] "O Poriadke i Usloviiakh Peredachi Vospitannikov Detskikh Domov v Krest'ianskie Sem'i Dlia Podgotovki k Sel'skokhoziaistvennomu Trudu," in Tizanov, Epshtein, eds., pp. 47–48.

[108] *Instruktivnoe pis'mo ob usynovlenii* (Sverdlovsk, 1926): 2.

[109] In certain cases this rule could be waived by the local executive committee and a maximum of two children adopted.

[110] Shishova, p. 113.

tract expired, he kept the plot of land. If he stayed in the *dvor*, he became a permanent member with full rights. In the meantime, the child was considered a temporary member of the *dvor*, entitled to the same privileges as other *dvor* members, but with no right to any of the buildings or agricultural inventory.[111] The degree was retroactive and could be applied to peasant families that had taken in children in previous years. Other conditions stipulated that the adoptee must be a minor; children 10 and over and parents (if available) had to agree to the adoption; priests, criminals, former tsarist officials, and insane people were not permitted to adopt. The state was so anxious to transfer the children that the Department of People's Education was instructed not to investigate kin ties between the children and the peasants who claimed them. The household would receive the promised benefits even if the child was a relative.[112]

Although a letter from the Commissariat of Enlightenment stated that adoption was permitted only in the interest of the child and "only by those individuals who are able and ready to provide satisfactory support, job training, and suitable preparation for socially useful activities,"[113] the terms of the decree were clearly designed to make adoption economically attractive. The households most likely to adopt were those in need of an extra worker or an additional plot. The children would be used as hired labor even though they had no rights to wages or a share in the property of the *dvor*. The peasant family received tax privileges, a lump sum, an extra plot, and a free laborer. The child received "job training."

The Commissariat of Enlightenment recognized that the decree was a far cry from the early plans to ensure socialized child care for all needy children. Its letter to the Departments of People's Education spoke of a forced retreat. It said: "On the one hand, the unprecedented hunger of 1921 enormously increased the number of orphans and *besprizorniki* who lost their parents or were abandoned by them, and on the other, the need to curtail the network of children's institutions due to diminish-

---

[111] The rights of the adopted child were specified in instructions from the Commissariats of Enlightenment, Land, and Finance in October 1926, in *Kak peredavat' besprizornykh i vospitannikov detdomov v trudovye khoziaistva i proizvodit' usynovlenie* (Viatka, 1928): 5.

[112] *Instruktivnoe pis'mo ob usynovlenii*, p. 10. [113] Ibid., p. 2.

ing state funds forced the organs of Peoples' Education . . . to use all possible means for saving the children." The provision of the 1918 Code forbidding adoption was recognized as "inefficient and impractical."[114]

The decree was straightforward: The state did not make a virtue of necessity. The commitment to socialized child rearing still existed in 1926, but it could not be realized. The practical tenets of social welfare policy were developed under severe constraints imposed by a ruined economy. Although educators dreamed of children's towns where every child could be "an artist and a composer," as early as 1921 children were placed in peasant families where they faced lives of endless work, poverty, and exploitation. The 1926 decree simply codified the final outcome of a decade of struggle between vision and reality. The fears of chronic *besprizornost'* and crime, and the unremitting shortage of funds had a far greater role in shaping policy than the early dreams and visions. The continuing refusal of educators and jurists throughout the 1920s to employ punitive sanctions against juvenile crime, and their support for rehabilitative, progressive, child-centered institutions was a testament to the strength of those earlier visions.

The family was resurrected as a solution to *besprizornost'* because it was the one institution that could feed, clothe, and socialize a child at almost no cost to the state. In 1925, the educator T. E. Segalov applied Fourier's famous comment on women to children. He wrote, "The manner in which a given society protects childhood reflects its existing economic and cultural level."[115] In the Soviet Union in 1926, 19,000 homeless children were expelled from state-funded children's homes and placed in extended peasant households to sow with a centuries-old wooden plough, and to reap with a sickle and scythe.[116]

---

[114] Ibid., p. 1.

[115] T. E. Segalov, "Poniatie i Vidy Detskoi Besprizornosti," p. 10.

[116] Shishova, p. 113. Shishova notes that among the 19,000 children, some were transferred from the homes to factories as well as to peasant families. Given the high levels of unemployment existing in 1926, however, it is likely that most of these children were sent to peasant families.

3

Law and life collide: Free union and the wage-earning population

The process of divorce is so simple that there is a loss of neither money nor time. Under the current law, the act of dissolving a marriage can be completed in fifteen minutes.

> *P. Zagarin*, writer on the family, 1927[1]

The broad mass of people do not regard registration of marriage as the basis of marital relations. De facto voluntary unions are becoming ever more widespread.

> *A. Stel'makhovich*, chairman of the Moscow provincial court, 1926[2]

The Bolsheviks believed that the freedom to divorce – to dissolve a union no longer founded on love – was essential to the freedom of the individual. The right to divorce was particularly important to women, whose true feelings and abilities were so often stifled by the unbreakable bonds of marriage. This idea was widely shared by most of the progressive, prewar intelligentsia. Liberal jurists tried repeatedly to reform Russia's unbending divorce laws. Tolstoy immortalized the desperate plight of a young mother in her struggle to free herself of a loveless marriage in his famous novel, *Anna Karenina*. And both Vera Figner, the leader of the terrorist People's Will, and Alexandra Kollontai, among countless others, struggled to escape the control of husbands and families.[3]

---

[1] P. Zagarin, *Oktiabr' v semeinom bytu* (Rostov na Donu, 1927): 16.
[2] A. Stel'makhovich, *Dela ob alimentakh* (Moscow, 1926): 60.
[3] On the women rebels of the nineteenth century see Richard Stites, *The Women's Liberation Movement in Russia. Feminism, Nihilism, and Bolshevism, 1860–1930* (Princeton University Press, Princeton, N.J., 1978): 89–138; Barbara Engel, *Mothers and Daughters. Women of the*

Yet the issue of divorce had a class as well as a gender dimension. The young women rebels who fought for their rights to emotional fulfillment, education, and careers at the end of the nineteenth century came mainly from upper- and middle-class families. Whereas they spurned marriage in their search for independence, the mass of Soviet working-class women in the 1920s had very different attitudes, opportunities, and prospects. Many of these women were mothers, unskilled and illiterate. For them, marriage frequently represented a form of security and survival.[4] Their dependence on the male wage earner was more than legal; it was also social and economic.

The 1918 Family Code made divorce easily available: A marriage could be dissolved upon the simple request of either party, and no grounds were necessary. Uncontested divorces were registered in ZAGS (offices for the registration of birth, death, marriage, divorce, and other statistics), while disagreements regard-

Intelligentsia in Nineteenth Century Russia (Cambridge University Press, Cambridge, 1983); E. H. Carr, *The Romantic Exiles. A Nineteenth Century Portrait Gallery* (Beacon, Boston, 1961). On Alexandra Kollontai, see Barbara Clements, *Bolshevik Feminist: The Life of Aleksandra Kollontai* (Indiana University Press, Bloomington, 1979) and Beatrice Farnsworth, *Alexandra Kollontai. Socialism, Feminism, and the Bolshevik Revolution* (Stanford University Press, Stanford, Calif., 1980).

4 For an excellent discussion of peasant and working-class women's attitudes toward the family in the years following the revolution, see Barbara Clements, "Working-Class and Peasant Women in the Russian Revolution, 1917–1923," *Signs*, 8, no. 2 (1982) and "The Effects of the Civil War on Women and Family Relations," in Diane Koenker, William Rosenberg, Ronald Suny, eds., *Party, State, and Society in the Russian Civil War. Explorations in Social History* (Indiana University Press, Bloomington, 1989). On women, see also, Beatrice Farnsworth, "Communist Feminism: Its Synthesis and Demise," in Carol Berkin, Clara Lovett, eds., *Women, War, and Revolution* (Holmes and Meier, New York, London, 1980): 195–259; Anne Bobroff, "The Bolsheviks and Working Women, 1905–1920," *Soviet Studies*, 26, no. 4 (1974): 540–567; Barbara Clements, "Bolshevik Women: The First Generation," Robert McNeal, "The Early Decrees of the Zhenotdel," and Alix Holt, "Marxism and Women's Oppression: The Bolshevik Theory and Practice in the 1920s," in Tova Yedlin, ed., *Women in Eastern Europe and the Soviet Union* (Praeger, New York, 1980); M. Donald, "Bolshevik Activity amongst the Working Women of Petrograd in 1917," *International Review of Social History*, 27, pt. 2 (1982): 129–160; Richard Stites, "Zhenotdel: Bolshevism and Russian Women, 1917–1930," *Russian History*, 3, no. 2 (1976): 174–193.

ing separation, alimony, custody, and child support were referred to the courts. Yet the conditions of NEP made it extremely difficult for women to exercise their new right to "free union." High unemployment, low wages, and lack of daycare not only reinforced women's dependence on the family, they created a sharp contradiction between the harsh reality of life and a legal vision of freedom long promulgated by reformers and socialists.

Popular use of the 1918 Family Code

One of the most important, although hardly the most radical provisions of the 1918 Code was the establishment of civil marriage. Designed to break the grip of the church, the provision stated expressly that civil marriage was the only legally binding form of marriage. After centuries of religious marriage, jurists considered civil marriage an indispensable weapon and attentively monitored the popularity of the new civil procedure. Goikhbarg, the author of the Code, proudly tallied the figures for the first registrations in ZAGS, although they were more symbolic of nascent Soviet power than statistically significant in their own right. In January 1918 in Moscow there were 8 civil marriages; in February, 9; March, 77; and April, 120. The figures steadily increased through the summer and fall, reaching a high of 1,497 civil marriages in November 1918. The Moscow registry offices reported a grand total, for the entire year, of 5,677 newlywed couples.[5]

The spread of registration was slowed during the civil war by the sheer difficulty in establishing and extending the network of ZAGS: many towns and more than two-thirds of the districts (*volosti*) lacked registry offices. Yet civil marriage still made significant progress. A study in Odessa province at the end of the civil war showed that although more than a quarter of the population still registered their marriages, births, and deaths in church, and another quarter registered in church as well as ZAGS, fully 50 percent used ZAGS alone. Studies in Smolensk

[5] A. Goikhbarg, "Eshche o Brakakh i Razvodakh," *Proletarskaia revoliutsiia i pravo*, 2–4 (1919): 83.

province and Moscow showed a similar pattern.[6] In 1921, the Commissariat for Internal Affairs (NKVD) took over the administration of ZAGS, and by 1923 had established a ZAGS in every *volost'*, amounting to 12,500 registries throughout Russia and the Ukraine. Yet compared to the 42,000 different parishes that had registered marriage, birth, and death under the old regime, the number of civil registries was still quite modest.[7]

By 1925 less than a third of the civil marriages registered in Moscow were accompanied by a church ceremony. And while Moscow was hardly representative of the country as a whole, the figures indicated a readiness, especially among city youth, to discard older religious traditions in favor of the simpler Soviet procedure. By the mid-1920s, jurists were confident of the ultimate success of civil marriage. The jurist Dmitri Kurskii assured the Central Executive Committee (VTsIK) in 1925 that "despite the peasant character of our country and the fact that we have remote corners where the law will only reach after a considerable period of time," Soviet family law was widely disseminated among the population. He confidently reported that the number of marriages registered in ZAGS had by 1922 surpassed the annual prewar figures of the church.[8]

Although Soviet citizens were slow to abandon church marriage completely, they availed themselves of the new divorce laws with striking alacrity. The crush of couples pushing through the doors of ZAGS in search of divorce easily overwhelmed the first blissful pairs of newlyweds straggling out. During the first four months of 1918 only 214 Muscovite couples registered their marriages, while 2,516 couples divorced. There were 98 divorces in January, 384 in February, 981 in March, and 1,053 in April. The number of divorces in these four months was almost twelve times the number of marriages. After April the number of divorces began to decline, dropping to 365 in December.

[6] Ibid., p. 140.

[7] Professor Mikhailovskii, "O Rozhdaemosti i Smertnosti Naseleniia Soiuza SSR," in *Trudy III Vsesoiuznogo s"ezda po okhrane materinstva i mladenchestva* (Moscow, 1926): 139. Hereafter cited as Trudy OMM.

[8] "Stenograficheskii Otchet Zasedanii 2 Sessii Vserossiiskogo Tsentral' nogo Ispolnitel'nogo Komiteta XII Sozyva 17 i 19 Oktiabriia 1925 goda po Proektu Kodeksa Zakonov o Brake, Sem'e i Opeke," in *Sbornik statei i materialov po brachnomu i semeinomu pravu* (Moscow, 1926): 110, 111.

Almost 7,000 divorces were granted in Moscow in 1918, out-numbering marriages by more than 1,000.[9]

Goikhbarg was neither surprised nor alarmed by the high divorce rate. The large numbers, he complacently explained, reflected the backlog of unhappy couples who were unable to divorce under tsarist law. Many of these divorce petitioners came from the upper classes and were not representative of the general population. "Among those getting divorced," he wrote, "one meets many extremely prosperous people (even former nobles)." Like Marx and Engels, Goikhbarg and his fellow jurists entertained a poor opinion of upper-class marriages and the first divorce statistics seemed to corroborate their view. These marriages – loveless matches based on property and preserved by hypocrisy – withered in an atmosphere of freedom. Goikhbarg actually applauded the "stormy tempo" of divorces, as a "process of purification." "In all probability," he wrote with lurid glee, "the pustulant abscess of abnormal family relations . . . has burst." He predicted that these "abnormal displays of marital life" would soon be replaced by new relations based on genuine love and respect.[10]

By 1922, the rise in divorce had leveled off, seeming to confirm Goikhbarg's contention that the high figures of 1918 represented an abnormal phenomenon. In 1921, there were 4,732 petitions for divorce in the Moscow city people's courts, but in 1922 the number dropped to 3,780. Although the ZAGS figures (for mutually agreed divorce) are not available for these years, the number of divorces, according to the court statistics, appeared steady. Yet the statistics for the following year belied Goikhbarg's complacency. The number of divorce cases in the Moscow courts began a steady rise from 5,377 in 1923, to 7,153 in 1924, and 8,233 in 1925.[11] These figures accounted only for

[9] A. Goikhbarg, "Eshche o Brakakh i Razvodakh," p. 83.

[10] Ibid.

[11] "Doklad: Predsedatelia M.S.N.S. Tov. Smirnova na Plenume Moskovskogo Soveta RK i KD. 3 oktiabria 1922 goda," *Proletarskii sud*, 1 (1922): 11; "Rabota Suda Moskovskoi Gubernii v 1923 gody. Doklad Predsedatelia Gubsuda I. A. Smirnova, 6 Iunia 1924," *Proletarskii sud*, 1–2 (1924): 8; I. A. Smirnov, "Sovremennye Zadachi Suda v Derevne," *Proletarskii sud*, 3 (1924): 2; A. Stel'makhovich, *Dela ob alimentakh*, p. 8. These yearly statistics are projections based on figures provided for the first quartile of 1921, the first half of 1922,

Table 3. *Soviet marriage and divorce rates, 1911–1926*

| | European USSR | | |
Year	Marriages (per 1,000 people)	Divorces (per 1,000 people)	Divorces (per 1,000 marriages)
1911–1913	8.2	0.0002	2.2
1924	11.5	1.3	113.0
1925	10.0	1.5	150.0
1926	11.0	1.6	145.4

Source: L. Lubnyi-Gertsyk, "Estestvennoe Dvizhenie Naseleniia SSSR za 1926," *Statisticheskoe Obozrenie*, 8 (1928): 85. On prerevolutionary divorce, *Estestvennoe dvizhenie naseleniia RSFSR za 1926 god* (Moscow, 1928): LII.

divorces contested in court. Added to the larger figure of divorces registered in ZAGS, the statistics clearly no longer represented a backlog of unhappy, upper-class marriages.

The rise in divorce in Moscow was paralleled by a nationwide increase. Both the marriage rate and the divorce rate grew steadily throughout the European part of the USSR in the 1920s. By 1926, the marriage rate in the European USSR was almost 35 percent higher than the prewar figures. The Central Statistics Bureau (TsSU) noted "an extraordinary growth of divorce." According to the TsSU, the high marriage rate was a direct result of the growing divorce rate and the number of remarriages.[12] In the European SSSR, there were 113 divorces for every 1,000 marriages in 1924, 150 in 1925, and 145.4 in 1926 (see Table 3). There was approximately 1 divorce for every 7 marriages in 1926, or 186,329 divorces for 1,244,030 marriages.[13]

The Soviet Union had the highest marriage and divorce rate

and the first three quartiles of 1924 and 1925. The divorce figure for 1925 is an average of Smirnov's 6,938 and Stel'makhovich's 7,639.

[12] *Estestvennoe dvizhenie naseleniia RSFSR za 1926 god* (Moscow, 1928): LII, XLVIII.

[13] L. Lubnyi-Gertsyk, "Estestvennoe Dvizhenie Naseleniia SSSR za 1926," *Statisticheskoe obozrenie*, 8 (1928): 86.

Table 4. *Marriage and divorce rates in the USSR and Europe,*
1925–1926

Country	Year	Per 1,000 people		Divorces per 1,000 marriages
		Marriages	Divorces	
Eur. USSR	1926	11.0	1.6	145.4
Germany	1925	7.7	0.56	72.7
France	1926	8.5	0.46	54.1
England and Wales	1925	7.6	0.06	7.9
Belgium	1926	9.2	0.31	33.7
Sweden	1925	6.2	0.28	45.1

Source: L. Lubnyi-Gertsyk, "Estestvennoe Dvizhenie Naseleniia SSSR za 1926," *Statisticheskoe Obozrenie*, 8 (1928): 89.

Table 5. *Divorce in the towns and countryside, 1925*

	Divorces	
	Per 1,000 people	Per 1,000 marriages
Town settlements	2.8	245.4
Rural areas	1.2	125.4

Source: *Estestvennoe dvizhenie naseleniia RSFSR za 1926 god* (Moscow, 1928): LIV.

of any European country in the mid-1920s: almost 3 times as high as Germany; 3.56 times as high as France; and 26 times that of England and Wales (see Table 4). The only Western country with a comparable marriage and divorce rate was the United States, with 10.2 marriages and 1.52 divorces per 1,000 people.

While the divorce rate for the Soviet Union was higher than that of any other country, the divorce rate in the cities and towns far surpassed even the national average. The divorce rate in the towns was more than twice as high as the rural areas and more than 1.5 times as high as the national average (Table 5).

The divorce rate was directly tied to the degree of urbanization. Cities (population over 50,000) had the highest divorce and

Table 6. *Marriage and divorce in cities, towns,
and rural areas, 1926*

				Per 1,000 people	
Area	Average population	Number of marriages	Number of divorces	Marriage	Divorce
USSR	125,051,927	1,350,062	198,076	10.8	1.6
Cities[a]	11,759,377	153,511	42,128	13.1	3.6
Towns	10,545,400	116,123	21,910	11.0	2.1
Rural	102,747,150	1,080,428	134,038	10.5	1.3
Eur. SU	113,366,512	1,244,030	186,329	11.0	1.6
Cities	10,859,884	142,350	39,555	13.1	3.6
Towns	9,786,783	108,374	20,653	11.1	2.1
Rural	92,719,845	993,306	126,121	10.7	1.4
RSFSR	90,571,005	947,277	134,507	10.5	1.5
Cities	8,921,920	115,544	31,958	13.0	3.6
Towns	7,213,105	76,344	13,820	10.6	1.9
Rural	74,435,980	755,389	88,729	10.1	1.2

[a]Population over 50,000.
Source: Lubnyi-Gertsyk, p. 86.

marriage rates: 13.1 marriages per 1,000 people and 3.6 divorces, or approximately 1 divorce for every 3.5 marriages (see Table 6). The more urbanized *raions* (districts) also had higher divorce rates. The Central Industrial Region, which included the city of Moscow, had the greatest number of divorces per 1,000 people, while the Central Black Earth region had the lowest with 1.9 and 1.1, respectively. Moscow's divorce rate in 1926 was highest of all: 6.1 divorces per 1,000 people, followed by Tver with 4.8, Iaroslavl 4.0, and Leningrad 3.6. Moscow had 477.1 divorces for every 1,000 marriages, Tver 359, Iaroslavl 279, and Leningrad 265.[14] In Moscow there was one divorce for every two marriages! The statistics showed that the new divorce law had a profound impact on popular practices as the centuries-old tradition of indissoluble marriage collapsed with the stroke of a legislative pen. Even in the rural areas, where the household constituted the primary unit of production, the divorce rate exceeded that of any European country.

[14] *Estestvennoe dvizhenie naseleniia RSFSR za 1926 god*, p. LIV.

The law was not solely responsible for the large number of divorces; it simply abetted a more profound process of social breakdown and transformation. Years of war, civil war, and famine had undermined family and community ties. Peasant migrants to the cities abandoned older customs and traditions. Women joined with soldiers, strangers, and temporary providers in casual, short-term unions. De facto "wives" flooded the courts seeking alimony and child support from the men who abandoned them. And for many, the new communist morality encouraged and justified looser forms of behavior. One social observer bemoaned the times:

The old rotten foundations of the family and marriage have collapsed and are heading toward a complete annihilation with every passing day. But there are no guiding principles for the creation of new, beautiful, healthy relations. There is unimaginable bacchanalia. Freedom of love is understood by the best people as freedom of depravity.[15]

By facilitating what some considered "free love," the law promoted what others considered "depravity," blurring the line between freedom and chaos. The statistics testified to the popularity of divorce, but offered little insight into its social consequences. Once the "rotten foundations of the family and marriage" collapsed, what happened to the family? One jurist proclaimed "the revolutionary freedom of divorce" to be "the best regulator of marital relations." Yet he added that, "after this, the struggle for existence remains, and here the chances of women, particularly with children, are still less favorable than for men."[16] Although the 1918 Code extended the right to divorce to men and women alike, the opportunity to benefit from this right was largely determined by the circumstances of class and gender.

First fired, last hired: Women's economic dependence

Until 1921, women constituted a growing percentage of the Russian industrial workforce. In 1901, 26% of all production

---

[15] S. Ravich, "Bor'ba s Prostitutsiei v Petrograde," *Kommunistka*, 1–2 (1920): 23.
[16] A. Stel'makhovich, *Dela ob alimentakh*, p. 3.

workers were women; by 1914 the number had increased to 32%; by 1917, 40%; and by the end of the civil war in 1920, 46%. By 1921, 1,360,310 (45%) of the country's 3,010,000 union members were women. Women predominated in many branches of the economy: They made up 75% of the workforce in People's Feeding (Narpit), 74% in sewing, 63% of medical workers, and almost 60% in the textile factories. Even in industries traditionally dominated by men, women constituted a significant share of the labor force, holding one-quarter of the jobs in the metal industry and one-fifth in the mines.[17]

After the civil war, 4 million men, demobilized from the Red Army, returned to the workforce, and veterans with higher skills replaced thousands of women in the factories.[18] Entire branches of industry closed in a shift to strict cost accounting under NEP. There were mass layoffs in August and September of 1921, and by the end of October, 13,209 women no longer had jobs (accounting for 60% of the unemployed.) There were sharp cutbacks in the social service sector where women workers predominated: Thousands of medical personnel, state employees, daycare staffers, teachers, as well as workers in Narpit, the consumer goods agencies, and communications suddenly found themselves without work.[19] Almost 280,000 women left the labor force.

Women clearly bore the brunt of the unemployment created by the transition to NEP. In an investigation of twelve provinces, the Commissariat of Labor estimated that by the end of 1921, 62% of the unemployed registered with the labor exchange (*Birzha Truda*) were women.[20] The Petrograd Labor Exchange announced in the beginning of 1922 that 67% of the 27,000 unemployed registered in the city were women.[21] One critic of NEP angrily described the reappearance of labor competition, a fea-

---

[17] A. Anikst, "Bezrabotnitsa i Zhenskii Trud v Rossii," *Kommunistka*, 2 (1922): 37.

[18] P. M. Chirkov, "Sovetskii opyt resheniia zhenskogo voprosa v period stroitel'stva sotsializma (1917–1937)," Dissertation for Doctor of Historical Science, Moscow State University (Moscow, 1979): 172.

[19] Anikst, p. 38.

[20] Ibid. The twelve provinces are: Vladimir, Viatka, Kostroma, Moscow, Nizhegorod, Penza, Samara, Smolensk, Ufa, the Urals, and Iaroslavl.

[21] V. L. "Vliianie Novoi Ekonomicheskoi Politiki na Byt Trudiashchikhsia Zhenschin," *Kommunistka*, 3–5 (1922): 15.

ture of capitalism often criticized in Marx and Engels's writings on women. He wrote, "The reconstruction of enterprises on the basis of cost accounting and the development of privately owned enterprises has inevitably created the disgusting phenomenon of capitalist thriftiness, giving rise to the competition between male and female labor."[22] The small industries that sprang up under private management could not rehire all the workers who had lost their jobs. Men and women competed for jobs in a tight labor market, and women invariably lost. Organizers at a meeting of the Petrograd Trade Union Soviet (Petrogubprofsoveta) in 1922 noted that women had been hit hard by the mass layoffs of staff. Conditions for women were "extraordinarily difficult."[23] Between 1921 and 1927, the numbers of unemployed women leaped from 60,975 to 369,800, a sixfold increase (see Table 7).

In 1927, the Women's Department of the Party (Zhenotdel) organized a large congress of working-class and peasant women in Moscow. The Zhenotdel was organized in August 1919, partially in response to pressure from women Party activists to provide separate, officially sanctioned and supported women's groups on the local level. Factory workers, peasants, housewives, and servants composed the rank and file of the Zhenotdel, and were elected as delegates to serve apprenticeships in various branches of the government. Although the Zhenotdel was often derided by Party men as the "*bab-kom*" or "*tsentro-baba,*" it had an important impact on thousands of women who became involved in its activities.[24] Delegates attending the Women's Congress (Second All-Russian Congress of Women Workers and Peasants) came from every corner of the country, arriving by rail, by cart, and on foot, to testify to conditions for women in their cities, towns, and villages. Numerous women complained bitterly about the problem of unemployment, one of the major concerns of the Congress. Ziuzina, a delegate from Akmolinsk province in

22 Anikst, p. 38.
23 GAORSSLO, fond 6262, op. 5, delo 9, p. 2.
24 Carol Hayden, "The Zhenotdel and the Bolshevik Party," *Russian History*, 3, II (1976): 155–157; and "Feminism and Bolshevism: The Zhenotdel and the Politics of Women's Emancipation in Russia," Unpublished Ph.D Dissertation, University of California, Berkeley, 1979.

Table 7. *Female unemployment, 1921–1929*

Date	Number	Percent of all unemployed
December 1921	60,975	62.0
July 1922	108,300	59.2
October 1922	142,600	58.3
January 1923	190,300	52.5
July 1923	154,578	41.4
October 1923	315,400	50.2
April 1924	383,200	45.9
July 1924	*b*	35.4
January 1925*a*	*b*	32.6
" "	167,200	39.2
April 1925	*b*	35.4
" "	217,100	39.2
January 1926	431,100	45.3
" "	*b*	44.4
January 1927	*b*	44.4
October 1927	369,800	45.5
January 1929	*b*	43.9
July 1929	*b*	49.9

*a*Where sources differ, both figures are included.
*b*No figure available.
Source: A. Anikst, "Bezrabotitsa i Zhenskii Trud v Rossii," *Kommunistka*, 2 (1922): 38; V. Usoltsev, "Zhenskii Trud v SSSR," *Voprosy truda*, 3 (1928): 56; G. Pavliuchenko, "Bezrabotitsa Sredi Zhenshchin," *Kommunistka*, 5 (1925): 39; G. Serebrennikov, "Zhenskii Trud v SSSR za 15 Let," *Voprosy truda*, 11–12 (1932): 61.

the Kazakh republic, noted that women who were fired after several years of work simply could not find other jobs.[25]

Moreover, the unemployment figures, generally understated, concealed a large, hidden pool of women in search of work. Up to 1925, the statistics included only the "officially" unemployed: workers who lost their jobs and registered with the labor exchanges. Peasants, housewives, and other job seekers looking for waged work for the first time were not eligible to register as unemployed, and thus did not show up in the official statistics.

[25] *Vsesoiuznyi s"ezd rabotnits i krest'ianok. Stenograficheskii Otchet. 10–16 oktiabria 1927 goda* (Moscow, 1927): 220. Hereafter cited as *S"ezd rabotnits i krest'ianok.*

A. V. Artiukhina, the head of the Zhenotdel in 1927, stated in her keynote speech to the Women's Congress that 84% of the women who needed jobs – wives of workers and peasant migrants – had never worked for wages. In the face of unemployment, the unions zealously protected the rights of their members and did little to advance the interests of new groups in search of work. Petrovskaia, a delegate from the Ukraine, explained that women were caught up in a vicious circle: They could not work because they were not union members and they could not join the unions without a job.

Another delegate described the problem in detail: "Women who are without work for three to four years are not able to get work," she flatly declared. "Why? Because wherever they apply everyone says, 'We cannot help you because you are not a union member, you have no social insurance.' The unemployed woman is hungry. She walks through the streets crying. She arrives at a factory and asks, 'Comrade women, help me somehow, I am without work, without a scrap of bread.'"[26]

The number of unemployed women fluctuated widely throughout the 1920s, reflecting periodic purges of the unemployment rolls, large influxes of migrants from the countryside, and expansions and contractions in industry. The sharp decrease in the number of unemployed women between 1924 and 1925 was, in part, a result of a purge of the unemployment rolls. Investigations in the early 1920s revealed that many employed workers took advantage of large-scale corruption in the labor exchanges to register as unemployed and collect insurance benefits. A sweeping purge of the rolls in July 1924 in Moscow significantly reduced the numbers of registered unemployed,[27] and the number of unemployed women dropped from 383,200 in April 1924 to 167,200 by January 1925. After 1925, the labor exchange lost its right to control job allocation and hiring to the managers of enterprises, and many unemployed stopped registering with the exchanges.

As the economy began to recover in the mid-1920s, workers

[26] Ibid., p. 237.
[27] William Chase, *Workers, Society, and the Soviet State. Labor and Life in Moscow, 1918–1929* (University of Illinois Press, Chicago, 1987): 140; V. Usol'tsev, "Zhenskii Trud v SSSR," *Voprosy Truda*, 3 (1928): 56.

Table 8. *Women in factory production, 1923–1929*

Date	Number	Percent of all workers
1923	416,900	28.4
1926	643,628	28.4
1927	713,822	28.5
1928	725,926	28.7
1929	804,030	28.8

Source: B. Marsheva, "Zhenskii Trud v 1931 godu," *Voprosy truda*, 1 (1931): 2.

experienced the odd phenomenon of a simultaneous rise in both employment and unemployment. Growing numbers of unemployed found new places in industry, but the economy still could not keep pace with the steady stream of migrants pouring into the cities in search of work.[28] Yet the recovery affected men and women differently. Although the number of women in factory production almost doubled between 1923 and 1929, women's share of the industrial labor force remained fairly constant at 28% (see Table 8). Thus although the number of jobs was rapidly growing and greater numbers of women were finding work, women were still not successful in expanding their share of the labor force. And women were not as quick to recover from the unemployment of the early NEP years as men. As late as 1929, they constituted fully 50% of the unemployed, but only 29% of the employed, despite the new, burgeoning job opportunities. And despite a significant improvement in the economy in the mid-1920s, women's share of unemployment actually increased from 40% in 1925 to 50% in 1929. Men were absorbed much more quickly into the expanding economy. Women, the first fired at the beginning of NEP, were the last hired at its end.

Many of the advocates of NEP rued the growth of female unemployment, but defended the policy of cutbacks, cost accounting, and rationalization that produced it. In their view, these measures were necessary to the speedy recovery of the economy and the reintegration of the returning Red Army vet-

[28] E. H. Carr, *Socialism in One Country, 1924–1926*, Vol. 1 (Macmillan, New York, 1958): 365.

erans.[29] Yet as the economy began to recover, it became clear that women were still suffering from a disproportionate amount of unemployment due less to the financial imperatives of NEP than persistent patterns of discrimination in the workplace. Given a choice, many managers clearly preferred to lay off women rather than men. Ironically, the more progressive features of Soviet labor legislation, such as paid maternity leave, the ban on nightwork for women, and work restrictions for pregnant women and nursing mothers, often prompted managers to fire women and replace them with men.[30] Women were considered more costly to employ. One writer indignantly declared, "Who does not know about those abuses that go on under the name of reduction in staff, where women, not just equally qualified, but more so, are dismissed because a woman costs an enterprise much more than a man."[31]

Delegates to the Women's Congress castigated the factory managers for their thoughtless, sexist practices. Ziuzina argued that managers fired women without any consideration for their family responsibilities. "Often they terminate those who have three or four children and no husbands or relations," she said. Another delegate angrily declared that factory managers discriminated against married women. "Even if she wants to work, they fire her anyway. They say, 'You have a husband – go home to your kitchen.'"[32] Despite the Commissariat of Labor's express instructions to consider men and women equally in event of a layoff, managers in male-dominated industries pursued an aggressive policy aimed at eliminating women and replacing them with men.[33] In a number of unions, the growing threat of unemployment led to a concerted drive against the female members.[34]

Delegates to the Thirteenth Party Congress in 1924 attempted

---

[29] See William Chase on the "productionist" position, p. 163; G. Serebrennikov, an economist in the 1920s, justified the dismissal of women in the early years of NEP on the basis of their low skill levels, but became more critical of these practices in the later twenties. See Serebrennikov, p. 61.

[30] P. M. Chirkov, "Sovetskii opyt resheniia zhenskogo voprosa v period stroitel'stva sotsializma (1917–1937)," p. 172.

[31] G. Pavliuchenko, "Bezrabotitsa Sredi Zhenshchin," *Kommunistka*, 5 (1925): 39.

[32] *S"ezd rabotnits i krest'ianok*, p. 225.

[33] Chase, p. 149.   [34] Carr, p. 387.

to halt the continuing expulsions of women from industry. Recognizing the awful predicament of the woman worker, the Congress noted: "In spite of the general improvement in the condition of the working class, the position of women workers, the majority of whom are in the least skilled, lowest paid section of the proletariat, still remains difficult." The delegates vowed to stop the layoffs of women, to raise their skills, and to involve them in those branches of production where women were traditionally excluded or underrepresented. Noting that women's employment was not merely a matter of economics, the Congress stressed "that the preservation of women workers in production has a political significance."[35] The party thus rejected a strictly "productionist" line oriented toward rapid economic recovery and maximization of profits, and reaffirmed its commitment to the humanist values embodied in its program for women's emancipation.

In line with the Party's resolutions, the Commissariats of Labor, Social Security, and Economic Planning, and the unions sent out a series of decrees aimed at stopping the discrimination against women. Factory managers were instructed that men and women with the same skills were to be terminated in equal proportions in a reduction of staff. Pregnant and nursing women on leave were not to be dismissed, and mothers with children under a year old had priority in remaining at work. Women who lost their jobs were permitted to keep their children in the workers' daycare centers. Single women were not to be thrown out of their lodgings.[36]

Yet the resolutions and decrees appeared to have little effect on the sexist practices of factory managers and the continuing discrimination against women workers. Managers, under pressure to raise profits and maximize efficiency, paid little heed to the Party's more humanist preachings. Their continuing intransigence soon forced a retreat from the high standards of protective labor legislation established on behalf of women after the revolution. After sharp debate, delegates to the Sixth Trade Union Congress in November 1924 voted to repeal the ban on nightwork for women and permit them to enter industries previ-

---

[35] *Trinadtsatyi s"ezd RKP (b). Mai 1924. Stenograficheskii otchet* (Moscow, 1963): 678, 680.
[36] Chirkov, pp. 173–174.

ously deemed hazardous to their health. In the harshly realistic words of a woman delegate from Rostov-on-the-Don, "It is better if the professional organizations offer the woman worker less protection so that she can have the chance to earn herself a crust of bread and not be forced to sell herself on the boulevard."[37] Even the Zhenotdel, the staunchest defender of women's interests, agreed on the need to repeal the ban on nightwork so that employers would have less excuse to lay off women workers.[38]

By 1925, industry had recovered sufficiently to experience a shortage of skilled labor. Yet the problem of female unemployment persisted unabated. The percentage of women among the unemployed actually rose after 1925 as factory managers gave preference to unemployed men. Even male peasant migrants were preferred to working-class women.

Ultimately, every level of the industrial and state apparatus bore some responsibility for discrimination against women workers. At the highest levels, the priority relentlessly placed on cost cutting and profit maximization at the expense of political values severely damaged women's opportunities. Factory managers perceived few alternatives to firing women if they were to keep costs to a minimum. As V. V. Shmidt, the commissar of labor, admitted, it was "economically unprofitable" to employ women.[39] The Party attempted to remedy some of the worst abuses by reaffirming its commitment to equality in the workplace. But despite its good intentions, both factory managers and union leaders continued to discriminate against women in their patterns of hiring, firing, and advancement. The resolutions at the highest levels had little effect on practice in local enterprises. The retreat from protective labor legislation demonstrated the Party's inability to end discrimination by decree. Apparently, the only effective method of eliminating discrimination against women was to abolish the protective labor legislation that recognized their special needs as mothers. One of the women delegates to the Sixth Trade Union Congress in 1924 spoke out fiercely against "the impairment" of women's "legal

[37] *Shestoi Vsesoiuznyi s"ezd professional'nykh soiuzov. Stenograficheskii otchet* (Moscow, 1925): 223.

[38] Carol Hayden, "The Zhenotdel and the Bolshevik Party," p. 169.

[39] *Shestoi Vsesoiuznyi s"ezd professional'nykh soiuzov. Stenograficheskii otchet,* p. 184.

achievements." Quickly grasping the essential problem, she noted that the constant push to increase labor productivity was at odds with the needs of women workers.[40]

Under these difficult economic circumstances, divorce entailed potentially tragic consequences for the housewife or the unskilled worker. For if her husband divorced or abandoned her, she was often unable to support herself or her children. Dziuba, a delegate to the Women's Congress from the Ukraine, emphasized the special difficulties of the housewife after divorce. "Comrade workers and peasants," she appealed, "I ask you to consider that the wife of the worker, your sister, has been overlooked. If a woman worker leaves her husband, she only loses a husband, she works independently. But when the wife of a worker leaves her husband she is considered a non-laboring (*netrudnyi*) element, left homeless in the street (*besprizornoi*). There is nowhere for her to turn, all is closed, and everyone turns away from her."[41] Without an independent wage, women were in no position to exercise their right to "free union." Vera Lebedeva, the head of the Department for the Protection of Maternity and Infancy (OMM), grimly summed up the future of many divorced women:

The weakness of the marital tie and divorce create masses of single women who carry the burden of child care alone. Imagine yourself such a woman, without support from your husband, with a child on your hands, laid off due to a reduction in staff, and thrown out of the dormitory . . . with no possibility to continue supporting yourself.

"Where do these thousands go?" Lebedeva asked. 'There is one exit – the street."[42]

On the street

The contrast between the socialist ideal of free union and the conditions of the time was nowhere so starkly depicted as in the spectacle of women selling themselves on the streets. Many observers noted the increase of prostitution during NEP. Women solicited men in the railroad stations, in the main squares, and in

[40] Ibid., p. 621.   [41] *S"ezd rabotnits i krest'ianok*, p. 452.
[42] V. L., "Vliianie Novoi Ekonomicheskoi Politiki na Byt Trudiashchikhsia Zhenschin," *Kommunistka*, pp. 15, 16.

the public toilets. "Nestled in front doors, in passenger and freight cars, in alleys, in baths, in other places,"[43] women sold sex for as little as 6 kopeks, for 5 rubles, for 10 rubles for the night. Homeless girls slept in train cars: the female *besprizorniki*. Abandoned women, peasant widows, mothers with small children, all desperate to earn money, turned to prostitution. Krupskaia wrote, "Poverty compels women to sell themselves. They are not prostitutes who make an enterprise out of this, but mothers of families." Poverty forced women into "sex for a crust of bread"; it was "the grave of human relations."[44]

Numerous contemporary studies highlighted the connection between prostitution and unemployment during NEP. A. Irving, a sociologist who published a study of prostitutes in 1925, noted that 80 percent of the 539 prostitutes he interviewed entered prostitution after 1921. Criticizing the effect of NEP on women, he wrote, "The extraordinarily high percentage of prostitutes with 'Nep-ovski' length of service, in contrast to the insignificant number of prostitutes in service since the first years of the revolution, demonstrates that NEP is by no means an advantage." Irving concluded that "NEP and its temptations and the unemployment of women workers are the main factors in prostitution."[45] Professor N. Duboshinskii found in his 1924 study of 601 Moscow prostitutes that 51% of the women had become prostitutes out of need. Surveying 340 women, he discovered that 84% had tried to leave prostitution but were unable to find a job. Duboshinskii concluded, "Hunger is the most powerful factor in prostitution."[46] Yet another study observed that while 44% of prostitutes had some work skills, only 15% were skilled enough to become self-employed. Most of these women were dressmakers, an occupation where wages were low, employment irregular and uncertain.[47] The remaining 85% were dependent on the unfriendly labor market for their employment. And even

[43] A. Uchevatov, "Iz Byta Prostitutki Nashikh Dnei," *Pravo i zhizn'*, 1 (1928): 52.

[44] N. Krupskaia, "Voina i Detorozhdenie," *Kommunistka*, 1–2 (1920): 18.

[45] A. Irving, "Vozrastnoi i Natsional'nyi Sostav Prostitutok," *Rabochii sud*, 5–6 (1925): 209.

[46] N. O. Duboshinskii, "Sotsial'nyi Sostav Prostitutsii," *Rabochii sud*, 3–4 (1925): 127–128.

[47] D. P. Rodin, "Iz Dannykh Sovremennoi Prostitutsii," *Pravo i zhizn'*, 5 (1927): 67.

employed women were occasionally forced into prostitution given their concentration in low-paid, unskilled jobs. A 1923 study found that many factory women used prostitution to supplement their wages.[48]

The majority of prostitutes in the 1920s came from working-class backgrounds. Duboshinskii's study of Moscow prostitutes showed that 60% were working-class. Of the remainder, 9% were from the aristocracy or the bourgeoisie, 5% from the intelligentsia, and 26% were self-employed in handicrafts, dressmaking, and sewing. Of the working-class women, 37% were former servants, 20% had worked in Narpit, 15% were factory workers, 14%, saleswomen, and 9%, medical personnel. The former occupation of the remaining 26% of the total was unknown. The statistics emphasized the impact of NEP: Almost 45% of the working-class women had entered prostitution from industries that experienced sharp cutbacks, such as Narpit, the factories, and medical services.[49]

Case histories revealed that many women became prostitutes because they were unable to find other work. Kh., aged 38, was described as a "sick, wandering, exhausted person with running eyes." Crying as she spoke of her life, she explained that she began work in a tobacco factory at age 11. She hawked goods on the streets from 1917 to 1923 and later worked briefly as a charwoman. Unemployed thereafter, she was arrested for angrily defending the pitiful remnants of her dignity: She threw a stone at a man on the street who called her a whore. V., a 29-year-old master dressmaker with two years of middle school, told a wrenching tale of her fruitless search for steady work. She worked in a textile factory up to the Revolution, when she was laid off. In 1920 she took another job but was sacked within the year. Another layoff followed a short stint as a hospital nurse. She sold her belongings piece by piece, and was eventually arrested for making *samogon* (home brew). When she come out of prison, she began working as a prostitute. V. w is described as "a devastated, slovenly woman, in dirty rags scarcely covering her body, with no shoes." In a defeated voice, she explained that she had lost all hope of ever getting a job.

---

[48] L. A. and L. M. Vasilevskie, *Prostitutsia i novaia Rossia* (1923): 4.
[49] Duboshinskii, pp. 125–126.

A number of women were homeless and prostituted themselves to buy food. P., aged 26, had lost her home when she split up with her husband. Sleeping in railroad cars and hanging around with *besprizorniki*, she prostituted herself to survive. S., a homeless 17-year-old, had wandered about, begging and stealing for years. At first, men had taken advantage of her by promising to take her home and feed her. Then she "learned how" and became a prostitute. She had sex with five or six men a night. Another homeless young woman described living in a train car, coupling with two or three men a night for 50 kopeks to 2 rubles. Many of the men were homeless too. Sometimes she got a beating instead of the money.[50]

While the female *besprizorniki* undoubtedly accounted for many of the prostitutes, one study published in 1925 found that fully 44% of Moscow prostitutes lived with parents, siblings, or other relations. Almost 40% lived in one room and slept in the same bed with a family member.[51] These women were not cut off from their families, but on the contrary, lived with them in close quarters, and in all likelihood, contributed their painfully gained earnings to the family budget. S., an 18-year-old prostitute, was typical in this regard. She lived with her parents and five brothers and sisters in one room. Her father, an elderly invalid, received a pension of 30 rubles a month. She began working as a prostitute at age 14 when she was abandoned by a worker who promised to marry her. Another young woman became a prostitute to support her younger brother and elderly mother. Neither family ever knew how the girls earned the bread that fed them.[52]

Many women worked as prostitutes to support their dependent children. One woman, abandoned by her husband after twenty years of marriage, explained, "I went to the street in tears. I had to support my daughter and protect her from this fate." She had sex with about four men a week, enduring their "poor treatment, beatings, and perverse demands." A., aged 26, was separated from her husband and supporting her baby daughter. She earned about 100 rubles a month as a prostitute

[50] Rodin, p. 68; Uchevatov, p. 53.
[51] Oleg Ol'ginskii, "Prostitutsiia i Zhilishchnyi Vopros," *Rabochii sud*, 5–6 (1925): 205.
[52] Rodin, pp. 67, 69.

and was saving her money to buy a sewing machine. K., aged 28, was divorced with an 8-month-old daughter. Ts., 30, was divorced with two small children and an elderly mother to support. One woman had been a housewife until her husband's death forced her to go to work. Laid off after five months in a sewing workshop, she had a small child, two younger sisters, and a mother-in-law depending on her earnings. "I wanted to remarry," she said sadly, "but no man would agree to take such a family."[53]

The two largest groups of urban prostitutes were the *besprizorniki*, who quickly found prostitution more profitable than beggary, and unemployed women who were unable to find steady work. Naturally, the categories overlapped, for the line separating the unemployed from the homeless was a thin one. Women told repeated tales of divorce, separation, and abandonment. They were frequently the sole support of small children, siblings, or aged relations. Prostitution represented the most painful, but not the most improbable, fate of the husbandless woman under NEP. It made a mockery of the idea that women were free, independent individuals who could enter a union on the basis of personal choice. Without an independent wage, women were forced into the most unfree of acts: to garner some portion of the male wage by selling their sexuality to whoever wanted them. Many of the women expressed a desperate desire to leave prostitution. Others felt deep shame at their situation. For most, it was the last resort before starvation.

Low wages and poverty

While unemployment stood as an unmistakable barrier to women's independence, the concentration of women in poorly paid, unskilled jobs further reinforced their dependence on men. However meager the pooled salaries of the working-class family, the man's higher wages ensured a better standard of living for his wife and children. Even if a woman worked, divorce signified a substantial drop in her standard of living.

Women earned only 65% of what men earned in the mid-

[53] Uchevatov, pp. 55, 52, 53.

1920s. In 1925, the average salary of women workers in industry was 32.60 rubles per month. The majority of women workers (57%) earned between 20 and 40 rubles; about 20% made less than 20 rubles, but only about 4% earned more than 60. There were strikingly few women at the higher end of the pay scale. Women's low pay could not be attributed to the fact that they worked fewer hours than men. Women and men worked approximately the same number of days per month and hours per day.[54] Women earned lower salaries because they were concentrated in unskilled, menial jobs at the bottom of the pay scale.

The cutbacks that occurred during NEP had the effect of shifting women away from heavy industry and back into the traditional jobs they held before the war. Women, thrown suddenly out of mining, metallurgy, and printing, filtered back into textile, food production, and sewing, the traditional, low-paid bastions of female labor. Women suffered layoffs in all industries because of their lack of skills, but the sharpest reductions occurred in industries that they had first entered during the war years. In the metal industry, for example, women's share of the workforce dropped from 15% in 1920 to 8% in 1928, a drop of 47%. In mining, women's share dropped from 13.7% in 1923 to 7.5% in 1928, and in machine production, from 13.8% in 1923 to 6.8% in 1929. As women's share of jobs in heavy industry decreased, it increased in light industry and the service sector. The percentage of women workers in Narpit increased from 55% in 1923 to 82% in 1928, from 61% to 65% among medical personnel, and 58% to 61% in the textile factories.[55] Their share in all branches of the food industry increased as well.[56] Between 1923 and 1928, 343,085 women entered the industrial workforce, yet fully 71% of these entered the traditionally female industries: 214,117 took jobs in textile factories, and 30,000 more in food production.[57] Women lost what they had gained

---

[54] B. Markus, "Zhenskii Trud v SSSR v 1924 gody," *Kommunistka*, 4 (1925): 49; and A. G. Rashin, *Zhenskii trud v SSSR* (Moscow, 1928): 39, 37.

[55] G. Serebrennikov, "Zhenskii Trud v SSSR za 15 Let," *Voprosy truda*, 11–12 (1932): 60–61.

[56] F. Vinnik, "Bezrabotitsa Sreda Zhenshchin y Pishchevikov," *Voprosy truda*, 2 (1929): 121.

[57] B. Marsheva, "Problema Zhenskogo Truda v Sovremennykh Usloviiakh," *Voprosy truda*, 2 (1929): 40.

during the war. As the economy gradually recovered, the prewar gender division of labor reasserted itself, concentrating women in the lowest paid sectors of the economy and the lowest paid, least-skilled jobs in every sector.

Delegates to the Women's Congress noted how women's lack of skills figured prominently in decisions regarding hiring, firing, and advancement. Factory managers frequently justified the dismissal of women workers on the grounds that they lacked the skills necessary to fill the higher-paid positions. And their lack of skills kept them in the ranks of the unemployed. Korotkova, a delegate from the Crimea, observed: "If you look at the labor exchanges you will find only women. No one wants to employ them because they have no skills."[58]

Yet other women noted that discrimination persisted even when women acquired new labor skills. Petrovskaia, a Ukrainian delegate, explained that the factory in her town employed 500 women: 205 had learned new skills, but only one or two were promoted into better positions. "With tears, with cries, you go everywhere," she said indignantly, "to the factory administration, to the supervisor, but our administration still preserves the old view of women workers. The administration thinks that women workers should only sweep." Women spoke bitterly not only about managers, but male workers as well, accusing them of sexist attitudes and practices that undermined equality in the workplace. Even when their male co-workers were not actively hostile, they nonetheless condescended to women and denigrated their abilities. The men in the railroad yards sneered at women workers, laughing among themselves and asking, "What will the *babas* make in the workshop?" "They interfere with us in everything," one delegate furiously declared, "they interfere with the promotion of women workers to higher, skilled positions."[59]

Statistics showed a sharp division between male and female labor in every industry except textiles, where women vastly outnumbered men. Almost 50% of male industrial workers in 1925 held skilled jobs; another 30% were in semiskilled positions, less than 20% performed unskilled labor. For women, the figures were reversed: Only 13% worked in skilled jobs, about 42% were

[58] *S"ezd rabotnits i krest'ianok*, p. 287.
[59] Ibid., pp. 237, 243, 255, 301.

semiskilled, and the remaining 45% were unskilled. The concentration of women in unskilled jobs was reflected in their job classifications. On an industrywide scale from 1 to 12, 89% of women workers were concentrated in grades 3 to 6. The vast majority of men (75%), however, were in grades 6 and above. Whereas less than 10% of male workers were in grades 1 to 3, almost 25% of women workers fell into this category. The average grade for male workers was 6, for women, 4.3.[60] By 1927, little had changed: Fully one-quarter of male workers occupied the higher job classifications (grade 8 and above), but only 1.1% of women.[61]

Moreover, even men and women who occupied the same positions received different wages. One delegate to the Women's Congress angrily noted, "A woman does not always receive a salary equal to a man's even if they do the same work." She complained that the skilled male workers received all the privileges. Even the overalls were not distributed equally![62] A salary survey of unskilled workers in various industries in 1928 revealed that women earned consistently less than their male counterparts in the same jobs: about 25% less in the metal, cotton, and rubber industries, 15% less in tobacco, and 33% less in shoe production.[63]

The women at the Congress were quick to connect women's lack of skills and low salaries to a host of other problems: Women were the most vulnerable to dismissal; men treated them with contempt at work; meager earnings reinforced their dependence on the family. One delegate noted that a woman's inability to support her family without a man was an important cause of *besprizornost'*. "Imagine the position of a woman, receiving a salary in the category of grade 3," she said, "who has four children on her hands, and does not even have the hope that she will be able to provide for them in the future." The problem of *besprizornost'*, she said, had to be solved at the root: by providing women with skills.[64]

The delegates to the Congress returned repeatedly to the im-

[60] Rashin, pp. 12, 13.　　[61] Serebrennikov, p. 64.
[62] *S"ezd rabotnits i krest'ianok*, p. 255.
[63] N. V., "K Voprosu o Planirovanii Zarplaty," *Voprosy truda*, 3–4 (1929): 45.
[64] *S"ezd rabotnits i krest'ianok*, pp. 240, 241.

portance of an independent wage. The vision of women's liberation through economic autonomy animated every discussion.
One delegate spoke for many when she proclaimed, "What gives
us, women, the basis of equal rights, what strengthens our independence? Our independent wage. All we women know that an
independent wage gives us our freedom and forces those
around us to treat us as an equal member of society and the
family."[65] Women from all parts of the country raised the stubborn problem of women's lack of skills. They clearly understood
that without skills and higher salaries, social equality was, at best,
an illusory proposition.

Reproductive dependence and the gender division of labor

Women's ability to enter the workplace, advance their skills, further their education, and participate in a wider public and political world was compromised not only by low wages but by their
unrelieved responsibilities for children. Vera Lebedeva, the
head of the Department for the Protection of Maternity and
Infancy (OMM), told the Women's Congress, "We have heard
from you about the difficulties women encountered in gaining
their right to work, the right and opportunity to demonstrate
their initiative. . . . These difficulties, in significant measure, are
created because women's hands are tied by motherhood."[66]

The number of childcare facilities available to women immediately after the revolution was pitifully small, though it increased impressively during the civil war years (see Table 9). The
number of factory and regional daycare centers grew from a
mere 14 in 1917 to 914 in 1922; special homes for single women
with infants were established throughout the country, and the
number of children's homes for orphans increased dramatically.
But NEP had a drastic effect on the facilities available to women
and children. Within the single year between 1922 and 1923,
more than half of the country's daycare centers and homes for
single mothers shut their doors and closings continued for two

[65] Ibid., p. 276.   [66] Ibid., p. 442.

Table 9. *Childcare institutions, 1917–1925*

Institution	1917	1918	1919	Jan. 1920	Jan. 1921	Jan. 1922	Jan. 1923	Jan. 1924	Jan. 1925	Oct. 1925	USSR Oct. 1925
Factory, *raion* creches	14	78	126	565	668	914	447	503	536	584	778
Rural creches[a]	–	–	–	–	–	–	–	–	–	5	5
Houses for mother and child	–	10	17	99	125	237	110	91	80	96	103
Children's homes	7	92	121	370	418	765	491	362	313	287	433
Konsultatsiia Children	6	39	58	133	161	179	137	165	262	372	521
Pregnancy	–	–	–	–	–	29	28	95	169	208	276
Rural	–	–	–	–	–	–	–	7	117	120	372
Legal	–	–	–	–	–	–	–	30	130	130	130

[a]Permanent creches.
Source: *Trudy III Vsesoiuznogo s"ezda po okhrane materinstva i mladenchestva* (Moscow, 1926): 12.

more years. Almost all services earmarked for women and children were sharply reduced.

Numerous delegates to the Women's Congress spoke of the impact of NEP and the need for more daycare centers and children's homes. Ziuzina, from Kazakhstan, observed that all the children's homes in her town had closed. A single mother had nowhere to turn for help with her baby. "She leaves it to the mercy of fate or throws it into some kind of abyss," noted Ziuzina, referring to the desperate practice of infanticide. Unemployed women were not covered by insurance and received no help with pregnancy, childbirth, or infant care. "All this falls upon the very poorest," Ziuzina said. "The unemployed mother can get neither work nor assistance." Another delegate appealed for more child care. "Nowhere is there such a destruction of the family as in Murmansk," she explained. Uraimagova, a delegate from Northern Ossetia, asserted, "In order to free women, we must create the necessary conditions, children's creches are needed, kindergartens and other children's organizations." Another delegate mentioned a new factory settlement built in the province of Ivanovo-Vosnesensk, a large textile center employing thousands of women. "But what did we do in this settlement?" she demanded. "Did we do anything to liberate women? There is almost nothing there – no public dining room, no daycare center, no creche . . . We must have the liberation of women in mind when we build housing."[67]

Daycare centers and other maternity institutions were not the only social services to suffer under NEP. During the civil war, large numbers of people, prompted by the increasing worthlessness of the ruble, ate their meals in communal dining halls (*stolovye*). When famine threatened Petrograd in 1918, the government quickly organized *stolovye* in the factories and workplaces, and by January 1920, they were serving close to 1 million people. After the decrees in 1919 authorizing free food for children, 80% of the city's young inhabitants began to receive free meals. In the surrounding Petrograd province, 1,892,513 people received government rations; 80% of the population took its meals in *stolovye*. In Moscow, communal dining was organized somewhat later, although by 1921, the city boasted over 2,000

67 Ibid., pp. 20, 231, 267, 300.

food stations serving 956,000 people, or 93% of the population. Hundreds of dining rooms, soup kitchens, food stations, and schools provided children with their daily meals. Communal dining was organized most effectively and rapidly in areas with large factory populations like Viatka, Perm, Iaroslavl, and Tula, but more than one-third of the population in 49 provinces (over 4.5 million people) received cooked food from communal dispensaries.[68]

The system of social feeding, like many hastily constructed emergency programs, suffered a great many problems. People waited in long lines to enter dirty dining rooms where the food was often spoiled, the meals meager, the dishes and utensils in short supply. Many went to the *stolovye* only because the shops were bare, and they received meals in lieu of wages. With the collapse of a money economy, the *stolovye* took the place of a more complex system of exchange. For the government, it became the most effective, albeit primitive, means of feeding the urban population.

Yet many saw the development of the *stolovye* as more than an economically expedient measure. They were considered a first step in the construction of a truly socialist economy and the emancipation of women from petty household labor. Advocates were quick to admit that the *stolovye* were inadequate, but it was the inadequacies, not the *stolovye* themselves, that were the product of shortage and economic collapse. Communal dining was a social advance, a victory over privatized family consumption, the embodiment of "a new communist way of life."[69] Like many of the features of war communism later dismissed as premature or illusionary, the sheer numbers of people participating in the new system led many to view it as a successful example of communism in action. Activists pointed with pride to the government's successful efforts to feed over 90% of the people in Moscow and Petrograd. I. Stepanov, a Party leader, later wrote with nostalgia, "During the years of war communism we managed to feed the children collectively. All we adults were insanely and dreadfully hungry, but we could justly say to the whole world: The children are the first privileged citizens of our republic. We could say that

[68] A. Sviderskii, "Razvitie Obshchestvennogo Pitaniia v Rykakh Zhenshchiny," *Kommunistka*, 8–9 (1921): 26–29.
[69] Ibid., pp. 30, 26, 29.

we were moving toward the realization of freeing love from those crippling and killing elements, freeing love from economics and women from household slavery."[70]

With the end of the rationing system in 1921, the communal dining halls began to close. Food stores reopened and workers began to receive a monetary wage. Although many were glad to leave the dirty *stolovye* and return to home-cooked meals, many women resented their return to the unpaid tasks of shopping and cooking for their families. Numerous working-class women complained that housework took up too much of their time and prevented them from participating in activities outside the home. One factory woman in Moscow province wrote, "A working woman comes home from work after an eight-hour day, eats dinner in 8 to 10 minutes, and once again faces a load of physical work: washing linens, cleaning up, etc." "There are no limits to housework," sighed another, for a woman is "charwoman, cook, dressmaker, launderer, nurse, caring mother, and attentive wife. And how much time it takes to go to the store and drag home dinner!"[71]

Clearly, the retreat from the system of communal dining did not affect men and women in the same way. Time budget studies showed that women were responsible for most of the domestic labor even if they worked outside the home. The factory woman worked the same eight-hour day as her male counterpart, but when she returned home, she faced about five more hours of housework; the male worker, only two. Men had about three and a half hours to relax during the day, a woman, only two hours and twenty minutes. Men slept for an average of eight hours, women, only six hours and 45 minutes.[72] Women spent, on average, two and a half times more time on housework than men and had barely half the leisure as a result.[73] Given their household responsibilities, it was not surprising that women had a

---

[70] I. Stepanov, "Problema Pola," in E. Iaroslavskii, ed., *Voprosy zhizni i bor'by* (Moscow, 1924): 205.

[71] Z. Rakitina, "Byt po Zametkam Rabotnits," *Kommunistka*, 12 (1926): 32.

[72] V. V. Sokolov, *Prava zhenshchinu po sovetskim zakonam* (Moscow, 1928): 16.

[73] Michael Paul Sacks, *Women's Work in Soviet Russia. Continuity in the Midst of Change* (Praeger, New York, 1976): 39.

higher rate of illiteracy and lower interest in politics and current affairs. A woman could hardly share her husband's concerns and interests when her horizons were blocked day after day by stacks of dirty sheets and dishes.

Many of the delegates to the Women's Congress in 1927 called for a return to the system of communal dining pioneered during war communism. Moirova, a delegate from Narpit, argued that women could not be free until cooking, cleaning, and other household tasks were fully socialized. "We are still not free from the family burden," she said, "even among the workers, who will be the first to liquidate all vestiges of the past in their families, it is clear that women factory workers are still forced to stand by the pots and fiddle around with the stove." She called for more public dining rooms, meals for children, and the distribution of cooked meals to people's homes. Moirova exhorted women to enter the service industries. If women were held back by the belief that "*Babushka* was not a lathe turner, so I should not be a lathe turner," "Then indeed," Moirova shot back, "all our *babushki* were good cooks." Women should use the skills they had for their own collective liberation. Another delegate suggested that the problems of housework and unemployment could be solved simultaneously by putting jobless women to work in new consumer service industries.[74]

While the law viewed women as the equals of men, women's role in the home undercut their independence. As long as work was segregated by gender, dependency was built into family life. Moirova argued that the socialization of housework was essential to an equal and companionate marriage. "We cannot consider the construction of socialism a success if we do not make a basic revolution in our own families," she declared. "We are accustomed to associating stoves, kitchens, pots, cradles, and crying babies with the family. In a socialist society, these parts of the family should not be. The family should consist of loving, equal comrades, each of which works where they are useful to the whole society."[75]

The plight of women prompted many advocates of women's liberation to vociferous criticism of NEP. Critics considered the sharp cutbacks in social services and childcare facilities, the in-

---

[74] *S"ezd rabotnits i krest'ianok*, pp. 243, 252.   [75] Ibid., p. 250.

crease in female unemployment, and the reappearance of prostitution as tangible signs of NEP's negative impact on women's
prospects for liberation. Trotsky, painfully aware of the social
ramifications of NEP, suggested that voluntarism and self-help
might offset the decreases in state spending. He urged families
to group together in "collective housekeeping units," and to
experiment with the socialization of housework, a task that the
state "cannot as yet undertake."[76] Yet other activists, often sup-
portive of NEP, were critical of a strategy for liberation based
solely on individual efforts. Lebedeva recalled an instance when
peasant women went from village to village, collecting flour and
eggs to support the daycare centers. Their initiative was laud-
able, but voluntarism had its programmatic limits. "This is not a
system," Lebedeva asserted, "and a network of daycare centers
cannot be created on the charity of the population. . . . The
daycare centers must be permanently entered in the budgets of
the district executive committees." She noted that the centers in
the towns served only 16% of the working population and the
childcare network was not keeping pace with the increase in
women workers. Lebedeva concluded pessimistically, "The position of women is not getting better, it is getting relatively
worse."[77] Many activists took the position that the revival of the
economy should not be engineered at the expense of women's
needs. Delegates to a meeting on female labor in 1922 angrily
called attention to "the catastrophic position of services designed
to protect mothers and infants due to state budgeting pressures
under NEP." The delegates demanded that the Central Executive Committee compel "the entire party, Soviet state, and the
unions" to consider "the problems of motherhood and infancy."
More important, they cautioned against separating women's issues from those of the state and the workers. Women's problems
were "closely connected to the overall position of the working
class and under no condition should be considered apart from
the proletarian state." The firm, uncompromising tone of the
resolution expressed the dissatisfactions numerous social activists felt with the "productionist" orientation of NEP. Yet as
Sophia Smidovich, the future head of the Zhenotdel, later

[76] Leon Trotsky, *Women and the Family* (Pathfinder, New York, 1970):
26, 27, 28.
[77] *S"ezd rabotnits i krest'ianok*, pp. 448, 450.

noted, "this resolution was but a voice wailing in the wilderness."[78]

Alimony

Given the obstacles to women's independence, thousands of divorced women turned to the courts to sue for alimony or child support from their former husbands. The very concept of alimony – the monetary expression of women's dependence on men – signified the persistence of the family as the primary form of social organization and security. The practice of alimony, ensuring that the male wage earner rather than the state took responsibility for the needy woman and the child, revealed the scarcity of social services and the paucity of options for women outside the family.

According to the 1918 Family Code, all children, regardless of whether their parents were married, were entitled to parental support until the age of 18. The provision was remarkably inclusive, making no distinction between "legitimate" and "illegitimate" children. The alimony provision of the Code, in contrast, was quite narrow. An ex-spouse was only entitled to six months of support after a divorce, and then only if he or she was disabled and in need. The provision thus excluded able-bodied women, no matter how poor. Given the limits on alimony, the vast majority of women who went to court were forced to sue only for child support, although Soviet jurists used the term "alimony" to cover monetary support of ex-spouses, children, and even dependent relations.

The number of alimony cases grew quickly after 1918. At first, requests for alimony were "negligible." Surveying seven Moscow court rooms in 1918, Goikhbarg noted that the number of divorces involving children was insignificant and that judges awarded alimony in less than 1% of the cases.[79] Yet as divorce

[78] S. Smidovich, "O Novom Kodekse Zakonov o Brake i Sem'e," *Kommunistka*, 1 (1926): 47.

[79] A. G. Goikhbarg, "O Brakakh i Razvodakh," *Proletarskaia revoliutsiia i pravo*, 5 (1918): 15. Soviet court statistics made no distinction between alimony and child support, so it is impossible to separate suits for support of a spouse from those on behalf of a child. The word *alimenti* covered both cases.

became more popular, the figures began to climb. In 1919, about 16% of the divorce cases in Moscow involved requests for alimony.[80] With the end of the civil war and the increase of unemployment, requests for alimony rose sharply. In 1923, about 33% of all divorce cases involved alimony. By 1924 the number had climbed to almost 45%.[81]

The number of alimony cases rose sharply as more and more women sought the help of the courts in supporting their children. The large number of alimony cases also included unmarried mothers who sued their partners for child support. By 1925, alimony cases outnumbered divorce cases in the courts. A. T. Stel'makhovich, the chairman of the Moscow provincial courts, noted "an uninterrupted increase in alimony cases."[82] In 1923, the people's courts of Moscow dealt with 2,662 alimony cases; by 1924, the numbers had almost doubled, reaching 2,592 in the first half of the year alone. By 1925, the numbers had almost doubled again, reaching 9,329.[83] Judges in the Moscow city and provincial courts heard approximately 1,300 alimony cases a month in 1925.[84]

Controversy flared over the ability of the courts to handle the influx of alimony cases. Some jurists charged that the courts were swamped, that the bailiffs could not search for all the errant husbands on their lists, and that women were unable to collect their court-ordered awards.[85] Others were less perturbed by the rapid rise in alimony cases and defended the ability of the courts to handle the consequences of the new divorce law. Nakhimson, chairman of the Leningrad provincial court, dismissed the critics in an angry speech to the court's Presidium in 1925. "Many people talk in fantasy about court practice," he snorted.

---

[80] A. Goikhbarg, "Eshche o Brakakh i Razvodakh," p. 85.
[81] "Rabota Suda Moskovskoi Gubernii v 1923 godu. Doklad Predsedatelia Gubsuda I. A. Smirnova," p. 8; and I. A. Smirnov, "Sovremennye Zadachi Suda v Derevne," p. 2.
[82] A. Stel'makhovich, *Dela ob alimentakh* p. 7; and A. T. Stel'makhovich, "Alimentnye Dela," *Proletarskii sud*, 4–5 (1926): 1.
[83] "Rabota Suda," p. 2.
[84] Stel'makhovich, *Dela ob alimentakh*, pp. 7–9.
[85] S. Smidovich, "O Novom Kodekse Zakonov o Brake i Sem'e," pp. 49–50; Li, "O Proekte Kodesksa Zakonov o Brake, Sem'e i Opeke," *Rabochii sud*, 2 (1926): 78; N. Zaks, "Zamechaniia po Prakticheskoi Rabote," *Proletarskii sud*, 2 (1926): 5.

"Some have alleged that alimony cases are flooding the courts. This is not true."[86] Several other judges supported Nakhimson, testifying that only 10 to 20 percent of the civil cases in their courts concerned alimony.[87]

The increase in alimony cases was also, in part, a result of Soviet successes in popularizing the new law. Emboldened by the legal *konsultatsiias* (free legal services) created to inform people of their rights, by the wide array of simple pamphlets for peasant and working-class women on family law, and by confidence in a potentially favorable judgment, poor and uneducated women flocked to the courts to assert their rights. Judges encouraged their initiative with sympathetic rulings on the issues of paternity and child support.

In 1925, Stel'makhovich conducted a detailed survey of 300 alimony cases in Moscow's city and provincial courts.[88] As chairman, he was privy to a panorama of courtroom scenes that dramatized marital life and sexual relations. Examining the class origin, marital status, and case histories of plaintiffs and defendants, his study offered a close look at popular use of the court system and the judicial response. Stel'makhovich's survey showed that the single largest group of women, fully 45% of the women who brought alimony suits, were unmarried. Despite the long tradition of tsarist law prohibiting women from demanding support for illegitimate children, single women were quick to take advantage of the law. Most of the women were poor and uneducated, either peasants, unemployed workers, servants, or laborers in unskilled jobs. About one-third had lived with their partners as "husband and wife" for over a year, and many had been abandoned once they became pregnant. Of this group, almost one-quarter of the women plaintiffs and male defendants were peasants, the women usually from the poorer of the two families. Although men denied paternity in about one-third of the cases, the woman received an award for child support 99% of

---

86 "Zasedanie Prezidiuma Leningradskogo Gubsuda," *Rabochii sud,* 1 (1926): 23.
87 See ibid., testimony of the judges, pp. 23–30; and "Diskussiia po Povodu Proekta Kodeksa Zakonov o Brake, Sem'e i Opeke," *Rabochii sud,* 3 (1926): 231–242.
88 All of the following material is drawn from A. Stel'makhovich, *Dela ob alimentakh.*

the time. One case concerned two peasants who had been involved in a long-term relationship. When the woman became pregnant for the first time, the man persuaded her to have an abortion. After the second pregnancy, however, she refused another abortion and had the baby. Her partner quickly abandoned her, but the Soviet judge did not: He awarded her child support. Despite the enormous stigma attached to illegitimacy in the village and the difficulties peasant women faced in pursuing their legal rights, many peasant women came to court and won their cases. In cases involving long-term relationships, the courts rarely denied women awards.

Two-thirds of the unmarried women who came to court were involved in brief, often casual unions lasting less than a year, or were victims of rape. Yet here too, women were remarkably successful in pressing their claims for child support. Judges generally refrained from passing judgment on a woman's sexual conduct and tried instead to meet her needs as a mother. In one case, a woman servant who lived in a dormitory with three male seasonal laborers slept with all three but named only one as the father. He vigorously denied the charge and pointed his finger at the other two. The judge, ignoring the ensuing protestations, calmly ordered all three men to pay the woman 3 rubles apiece per month until the child reached 18 years of age. In another case, a servant woman brought suit against a cabinetmaker who lived on her floor. She claimed he was the father of her child. He countered that she had only visited him for firewood. Although there were no witnesses, the woman left the courtroom with a monthly award. Judges even ruled in favor of women when considerable time had elapsed between conception and the lawsuit. A young student who had lived with her boyfriend for a short time in 1919 became pregnant. They soon broke up, she was forced to drop out of school, but he finished his studies. Six years later, after she became ill and lost her job, she brought suit. The judge awarded her 10% of her former lover's salary.

In some of the cases involving short-term unions, the women had been coerced into sex or raped. Women servants and *sluzhashchie* were frequently forced to submit to the sexual advances of their employers or co-workers. Unemployed women were occasionally promised work in exchange for sexual favors. In these cases, judges relied heavily on the testimony of the women involved. A deaf, retarded maid who became pregnant after a rape by a peasant bachelor who employed her was awarded 5 rubles a month for her child. And a widowed cleaning woman with two children was awarded 6 rubles a month from a fellow worker who raped her while she worked swabbing out empty box cars. He was a married father of five children. In both cases, the women's testimony was supported by witnesses who provided only circumstantial evidence.

More than 70% of the men in cases involving short-term union denied paternity. In the towns, the figure reached 92%. Stel'makhovich noted that many of the men had "a very cynical approach" to women. By and large, other judges agreed, often crediting the woman's side of the story over the man's. If one man could not be identified as the father, all of the men who had sexual relations with the women were held responsible for the support of her child. Evidence frequently consisted of a single witness who saw the couple strolling around together. An unskilled woman worker who became pregnant after a vacation in the countryside was awarded 10 rubles a month from a peasant bachelor. The man denied responsibility, but witnesses testified to seeing the couple together. An unemployed woman in Moscow became pregnant after sleeping with a Red Army veteran who visited the city. Although he claimed not to remember her, the judge awarded her one-third of his monthly income. The overwhelming majority of women won their cases despite a lack of "hard" evidence. Stel'makhovich cited only one instance in which a woman was found to be lying. A poor peasant (*bedniachka*) who lived with one man claimed child support from another. She later revealed that she had filed suit simply because the defendant "had two cows."

Judges generally employed very flexible criteria to "prove" paternity. They usually relied on the probability rather than the proven fact of a sexual tie to identify, in Stel'makhovich's words, "the candidate comparatively the closest to being the father." Moreover, the judges were not unduly worried about mistakes. Establishing support for the child took priority over protecting the financial interests of the male defendant. Stel'makhovich wrote: "In the final analysis, the task of the court is to protect the child by providing a father who will be materially responsible. From this point of view, if the court is mistaken and selects someone as the father who was not guilty of conception, then it still has not sinned against the interests of the mother and the child."[89]

The second largest group of cases (37%) involved couples who were married (in church or in ZAGS) and subsequently divorced. Here, the size of the child support payment, rather than the fact of paternity, was the central issue. Among the divorcing couples, the number married in church (28%) was far smaller than the group wed in ZAGS (72%). Generally, the church-wed couples had already been living apart for a long time. Mostly older couples with teenaged children, they had remarried and had new families. Fully 40% of the women were either unemployed or housewives, 23% earned an independent wage, and slightly over one-third were peasants. The men were mostly *sluzhashchie* and workers. In contrast to the women, only 10% of the men were peasants, suggesting that many of these couples had divorced after the man left his wife to find work in the city.

Custody and the amount of child support were recurring points of contention in cases where the defendant had a new family to support. One case concerned a mill director who earned 80 rubles a month and his former wife, a worker earning 24 rubles a month. Petitioning the court for custody of his 7-year-old child, he explained that he had four children by his second marriage, and simply could not afford the payment of 50 rubles a month set by the court in 1918. The court ordered him to pay 15% of his salary, reducing the payment to 12 rubles a month. Another woman with a child was married for twenty-one years before her divorce. Her former husband, a factory manager earning 145 rubles a month, was remarried with five children. Sick and unemployed, she requested 35 rubles a month to support herself and the child. He offered 10 rubles and asked for custody. The court awarded her and the child 20 rubles, a sum that would scarcely cover their monthly expenses. These cases all shared a common theme: The women were unemployed and needed money; the men had remarried and had financial obligations to their second families. There was no entirely just solution to the problem. Simply put, even men who were relatively well-off could not support two families on their wages.

[89] Ibid, pp. 49–50.

The cases involving ZAGS marriage differed somewhat from the marriages concluded in church. Naturally, the couples tended to be younger with fewer children. Only a small percentage had remarried and far fewer had second families. None of the women were housewives, although about 14% were unemployed, and fully half were peasants. The men were workers (42%), peasants (23%), or *sluzhashchie* (21%). Here, too, both peasant and wage-earning men found it difficult to pay the court-ordered awards. The largest group of couples consisted of peasant women and working-class men, and many of these cases involved particularly complicated issues of alimony.

The difficulties of establishing a payment system for peasants living in a nonwage economy based on family self-sufficiency cropped up repeatedly among couples regardless of whether they were wed in church, registered in ZAGS, or never married at all. Peasant men, without access to a regular monetary wage, frequently contended that they had no money. A typical example concerned an unemployed factory woman who had a 3-year-old child from her former marriage to a peasant. He had married again and fathered another child. Living in a small, impoverished household, he claimed he had no money to pay child support. The court awarded his ex-wife 3 rubles a month, a sum too small for her and too large for him. Peasants often paid alimony in kind (flour, milk, produce, etc.), but if an ex-wife and child moved to an urban area, such an award no longer sufficed. One young peasant woman received 36 pounds of flour a month for the support of her child, but when she went to the city to look for work, she requested 25 rubles in place of the flour. Her husband explained to the court that he could not pay and asked for custody of the child. The definition of a "just" sum was next to impossible to establish when families were split between two widely differing economic systems. Two peasants with an 8-year-old son had divorced in 1920. At that time, the man gave his ex-wife and child one-third of the house and land. Both eventually remarried, the man moving to Moscow and taking a job paying 52 rubles a month. This prompted his ex-wife to return to court to sue for alimony in monetary form. He indignantly referred the judge to the earlier settlement: a traditional peasant division (*vydel*). Although a lower court initially refused the woman, the decision was reversed and she was eventually awarded 15 rubles a month out of her husband's new salary. Such cases were com-

mon. The judges tried daily to resolve the complicated consequences of divorce in families still rooted in a nonwage economy,
or split between the worlds of wage labor and peasant self-
sufficiency.

The remaining group of alimony cases, constituting a significant 18%, concerned couples who were still married. Among the
most tragic cases in court, they revealed marriages ruined by
alcoholism, poverty, abandonment, and abuse. More than half of
the women in this group were peasants. Many had stayed in the
countryside when their husbands left to work in the towns; they
sought the help of the court when their men stopped sending
money home. The men pleaded large expenses and small salaries. The women told the judges, "He drinks," or "He is living
with another woman." Numerous peasant men had left their
families in the village and found a new, urban "wife." In other
instances, peasant women left their husbands' households because they were beaten or abused. Sometimes peasant men
tossed their wives out because they were sick or disabled. One
peasant man informed the judge that his sick wife, "eats bread
for nothing." In other cases, women tried to gain some control
over the paycheck of an alcoholic husband.

The courts clearly favored the needs of women and children
in their interpretation of the 1918 Code. Judges used flexible
criteria to determine paternity by assessing whether the defendant "in the natural course of events could be guilty of impreg-
nation."[90] And they tried to force men to assume a continuing
responsibility for their children. Yet even the best intentions
could not redress other, more serious problems. Although the
courts did not pass judgment on a woman's sexual conduct, usually crediting her testimony in assigning paternity, the awards
were nonetheless small. Moreover, a woman had no claim to
personal support. Abandoned with an infant, with little hope of
employment or of access to daycare, she had limited legal recourse. She faced a dismal future of trying to support herself
and an infant on 10 to 20 rubles a month, sometimes even less.

Moreover, the courts were severely restricted in determining
the amount of the award, for men's salaries were frequently too
small to support an ex-wife and a child. Although men pleaded

[90] Ibid., p. 49.

poverty with a suspicious constancy, in most cases they were telling the truth. If a man remarried or if his ex-wife was unemployed or had children, everyone suffered. Women seldom could live on the court-ordered awards, men could rarely afford to pay them. Poverty, coupled with female dependence, produced a situation that even King Solomon could not resolve.

In Moscow, the average worker heading a family in 1924 earned about 82 rubles a month. Under optimal circumstances, a second income from a working wife or teenager brought the monthly family earnings to 125 rubles. The monthly expenses for this average family of three amounted to 107 rubles.[91] If the male worker became involved with another woman who subsequently had a child by him, the court was likely to order him to pay one-third of his wages in child support. This left his original family in serious financial trouble, about 10 rubles short of meeting their monthly expenses. If the same male worker left his wife and child for the other woman, the court would have ordered him to pay one-third of his income to his former wife. Without the male wage earner, the family's income amounted to only 43 rubles a month, with child support, it might reach 70 rubles. Yet the monthly expenses for a woman with one child amounted to about 72 rubles a month: Her earnings and his payments could not quite cover the family's basic expenses. And if a woman did not work, or only worked part time, or had more than one child, the family's financial prospects were even more dismal.

Men were victims as well as women. A surprising number of men requested custody of their children because they were unable to pay the child support ordered by the courts. Although these requests were common among peasant men, they were made by wage earners as well. Once a man remarried and had a second family, he often could not afford to send the court ordered "third" of his wages to his first wife and child.

Given the great financial obstacles to divorce, men and women tended to blame each other for their hardships. Judges received "venomous notes" from men, complaining about the court settlements. Men grumbled that alimony led to "unfree Soviet marriage," that it interfered with their freedom, that women were

[91] E. O. Kabo, *Ocherki rabochego byta* (Moscow, 1928): 19.

liberated at the expense of men. They claimed that the courts were unfair, always threatening "to swoop down 'on the third'." Women used the courts to trap and blackmail men. Alimony was "punishment without a crime."[92]

Thousands of men simply refused to pay the court ordered awards. They left town or changed jobs. Sofia Smidovich, head of the Zhenotdel in 1924, observed that there were "a hundred subterfuges to avoid paying alimony." She argued that the courts were "overburdened with alimony cases." "Even on the occasion of a favorable settlement," Smidovich asserted angrily, "the woman (and practice shows that it is always the wretched woman who is importuning the courts for alimony) vainly strives to collect it. Her former spouse either leaves for the North Pole or claims he is unemployed, orphaned, etc."[93] The bailiffs had great difficulty collecting from men who refused to pay: Only about half of the men listed on the court orders were ever apprehended.[94]

The problems created by alimony combined with the hardships women faced under NEP engendered great pressure to revise the law. One popular solution was to change the law to permit child support only to children from registered marriages. While this favored the married woman and reduced the bailiffs' caseload, it did little to solve the problems of the abandoned de facto "wife." Stel'makhovich, who called divorce "one of the greatest gifts of the Revolution," cautioned that such freedom entailed "a particularly careful and cautious approach to marriage." Viewing the misery created by divorce, Stel'makhovich issued a warning to men. "In no sense can one interpret this freedom of choice as the right to debauchery, as the right to exploit women's physical and material weakness."[95]

Yet the rising divorce statistics and the desperate requests for alimony showed that Stel'makhovich's warning went largely unheeded. While judges did what they could to protect women and

---

92 A. Stel'makhovich, "Alimentnye Dela," *Proletarskii sud,* 12 (1925): 1.
93 S. Smidovich, "O Novom Kodekse Zakonov o Brake i Sem'e," pp. 49–50.
94 "Diskussiia po Povodu Proekta Kodeksa Zakonov o Brake, Sem'e i Opeke," p. 233.
95 A. Stel'makhovich, "Alimentnye Dela," *Proletarskii sud,* 12 (1925): 1–2.

children – by taking a lenient view of proof in paternity cases and awarding alimony whenever possible – they could not solve the larger social problems that drove women to court. Unemployment, low skills, lack of social services, and terrible poverty all mitigated against women's independence from the family unit. The idea of "free union" had tragic and unforeseen consequences for women as long as they were unable to support themselves and their children. The law, born out of the socialist-libertarian tradition, was painfully at odds with life. In Stel'-makhovich's own words, "The liberation of women . . . without an economic base guaranteeing every worker full material independence, is a myth."[96]

[96] Ibid., p. 2.

4

Stirring the sea of peasant stagnation

A chicken is not a bird and a *baba* is not a human being.
Traditional peasant proverb

It is necessary to say that a women's mind is exactly the same as a man's, that a *baba* is a human being.[1]
Pichurina, peasant delegate to the All-Union Congress of Women Workers and Peasants, Moscow, 1927.

In the late 1920s, the overwhelming majority (84%) of Russians were peasants, living within an agricultural system that was centuries old. One historian observed that it was not unusual to see a peasant or even his wife dragging a wooden plough "dating back to the time of the flood" across the fields.[2] Four of five Russians lived in villages; three of four employed people worked in agriculture.[3] Urban life was concentrated in small industrialized islands around Moscow, Leningrad, the Urals, and parts of the Ukraine and Azerbaidjan. In the great majority of provinces, 85% to 95% of the people lived in the countryside. People lived in tiny, isolated hamlets with an average size of 200 people, thirty to forty households. And most of these settlements, in the words

---

[1] *Vsesoiuznyi s"ezd rabotnits i krest'ianok. Stenograficheskii otchet* (Moscow, 1927): 274.

[2] Moshe Lewin, *Russian Peasants and Soviet Power: A Study of Collectivization* (Norton, New York, 1975): 29.

[3] Teodor Shanin, *The Awkward Class. Political Sociology of Peasantry in a Developing Society: Russia 1910–1925* (Oxford University Press, Oxford, 1972): 19.

of the rural historian V. P. Danilov, "were truly God-forsaken places."[4]

The Revolution had done little to improve the productive basis of agriculture, and in many ways it had actually undermined it. In redistributing the gentry's estates, the peasants eliminated large holdings and revived many age-old features of peasant life, like the village commune.[5] Peasants still relied mainly on manual labor with primitive tools. Few owned machines and most survived with minimal dependence on the market. Only a tiny fraction of the rural population was employed in factories (1.1%) or cottage industry (1.6%).[6] Rural, roadless Russia, rooted in an archaic mode of production and long-held customs and traditions, stretched endlessly beyond the towns and the cities.

The application of Soviet family law to the countryside posed unique problems for peasants and jurists alike. The law granted the peasants the right to live apart from one's spouse, to divorce, and to receive alimony and child support, but all of these rights directly conflicted with a system of family-based agricultural production that placed little emphasis on individual rights. Unlike the urban working-class family, members of the peasant household did not labor for individual wages. They worked together, collectively consuming what they produced. Soviet family law, emphasizing the values of personal freedom, gender equality, and independence, was strikingly at odds with the economy and social customs of the village.

The weight of the old: Women, the household, and customary law

The ancient institutions of the household (*dvor*) and the commune (*mir* or *obshchina*) still governed agricultural production and village life in the 1920s. The family-household, often spanning several generations, was the basic unit of production. The

[4] V. P. Danilov, *Rural Russia under the New Regime* (Hutchinson, London, 1988): 49.
[5] Ibid., p. 88. [6] Ibid., pp. 260, 262, 55.

commune, composed of all member households, constituted a local governing structure that distributed land, settled disputes, operated its own businesses, and handled the daily problems of life. According to custom, the commune, not the individual peasant, held the land and distributed it periodically to its member families according to household size. The size of the Russian peasant family did not "adjust" to the availability of land, as did its European counterpart, but rather landholding was adjusted to the size of the family.[7] Communal decisions were made by the *skhod*, a governing body composed of all the heads of households. After the revolution, the peasants resurrected the commune to divide the estates of the dispossessed landlords. The ancient system of land redistribution received "a miraculous new lease on life."[8] Peasants placed between 85 and 97 percent of the expropriated land under the control of the revived communes.[9]

The household or *dvor* was a kin-based, patrilocal unit composed of one or more family groups. Women who married went to live in their husbands' households; men remained in the *dvor* of their fathers. A *dvor* might thus include a group of brothers and their wives and children as well as parents and grandparents. Before the Revolution, the large, multifamily household predominated. Peter Czap notes, "The large multifocal household was widely accepted as . . . the virtually exclusive basis of life for the individual."[10] A household's ability to survive and prosper depended on its size and its number of male workers. Richer households were large, multifamily units with strong, able-bodied sons whose labor power was necessary to

---

[7] Peter Czap, "The Perennial Multiple Family Household, Mishino, Russia, 1782–1858," *Journal of Family History*, 1 (1982): 5.

[8] Lewin, p. 85.

[9] Danilov, p. 104. As a result of the Stolypin reforms (1906–1911), less than half of all Russian peasants were members of a commune in 1917. But by 1927, over 95% of all land was held communally. On the history of the commune, see Dorothy Atkinson, *The End of the Russian Land Commune, 1905–1930* (Stanford University Press, Stanford, Calif., 1983).

[10] Rose Glickman, "Peasant Women and Their Work," in Ben Eklof, Stephen Frank, eds., *The World of the Russian Peasant. Post-Emancipation Culture and Society* (Unwin Hyman, Boston, 1990): 46; Peter Czap, "The Perennial Multiple Family Household," p. 6.

farming. Widows and old couples featured prominently in poor households with a "high extinction or merger rate."[11]

All households, regardless of size, were based on common principles. The family held the land, livestock, implements, buildings, and other property in common. Apart from the wife's dowry, small personal items (watches, musical instruments, clothes, etc.) and some money wages, all crops and income belonged to "the common pot." The household collectively consumed what it produced; property or profits were not divided into "definable shares."[12] Peasants who responded to a questionnaire distributed in 1926 by the Communist Academy repeatedly explained that it was contrary to the principles of the *dvor* for individuals to accumulate their own property. One peasant from Samara province unequivocally noted, "There are no such families where the members have income or property separate from that of the *dvor*." A peasant from Penza province said flatly, "It is not possible to accumulate separate means within the household." Peasants found the very idea of separate incomes for family members nearly inconceivable. Many simply viewed it as a form of "hoarding" or a warning sign of the breakup or partition (*razdel*) of the family. "There is no accumulation of separate family means from the agricultural income in a many-familied *dvor*," another peasant explained; "this cannot be allowed because it would involve a split (*razdel*)." According to the peasants, if family members withheld means or income, the *dvor* lost its very reason for being; such actions were tantamount to a de facto division. Peasants repeatedly stressed the importance of the common pot. In the words of a peasant from Ivanovo-Vosnesensk province, "As long as there are no separate pockets in the family, it is still a family, but as soon as each family member begins to live out of his own pocket, then you know that tomorrow will bring *razdel*."[13] For the peasants, the *dvor* was a joint enterprise: Everyone contributed their labor and shared in the fruits. Separate income was tantamount to deception: Family members who withheld income violated a cardinal rule and lost their right to be a part of the household.

[11] Shanin, p. 85.   [12] Ibid., p. 31.

[13] N. Semenov, "Krest'ianskii Dvor," *Revoliutsiia prava* 1 (1927): 192–194.

The right to use the family property and share in the produce was based on two principles: family ties and labor contribution. A son, for example, who left the countryside permanently to work for wages in the city eventually lost his right to a share in the household, while an unrelated man who worked in the household could become a member with full rights. Membership in a *dvor* was acquired by birth, marriage, or the custom of "acceptance" or *primachestvo*. If a household lost its men – to the city, to disability, to infirmity – it could take in a son-in-law or an unrelated outsider who would then take the family's last name. The accepted male, known as a *primak*, received a share in the land and the same rights as other family members. Because he was entitled to a share in the community's land, the *primak* had to be approved by the commune as well as the *dvor*. And in areas where land was scarce, the commune might reject the *primak*. The labor principle did not by itself, however, entitle a person to rights in the *dvor*. Neither agricultural laborers hired for a day or a season nor de facto wives were considered part of the household, and by custom, neither had property rights within it.[14]

Although the members of the household owned the property in common, the household was not managed democratically.[15] The head of the household (*domokhoziain*) exercised strong patriarchal control over the entire family, and although he did not own the property of the *dvor*, he did have the final say in its management. He was responsible for distributing the products of the *dvor's* labor and allocating property in the event of *razdel*. The larger and richer the household, the greater the power of the *domokhoziain*. But despite his commanding position, he could be replaced by the common consent of the family if he squandered its resources, grew too old or too sick, or otherwise proved incapable of proper management.[16] The selection of a new household head, according to the peasants, occurred "without a

---

[14] A. Panferov, "Obychnoe Pravo v Uklade Krest'ianskogo Dvora," *Revoliutsiia prava*, 2 (1927): 110–111. Many landless female laborers, thrown out of the household for pregnancy after many months of work, took their cases to court in the 1920s and won property settlements.

[15] Shanin, p. 221.

[16] Panferov, pp. 108, 113, 107; William T. Shinn, "The Law of the Russian Peasant Household," *Slavic Review*, 20, 4 (1961): 605.

meeting and without official discussion." One peasant from Briansk province, questioned about the idea of voting for the *domokhoziain* within the family, replied, "There is no sort of election, there is not voting, and as far as I am concerned, this question seems very odd. It occurs spontaneously." Often an old man who was no longer capable of managing continued to be listed as the head of the household "out of respect." As one peasant indulgently mused, "Let him lie on the stove, no harm comes from this."[17]

In a fatherless family, the *domokhoziain* was usually the oldest son. A woman only became the head of a household if she was widowed in a single-family *dvor* with no adult males, if her husband worked outside the village for long periods of time, or if he was chronically ill, disabled, or mentally incompetent. If a father died, leaving more than one grown son within the family, the mother might assume the role of *domokhoziain* to avoid arguments among her sons. Yet even if a woman attained this position, she was still limited in her rights and powers. According to peasant custom, a woman could not sell or buy cattle, tools, or machines, or lease or rent land without her husband's consent, and all documents, taxes, and so on were in his name.[18]

The principle of common ownership imposed a unity on family members that obviated certain conflicts and generated others. The practice of delaying *razdel* or household division until the third generation often led to bitter fighting between family members. Yet unlike the European peasantry, where a single individual inherited property, Russian peasants did not struggle over the household's property when the *domokhoziain* died, for the entire family inherited or, more accurately, retained the land and property in its collective possession. The concept of inheritance was unknown in Russian peasant customary law.[19]

The practice of *razdel* determined the allocation of property among household members in the event of a split, but it was not necessary for the *domokhoziain* to die for *razdel* to take place. The partition of the household was usually initiated by family members, but required the approval of both the *dvor* and the commune. The *domokhoziain* divided the property according to both

[17] Semenov, pp. 188, 186.   [18] Ibid., p. 187–188.
[19] Peter Czap, "The Perennial Multiple Family Household," p. 22.

the amount of time and labor each member had invested in the *dvor* and the number of "mouths" in each of the new households. *Razdel* could occur only if the divided land and property was sufficient to maintain two households. If the household had too little land, too few workers, or insufficient livestock and implements, *razdel* was forbidden by the commune.[20]

Like inheritance, the process of partition revealed the difference between male and female property rights. According to customary law, all males had a claim to the property of the *dvor*, but women had almost no rights at all. All male members, including *primaks* and males under 18, were entitled to an equal share, with an additional portion for the men who accepted responsibility for women and the elderly. Women did not receive their own shares. Women were not considered household members because they could not "perpetuate a family." The peasant view of a daughter's worth was summed up in the following proverb: "By supporting my parents I pay my debts, by helping my son I give a loan, by giving to my daughter, I throw away." According to the peasants, "Every daughter is someone else's booty."[21]

Although women did not have the same property rights as men, they were not entirely dispossessed. A woman was entitled to a dowry, and if her father died, her brothers were required to provide it. A woman's dowry, consisting of linens, towels, clothing, livestock, and money, was considered her private property. Women frequently had the right to income from the garden produce, poultry, dairy products, needlework, and spinning.[22] The cow was often part of the woman's dowry, and was hence excluded from the common property of the household. In some areas, women actually controlled small plots of land and provided their daughters with dowries. A man could keep his dead wife's dowry if she had lived with him for more than a year; if not, it reverted to her father's family.[23]

Widows usually had greater rights than other women and

20 Shanin, pp. 222–223.
21 A. Petrov, "V Narodnom Sude," *Sud idet!,* 12 (1925): 729; ibid.
22 Semenov, p. 191; Panferov, pp. 106–108.
23 Beatrice Farnsworth, "The Litigious Daughter-in-Law: Family Relations in Rural Russia in the Second Half of the Nineteenth Century," *Slavic Review,* 1 (1986): 56; Shanin, p. 222.

were sometimes permitted a share in the *dvor's* property. In some regions, a widow could become a *domokhoziain* and hence control the property of the *dvor*; but in others, the widow had no rights at all. Sometimes, a widow received a fixed portion of the property in accordance with the length of her marriage and the amount of labor she had invested in the household. By some customs, a widow with minor children received a full share, while a widow with no children received only one-seventh of a share. Although widows had more rights than wives or daughters, their rights varied widely from region to region.[24]

A woman's limited rights made her position in the *dvor* less secure than a man's. A married woman's tie to the *dvor*, for example, frequently depended on the presence of her husband or male children. If a women's husband died leaving her childless, his family could disown her. Even a widow with children or the wife of soldier (*soldatka*) could be thrown out of her husband's *dvor* by his family. Before the Revolution, many such women appealed to peasant courts for redress. Custom formally obliged the *domokhoziain* to support his son's family, although peasant judges were more likely to give the woman a property settlement than to force her in-laws to take her back.[25]

Divorce was rare in prerevolutionary Russia, although peasant courts occasionally permitted separation by mutual consent. A husband who refused to live with his wife was still obliged to support her. Peasant courts thus provided a rudimentary type of alimony for women who were banished from the household. In one case, a pregnant woman appealed to a peasant court after banishment, and the judge ordered her husband's family either to take her back or pay her 3 rubles a month in child support.[26]

Peasant customary law provided for the widow or the woman who was banished not because the law recognized a woman's right to independence, but because families were required to care for their own. Mutual obligations were enforced by custom, but there was neither monetary nor moral support for the

---

[24] Farnsworth, p. 56; Peter Czap, "Peasant Class Courts and Peasant Customary Justice in Russia,1861–1912," *Journal of Social History* (Winter 1967): 164–165.

[25] For an excellent treatment of the daughter-in-law's role in the household, see Farnsworth.

[26] Ibid., p. 62.

woman who willfully left her husband's family. Women were not considered equals. Despite their crucial contributions to the productive and reproductive life of the household, they had limited property rights, little say in the household, and no say in the commune and the *skhod*. There was no place for the single, independent woman in the system of agricultural production, in the practices of customary law, or in the traditional peasant view of life. The *dvor* was a deeply patriarchal institution in which the individual wants of its members were strongly subordinated to the economic viability of the whole. Family members depended on each other, for without common labor, survival itself was threatened. And although both men and women were subjugated to the rule of the household, the position of women, in the households of their husbands, was infinitely worse than that of the men.

The Russian Land Code

The Land Code, approved by the Central Executive Committee in 1922, combined peasant customary law with a new, revolutionary affirmation of gender equality. The Land Code abolished private ownership of land, water, forests, and minerals, and placed all land in the hands of the state. The peasants would distribute the land through what the Land Code termed the "*zemel'noe obshchestvo*," or commune. The Land Code thus recognized the role of the commune, although it stipulated that the commune consisted of all *dvor* members, "independent of sex or age." All citizens, "regardless of sex, religion, or nationality," had rights to the land, which derived from labor usage. Women, therefore, had the right to participate fully. In accordance with custom, communal affairs were to be decided by the *skhod*, but this decision-making body was to be enlarged to include not only the heads of households, but all adult members of the commune "without distinction to sex." The Land Code substantially broadened and democratized the composition of the *skhod* although power still rested with the heads of households. All adults could now attend, but no less than half of the household heads had to be present for its decisions to be valid. Two-thirds of the heads along with no less than half the members had to be present to decide on questions of land use and distribution. Land use questions were to be decided by a two-thirds majority vote; all other matters by a simple majority. Everyone over 18, male and female, had the right to participate and vote.[27] Thus although the presence of the *domokhoziain* was required in the *skhod,* voting itself had been widely democratized.

The Land Code also redefined the *dvor* in accordance with the principles of gender equality. It constructed the *dvor* as "a family/labor unit of individuals within a common agricultural household," but added that a "*dvor* can be composed of a single person (regardless of sex)." All participants in the *dvor* were considered members, including children and the elderly. As in customary law, a *dvor* could increase its size only through marriage or *primachestvo,* decrease only if a member left or died. Those who entered by marriage or *primachestvo* acquired rights in the *dvor's* land and property; they simultaneously lost rights in all other *dvors.* Unlike customary law, in which the woman's rights depended on the presence of her husband or sons, the Land Code stipulated that a daughter-in-law, entering a *dvor* by marriage, had the right to an equal share. The Code repeatedly stressed that rights to the land, buildings, and inventory of the *dvor* belonged to all household members, regardless of age or sex.[28]

Like customary law, the Land Code recognized the role and power of the *domokhoziain,* although it specified that this role could be filled by a woman. It defined the *domokhoziain* as "the representative of the *dvor* in all economic matters," but did not specify right and powers. It stipulated that the *domokhoziain* was the representative, not the owner, of the household's property. Following the customary understanding, the Land Code affirmed the economic indivisibility of the *dvor.* No member, including the *domokhoziain,* could use the common property, or even his or her share, to pay personal debts or obligations. The Code stated, "The property of the *dvor* cannot be awarded in payment for the share of an individual *dvor* member, or given out by them for their personal needs." The property of the *dvor* remained inviolable and indivisible.[29]

The Land Code provided for *razdel* of property along custom-

[27] *Zemel'nyi kodeks RSFSR* (Moscow, 1922): 5, 6, 10–12.
[28] Ibid., pp. 13–14.   [29] Ibid., p. 14.

ary lines, but with new and crucial differences. Land was to be divided not only among the male members of the household, but among all members, regardless of age or sex. Yet only members who were over 18 and had participated in the *dvor* for more than two sowing cycles (approximately six years) had the right to demand *razdel.* As in customary law, property division could occur only if a new household was economically viable on the smaller share. If a family disagreed about the division of the land, the district (*volost'*) land commission would decide the issue. Arguments over other forms of property would be adjudicated in people's court. The provincial (*guberniia*) executive committee had the right to set criteria for *razdel*, to ensure that the plots and the households would not become unworkably small (*izmel'chaniia dvorov*).[30]

A. V. Artiukhina, the head of the Zhenotdel, summed up the advances of the Land Code at a meeting of over 1,000 women workers and peasants in 1927: Every person, regardless of sex, now had a right to the land; a *dvor* could consist of a single woman; a woman could be a *domokhoziain;* and a peasant woman was entitled to her own share.[31] Popular journals and pamphlets stressed peasant women's new rights and urged them to take advantage of their new status under Soviet law. While the Land Code standardized and formalized the broad lineaments of peasant customary law, it also gave the peasant woman, for the first time in history, equal rights to land, property, and participation in the decisions of village life.

The vacillations of Soviet law: Women versus the household

The Land Code represented a compromise between the Bolsheviks and the peasantry on the issue of gender relations. Despite the Code's emphasis on gender equality, it legitimized the traditional relations of production in the countryside and affirmed the centrality of the household. The household was still the main unit of production, its property remained indivisible, and the power of the *domokhoziain* was largely perpetuated. Al-

30 Ibid., pp. 14–16.
31 *S"ezd rabotnits i krest'ianok*, pp. 187–188.

though the Land Code granted women the right to land and property, it did little to alter the patriarchal structures of peasant life. A woman still left her father's *dvor* to enter the *dvor* of her husband. Peasant society remained patrilocal.

The Family Code, however, offered a more radical vision of change by extending rights to individuals that undermined the unity and economic interests of the household. Women not only had the right to land and property, but now had the right to leave the family as well. While the Land Code guarded the interests of the household unit, the Family Code emphasized the rights of the individual. Not surprisingly, the conflicts between the household and the individual, between the Land Code and the Family Code, emerged most clearly around the issue of property. The extension of gender equality and "modern" notions of individuality to a patriarchal social order raised a host of questions concerning women's and children's property rights that neither the Land Code, Family Code, or subsequent juridical decisions could resolve.

One of the main contradictions between the Land Code and Family Code concerned the property rights of marriage. According to the 1918 Family Code, marriage did not create community property; both spouses remained independent and retained the right to their own property and earnings. Yet the peasant household was based on the principle of joint ownership. Community of property was the single most important economic feature of the *dvor*. The notion that each member retained the right to his or her own property contradicted a fundamental tenet of the peasant household.

Moreover, the Land Code clearly stated that the peasant wife had an equal share in her husband's household by virtue of her membership in the *dvor* by marriage. In a landmark divorce case in 1922, the higher courts ruled that a woman had the right to property acquired with her husband's earnings in the course of marriage. The Commissariat of Justice added that the peasant wife had the right to *vydel* (movable property, excluding the land, and buildings) if there was "significant labor contributed by the wife to the general household in the course of her marriage."[32] The case thus clearly affirmed the peasant woman's

---

[32] "Iz Deiatel'nosti Narodnogo Komissariata Iustitsii," *Ezhenedel'nik sovetskoi iustitsii*, 11 (1922): 12.

right to a share in the movable property of her husband's household after divorce. Although the ruling removed one of the most glaring contradictions between the Family Code and the Land Code, it left open many questions concerning the limits of the peasant woman's share. Women had the right to movable property after divorce, but what rights did they have to the land and buildings? According to the Land Code, the peasant woman had the right to an equal share as long as she remained in the household, but what claims could she make if she decided to leave?

According to the Land Code, only *dvor* members who were 18 or older and who had participated in the *dvor* for two sowing cycles (or approximately six years) could demand *razdel*. A woman lost her rights in her father's *dvor* when she married, but did not gain full rights in her husband's *dvor* for six years. The jurist, Nezhdanov, noted that the Land Code placed women in a difficult position. If a husband divorced his wife or threw her out before six years had elapsed, she had no rights in either her husband's or her father's *dvor*. Although the *dvor* needed protection against the land claims of new members, its interests were clearly at odds with the interests of women, "the socially weaker element." Nezhdanov argued that Soviet law should protect the weak in a clash with the "economically strong."[33] But other jurists and judges vacillated between the interests of the woman and the household. The law itself seemed to follow a crooked, contradictory paper trail of circulars and explanations, veering first toward the woman, then toward the household.

As early as 1922, several months before the publication of the Land Code, the jurist G. Ryndziunskii tried to clarify the rights of the peasant wife. Many cases concerning peasant women's property rights had already come to court. As in the prerevolutionary period, the great majority of female plaintiffs were either widows of the brother or son of the *domokhoziain*, or women who had been banished from the household, although divorced women too began to appear in increasing numbers. The cases followed similar lines: The woman left the household, often with children, and filed suit for property or support from her husband or his family. In Ryndziunskii's opinion, a woman had the

[33] *Zemel'nyi kodeks RSFSR*, p. 14; Nezhdanov, "Iz Tekushchei Praktiki: Bol'noi Vopros Krest'ianskogo Dvora," *Pravo i zhizn'*, 7–8 (1924): 115–116.

right to her dowry or "any property she brought to her husband's house that was not used in the common life." If her dowry was already used up, she could not demand substitution or repayment. She had the right to money she acquired apart from the common household, such as income from her kitchen garden or the milk of her cow, and more generally, a right to a share in the family's "material prosperity" in proportion to the amount of labor she had contributed to the household. She did not have the right to *razdel,* for a household could not be expected to divide the land every time a divorce took place. And even *vydel* was not always possible. Ryndziunskii cited two decisions of the Higher Court Control as guidelines. In one case, the Higher Court granted a peasant woman's claim to a horse she had brought to her husband's family as a foal. And in the other, a woman was denied the calves from her dowry cow. Yet even these guidelines were murky. Ryndziunskii himself raised a thorny question: What if a woman's dowry had already been converted into another form of property? What if her money was used to build a shed? Or her cow sold to buy a horse?[34] He had no ready answers to these pressing questions.

According to Ryndziunskii, a woman had the right to her dowry, her separate income, *vydel* in proportion to her labor contribution, and alimony and child support if necessary. Her right to *vydel* did not interfere with her right to alimony. She had no claim to the land, livestock, tools, or other inventory of the *dvor.* Although the terms seemed generous, they in fact amounted to very little. A woman from a poor or even a middle household had no "material prosperity" to share in, even if she had worked for years. Under these terms, a divorced peasant woman could easily be left without land, livestock, or dwelling place, without rights in any household, and with nothing but the threadbare towels and linens she had brought to her marriage years before.

As the government attempted to adjudicate between the rights of the woman and the integrity of the peasant household, its directives grew increasingly contradictory. A notice to the

[34] G. Ryndziunskii, "Voprosy Deistvuiushchego Semeinogo Prava," *Ezhenedel'nik sovetskoi iustitsii,* 14–15 (1922): 11–12; Ryndziunskii, "Voprosy Deistvuiushchego Semeinogo Prava," *Ezhenel'nik sovetskoi iustitsii,* 18 (1922): 4.

Northern Dvinsk provincial land administration (*gubzemuprav-
lenie*) in April 1923 contained guidelines for *razdel* that were
even stricter than those established by the Land Code. The notice specified that people who left the *dvor* were entitled only to
"part of the property of the *dvor*," and to recompense for "special expenditures." They had no right to a share in the land.
Thus a woman who left her husband's *dvor*, even after six years
had elapsed, had no right to a share in the land. The notice also
stressed that all cases that did not involve land should be tried in
people's court, not the land commissions.[35]

Eight months later, in December, further instructions from
the Special Collegium of Higher Control (*Osobaia Kollegiia
Vyshego Kontrolia*) took a slightly more generous view of women's
land claims. The directive stated that article 75 of the Land
Code, which granted the right of *razdel* only to individuals who
had participated in the household for six years or more, did not
apply to members by marriage or *primachestvo*. The rights of
wives and *primaks* were to be decided by the land commissions
according to the circumstances of each case. The land commissions would be guided by the amount of labor the individual had
invested, as well as the material position of the household. The
ruling was reaffirmed in 1924 by the Commissariat of Land.[36]
Although the instructions never stated that wives and *primaks*
with less than six years' tenure had the right to land, according to
this new interpretation they were not prohibited by the Land
Code from demanding *razdel*. It was an ambiguous declaration
at best, leaving the ultimate decision to the discretion of the local
land commissions.[37]

One jurist drew up an unusual proposal designed to solve the
problems of women's property rights in a patrilocal system. He
recommended that a woman retain the right to *vydel* in her
father's *dvor* for six years after marriage, until she was fully
vested in her husband's household. Her dowry would be considered part of her *vydel*. While a peasant with several daughters

---

[35] N. V. Gendzekhadze, I. B. Novitskii, eds. *Zemel'nyi kodeks s dop-
olnitel'nymi uzakoneniiami i raz'iasneniiami narkomzema RSFSR na 1
avgusta 1927 goda* (Moscow, 1927): 104. Hereafter cited as *Land Laws*.

[36] Ibid.

[37] For a discussion of the rights of wives and *primaks*, see E. Dombrovskii, "O Krest'ianskikh Semeino-Imushchestvennykh Razdelakh,"
Proletarskii sud, 8–9 (1925): 7–10.

could have been bankrupted by the scheme, it revealed the lengths to which jurists were willing to go to counteract the patrilocal focus of the family and to establish some form of gender equality in the countryside.[38]

In December 1924, the Commissariat of Land captured the prevailing confusion in a reminder to the Tver land commission. The Commissariat explained that decisions on *razdel* should be based not only on the principle of equal shares, but on the economic efficacy of *razdel*, the amount of labor invested by each of the members, and the material position of the member demanding *razdel*.[39] Unfortunately, the instructions were still not very clear. Did a woman's poverty affect her demand for *razdel* favorably or unfavorably? Should the land commission side with the weak and vulnerable or the strong and viable? The instructions listed three determining factors, but how would the land commissions resolve a case in which the three guidelines contradicted one another, in which the economic interests of the woman conflicted with the economic efficacy of the household as an undivided unit? The Land Code stated that every member of the household was entitled to an equal share of land and property, regardless of sex or age. But the circular urged the land commission to consider such factors as the member's labor contribution, tenure in the household, and means invested, all factors that were potentially sex- and age-linked. The labor principle also conflicted with the family principle, which ensured each member an equal share.[40] It was not surprising that a chairwoman of the village soviet in Novgorod province made a desperate request for "live instruction" from the center. "They only send us papers," she said, frankly admitting her confusion, "but we are not developed enough and we don't understand them."[41] Many officials in similar positions undoubtedly shared her confusion.

In March 1927, the Commissariats of Land and Justice issued new instructions on *razdel* designed to prevent economically unviable divisions of the land. The instructions established two criteria for *razdel:* The partitioners had to form a new, independent household, and both the new and the old households had to have enough land and implements to be economically viable.

---

[38] Ibid., p. 9.   [39] *Land Laws*, p. 104.
[40] *Zemel'nyi kodeks RSFSR*, pp. 15, 14; *Land Laws*, p. 105.
[41] *S"ezd rabotnits i krest'ianok*, p. 247.

In the absence of either criteria, a family member who wanted to leave the *dvor* was entitled only to a share in the household property. Although the instructions legalized the division of buildings and other property apart from land, they clearly, according to Danilov, "contradicted rural reality." For how could a family split a house, a cow, or a plough? The instructions explained that shares might be paid out over a period of five years, in cash or in kind. Yet "the market exchange of the vast majority of peasant households was insufficient to allow half or even a third of the value of the household to be paid out for five years."[42]

By limiting *razdel*, the instructions worked to the detriment of women. The criteria excluded the divorced woman who could not establish an independent household from her rightful share to the land. As the Leningrad regional executive committee later noted in an addendum to its own resolution limiting *razdel*, by upholding the principle of the indivisibility of the land, the committee "placed separated household members, especially women, in a difficult position."[43]

The issue of children's rights also highlighted differences between custom, the Land Code, and the Family Code, and produced in turn a bewildering body of conflicting opinion. Here too, jurists steered a difficult course between the integrity of the household and the rights of the individual. The 1918 Family Code had abolished the concept of illegitimacy, but custom and the Land Code maintained a rigid distinction between the property rights of a child born in or out of wedlock. The children of the "legal" wife had a share in their father's *dvor*, but the children of the de facto wife had no claim to the household's property.[44] Here jurists largely affirmed customary relations and sided with the household, for the extension of property rights to children born outside marriage threatened the very foundations of the household.

Divorce further complicated the question of children's property rights and created a thicket of problems concerning child custody in a patrilocal society. If a woman with children remarried, to which *dvor* did her children belong? According to the Land Code, one could only enter a *dvor* by birth, marriage, or

[42] Danilov, pp. 248–249.   [43] As quoted ibid., p. 250.
[44] E. Sedliarov, "Bespravie Vnebrachnogo Rebenka po Zemel'nomu Kodeksu," *Ezhenedel'nik sovetskoi iustitsii*, 23 (1927): 708.

primachestvo. Children had rights in their father's *dvor* by birth, but they could not accompany their mother to a new household unless its members and the commune agreed to accept them. The Land Code, upholding the patrilocal principle of peasant society, maintained that after a divorce, children were to remain in their father's household.[45]

In March 1925, a circular from the Commissariat of Land reversed this rule, and declared that a woman's children by a previous marriage automatically became members of her new *dvor.* The consent of the other household members or the commune was not required for their admission. The ruling had far-reaching implications, for once the children became members of the new household, they were entitled to share in its property. The significance of the ruling was underscored by a Supreme Court decision one month later in April 1925, stating that a parent who left a *dvor* with children was not only entitled to his or her own share, but the children's shares as well.[46] In both of these rulings, jurists subordinated the interests of the household to those of the mother and the child.

The most significant contradiction between the Land Code and Family Code concerned alimony and child support. Whereas the Family Code entitled a needy or disabled spouse to alimony, and a child born in or out of wedlock to parental support, the Land Code strictly limited the individual peasant's ability to fulfill these obligations. According to the Land Code, the common property of the *dvor* could not be used by a member to meet personal debts or obligations. If a peasant divorced his wife or had a child outside of marriage, he could not use the money, produce, livestock, or land of the *dvor* to pay alimony or child support.[47] Yet most peasants had no other source of income. Personal possessions often amounted to nothing more than some ragged clothing and other insignificant items. The combination of poverty and joint property deprived women and children of the rights granted to them by the Family Code.

In July 1923, the Commissariats of Land and Justice ruled

---

[45] *Zemel'nyi kodeks RSFSR,* p. 13; A. N. Granina, "Lichnyi Sostav Krest'ianskogo Dvora," *Pravo i zhizn',* 10 (1924): 22–23.

[46] *Land Laws,* p. 97; I. Kabakov, "Razdel Imuschestv," *Proletarskii sud,* 4 (1923): 4; "Zametki po Voprosam Praktiki," *Rabochii sud,* 17–18 (1925): 778.

[47] *Zemel'nyi kodeks RSFSR,* p. 14.

that the child had the right to support from the common property of the *dvor*, if the personal means of a peasant was insufficient to provide support. Thus in the matter of child support,
the *dvor* was liable for the debts of its members. In April 1926,
the Plenum of the Supreme Court broadened this ruling to
include alimony, adding that all the property of the *dvor* could
be drawn on, excepting essential tools, one cow, one horse (or
draught animal), and a three-month reserve of food.[48]

Here the law clearly sided with the interests of the woman and
child against the household. Yet even these rulings offered limited protection given the reality of peasant life. For even when
the law sided with "the socially weaker element," it could not
restructure the peasant household. Many *dvor* members fiercely
resented being forced to meet the financial obligations of others,
and more important, peasant agriculture was so inefficient that
frequently the household simply could not afford to support a
member who lived apart.

Jurists never worked out a clear policy on women's rights,
which meant that local land commissions continued to decide
cases more or less independently of the conflicting instructions
issued by the Commissariats of Land and Justice. From the peasants' perspective, the bewildering tangle of directives from the
center often contradicted the most self-evident customs and
practices. In response to an inquiry by the Commissariat of
Land, provincial authorities reported that the instructions on
razdel "were incomprehensible to both the peasants and the local
administrators," and had no discernible effect on the process of
partition.[49] The peasants expressed the same view in the livelier
form of a *chastushka*, or popular short song:

> Comrades, your new laws
> Are really quite insane,
> It's clear they were devised,
> By someone without a brain.[50]

The problem, of course, was not that the jurists lacked sense.
Rather, their attempt to impose a system of individual freedom

---

[48] Abramov, "Vzyskanie Alimentov s Chlena Krest'ianskogo Dvora po
Novomu Kodeksu o Brake, Sem'e, i Opeke," *Ezhenedel'nik sovetskoi
iustitsii*, 9 (1927): 251.
[49] Danilov, p. 249.
[50] N. I. Morev, N. G. Shirintsina, "Sovremennaia Chastushka," in V. G.
Tan-Bogoraz, ed., *Staryi i novyi byt. Sbornik* (Leningrad, 1924): 123.

and gender equality upon relations of production that were organized around the patriarchal household produced irreconcilable conflicts. Peasants themselves were divided. With the growing number of divorces and *razdely,* the interests of men and women, of the individual and the household, diverged, forcing the courts and the land commissions to adjudicate in practice what was irresolvable in principle.

Small changes

The basic structures of peasant life clearly lagged far behind the principles embodied in the Land and Family codes, yet the villages of "roadless Russia," what the ethnographer Tan-Bogoraz called "Russia No. 2," were not untouched by new, revolutionary ideas. The legal experts in the Commissariats of Land and Justice dispatched their directives to peasants who still believed in satyrs, devils, *domovoi* (house spirits), and *kolduns* (shamans), yet slowly and unevenly the villages were changing.[51] Soldiers who had learned to read returned home with leaflets in their pockets. And in a number of households, these literate Red Army veterans, respected for their surer understanding of Soviet law, replaced their elders as *domokhoziain.*[52]

The young, in particular, began to question the old beliefs. While older peasants told stories of the strange punishments that befell those who dared remove their icons, young rural Komsomol members mocked the old beliefs with obscene *chastushki.* They sang:

> God, oh God,
> What are you doing?
> Instead of working,
> The Virgin Mary, you're screwing.

[51] N. Morev, "Staroe i Novoe," in Tan-Bogoraz, pp. 46–48. Peasant belief was based on both magic and the teachings of the church. Pagan rituals and the ceremonies of orthodoxy affected virtually every area of life. Anyone who wanted to begin sowing, build a hut, move, or bring a bride before a groom could not ignore certain customs. For a discussion of the role of religion and magic in the peasants' worldview, see Moshe Lewin, "Popular Religion in Twentieth Century Russia," in his *The Making of the Soviet System. Essays in the Social History of Interwar Russia* (Pantheon, New York, 1985): 57–71.

[52] Danilov, p. 231.

Even the most superstitious admitted, "Now there are no such things as there were earlier. Even the *kolduny* are not the same. Before they actually had power, but now it is all based on illusion." Thus magic still existed in the minds of the old, but mysteriously, it had lost much of its strength in the face of Soviet power.[53] Although the old may have brooded over the peculiar incompatibility of socialism and magic, the young were largely occupied with other questions. And the rural population was overwhelming young: fully 59 percent was under the age of 25 in 1926.[54] Demography, it appeared, was on the side of change.

The expropriation of the gentry lands after the revolution not only reinvigorated traditional institutions, but also promoted social change. With the increased availability of land, the large, multifamily peasant household began to break up into smaller units. The growing number of *razdely* resulted in an additional 10 million households between 1917 and 1928. The average household size dropped from 6.1 to 5.1 between 1917 and 1924. Simply put, the large, multifamily household ceased to predominate in the countryside. It still prevailed in provinces like Samara and Orlov, but in many areas, particularly in the central factory regions, it was superceded by smaller, nuclear units.[55]

The breakup of the multifamily household naturally affected peasant social relations, especially the roles and status of women. *Razdel* undermined the power of the *domokhoziain* and gave the younger married woman more control over her own household affairs. It also, however, undercut the power of the wife of the *domokhoziain* and thus eliminated one of the most important positions a woman could occupy or aspire to within the household. The daughter-in-law's increased independence came at the expense of her mother-in-law's diminished authority. Moreover, a woman within a smaller, poorer household struggled harder to

[53] N. Morev, "Staroe i Novoe," p. 49; V. G. Tan, "Staryi i Novyi Byt," in Tan-Bogoraz, pp. 6–7.

[54] Danilov, p. 43.

[55] N. Semenov, p. 185; Christine Worobec, "Reflections on Customary Law and Post-Reform Peasant Russia," *Russian Review,* 1 (1985), and Moshe Lewin, "Customary Law and Russian Rural Society in the Post-Reform Era," and Michael Confino, "Russian Peasant Customary Law and the Study of Peasant Mentalities," in the same issue; William T. Shinn, "The Law of the Russian Peasant Household," p. 612; Danilov, p. 230.

assure its economic viability and therefore assumed a greater burden of labor. Numerous peasant women remarked that *razdel* made it more difficult to integrate work with pregnancy and child rearing.

The expansion of commodity production and the new opportunities to earn an independent wage in handicraft and factory work, changes begun well before the Revolution, also eroded the traditional customs of the village. By creating a new economic basis for individual independence, waged work undermined the power of the *domokhoziain* and the principle of common ownership. A peasant who left the village to work for wages had some control over how much money he would send back to the *dvor*. And in areas where many peasants left the village to work in factories, individual hands began to take their share from the common pot. The introduction of a separate wage upset the traditional power arrangements and the cooperative balance of the *dvor*, introducing new questions about control and ownership. Waged work that could be done within the household (handicraft or *kustar*) or close to the village posed fewer problems. An ethnographer noted that "this work gradually enters the daily circle of the household's customary labor and merges with it." But when a person left the village to work for wages, the tie to the *dvor* weakened and "little by little, the working member of the *dvor* changes his view toward his salary and begins to see it as his own property." In some areas, peasants developed rules within the framework of customary law to govern the apportionment of wages. Peasants from Moscow, Briansk, Tver, Northern Dvinsk, Viatka, and Novgorod provinces, areas with long traditions of *otkhod* (seasonal wage labor), recognized the right of a wage-earning member of the *dvor* to retain half his earnings. Although many peasants working in the cities maintained strong ties with their villages, the separate wage-earning of individuals eroded the principle of commonality on which the *dvor* was based.[56]

Courtship and marriage were also changing slowly, showing signs of both the old and the new. Young people still organized get-togethers in the evenings, known variously as *besedy, posedelki, posedki, positki,* and *posetki,* depending on the region. Beginning

[56] Semenov, pp. 192–194.

in the fall and continuing through the winter, the unmarried boys and girls gathered in a girl's hut, laughing, talking, singing, and playing the accordion until late at night. The girls brought their needlework and spinning and worked through the evening; when the gathering broke up, the boys walked them home. In the summer, and on Sundays and holidays, the young people gathered to sing *chastushki,* to dance, and to gossip. Boys and girls walked together (*guliat'*) arm in arm. On warm evenings they danced in the fields beneath the starry sky and strolled about the countryside.[57]

There were many variations on the *posedki* or *besedy.* In the northern provinces, a serious "work atmosphere" prevailed, especially among the girls. M. Ia. Fenomenov, an ethnographer who studied village life in Novgorod province, noted that the *posedki,* an "archaic phenomenon" with a "basis in production," still existed in the 1920s. The girls organized the gatherings, worked on the linens for their dowries, and appeared in their future role of *khoziaiki* (housewives). In the southern provinces, there was much less work and more merrymaking. The young people rented an *izba* (hut) to which the girls brought food. Around midnight, the boys returned to their homes, leaving the girls to spend the night together on the floor. In some of the districts south of Moscow, parts of the custom had already disappeared by the 1920s, replaced by new forms of socializing. The boys rented a house for an evening, and dancing took the place of spinning, weaving, and sewing. And in yet other areas, the local soviets set up *narodnye doma* or "people's houses" for educational programs, social activities, and spectacles for the young people.[58]

Courtship rituals were everywhere changing: Boys, rather than girls, began organizing the gatherings; a rented *izba* replaced the homes offered by the girls themselves; and the work-related aspect of the evenings began to disappear. The activities sponsored by the local soviets were one more step in the transition to more urban patterns of courtship. There were other changes as well. Young people no longer sang the "long"songs,

[57] Morev, Shirintsina, "Sovremennaia Chastushka," p. 118; A. Borisova, "Vzaimootnosheniia Polov u Chukharei," in Tan-Bogoraz, pp. 61–62.

[58] M. Ia. Fenomenov, *Sovremennaia derevnia. Opyt kraevedcheskogo obsledovaniia odnoi derevni,* Vol. II (Leningrad-Moscow, 1925): 6–8.

but chanted *chastushki* instead. Older dances like the *pliaska* and *korovod* were replaced by new town dances like the quadrille, the *lans'e*, and the *tsyganochka*. The young people dressed more diversely: Boys topped homespun trousers with English cloth coats, as girls showed off galoshes, and highheeled, lacquered shoes in place of traditional bast sandals. Umbrellas, gloves, and bracelets made their way into the countryside.[59] Young people sang *chastushki* that reflected the changing fashions:

> Don't spare the money, papa,
> Twenty-five rubles is enough,
> Buy an umbrella and galoshes,
> Like the finer people's stuff.[60]

Yet beneath the shoes and bangles, the prevailing attitudes in the village toward premarital sex and marriage remained traditional. If a boy courted a girl, the peasants said he "*guliaet no dniam*," or "strolled about by day." If he had a more intimate tie, he "*guliaet po nocham*," or "strolled by night." Peasants described premarital sex by the biblical phrase "to know," in the sense, "*Pet'ka znakom s Niutkoi*," or "Peter 'knows' Niutka." A girl who "*guliaet*" with many boys, or who was "*zhakomoi s parnem*," "familiar with a lad," risked a bad reputation. She would become "*slava*" or "well known," among the village gossips.[61] One *chastushka* metaphorically described the consequences of intimacy under the watchful eyes of the village:

> Whoever carries water from the well
> Also drinks to satiation,
> Whoever loves in their own village,
> Gets a reputation.[62]

In the summer months, the girls often slept outside, in haystacks, sheds, and abandoned huts. Sometimes the boys would visit them and spend the night. The boys sang:

> Fear not, my little sweet one
> That I will stop loving you,
> Darker nights are coming
> We will spend the whole night through.

[59] Morev, Shirintsina, "Sovremennaia Chastushka," p. 118; V. G. Tan, "Staryi i Novyi Byt," p. 7.
[60] Morev, Shirintsina, p. 120.
[61] Fenomenov, pp. 8–10.
[62] Ibid., pp. 10–11.

And the girls proudly flaunted their new maturity:

> When I was just a little girl
> Mama made my bed at home
> But I bed down in the hay
> Now that I am grown.[63]

Boys and girls had ample opportunity for sexual intimacy, but "*gulian'e*" still usually ended in marriage. There were instances when a girl became pregnant and the boy refused to marry her, but these were not common.[64]

An illegitimate child still brought terrible shame to a girl and her family. The village viewed the girl "almost like a criminal."[65] The strictness of peasant morality resulted in part from powerful economic considerations: Land rights derived from the male line and a fatherless child had no share in village land. Girls resorted to illegal abortions and even infanticide to avoid the stigma of illegitimacy. And the parents of a pregnant girl would often try to marry her off to a poor boy to avoid the shame. Before the Revolution, illegitimate children were forced to leave the village after they grew up, the boys to enter a trade, the girls to get married.[66]

There were small indications, however, that by the mid-1920s the Family Code's provision on child support had begun to alter traditional peasant calculations about marriage. In a village in Tver province, a boy got a girl pregnant but declined to marry her. Refusing an abortion, the girl had the baby and promptly filed suit in people's court. The judge sentenced the boy to pay a monthly sum to support the child. The boy's family, anxious to avoid payment, hastily tried to arrange a marriage, but the girl's family was not quite so eager once they glimpsed the possibility of a regular monetary payment. The old ways eventually prevailed and the couple wed, but the case made a strong impression on the young people of the village. Several girls regretted their abortions and the boys grew less cocky about sexual conquest. The married *babas* joked, "If they levy such strict awards

---

[63] Ibid., pp. 15–16.
[64] Ibid., pp. 8–10; On changing mores in the prerevolutionary period see Barbara Engel, "Peasant Morality and Pre-marital Relations in Late 19th Century Russia," *Journal of Social History*, 23, No. 4 (Summer, 1990): 695–714.
[65] Panferov, p. 110.
[66] Fenomenov, p. 19.

for the illegal children, then our husbands should pay us even more for the legal ones!" The ethnographer M. Ia. Fenomenov concluded that child support had a positive effect on the position of peasant women. They could "raise their heads and feel they are not unprotected."[67]

Parents still exercised great power over their children's choice of a spouse, although their influence was waning. Young people who earned a wage increasingly demanded the right to choose their own partners, defying the will of their parents.[68] Young people made their choices by eloping or marrying *samokhodkoi*, without parental knowledge or consent. Elopement was a simple affair. The girl quietly left her parents' home at night, took her dowry, and moved in with her future husband. There was no feast, no priest, no wedding, no *koldovstvo* (sorcery) of a *koldun*. The spread of civil marriage and the simplicity of the registration procedure made elopement quite easy. Eventually, the couple would register their marriage or perhaps even be blessed in church. The case of Nikolai Trofimov, a 20-year-old clerk in the executive committee, was typical. Nikolai arrived late one evening at his waiting sweetheart's *izba*. Her parents were asleep. "Let's go!" he said, and taking her by the hand, he led her back to his house. Their story followed the simple lines of the *chastushka:*

> I don't tell anyone,
> Where I go in the evening,
> I put my feet on the road,
> And walk on down the line.

The next morning the girl was up and working in the fields of Nikolai's family. Within several days, they registered their marriage at the local soviet. They planned a church wedding at Easter.[69]

In the prerevolutionary period, elopement was considered a great shame to the girl and her parents.[70] Sometimes, the girl's

[67] Ibid., pp. 16–17.
[68] Engel, pp. 695, 702, 703. Engel also makes an important gender distinction, noting that even in industrialized areas where parental authority had weakened, young women rarely had the same freedom as young men.
[69] Borisova, pp. 63–64; Morev, "Staroe i Novoe," p. 50.
[70] Engel notes that by the late nineteenth century, elopement was already considered respectable. Although women were not shamed

parents forced her to return home and marry by "an honest path." One peasant woman, forced to marry an older man who mistreated her, looked back over her many years of marriage and said with regret, "If it would have been the present, I would have eloped (*ushla samokhodkhoi*). But then I was afraid to bear the shame. People would have censured me for an entire year."[71] Two *chastushki* reflected the new values of the young people and their willingness to defy their parents:

> My sweetheart asked me to elope,
> But mama scared me so,
> Yet even if she hurt me,
> I would have to go.
>
> I will elope,
> I will make father weep,
> I will make father grieve,
> I'll take a cow and a sheep.[72]

Parents insisted so heavily on control over marital choices because peasant marriage was an economic institution in which property took precedence over sentiment. Peasants believed that the marital bond should be "*pripechaten*" or "sealed" as tightly as possible. Although many peasants registered their marriages, the majority still took the additional precaution of marrying in church.[73] Many distrusted civil marriage, considering it "unstable" and "a disadvantageous union for the woman."[74] Yet the practice of civil marriage was slowly increasing in the rural areas, prompting young people to sing the virtues of registration over a church wedding:

> Now we have new laws,
> We don't need to marry in church,
> In the executive committee, by a table,
> You simply sign your name.[75]

for eloping, a son still risked being disinherited if his father disapproved of his choice. See p. 704.

[71] Borisova, pp. 65, 71; Morev, "Staroe i Novoe," pp. 50–51.
[72] Morev, Shirintsina, "Sovremennaia Chastushka," pp. 121–122.
[73] A. M. Bol'shakov, *Derevnia, 1917–1927* (Moscow, 1927): 319.
[74] Borisova, p. 69.
[75] Morev, Shirintsina, "Sovremennaia Chastushka," p. 122.

Divorce and alimony

Despite the enthusiasm of some *chastushki* sung by youth, the reaction to Soviet family law was mixed. Many older peasants in particular believed that the Family Code encouraged promiscuity and hurt the economic interests of the household.[76] Others seemed to accept the changes more willingly. In one village, a peasant took a wife without a church marriage and soon abandoned her for another. The other villagers regarded his actions with amused toleration. "Now there are new laws," they said; "Everything is possible."[77] Young men sang happily of the new sexual freedom created by civil marriage and easy divorce:

> You should not smoke tobacco
> You should not drink much home brew
> Love more girls instead
> Now we have a law that's new.[78]

And women, too, celebrated the new laws, confident that the threat of divorce strengthened their position in the family. Rural women sang:

> Time was when my husband,
> Used his fists and force,
> But now he is so tender,
> For he fears divorce.

and:

> I no longer fear my husband,
> If we can't cooperate,
> I will take myself to court
> And we will separate.[79]

The Family Code thus began to erode the traditional conservatism of the village. The divorce rate in the countryside in the 1920s was lower than the national average, and considerably lower than in the towns, but the figures were nonetheless note-

[76] See Chapter 6 for peasant attitudes toward marriage, divorce, and the Family Codes.
[77] Morev, "Staroe i Novoe," pp. 51–52.
[78] Morev, Shirintsina, "Sovremennaia Chastushka," p. 122.
[79] A. S. Kalygina, *Krest'ianka v brake i sem'e* (Moscow-Leningrad, 1926): 29.

worthy. In 1925, the divorce rate in the towns was about twice as high as the rural areas (2.8 divorces per 1,000 people in the towns, and 1.2 in the countryside). Yet by 1926, there was roughly 1 divorce for every 10 rural marriages. By 1927, almost 11% of men and 9% of women entering marriage in the countryside had been previously divorced. One demographer noted, "The influence of the freedom provided by the Family Code is clear."[80]

Most divorces, both urban and rural, occurred between people married for a short period. In the rural areas, the average duration of a marriage ending in divorce was only 2.4 years. In the towns, marriages ending in divorce tended to last somewhat longer, about 4.4 years. The median age of people who divorced in the countryside was only 23 for men and 22 for women; and in the towns, it was somewhat higher (28 and 25). The overwhelming majority (about 80%) of divorcing rural men and women were dissolving their first marriages. But a significant number, roughly 17% of the men and 16% of the women, were getting divorced for the second time. In the towns, the percentage of people ending a second marriage was slightly higher (about 19%).[81]

The brief duration of marriages ending in divorce complicated women's property claims, for the average length of marriage fell considerably short of the six years a women needed to claim a share in the *dvor's* land. A woman could return to her parents' household, but often they were not happy to take her

---

[80] M. Kaplun, "Brachnost' Naseleniia RSFSR," *Statisticheskoe obozrenie*, 7 (1929): 91.

[81] Ibid., p. 96. People in the countryside married earlier than those in the towns, but the mean age at marriage was rising. In 1900, in European Russia, 32% of men and 56% of women entered marriage before age 20. Although the figures for rural areas alone are not available, the percentages were in all likelihood even higher. By 1927, far fewer men and women were married before the age of 20 – only 22% of the men and 35% of the women in the rural areas; only 4% of the men and 19% of the women in the towns. By the age of 24, 71% of all rural men and 80% of the women had married – Russia still had higher rates of early marriage than Europe – but the marriage age was rising in both the countryside and the towns. Kaplun, p. 94; *Estestvennoe dvizhenie naseleniia za 1926 god* (Moscow, 1928): L.

back, especially if she had children. From the parents' point of view, a divorced woman was like a discarded piece of the whole that no longer fit: an *"otrezannyi lomot',"* or literally, a slice from the loaf. She was *"ni baba, ni devka,"* neither married woman nor maid. There was little place for her in village life.[82]

Divorce posed serious economic problems for both the woman who left the household and the family members obligated to support her. As one well-to-do Ukrainian peasant man put it, "As long as I do not split off from them (the household), I am rich. If I split off, we will all be like *bedniaks* (poor peasants)."[83] Although he was referring to the process of *razdel,* the same rule held true for divorce.

Peasant women complained bitterly about their problems after divorce. Belitskaia, a peasant delegate from Belorussia to the All-Union Congress of Working and Peasant Women in 1927, rhetorically asked her fellow delegates, "What rights does a woman have in the countryside?" She posed the hypothetical case of a husband and wife who got a divorce. Their two children stayed with the mother. "What part of the household does she get?" Belitskaia asked. "Only one-third and only from the movable property. The land is not divided because we have too little suitable land to divide. What remains for the peasant woman to do?" The woman received a court order detailing her award: a shed, a pig, perhaps 2 or 3 rubles a month. But she had nowhere to go and no way to support herself. Moreover, men often refused to pay the awards, small as they were. Belitskaia explained angrily, "Half a year goes by, a year, by now she needs 10 rubles. Her former husband gives her 5 and again the woman has nothing." Zhuravleva, a delegate from the Chuvash republic, spoke passionately about the same problems. "The division of land to the divorced wife is delayed," she said. "Women and children are tormented and do not receive their plot for eight months." Zhuravleva suggested that the bailiffs enforce the law more strictly and efficiently "so that women will receive alimony and their plots of land more quickly."[84]

While women struggled to collect their often meager awards, households fought back to protect their property. Many peas-

[82] Bol'shakov, p. 318; Fenomenov, p. 18.
[83] Semenov, p. 191.
[84] *S"ezd rabotnits i krest'ianok,* p. 249, 299.

ants swore that alimony could only lead to the ruin of the *dvor*. A member of the land commission in Briansk noted that the peasants developed numerous ruses for avoiding alimony payments. Sometimes the household would make a fictitious *razdel*, granting very little property to the member responsible for alimony, and absolving its other members of liability for his debts. Local executive committees frequently winked at these tricks and officially registered the fictitious *razdel*. Sometimes peasants deliberately cut back on production, raising only what the household needed. If the defendant did wage-paying work, he might contract privately and fail to report his income.[85]

The courts, especially at the higher levels, tried to enforce the law and tended to side with the woman and child against the household. Jurists were especially strong advocates of the woman's rights if they felt she was being deceived by a rich, powerful household, for such cases had class as well as gender implications. A. S. Romanova, for example, was an illiterate peasant from Votskaia autonomous region who took her case to the Supreme Court and in the process established an important legal precedent. Romanova had lived with her husband and worked in his household for almost three years. In the winter of 1923, her husband threw her out, despite her pregnancy. She went home to live with her father. Her child was born and registered in her husband's name. Her father, a poor peasant burdened with a large family, refused to support her and the baby. He brought suit against her husband for child support and *vydel*. The local people's court awarded her 35 rubles (the cost of a cow), but refused her child support, claiming that the paternity of Romanova's child was unproven. The Supreme Court angrily reversed the people's court decision, charging that it was "completely without foundation, and belittled the rights of the plaintiff." The Supreme Court stressed that the lower courts must consider the size of the *dvor* and the amount of its property in deciding alimony and child support cases.[86]

The most intractable problem in the great majority of cases

[85] Fisunov, "Stranitsa Praktika," *Ezhenedel'nik sovetskoi iustitsii*, 24 (1927): 739; V. Solov'ev, "Stranitsa Praktika," *Ezhenedel'nik sovetskoi iustitsii*, 22 (1927): 673.

[86] "Zametki o primenenii kodeksa zakonov o brake, sem'e i opeke v derevne," *Ezhenedel'nik sovetskoi iustitsii*, 4 (1929): 86–87.

was that peasant poverty stood in the way of equitable alimony and child support settlements. From the revolution until 1926, most peasants lived at a level of bare subsistence. As late as 1929, more than one-third of peasants were *bedniaks*, which meant that they cultivated less than 5.4 acres of land, did not own a horse or cow, and were forced to rent their tools and draught animals. Fifty percent had only one draught animal.[87] According to a study of alimony in Kostroma province, more than 80 percent of the cases involved middle or poor households. The courts usually levied a sum of 3 to 10 rubles a month, but this amount simply could not be met by many of the households. The average annual income of a peasant household in Kostroma province in 1924 was 180 rubles, which had to cover taxes, repairs of agricultural and household tools, food from harvest to harvest, and numerous other expenses. An alimony award of even 5 rubles a month amounted to almost one-third of the average peasant's annual income. The peasants could barely pay annual agricultural taxes, which were a much smaller sum.[88] It was thus virtually impossible for the overwhelming majority of peasant households to pay alimony or child support. Not only did the woman's ex-husband often have nothing to give her, the household itself had little or nothing. Even if they owned a horse or a cow, the animal could not be cut in half.

Many of the cases that came to court were simply unresolvable. One divorced woman with several children petitioned the court for alimony. She had already received her share of property and land. The Kostroma alimony commission wondered how alimony could be awarded when the main source of peasant income was land. If the land was divided, the household would be even poorer. Where would the payments come from? Was a woman still entitled to alimony after she had exhausted the customary sources of rural wealth, a portion of land (*razdel*) and part of the movable property (*vydel*)? In another case, the local people's court judge wrote, "Neither of the sides had anything. It is a good thing they were reconciled in court. But how do we handle similar cases in the future?" The judge noted grimly that

---

[87] Lewin, *Russian Peasants and Soviet Power*, pp. 36, 30.
[88] A. Sidorov, "K Voprosu Alimentnogo Prava v Derevne," *Rabochii sud*, 1 (1926): 13–14; V. Solov'ev, "Stranitsa Praktiki," p. 673.

collecting alimony in the countryside was "hellish work." About half of the peasant women who were awarded alimony were unable to collect anything.[89]

In the mid-1920s, the Commissariat of Justice set up several commissions to investigate the problems of alimony in the countryside. The Kostroma commission came to the conclusion that "court decisions are made in vain," for there was "no possibility of carrying out the verdict." Although the courts usually sided with the woman and the child, their rulings were meaningless if the households could not pay the awards. In several Moscow districts, 30 percent of the women who received alimony awards were unable to collect. Both the Kostroma and Moscow commissions recommended that judges make awards commensurate with the household's assets. Awards from poorer households should be reduced. Alimony payment should be make in kind, rather than money, and at flexible intervals rather than on a strict monthly schedule. In cases where both spouses were destitute, the state should intervene. And finally, criminal sanctions should be applied to people who could afford to pay but refused. In desperation, the Kostroma commission urged the courts to use greater "creativity and initiative." Employing both skills freely in its own recommendation, the commission suggested a new and strange sort of gender *corvee:* If a woman's ex-husband could not pay her alimony, he could pay off the debt by working as her laborer.[90]

While the commissions sought to be helpful and fair, their suggestions only highlighted the difficulty of applying Soviet family law to the countryside. Household members adamantly declared their opposition to alimony in local meetings. The *dvor* was an indivisible unit, merging land, labor, tools, and livestock into a single unit of production. Survival of the individual depended on the unity of the household.

A woman alone

The obstacles to divorce and women's independence were not only financial, in the narrow sense, but linked with the broadest

[89] Solov'ev, p. 673.
[90] Sidorov, p. 15; F. Vol'fson, "Voprosy Alimentnogo Protsessa v Derevne," *Rabochii sud*, 37–38 (1925): 1386–1389.

economic, social, and political structures in village life. The divorced or widowed woman living apart from a household, found it quite hard to survive in the countryside by herself. Even if she received a plot, there was often little she could do except rent it to someone else. Kiselev, a delegate to the Women's Congress from Saratov province, noted that many women were forced to give up their land because they had no livestock and no way to plough it. He said, "Those who do not give out their land, but till it themselves – their land is always unploughed because they do not have the strength."[91] Often the peasant woman had not only to rent out her land, but to work as a day laborer so that she, in turn, could pay a man to do the heavy jobs – hauling timber, repair and construction work, digging wells – that she could not handle. One writer wrote: "Single peasant women without husbands know no rest. In the summer, they till the fields, sow, harrow, work in the kitchen garden, mow and gather in the meadows, thresh, etc. They do a man's and a woman's work." In the winter, they had to cut and drag firewood and hay, look after the cattle, spin, sow, mend clothes, and wash linens, not only for themselves, but also for their neighbors.[92]

The single woman not only labored day and night, but was frequently cheated by the commune. The commune might take her allotment or encroach on her farmland and meadow in order to provide a returning soldier or worker with land. The writer explained, "If they take away the land of Ivanov or Petrov, they will resist and commit violence with drunken hands. But Maria or Akulina, they will not contradict the *mir*. They will not dare. They can scarcely complain or file a lawsuit because they are illiterate. And so the land of Maria or Akulina is taken away."[93]

Women like Maria or Akulina were virtually helpless against the depredations of their neighbors. The story of the widow, Nastasia, in Chernovtsy province, revealed the vulnerability and dependence of the single woman. Widowed for five years, Nastasia, according to her neighbors, lived "decently" for a long time. Then she became involved with a worker. She wanted to marry him but she still feared her father-in-law, and eventually

---

[91] *S"ezd rabotnits i krest'ianok*, p. 262.
[92] V. Romanov, "Krest'ianka i Derevenskii 'Mir'," *Kommunistka*, 8–9 (1922): 35–36.
[93] Ibid., p. 36.

ended their relationship. When Nastasia discovered she was pregnant, she tried to hide her condition by putting a tight belt around her waist. But the village soon discovered the truth and condemned her. After the child was born, many of the *muzhiki* (male peasants) began to take advantage of her. In the autumn, she killed a bull and hung the meat outside to dry under the roof of her *izba*. The *muzhiki* stole the meat, forcing her to dry the rest inside, by the stove. During the summer, they took part of her meadow and her hay.[94]

Landless women who worked as laborers (*batrachki*) were among the most vulnerable and exploited of the village poor. Even the small number of *batrachki* who worked on state farms had few protections. Dismissed from their jobs if they became pregnant, they had no social insurance and nowhere to turn. Many drifted into the cities and became prostitutes. One delegate to the Women's Congress described how these women dragged through the fields during harvest time with babies at their breasts. "These women take their tiny babies in rags, like ragamuffins. Why is this? Because they have no one to help them, no livestock and no machines."[95]

Batrachki were frequently exploited sexually as well as economically. A household would hire a *batrachka* for several months or more, and often she would live with one of the men as his "wife," and work in the fields beside his family. These women, known as "wives for a season," were thrown out of the household as soon as they became pregnant and were no longer able to work. The practice was so common that one official in Tver province actually witnessed, signed, and sealed a contract between a peasant and *batrachka* in 1924 that formalized the practice of a "seasonal" wife by absolving the man of all legal responsibility. The peasant, S. P. Kovalev, promised to support Anna Romanenko, a *batrachka*, as his wife for three years. After that time, he disclaimed responsibility.[96] At the end of this period, Anna, the *batrachka*, would in all likelihood find herself homeless with a small child to support. She probably signed the contract, which was clearly illegal, in a desperate bid for short-term security.

[94] Borisova, p. 76.
[95] *S"ezd rabotnits i krest'ianok*, p. 262.
[96] Bol'shakov, p. 349.

One poor peasant woman, Matrena Mel'nikova, from the Urals, scrambled all her life for a secure niche. Thrown out of her husband's household, she told her bitter tale in court:

I stayed with my parents until I was 13 years old, then I went to work for other people. I worked as a *batrachka* until the age of 18, then I married. Neither my husband nor I had anything. Soon he fell sick and died, and again I went to work for others. Two years ago, Mel'nikov began to pester me. "What will be," I thought, "I have neither horse nor cow, but these people are well off, even prosperous one might say, and he wants to marry me." I believed his words and I agreed. We married, everything proper, married in church and the village soviet. So, I thought, now everything will be solid. Life will begin. All went well, we liked each other. I worked a lot, but all the same, compared to the past, this was easy. Within a year, I had a baby. Life changed. I had to work in the fields and in the house, but now I had a child on my hands. At home, my mother-in-law began to find fault, my father-in-law would not talk at all. I felt misfortune hanging over my head and I thought – I thought for days and nights on end – Why can't I please them? I racked my brains, but soon an event opened my eyes. My child died. My husband and in-laws were happy at this. My husband began to chase me away from the *dvor* saying that although I lived with them in the household, I was not his wife, but a *batrachka*. And what about the fact that I had born a child? My husband said, "Why did you lie down with me, no one forced you." I was forced to leave them. Again I began to work by the day, to work and to wait for what the court would say.

She had heard that a new law might help her, but she was still afraid. She concluded, "Indeed we are dark, we do not have the words to speak, I knew I would have to speak about the case, but my tongue says something else." Fortunately, Matrena "had the words to speak"; she told her story well. The Mel'nikovs, who owned three houses, a sheepskin factory with hired workers, 8 horses, 11 cows, 25 sheep, and 3,270 acres, were forced to give her 4,000 pounds of wheat, a horse, a cow, and 6 sheep.[97]

Matrena's story, combining all the elements of a peasant fairy tale with a socialist passion play, was unusual: the Mel'nikovs were very prosperous and Matrena received a substantial award after her suit. Not only was she instantly transformed from *batrachka* to *kulachka*, but she did it with the help of Soviet law. Yet most stories did not have such happy endings. Ledkodukhova, a peasant delegate to the Women's Congress from the Ukraine, summed up the problem very simply: "The harvest begins –

97 A. Malkov, "Byt v Sude," *Sud idet!*, 5 (1927): 269–270.

they take a wife, and when the harvest is finished – the wife is divorced." And although a woman, married or not, could claim support from the father of her child, it was very difficult to collect the award. Ledkodukhova exclaimed indignantly, "The Land Code states it is impossible to ruin the *dvor*, therefore it is useless to levy an award of 3 rubles a month for the child when the father has only one horse and a hut." All the same, she added, something must be done to ease the suffering of the *batrachka*.[98]

Women were especially vulnerable in the countryside because they traditionally had no power in the governing institutions of village life. The Land Code gave them the right to participate in the *skhod* (decision-making body of the commune), but this was difficult to enforce in practice. Bykhtiaeva, a *bedniachka* (poor peasant) and widow with five children from Nizhegorod province, described the problems she encountered with her commune. After her home and all her possessions had been destroyed in a fire, the commune took away her land. In her words, she "went out among the people" and after threatening the men with the Land Code, demanded, "Whoever is against the law, speak and show yourself." But the commune still refused to take her back. She proudly told her fellow delegates, "I was forbidden to show my nose in the commune's meeting, but I was there anyway." Bykhtiaeva concluded that it was possible to advance women's interests in the countryside only if women "were willing to break down every door with their heads." Even then, she added gloomily, there were still "men who will not give way to women."[99]

Many peasant women at the Congress harshly criticized the domineering attitudes and arrogant behavior of the men in their villages. Pichurina, a peasant woman from Voronezh province, described how she successfully turned the consumer cooperative in her village into a profitable enterprise. When someone suggested that she take over the leadership of the failing agricultural cooperative, many men balked. "Why should a *baba* lead us so that everyone will laugh at us?" they asked. "Perhaps a *baba's* business is to fiddle with a tractor, to plough, and to store

[98] *S"ezd rabotnits i krest'ianok*, p. 228.
[99] Ibid., p. 286.

the grain? This is not a *baba's* business. There is no reason to make a mockery of things."[100]

Uraimgova, a woman from Northern Ossetia in Georgia, complained, "Even the conscious men, even Party members, do not allow women to go to the meetings." Speaking in her native language, she explained how men consistently excluded women from positions of power. "Men act very badly in regard to electing women," she said. "When the candidacy of a woman comes up, none of the men raise their hands for her. And if a woman comes to the soviet, then the men begin to talk in Russian, so she will not understand." Another woman from Tver province added, "The men try to hold the elections while the women are busy with the milch cows." Sentsova, the chairwoman of the provincial land commission in Kostroma, summed up the difficulties, "Although we have achieved much among women, our work is undermined by men. It is particularly hard to work among the peasants." She said, "When we go to a meeting, they snub us. There was a time when we had to come in through the back entrance, not through the same door the men used, although everyone participated in the meeting." Men refused to respect women or acknowledge them in positions of leadership. "I try with all my strength to explain our legislation to men," Sentsova said with frustration, "but they do not even want to listen. They walk away and ask the first man they come across." Sentsova concluded, "There is much darkness in the countryside." Numerous speakers testified to men's efforts to keep women from participating in local government, the land commissions, the village soviets, and the district executive committees. One peasant woman, expressing her disgust for the men in her village, said they were "unconscious, uncultured," and "nasty to look at"; they "undermined the work of women at every step." When a male speaker asked the women delegates if there were many uncultured and ignorant men who made women's work harder, one voice shot back indignantly, "Many, almost all!"[101]

Several Party organizers and delegates urged women to participate in local government so they could advance their own interests in the village. One organizer counseled women not to

[100] Ibid., p. 274.   [101] Ibid., pp. 266, 223, 258.

rely on "male goodness and consciousness," which was all too often in short supply. "Sometimes in the struggle with men's backwardness, you must shove them along the road with your fist," he explained. Another organizer urged, "Everything is in the soviets, all the money, all the power. It is one thing when you ask for money, another when you have the right to manage it." Afaneseva, a delegate from Iaroslavl province, urged the women to take power away from the men. "I have heard many women cry out," she said, "that a single woman cannot change anything in the district, that they give only to the men, and to the *babas* they give nothing." Speaking in a powerful feminist voice, she exhorted her fellow delegates, "Comrade women, go to the co-operatives, promote your women in the elections so that they will manage, and do not give the power to men, for they have dominated up to this time."[102]

Tradition and change

The testimony of the peasant delegates before the Women's Congress amply confirmed the enormous difficulties involved in transforming village life. Centuries of patriarchal power, structuring the most basic social, economic, and cultural institutions, could not be easily dislodged by law alone. Jurists committed to extending gender equality in the countryside encountered the obstacles of extreme poverty, the relative absence of independent wage earners, the economic indivisibility of the household, the importance of physical strength in the division of labor, the powerful dependence of women on men, and the patrilocal focus of family relations. The liberation of peasant women required no less than a complete transformation of the mode of production – the development of the primitive level of production, the establishment of wage relations, the introduction of machinery, and the abolition of the family as the basic unit of production – as well as a corresponding revolution in traditional social values and practices.

Yet life in the village was changing, slowly affected by economic and demographic processes begun long before the Revo-

[102] Ibid., pp. 260, 296.

lution, suddenly confronted by new revolutionary ideas, laws, and activism. The old, multigenerational patriarchal family was breaking up, family size was decreasing, the incidence of *razdel* increasing, and wage relations were slowly undermining the rule of the "common pot." Courtship patterns were changing too as parents lost control over their children's marital choices and girls increasingly married without their consent. Civil marriage and divorce were becoming more common. Peasant women were beginning to take advantage of their new rights.

The Family Code, with its emphasis on individual rights and freedoms, challenged centuries of patriarchal values and undermined the collective principle of the household, the very basis of agricultural production. It contradicted both peasant custom and the Land Code, prompting a bewildering tangle of instructions and directives, in which jurists tried to reconcile their ideal of gender equality with the productive primacy of the peasant household. The Code generated intense conflict in the countryside. Women often used the law to gain a greater measure of freedom; the household fought back fiercely to protect its common property. Extreme poverty exacerbated the gap between law and life, making it almost impossible for many households to pay women their legal due. As long as the family remained the basic unit of production, as long as patriarchy structured the institutions of village life, neither peasant women nor men could realize the freedom promised by the Code.

Yet the jurists upheld their commitment to individual freedom and gender equality in the face of powerful peasant opposition. Officials in the Commissariats of Land and Justice repeatedly refused to accede to peasant demands to abolish divorce and alimony, and continued to support the rights of the vulnerable, the weak, and the landless peasant woman. Although increased grain production was clearly a major state priority, the Land and Family codes established rights for women that could only engender a decrease in plot size and production. The Moscow commission declared: "To agree that the *dvor* should bear no responsibility for alimony means to flood our Soviet law in a sea of peasant stagnation."[103] Clearly, this was something the jurists were unwilling to do.

[103] Vol'fson, p. 1385.

Despite the structural obstacles to women's liberation, a small minority of peasant women were strongly empowered by the Party's educational efforts, the activities of the Zhenotdel, and their new legal rights. Delegates to the Women's Congress spoke proudly of their struggle as single women to retain their share of the land, to attend meetings of the *skhod,* and to organize agricultural cooperatives for women. Mothers of illegitimate children and divorced peasant women defied centuries of patriarchal tradition to fight the household in court for the right to child support and alimony. One peasant woman, hardly representative of the majority but noteworthy nonetheless, wrote, "In the countryside they look at a woman like a work horse. You work all your life for your husband and his entire family, endure beatings and every kind of humiliation, but it doesn't matter, you have nowhere to go – you are bound in marriage. So it has always been under very strong marriage. I myself am a peasant and I was in this bind. We don't need such strong marriage now."[104]

The Land Code and the Family Code offered a measure of protection to the unmarried, the outcast, and the landless, and a new sense of entitlement for all. Although the Family Code prompted gender conflict in the countryside, promoting irresolvable contradictions between the individual and the household, it also offered a new vision of gender relations that a small but significant number of peasant women eagerly embraced. Perhaps the story of Mel'nikova, the impoverished *batrachka* who had labored since childhood, captured the small stirrings of change most clearly. Thrown out of her husband's *dvor,* she stood terrified before the judge. "I heard in the village that now there was this law," she said simply, "that they could no longer insult women in this way."[105]

[104] "Chto Predlagaiut Rabotnitsy," *Rabotnitsa,* 14 (1926): 15.
[105] Malkov, p. 270.

5

Pruning the "bourgeois thicket": Drafting a new Family Code

> The period of human struggle and war will become a matter of legend. . . . Coercion will begin to disappear in relations between people. Law, as the instrument of coercion in human relations, as the expression of constant struggle between individuals, groups, and the state, will also disappear. With the decisive consolidation of collectivism, not only civil law, but all law will disappear. The harmonious existence of people will be built not on the basis of social coercion and social necessity – in other words, law – but on the basis of full social freedom.
>
> *A. G. Goikhbarg, 1918*[1]

Throughout the early 1920s, jurists tried repeatedly to reform the Family Code of 1918. Prompted by the more radical proponents of free union, as well as the need to redress the social problems of NEP, the Commissariats of Justice and Internal Affairs prepared several drafts of a new Family Code. Their efforts were clearly influenced by Evgeny Pashukanis, a young Marxist jurist, whose ideas on the origins of law dominated Soviet jurisprudence after 1924. Pashukanis's work on the withering away of the law provided a powerful, comprehensive framework for those who sought to hasten the withering away of the family. The process of drafting the new Family Code clearly bore the stamp of his thinking. With each successive draft, the jurists further pared the provisions of the Code and minimized the role of law. The final draft, which was submitted for nationwide debate in 1925, was considerably shorter and sparer than the 1918 original. In its language and its content was evident a curious partnership between the radical, libertarian jurists who sought to promote the withering away of law and the family and

[1] A. G. Goikhbarg, "Proletarskaia revoliutsiia i grazhdanskoe pravo," *Proletarskaia revoliutsiia i pravo*, 1 (1918): 9–10.

185

their more cautious colleagues who sought to protect women and children from the social and economic strains of NEP.

Challenging the Family Code

The radical proponents of free union had derisively rejected the Family Code when it was first discussed in 1918 in the Central Executive Committee (VTsIK). They insisted that the provision on civil marriage, in particular, permitted the state undue influence in the private lives of its citizens. The sheer struggle for survival during the civil war had of necessity imposed a brief moratorium on further debate, but no sooner did the war end than the libertarian critics of the Code resumed agitation for an end to marriage registration. Although they constituted a minority among jurists, legislators, and social activists, their ideas had considerable impact. They sparked a spirited discussion of the 1918 Code and played an important role in the decision to redraft it.

The main difference between the radical proponents of free union and their more mainstream colleagues centered not on whether law and the family would wither away, but when. The radical jurists maintained that marriage registration was largely unnecessary in the transition period. They advanced a more libertarian approach to law, stressing the right of the individual to be free of state interference. The majority felt they wanted to move too quickly, claiming that the young Soviet state still needed marriage and law for social purposes. These two groups agreed on the ultimate goal, but differed on its proper timing.

The libertarian critics of both marriage and family law found new ideological strength in the experience of the civil war. The disappearance of money, the organization of large-scale, communal dining, the fluidity of personal relationships, and high revolutionary morale all conspired to convince many that the withering away of the family and its supporting law was imminent. Alexandra Kollontai expressed these idealistic sentiments in a series of lectures at Sverdlov University in 1921. Kollontai argued that marital relations should not be subject to legal regulation except in terms of health and hygiene. (People with tuberculosis or venereal diseases, for example, should not be permitted to marry.) She dismissed provisions on alimony and child support as "survivals of the past, contradicting the interests of the collective, weakening its unity, and therefore, subject to reconsideration and change." Even recognition of paternity should be voluntary. Drawing on the popular juridical idea that social norms would soon supplant law, Kollontai envisioned a society where communist morality, based on the principles of comradeship and collectivity, reigned in place of "marriage regulation." Marriage detracted from the collective by fostering "the illusion that the collective should recognize the separate and isolated interests of two married members," Kollontai told her student audience; "The stronger the ties of all members with the collective, the less the need for the creation of strong marital relations." She stressed the importance of recognizing "the freedom of others in the area of love experiences." In place of marriage, Kollontai advocated relationships based on love, comradeship, mutual respect, and strong social bonds.[2]

Kollontai's belief that norms should replace law was shared by a number of jurists. Throughout the early twenties, the legal journals, including *Ezhenedel'nik sovetskoi iustitsii*, the official journal of the Commissariat of Justice, carried lively critiques of the 1918 Code, suggestions for reform, and rebuttals. The jurist A. Zelenetskii opened the debate in 1921 with an sweeping attack on the 1918 Code. "The centuries-old established conceptions and constructions of civil law are a survival of the bourgeois era," he declared, a perfect example of Marx's phrase, "the dead holding onto the living." In Zelenetskii's view, the 1918 Code was outdated, its provisions on marriage too conservative. Social practice had already surpassed the law. Zelenetskii argued that proletarian marriage needed no regulation. He wrote, "Our proletarian conception of marriage as the private, intimate business of every individual is legally expressed by an obsolete construction, a survival of either church law or the conditions of the bourgeois order."[3]

Like Kollontai, Zelenetskii believed that the civil war had created the conditions for the abolition of marriage registration.

[2] A. Kollontai, "Tezisy o Kommunisticheskoi Morali v Oblasti Brachnykh Otnoshenii," *Kommunistka*, 12–13 (1921): 29–34.
[3] A. Zelenetskii, "O Nashem Brachnom Prave," *Proletarskaia revoliutsiia i pravo*, 15 (1921): 17.

The Family Code might have been useful in 1918 "insofar as the new conception of marriage still did not have a base in corresponding changes in social conditions," but "even then it was clear how little basis the old conception of marriage had, and how insignificant the area of mutual relations which needed regulation by state power." The entire foundation of marriage was rapidly eroding under the new Soviet system. "What remains of marriage as a legal institution?" he asked. "So little that the law on marital rights will soon regulate nothing, because the old social institutions are disappearing before our eyes." Marriage registration was thus nothing more than an unnecessary hindrance. "What is the point of this comedy?" Zelenetskii queried sarcastically. "It is time to say loudly that without an intimate moral tie and mutual sympathy, there is no marriage in our sense, and we do not need punitive marriage."[4]

Zelenetskii thus claimed that the marriage contract itself was an outdated relic of bourgeois social relations. The rights and responsibilities it enumerated – protection of property, inheritance, and support for the needy and disabled spouse – were irrelevant to the needs of the working-class family and, moreover, increasingly meaningless under the Soviet system. Moreover, if necessary, these rights could be regulated apart from the marriage contract. Property rights could be subsumed under criminal law, which already established penalties for forced or harmful contract. Inheritance could either be abolished or individuals could be permitted unrestricted freedom in bequeathing their property. And the state, not the husband or wife, would assume responsibility for the needy and disabled. Zelenetskii wrote, "From the point of view of planned socialist construction, it is inefficient to establish the care of needy, disabled citizens on the basis of whether they have a 'well-off' spouse." Invoking the familiar Marxist view of socialist marriage as a freely chosen union, he wrote, "It is clear that in the absence of a moral tie between spouses there is no sort of marriage in our socialist sense. Therefore, by insisting on the fulfillment of these responsibilities (alimony and child support), our state simply upholds the existence of a marriage where it has already ceased to exist." Summing up his position, Zelenetskii declared, "Now, almost

[4] Ibid., pp. 19, 21.

three years after the publication of the Code, so little remains of the old social conditions that served as the basis for the regulation of marital rights that the time has come for their full abolition; i.e., for the recognition of marriage as the personal business of every citizen, and the end to the interference of state power."[5]

Zelenetskii's view of state authority typified the libertarian strain in Bolshevik juridical thought. His position, however, was not supported by the majority of Soviet jurists, who took a more functional approach to the law. They insisted that law was an important weapon in the struggle with the old order. Moreover, they differed with Zelenetskii in their assessment of social conditions. The Soviet people were not yet ready for the abolition of marriage. Zelenetskii's prescriptions would only harm the more vulnerable sections of the population: women and children.[6]

In a sharp rejoinder to Zelenetskii, the jurist A. Prigradov-Kudrin argued that civil marriage was still needed to combat the reactionary influence of the church. "It is necessary to consider the implanted psychology of the masses," he cautioned. The majority of the Soviet people was psychologically unprepared for free union. Moreover, with the recent adoption of NEP, marriage had acquired even greater significance because the new property relations required increased regulation. Zelenetskii's suggestion to abolish inheritance was utterly impractical. If the state became the sole heir to property, how could it possibly collect, use, and dispose of the petty goods of millions of citizens? More important, a new decree, permitting inheritance of property amounting to less than 10,000 prewar rubles, had rendered Zelenetskii's suggestion irrelevant.[7]

Prigradov-Kudrin also raised a question that would be discussed for years to come: in the absence of a civil procedure or religious ceremony, how did the state recognize and define a "marriage"? Challenging Zelenetskii to produce a definition, he asked, "What does he consider marriage to be, given the elim-

[5] Ibid., pp. 18–21.
[6] In the debate over the draft Code in 1925–1926, almost all the jurists agreed that some form of civil marriage was necessary. See Chapter 6 for an extensive discussion of the debate.
[7] A. Prigradov-Kudrin, "Brachnoe Pravo i Nasledovanie," *Ezhenedel'nik sovetskoi iustitsii,* 12 (1922): 4–5. Hereafter cited as *ESIu.*

ination of the external form which marks its presence?" In short, Prigradov-Kudrin charged that Zelenetskii's ideas were too advanced for the prevailing psychological attitudes and material conditions; he was out of touch with the realities of Soviet life. Prigradov-Kudrin concluded sharply, "To say simply that marriage as a legal institution should not exist now, that the conception already has neither meaning, nor content, nor significance in contemporary life, means to lose contact with life itself and to soar into outer space."[8]

Zelenetskii responded several months later, maintaining that the onset of NEP had in no way altered the substance of his argument. "The New Economic Policy is a retreat from the communist program only on several specific branches of the social front (primarily in the areas of production and distribution)," he explained, "not from the entire front or in the general area of culture." He reiterated that once marriage ceased to entail property rights, all the rules governing the formal conclusion, dissolution, and existence of marriage were irrelevant. Without property, there was no point in registering marriage, just as "there was no legal significance to registering the names of a steamship's passengers if there are no passports."[9]

Zelenetskii and Prigradov-Kudrin agreed that the primary purpose of the marriage contract was to regulate property, yet they differed in their assessment of property relations in the transition period. While Prigradov-Kudrin stressed the continuing need to regulate property relations under NEP, Zelenetskii downplayed their importance and emphasized those aspects of individual and property relations that no longer required regulation. Prigradov-Kudrin argued the state's continuing need for law, but Zelenetskii insisted that certain areas of law had already been rendered obsolete by new socialist economic relations. This debate, captured in embryonic form in the exchange between these two jurists, continued in one form or another up to 1936. Eventually, the functionalist idea of law as a tool of state power, expressed so reasonably by Prigradov-Kudrin, would be used to annihilate those jurists who promoted theories on the withering away of law and the family.

[8] Ibid., p. 4.
[9] A. Zelenetskii, "Nuzhna li Registratsiia Braka," *ESIu*, 24–25 (1922): 9–10.

Throughout 1922 and 1923, the debate on the 1918 Code expanded and intensified. The jurist I. Slavin strongly defended Zelenetskii, asserting that "the current legislation on marriage and the family" had "come to an impasse." The legislation was entangled in contradictions that could only be resolved by "the full freedom of marriage." The most glaring of these, in Slavin's opinion, was between the Code's construction of the family and its insistence on marriage registration. The family was constituted on the basis of biological ties: A child was entitled to support regardless of whether his or her parents were married and a married woman could confer paternity on a man who was not her husband. The rights and responsibilities binding parents and children were construed on the basis of blood, not a marital contract. Yet despite the separation of the family from marriage, the Code preserved registration. If marriage was irrelevant to the juridical construction of the family, why retain marriage registration? Moreover, the terms of the Code itself diminished the significance and scope of the marriage contract: Spouses were permitted to keep their own residences and property, and to divorce at any time. Slavin reasoned, "It would only be consistent to go further and abolish the institution of marriage, permitting all citizens to define their mutual sympathies according to their own judgment, without any sort of registration, and to preserve only the registration of birth according to the stated parent." There was no reason to preserve the tattered contractual remnants of marriage.[10] In Slavin's view, the only significant contractual right that marriage still provided was alimony. He asked rhetorically, "Is it necessary to retain such a cumbersome institution, burdened with thousands of years, entire layers of prejudices, superstitions, and psychological chains . . . simply to

[10] I. Slavin, "Brak i Sem'ia po Nashemu Zakonodatel'stvu," *ESIu,* 42 (1922): 3–5. For a discussion of the construction of the family according to biological descent, see S. Glikin, "Nezakonnye Deti," *Rabochii sud,* 6–7 (1924): 19–27. Glikin explained, "According to Soviet law, the family is constructed according to de facto descent, not by marriage. Marriage creates defined mutual relations only between spouses. Relations between parents and children, i.e., family relations, are defined by actual descent. The natural tie between a father and an illegitimate child, which is torn apart and destroyed by legal norms in bourgeois society, is restored in full measure here" (p. 26).

ensure help for the needy and disabled spouse?" His answer, not surprisingly, was a resounding "No!"[11]

Other jurists, however, troubled by the enormous social problems women faced under NEP, answered strongly in the affirmative. R. Lopato, for one, countered Slavin's arguments with the observation that the freedom of marital relations was working to women's disadvantage. His colleagues' eagerness to free both spouses from the constraints of "purely feudal marriage law," had unfortunately, "painfully affected the weaker side, particularly the rights of women." Lopato argued that men and women had very different social roles, and that women were still not equal, independent individuals. Work and marriage had different meanings for men and women, and legal rights alone could not redress the longstanding imbalance of power between the sexes. True equality would be years in the making. Lopato explained, "In spite of equal political rights, women have always been, and for a long time will be, weaker than men in the life struggle. Marriage has greater meaning for them than for men, because it completely destroys their former lives." The urban woman usually gave up her trade or occupation when she married, and the rural woman left her family to enter a new household. In both cases, the woman entered new relationships of dependency. Lopato continued, "For the man it is quite different. Not only does he not throw away his occupation, but under the pressure of new demands, he redoubles his energy." As a result, Lopato argued, women always suffered most from divorce. A woman without ties to family or occupation was left defenseless. Lopato noted the common phenomenon whereby many women, "at the present difficult time, unable to find work, often take the only steady path open to them – prostitution." Lopato recommended that the state levy a monetary penalty on men who divorced their wives without cause, and that all needy women, not only the disabled, be entitled to alimony. He strongly hoped that such measures would discourage divorce, curtail prostitution, and grant women protection they desperately needed.[12]

Sergei I. Raevich, a young jurist who wrote several important

[11] Slavin, p. 4.
[12] R. Lopato, "Odin iz Voprosov Brachnogo Prava," *ESIu*, 4–5 (1923): 94–95.

books on civil, international, and patent law in the 1920s, invoked the exchange relations of NEP to demand "strong measures" and "firmer limits." In Raevich's opinion, the main reason to change the 1918 Code was "to protect the interests of the weaker sections of the population." During the civil war, Raevich explained, the state had fed and cared for thousands of children. There had been few wage differentials, and thus, more equality between men and women in regard to marriage and divorce. But NEP had brought greater inequality and the new social conditions had hurt the position of women.[13]

Raevich proposed several specific changes in the 1918 Code that would help "the weaker side," "without violating the freedom to contract and dissolve marriage." To prevent men from marrying over and over again, he suggested that every citizen carry a document noting their current marital status as well as the number of times he or she had been divorced. Although there would be no legal restrictions on the number of permissible marriages or divorces, each person's marital history would be made available to their intended spouse, and a woman could discover how many former wives her fiance already had. (This suggestion would be adopted in 1936 in the shift toward a more conservative approach to the family.) Raevich also proposed that spouses have more rather than fewer responsibilities to each other. Arguing against increasing independence and autonomy within marriage, he held that unemployed, as well as needy and disabled, women have the right to alimony. "Finding work is not easy for anyone now," he explained. "Women in particular, and divorced women even more, do not have any income, although they are not disabled. This provision, which actually deprives women of alimony, is very cruel." In the interests of women and children, he also recommended a reevaluation of the Code's prohibitions on joint marital property and adoption.[14]

Raevich, Zelenetskii, Prigradov-Kudrin, Slavin, and Lopato all expressed positions and concerns in 1922 and 1923 that foreshadowed the more far-ranging debates over the Family Code in 1925–1926. Zelenetskii and Slavin, optimistic about the growth of new social relations and eager to advance the socialist experi-

[13] S. I. Raevich, "Brachnoe, Semeinoe i Opekunskoe Pravo v Usloviiakh NEPa," *Vlast' Sovetov*, 3 (1923): 43–44.
[14] Ibid., pp. 45, 49.

ment, called for the abolition of marriage and the creation of new forms of love and family. Advocating the abolition of law, they impatiently awaited the time when the state would have no right to interfere in the private lives of its citizens. Prigradov-Kudrin, Lopato, and Raevich, representing the majority of jurists, were more cautious in their assessment of the transition period. Prigradov-Kudrin worried about the influence of the church and appreciated the need to combat old customs with transitional measures. Raevich and Lopato were concerned by women's economic dependency and vulnerability. All three recognized that freedom was not merely a matter of law, or more precisely, the abolition of law. They justified the continuing need for law by women's lingering need for protection.

Court practice

As the libertarian jurists challenged the validity of the 1918 Code in print, judges in courtrooms around the country quietly revised the Code in their daily practice. The conflicts between law and life were clearest in the courtroom, where judges witnessed a troubling procession of personal tragedies created by poverty and social instability. Called upon to solve the problems engendered by divorce, judges began to interpret the law in new ways. A number of cases provoked far-reaching decisions by the Supreme Court that significantly altered and even contradicted provisions of the Family Code. By 1925, judges were recognizing the right to joint marital property, extending rights to de facto spouses, and devising unusual forms of alimony payments for peasants. In the absence of a standard legal definition for de facto marriage, they were devising their own criteria to determine whether a woman had lived with a man as his "wife."[15]

The first landmark decision to have a significant effect on the Family Code was handed down in 1922 by the Higher Collegium of Control (soon to become the Supreme Court).[16] Originating

[15] See comments of the judges at the meeting of the Society of Workers in Soviet Law in *Leningradskaia pravda* (December 12, 1925): 6.

[16] The Supreme Court was not established until 1923. Before 1923, civil cases were subject to review by the Higher Collegium of Control, also termed the Division of Juridical Control by Vladimir

in a common divorce case of a couple named Abukomov, the decision reversed the provision in the 1918 Code that held that marriage did not entail joint property. According to the Family Code, an urban housewife had no right to the property acquired with her husband's wages during their marriage, and the peasant wife had neither a claim on the wages of a husband working in the city nor a share in the property of his household. While the Family Code sought to guarantee the woman's independence by protecting her property from her husband, it failed to take into account that most peasant and urban women had no real property to protect. In effect, the provision cut a woman off from any claim to the property acquired with her husband's wages. In the Abukomov case, the Higher Collegium of Control ruled that a woman had the right to property acquired with her husband's wages in the course of marriage.

The Abukomovs had been married for sixteen years, during which time the husband had lived and worked in Petrograd, while his wife remained in the village with their three children. In 1920, Abukomov requested and was granted a divorce in Petrograd court. He was ordered to pay 900 rubles a month (in wildly inflated currency) for child support and alimony to his ex-wife. His wife then filed suit for a portion of the household's movable property. The court refused her, arguing that she was not entitled to the goods acquired with her husband's wages. She appealed the case, and finally the Collegium reversed the decision.[17]

The Collegium made the unprecedented judgment that housework, like wage work, constituted a form of socially necessary labor. The Commissariat of Justice proclaimed: "A lengthy, mutual marital life inevitably creates such a situation whereby an entire series of household items are acquired as a result of joint labor. Customarily, a man works to provide support for his family's existence, and the woman contributes her labor within the home, by caring for her husband, children, and others. This labor should undoubtedly be considered productive labor, creating rights to share in the fruits of this labor, i.e., the com-

Gsovski. See Gsovski, *Soviet Civil Law*, Vol. 1 (University of Michigan Law School, Ann Arbor, 1948): 262–263.
[17] "Iz Deiatel'nosti Narodnogo Komissariata Iustitsii," *ESIu*, 11–12 (1922): 12.

mon household property." The Collegium's decision in the Abukomov case gave both the peasant and the urban wife a share in the property acquired in the course of marriage even if they had never earned a kopeck.[18]

The Collegium reasoned that a woman's right to property was based on her labor in the household, not her rights as a spouse. It followed that a housewife who hired servants to do her housework did not deserve a property settlement, and indeed when a recently divorced woman brought suit in Leningrad provincial court, she received only a small portion of the property once the court determined that she had never worked for wages and had hired servants to do the housework.[19] Yet the majority of women who came to court were not wealthy wives with servants. Most were working-class or peasant women who either worked sporadically for wages or as housewives. The ruling on the Abukomov case ensured that they would not be left destitute after a divorce.

Other decisions further revised the 1918 Code. In 1925, the Supreme Court officially sanctioned the local court practice of extending inheritance rights to the de facto wife. The case concerned two women who both claimed the right to a dead man's pension. One woman was the man's "legal" wife, although she had been separated from him for several years. The other was his de facto wife who had lived with him before his death. Both women were financially dependent on the deceased. The court decided to split the pension equally between the two women. Anxious to avoid a position that condoned bigamy, the court argued that both claims were valid because each woman was dependent on the deceased. Their respective marital positions were not relevant to the case.[20] Yet the court effectively affirmed the rights of the de facto wife by acknowledging the legitimacy of her claim. Thus by 1925, the rights of the de facto wife, unrecognized by the 1918 Code, were officially acknowledged at the highest level of the court system.

In neither the Abukomov case nor the 1925 Supreme Court decision on inheritance had the Collegium or the Court invoked

[18] Ibid.
[19] N. Toporov, "Prava Suprugov na Imushchestvo," *Rabochii sud*, 15–16 (1925): 635.
[20] "Kassatsionnaia Praktika," *Rabochii sud*, 17–18 (1925): 781–782.

marital rights to justify their rulings. In both cases the higher judicial organs refused to establish precedents concerning conjugal rights; they appealed instead to the principle of labor. Both decisions reflected the jurists' belief that the family would eventually "wither away." Loathe to strengthen the web of rights binding the marital pair, the higher court proved eager to undercut the rights entailed by marriage. In substituting the socialist principle of labor for the rights of the marriage contract, it narrowed the sphere of marital responsibilities, yet still succeeded in protecting the woman's interests.[21]

Other provisions were also superceded by practice. The 1918 Code had prohibited adoption in the expectation that the state would be able to shelter and raise the country's needy children. Yet in light of the large numbers of homeless children and the inadequacy of state resources, the prohibition quickly proved unrealistic. Officials had begun permitting adoption as early as 1922 in a desperate effort to alleviate the overcrowding in state institutions and to provide food and shelter for the *besprizorniki*. By 1925, the Commissariats of Land and Enlightenment had launched a vigorous campaign to encourage peasant families to adopt homeless children from the impoverished state homes and institutions. The Code's prohibition of adoption had clearly proved premature.[22]

Independent of higher rulings, local judges also began to ignore certain provisions and revise others. The 1918 Code had prohibited the payment of alimony or child support in a lump sum. Drawing on the court experiences of the European countries, the authors of the Code feared that poor women might be tempted to take a lump sum of money even when it was not in their long-term financial interest to do so. By including this provision, the authors of the Code tried to prevent wealthy men from taking advantage of poorer women. Yet rural judges quickly discovered that peasants found it difficult to pay regular monetary sums of alimony or child support. Judges ruling on peasant divorce began ordering lump-sum payments and even payments in kind, despite the expressed prohibition in the

---

[21] See G. Ryndziunskii, "K Proektu Kodeksa Zakonov o Brake, Sem'e i Opeke," *ESIu*, 7–8 (1924): 150, on the labor principle as a basis for recognizing de facto marriage.
[22] See Chapter 2 for details.

Code. Practice showed that the provision, initially motivated by good intentions, worked to the disadvantage of peasant women and their children.

The problems of de facto relations, *besprizornost'*, and peasant poverty thus compelled jurists, judges, and officials to interpret the 1918 Code in new ways. In their daily practice, they reinterpreted and sometimes flouted the law in order to accommodate the difficult realities of life. Their revision of the law was generally guided by a desire to offer greater protections to women and children, but their recognition of de facto relations also helped provide practical legal justification for the abolition of marriage registration.

The withering away of law

Efforts to revise the Family Code were reinforced by the prevailing juridical opinion that all branches of law would eventually wither away. Ideas about the withering away of the family found strong parallels in the political commitment to the withering away of law. The great majority of jurists shared the view that under socialism, morality and limited norms would supercede law and the state in governing social relations. A classless society would have no need of law to regulate and coerce human behavior. In the words of the jurist M. Kozlovskii, "Law is born with the division of society into classes and it dies with the death of class society."[23] The first decree on law, for example, issued in November 1917, abolished all the prerevolutionary legal institutions. At the time, Goikhbarg considered the decree part of a broader shift from legislation to administration, a transition, in his opinion, that constituted the main difference between bourgeois and proletarian methods of governance.[24] In 1922, a number of Party members argued that communists should not be encouraged to join the bar and work in the court system because their efforts would be wasted on organizations that had no future under socialism.[25] Pashukanis provided strong theoretical

[23] M. Kozlovskii, "Proletarskaia revoliutsiia i ugolovnoe pravo," *Proletarskaia revoliutsiia i pravo*, 1 (1918): 22.
[24] Goikhbarg, "Proletarskaia revoliutsiia i grazhdanskoe pravo," p. 14.
[25] Eugene Huskey, *Russian Lawyers and the Soviet State. The Origins and Development of the Soviet Bar, 1917–1939* (Princeton University Press, Princeton, N.J., 1986): 106.

justification for these beliefs and the larger withering-away doctrine. But similar ideas – about the imminent disappearance of family, law, and the state – were widely popular before he published his work in 1924.

These ideas, denounced in the 1930s as "legal nihilism," guided the Bolsheviks' approach to law in the years immediately after the Revolution. During the civil war, justice was enforced summarily, frequently at the point of a gun. Revolutionary tribunals, operating with few sanctions or guidelines, took the place of the courts.[26] Jury trials were abolished and the number of legal representatives plummetted from 13,000 in 1917 to 650 in 1921.[27] In the words of one observer, "revolutionary anarchy" reigned. "Every firm, established, regular aspect of relations that had a place prior to the revolution," he wrote, "is now replaced by free self-determination, by creative autonomous activity, and by disregard for all habits and customs, morals and rights, norms and laws, traditions and forms."[28]

Many historians view the adoption of NEP as marking a new stage in Soviet legal theory and practice. The swift, arbitrary enforcement of revolutionary justice, congruent with the exigencies of the civil war period, was replaced by the development of detailed legal codes, a hierarchical court system, a procuracy, a bar, and an organized, professionalized approach to legal training. Drawing on European and prerevolutionary models, the jurists drafted new codes on land, labor, civil, and criminal law.[29] Yet the hard distinction between the civil war and NEP, based on the degree of legislative activity, is largely belied by developments in family law and juridical ideology. Although NEP brought a resumption of law building interrupted by the civil war, it did not bring a corresponding belief in the need for strong, stable law. In the area of family law, the introduction of NEP actually stimulated a resurgence of earlier radical ideas

[26] On the struggle between "legal nihilism" and "legal revival" in the early years after the revolution, see Eugene Huskey, "From Legal Nihilism to *Pravovoe Gosudarstvo:* Soviet Legal Development, 1917–1990," in a forthcoming collection edited by Donald Barry.

[27] Huskey, *Russian Lawyers and the Soviet State*, p. 75.

[28] N. Totskii, "Pravo i revoliutsiia," *Pravo i zhizn'*, 1 (1922): 9.

[29] Harold J. Berman, *Justice in the USSR. An Interpretation of Soviet Law* (Harvard University Press, Cambridge, Mass., 1963): 33–37; John Hazard, *Communists and Their Law* (University of Chicago Press, Chicago, 1969): 108–113.

about the withering away of law and the family. While a number of jurists directed unprecedented attention to the codification of civil law, others actively agitated for the minimization and even abolition of the Family Code. Moreover, the great majority of jurists did not view the newly written codes of NEP as immutable instruments of state power, but rather as part of a "legal transfer culture" aimed at transforming Russia into "a classless society without coercion."[30]

The simultaneous impulses for both creating and eliminating law reflected the absence of a monolithic, hegemonic ideology defining the role of law in Soviet society in the early 1920s. Although jurists broadly agreed that the law would wither away, they differed widely on what function family law, and law in general, should serve. Even more fundamentally, they differed on the very meaning of law. What was law? Was it an instrument promoting and protecting the interests of whatever class happened to be in power, be it the aristocracy, bourgeoisie, or even the proletariat? Was it an evolving expression of competing class interests, reflective of popular struggles and gains? Or was law itself a product of capitalism and commodity relations? Was Soviet law socialist? If not socialist, was it proletarian? Or was it simply a legacy of the bourgeois era that was still indispensable at the present moment?

Apart from Lenin's work on the state and some general comments set down by Marx and Engels, there were few Marxist studies of law available to the Bolsheviks in 1917. In January 1921, the Orgburo (Organizational Bureau) of the Central Committee sought to remedy this gap by commissioning P. I. Stuchka, the first head of the Commissariat of Justice (1917–1918), to write a *Textbook on the Theory and Practice of Soviet Law.* Stuchka, the son of a Latvian peasant, had studied in the juridical faculty of St. Petersburg University before his arrest and exile for revolutionary activities. He joined the Bolsheviks in 1903 and helped to organize the Latvian Communist Party. Given a three-month deadline to complete his text, Stuchka retreated to his study and doggedly ploughed through volumes of "bourgeois" legal theory in an attempt to produce a comprehensive

[30] Robert Sharlet, "Stalinism and Soviet Legal Culture," in Robert Tucker, ed., *Stalinism. Essays in Historical Interpretation* (Norton, New York, 1977): 158–159.

Marxist analysis of the history and function of law. In the long, rambling critique of bourgeois jurisprudence he produced, he proposed three postulates for a Marxist approach to law. First, that law was not an eternal category, but a social phenomenon expressing the prevailing relations of production. Second, that law existed wherever society was divided into classes and one class dominated the others. And third, that law safeguarded the interests of the dominant class through the use of organized force.[31]

Stuchka's work ranged widely over history and legal philosophy, but ultimately failed to persuade his colleagues, who continued to disagree over the role of law in the transition period. Stuchka, for example, argued that among all the branches of Soviet law, only civil law expressed the bourgeois social relations that still flourished under NEP. Other branches, such as family, land, labor, and criminal law, were socialist in both form and content.[32]

Mikhail Reisner, on the other hand, a Party member and head of the Department of Legislative Plans and Codification in 1918, who had worked on the committee to draft the first Family Code, offered a different conception. He saw Soviet law as an expression of competing class interests. Influenced by the pre-revolutionary legal philosopher and Constitutional Democrat L. I. Petrazhitskii, Reisner argued that the NEP period encompassed elements of bourgeois, proletarian, and semifeudal or peasant legal systems. Although Reisner's ideas were dismissed by Marxist jurists in the late 1920s, the Land Code of 1922, with its blend of peasant custom and Soviet law, was a perfect example of his argument.[33]

---

[31] P. I. Stuchka, "The Revolutionary Part Played by Law and the State – A General Doctrine of Law," in Hugh Babb, trans., V. I. Lenin, et al., *Soviet Legal Philosophy* (Harvard University Press, Cambridge, Mass., 1951): 20, 25; and P. Stuchka, "Moi Put' i Moi Oshibki," excerpted in Zigurds L. Zile, ed., *Ideas and Forces in Soviet Legal History: Statutes, Decisions and Other Materials on the Development and Processes of Soviet Law* (College Printing and Typing, Madison, Wisc., 1967): 221.

[32] Rudolf Schlesinger, *Soviet Legal Theory. Its Background and Development* (Routledge, Kegan Paul, London, 1951): 204–205.

[33] On Reisner, see John Hazard's introduction to *Soviet Legal Philosophy*, and Mikhail Reisner, "The Theory of Petrazhitskii: Marxism and Social Ideology," in same, and Vladimir Gsovski, *Soviet Civil Law*, Vol.

The greatest contribution to the debate, however, was made by Pashukanis, whose theories about the origin and nature of the law had a powerful impact not only on Soviet jurisprudence but on the international academic community as well. Pashukanis first presented his ideas in a modest monograph, *Obshchaia teoriia prava i marksizm* (A General Theory of Law and Marxism), published in 1924. By 1929, the book had been republished three times in Russian and translated into German and Italian. Quickly acclaimed by Soviet jurists and philosophers, it catapulted Pashukanis into a leading position in juridical circles. As the originator of what came to be known as the "commodity exchange school," Pashukanis argued that the essence of law lay "in the conception of contract."[34] Law first developed as a means of regulating the market and commodity exchange under capitalism. Not just civil law, but all law – family, criminal, labor – was based on a contractual model that originated in barter and trade in the cities and reached its apogee under capitalism.

Pashukanis rejected the idea, put forward by Stuchka in his textbook, that state coercion was the defining feature of law. Law was not simply a superstructural expression of ruling class power, but itself the product of commodity exchange relations. All societies, regardless of their mode of production, had rules and norms, but not all rules or norms were law. Pashukanis was the first to analyze not simply the content of law, but "the legal form itself." Opposing the idea that law was capable of expressing the interests of any class, Pashukanis believed that "proletarian law" or "socialist law" was an oxymoron. Since law was essentially the product of market relations, and since the market would not exist under socialism, there could be no such thing as "socialist law." Soviet law under NEP was unequivocally "bourgeois law": It existed to regulate the free-market features of

1 (University of Michigan Law School, Ann Arbor, 1948): 166–167. A. Ia. Vyshinskii denounced Reisner, along with many of his critics from the late 1920s, in his *The Law of the Soviet State* (Macmillan, New York, 1948): 58.

34 Evgeny B. Pashukanis, *Law and Marxism: A General Theory* (Pluto, Worcester, 1989): 80–82, ch. 3–4; Eugene Kamenka, Alice Erh-soon Tay, "The Life and Afterlife of a Bolshevik Jurist," *Problems of Communism* (January-February 1970): 76.

NEP. With the development of socialism, it would eventually "wither away."[35]

By the late 1920s Pashukanis's commodity exchange school had come to dominate Soviet jurisprudence. It gave new meaning to the libertarian critique of marriage registration and family law, significantly influencing the final draft of the Family Code. Pashukanis and his adherents aimed to replace the existing bourgeois legal culture of NEP and hasten the process of the withering away of the law. In the words of one legal historian, they sought to prune "the bourgeois thicket" of laws so that law itself would become increasingly superfluous. They attempted to replace the NEP codes "with shorter, simpler models which would compress (and hence eliminate) the finer distinctions of bourgeois justice."[36] By replacing the more elaborate Family Code with an abbreviated and simpler version, jurists followed Pashukanis's injunction to eliminate "bourgeois" law.

Changing the 1918 code: The first draft

Between 1923 and 1925, the jurists in the Commissariat of Justice worked out three drafts of a new Family Code, each diverging more sharply from the 1918 Code than its predecessor. Each successive version was shorter and simpler, and each further undermined the significance of registered marriage. The final draft clearly showed the influence of both the libertarian jurists who sought to hasten the withering away of the family and the adherents of the commodity exchange school who sought to hasten the withering away of the law.

In July 1923, Iury Larin, an economist and Party member, formally proposed to the VTsIK that certain changes be made in the 1918 Code. "This is necessary," he explained, "because the current laws in this area abound in survivals of an older period

[35] See Chris Arthur's introduction in Pashukanis, pp. 34, 18–19; and Robert Sharlet, "Pashukanis and the Rise of Soviet Marxist Jurisprudence, 1924–1930," *Soviet Union*, I, 2 (1974): 103–121, for a detailed discussion of the commodity exchange school and Pashukanis's career and ideas.

[36] Sharlet, "Stalinism and Soviet Legal Culture," p. 161.

and are completely unsuitable for our epoch." Although Larin
never specified which survivals he had in mind, he thoroughly
amused his fellow delegates by deriding the more idealistic and
impractical features of the Code. Larin's description of the provision permitting a married woman to name a man other than
her husband as the father of her child provoked a hearty round
of ribald laughter. Nikolai V. Krylenko, the deputy People's
Commissar of Justice and one of Pashukanis's most influential
supporters, stiffly objected to Larin's flippancy, but agreed that
the Code should be reviewed. The jurist Iakov Brandenburgskii
also agreed, suggesting that Larin bring his recommendations to
the Commissariat of Justice, which would establish a committee
to reconsider the Code.[37] Following the VTsIK's suggestion, the
Commissariat of Justice quickly set up a committee, chaired by
Goikhbarg, to revise the 1918 Code. Taking into account current
court practice, the conditions of NEP, and the criticisms of the
1918 Code, the committee made a number of revisions and
quickly drafted a new version.

The new draft streamlined the older Code, thereby undermining the significance of several important original provisions.
It differed from the Code in eight basic ways. First, the 1918
Code had heavily stressed the need for civil marriage. The new
draft reduced the Code's lengthy introductory provision on marriage to a simple sentence: "Only marriage registered according
to the established legal order is valid." Second, the 1918 Code
had made no mention of de facto relations. Only spouses in a
registered marriage were entitled to the rights and responsibilities of marriage. The draft, however, invited spouses in a de
facto relationship to register their union at any time; their marriage would be considered retroactively valid for as long as their
union had existed. Third, the 1918 Code had stipulated that
both spouses retained the right to their own property. The draft
retained this provision, but added joint rights for property acquired in the course of marriage. Moreover, it extended the
right of joint property to partners in de facto unions. Fourth, the
1918 Code had entitled the needy, disabled spouse to an unlimited term of alimony. The draft expanded this provision to in-

---

[37] *II Sessiia Vserossiiskogo Tsentral'nogo Ispolnitel'nogo Komiteta, X sozyva.
Biulleten' VTsIKa*, 7 (Moscow, 1923): 253–255.

clude the ablebodied, unemployed. It did not, however, extend alimony rights to the de facto spouse. Fifth, the Code had permitted spouses three choices for a last name (the man's name, the woman's name, or a jointly chosen last name) but had specified that the husband and wife must share a common name. The draft permitted the spouses to take the name of the man, the woman, or to retain their own premarital last names. Sixth, the 1918 Code had stipulated that a pregnant woman must register a paternity claim no later than three months prior to the birth of her child. The draft placed no time limit on paternity declarations. Seventh, the Code had prohibited a lump-sum payment in lieu of regular alimony payments. The draft, in deference to the problems the peasants faced, omitted any instruction on the method of payment. Finally, the 1918 Code had expressly forbidden adoption, but the draft did not mention the practice.[38]

Most jurists appeared to favor the changes in the draft, although both Grigorii D. Ryndziunskii, a jurist who wrote on women's and children's rights and on land and civil law, and Raevich, a strong adherent of Pashukanis's ideas, offered numerous suggestions for improvement. Both jurists noted that the provision permitting partners to formalize de facto unions at any time made no sense. The length of a union had no bearing on property, alimony, or inheritance rights, and the provision did nothing to protect the rights of one partner if the other refused to register.[39] Ryndziunskii aptly observed that people who mutually agreed to register their unions had no need for legal protection. Partners in unregistered marriages needed protection precisely at the point when the union dissolved. The provision offered the stable partners an opportunity to register (which they did not need), and it offered the abandoned and impoverished partner nothing. Ryndziunskii argued that the law

---

[38] "Iz Deiatel'nosti Narkomiusta: Proekt Kodeksa Zakonov o Brake, Sem'e i Opeke," *ESIu*, 36 (1923): 827–828; Ibid., 37 (1923): 851–852; Ibid., 49 (1923): 1142–1143; "Iz Deiatel'nosti Narkomiusta. Prilozhenie k Kodeksu Zakonov o Brake, Sem'e i Opeke," *ESIu*, 10 (1924): 235; Ibid., 14 (1924): 330–332.

[39] G. Ryndziunskii, "K Proekta Kodeksa Zakonov o Brake, Sem'e i Opeke," *ESIu*, 7–8 (1924): 150–151; S. Raevich, "Po Povodu Proektu Kodeksa Zakonov o Brake i Sem'e," *Vlast' Sovetov*, 3–4 (1924): 26.

should simply extend all rights of registered marriage to de facto unions. He also advised that the right to alimony be limited to a term of six months.[40]

Raevich agreed that alimony rights should be extended to the de facto spouse. Anything less was "unacceptable." He pointed out that de facto marriage often resulted in class as well as gender exploitation. NEPmen and well-off officials frequently entered liaisons with poor girls, but avoided marriage because of the girls' low social status. Rich men may have exploited poor women in this way for centuries, but Soviet law should not allow it to continue. Men should be forced to pay alimony to the women they abandoned regardless of whether they were married to them.[41]

Ryndziunskii pointed to other problems. The draft established that property earned in the course of marriage belonged to both spouses, while property acquired before marriage remained private. Yet this article contradicted the Land Code, which held that a woman had a share in all the property of the *dvor,* acquired both before and after marriage. Noting that peasants constituted the majority of the population, he exclaimed in disbelief, "How can there be no community of property between peasant spouses?"

But the greatest drawback to the draft, in Ryndziunskii's opinion, was that it failed to define de facto marriage. By what criteria did an unregistered union constitute "a marriage?" If the draft was to extend rights to partners in de facto unions, it had to provide a definition that judges could use to render their decisions. Ryndziunskii supported recognition of de facto marriage, but he foresaw numerous complications. What would happen if a man had both a registered and a de facto wife? What if an estranged registered wife demanded support from a husband who had entered a new de facto marriage? The jurist understood that the legal recognition of de facto marriage opened a Pandora's box of problems concerning polygamy, property, and support.[42]

[40] Ryndziunskii, "K Proektu Zakonov o Brake, Sem'e i Opeke," *ESIu,* 7–8 (1924): 151.
[41] Raevich, "Po Povodu Proektu Kodeksa Zakonov o Brake i Sem'e," p. 28.
[42] Ryndziunskii, "K Proektu Zakonov o Brake, Sem'e i Opeke," *ESIu,* 7–8 (1924): 153–154.

Ryndziunskii also questioned the practice of collective paternity. Both the 1918 Code and the draft stipulated that if an unmarried woman was involved with several men at the time of conception, all the men would collectively bear paternal responsibility for the child. Soviet citizens jokingly referred to this practice as a "cooperative of fathers." Emerging directly from the Code's construction of the family as a biological unit, the provision was one of the more unusual features of Soviet family law. Ryndziunskii questioned whether a "cooperative of fathers" could be realistically responsible for fulfilling a paternal role. His question drew attention to the problems inherent in a practice that expected a group of men not only to make regular support payments, but to make important parental decisions collectively, maintain bonds with the mother, and take an active role in raising the child.[43]

The second draft

In December 1924, the Commissariat of Justice published a second, revised draft of the Code, which took Ryndziunskii's and Raevich's suggestions into account. The second draft, even shorter than the first, went still farther in extending rights to de facto spouses and in diminishing the significance of registration. In place of the provision establishing the validity of civil marriage, the second draft offered the following: "Registration of marriage is established with the aim of easing the protection of personal and property rights, and in the interests of spouses and children." Whereas both the 1918 Code and the first draft had defined marriage as synonymous with the act of civil registration, the second draft separated the concepts. It reduced civil marriage to nothing more than a useful means of protecting property rights in the event of marital breakup. The second draft also extended alimony rights to the disabled or unemployed de facto spouse, although a person who was already married and living with his or her registered spouse was not required to pay alimony to a de facto partner. Thus a man who lived with his wife in a registered marriage was exempt from

[43] Ryndziunskii, "K Proektu Zakonov o Brake, Sem'e i Opeke," *ESIu*, 19–20 (1924): 445.

paying alimony to his mistress even if he had lived with her too. The second draft also expressly permitted adoption. All other provisions remained the same.[44]

Iakov Brandenburgskii, a Bolshevik since 1903, graduate of the Sorbonne's juridical faculty, and a member of the Kollegiia of the People's Commissariat of Justice, enthusiastically endorsed the new plan. He believed that civil marriage was still necessary to counteract the church's influence in the more backward sections of the population. He wrote contemptuously, "The average philistine still faces the dilemma: to go to church or to leave this day (marriage) unmarked in any way, and due to the strength of his prejudices, he will prefer the former. Yet if he has the opportunity to officially register in ZAGS, it will be easier to wean him from the harmful habit of qualifying his marriage with the blessing of heaven." Yet despite the retention of civil marriage for "the average philistine," Brandenburgskii was gratified by the custom's dwindling importance. He warned that undue emphasis on the official act of registration would ultimately mislead the population, hinder the development of new views, and retard "the transition to a higher form of completely free marital union." He also opposed the idea of collective paternity on the grounds that it created too many problems for the child.[45]

Like Brandenburgskii, Professor V. Verkhovskii believed in "the full freedom of marital relations," with no bars to divorce. But unlike Brandenburgskii, he was highly critical of both drafts of the Code. Arguing vigorously in favor of defining de facto marriage, he noted that the draft created the possibility of polygamy by failing to establish a procedure for officially ending a de facto marriage. Moreover, he contended that the material conditions for full freedom of marital relations did not yet exist. Economic independence for women, state care for children, pregnancy insurance for all women, and the elimination of housework were all prerequisites for "free union;" and these basic requirements for freedom existed in neither the towns nor the countryside. Verkhovskii wrote, "It is clear that we are still far from eliminating the household, and inevitably, this compli-

---

[44] "Iz Deiatel'nosti Narkomiusta. Proekt Kodeksa Zakonov o Brake, Sem'e i Opeke," *ESIu*, 48 (1924): 1160–1163.

[45] Iakov Brandenburgskii, "Neskol'ko Slov o Brake i Sem'e," *ESIu*, 37 (1924): 871–872.

cates property relations between spouses." Given the shortcomings of the moment, the line between de facto and registered marriage could not yet be dissolved.[46]

A third draft: The Commissariat of Internal Affairs

Verkhovskii drew his reasoning from still another draft of the Code that had been worked out by the Commissariat of Internal Affairs (NKVD) with the help of the Commissariat of Enlightenment in 1924. The NKVD, dissatisfied with the ambiguities of the first draft prepared by the Commissariat of Justice, created its own version of the Code. In contrast to the brief provision on marriage that introduced the two drafts prepared by the Commissariat of Justice, the NKVD draft opened with a lengthy exposition of the purposes of Soviet family law. The NKVD draft explained that "revolutionary life" was built on "the full freedom of marital relations," "the total liberation of the woman from the power of her husband through her economic independence," "the blood tie as the basis of the family," full protection of needy spouses, mothers, and children, and equal property rights for men and women.[47]

Most important, the NKVD draft offered a definition of marriage apart from the act of civil registration. "Marriage," it stated, "is an unlimited term of voluntary cohabitation, entailing all juridical consequences, and based on the free contract of the man and the woman whereby they acknowledge each other as spouses." A marriage could be concluded orally or in writing, but in both cases, the mutual, voluntary consent of the contracting parties was essential. A casual sexual relationship in which the lovers did not regard each other as spouses was not a marriage. In order to be "married," a man and woman had to appear "before the state, Soviet society, and citizens as husband and wife." To enter a marriage, a man and woman had to meet four conditions: both parties had to be old enough to marry (16 for women, 18 for men); they had to be mentally healthy; they could not be direct relations (brothers and sisters, parents and

[46] V. Verkhovskii, *Novye formy braka i sem'i* (Leningrad, 1925): 31–33.
[47] Ibid., p. 43. For a complete text of the NKVD draft, see Verkhovskii, pp. 43–50.

children); and neither could be party to another marriage contract.[48] Apart from these restrictions, the NKVD definition was premised on the spouses' mutual, voluntary recognition of a marital state. Conceiving "marriage" as based on freely proferred, mutual affection, the definition clearly drew on the socialist ideal of "free union."

The NKVD version, like both Commissariat of Justice drafts, established spousal rights to property earned in the course of marriage and extended alimony rights to the needy, unemployed spouse. Although the NKVD draft did not explicitly extend the rights and responsibilities of registered marriage to de facto unions, its definition of "marriage" permitted recognition of the de facto union in court. And like the second draft prepared by the Commissariat of Justice, it permitted the practice of adoption.[49]

The significance of the NKVD draft lay in its attempt to provide a working definition of marriage apart from the act of civil registration. This effort distinguished it from both the 1918 Code and the drafts of the Commissariat of Justice. Yet the NKVD's attempt to dispel the ambiguity surrounding de facto marriage by providing a definition raised a storm of criticism and revealed how little agreement existed as to what actually constituted a "marriage."

Krylenko, the deputy People's Commissar of Justice and Assistant Procurator of the RSFSR, blasted the NKVD definition as a "miserable formula" that "said nothing." The main problem, in his view, was that the definition revolved around the partners' voluntary recognition of each other as spouses. The definition was, therefore, a tautology: Marriage was defined as the mutual recognition of "marriage." The definition was strictly subjective, lacking any objective criteria for the courts to use in determining whether or not a marriage existed. Marriage, according to the NKVD, was a *folie à deux*, a shared fantasy existing solely in the minds of the participants. But more important, the definition excluded the very group that showed up most often in court: women in de facto marriages whose partners refused to acknowledge them as spouses. If the relationship was stable, and both partners were content, they had no reason to go to court.

[48] Ibid., p. 43.   [49] Ibid., pp. 46, 44.

The law had no need to define their relationship. By the time a judge had to determine whether a de facto marriage existed, the man had in most cases already abandoned the woman and denied his tie with her. Krylenko wrote, "The main question does not concern cases where people recognize each other as spouses. Then there is no argument. Arguments emerge when there is no agreement and the court must decide the question of whether there is a marriage, in the absence of an agreement between the spouses." Women abandoned by their de facto spouses were excluded from receiving alimony by the NKVD definition, unless their partners voluntarily agreed to recognize the relationship. And it was hardly in a man's self-interest to acknowledge his former girlfriend as his wife and then to pay her part of his salary every month. The NKVD draft revealed many of the difficulties involved in defining de facto relations.[50]

Krylenko observed that many jurists had tried, unsuccessfully, to define marriage. What was the difference between marriage and a casual affair? Did the difference lie in the duration of the tie, in the degree of commitment, in a shared economy, or in joint cohabitation? What were the defining features of a "marriage"? Some people were married, but lived apart. Others were unmarried but lived together. Some pooled their resources, others kept them separate. The degree of variation in human relations made it almost impossible to quantify the illusive, shifting factors that ultimately created a marriage.

The final draft

By 1925, the Commissariat of Justice had redrafted its own third version of the Code, the fourth altogether. The final draft was submitted to both the Council of People's Commissars (Sovnarkom) and little Sovnarkom. It was approved for submission to the VTsIK in October 1925. The new draft resembled its predecessors, although it retained a section on the rights and responsibilities of marriage that the authors of the previous drafts had rejected. The third draft granted even greater rights

[50] N. V. Krylenko, "Proekt o Brake i Sem'e," in D. I. Kurskii, ed., *Sbornik statei i materialov po brachnomu i semeinomu pravu* (Moscow, 1926): 64.

to de facto unions than had the first two, requiring a de facto partner to pay alimony even if he or she was still involved in a registered marriage. The 1925 draft also simplified the divorce procedure by transferring contested divorces from the court to ZAGS, where such matters would be processed administratively by simply filling out a form. The draft extended the period in which a man could protest a paternity declaration from two weeks to one month. And it abolished the practice of collective paternity, charging the judge with choosing one man as the father of the child. Last, both the 1918 Code and the Commissariat of Justice's first two drafts had stipulated that family members could turn to each other for support if necessary. The Code and the first two drafts construed the family on a wide basis, encompassing all relations in direct ascending and descending lines (children, parents, grandparents), as well as brothers and sisters. In a further effort to undermine the importance of the family unit, the 1925 draft narrowed the legal definition of the family to include parents and children only, thus replacing the larger, extended family with the smaller nuclear unit in terms of legally enforceable obligations and responsibilities.[51]

By 1925, four versions of a new Family Code had been published, discussed, and criticized.[52] With each draft, the jurists moved closer to the goal of "free union." Whittling away at both the law and the family, the final draft encouraged Soviet citizens to think of marriage registration as no more than a means of proof that a marriage actually existed. It retained civil marriage, but extended every significant right of marriage to people in de facto unions. By transferring contested divorces from the courts to the registry offices, the draft removed the law's last vestige of authority over the dissolution of marriage, thereby circumscribing both the power of the law and the strength of the marital union. And it further undermined the institution of the family by reducing the legal obligations of its members. The draft

---

[51] For the complete text of the 1925 draft, see "Kodeks Zakonov o Brake, Sem'e i Opeke," in *Sbornik statei i materialov po brachnomu i semeinomu pravu*, pp. 205–223.

[52] In *U istokov Sovetskoi demografii* (Moscow, Mysl', 1987): 79, V. Z. Drob-izhev mentions that according to archival sources, the Zhenotdel also worked out a version of the Family Code in March 1925 that was circulated for discussion.

shortened the 1918 Code considerably; Pashukanis had urged jurists to prune "the bourgeois thicket," and indeed entire sections were eliminated.[53]

At the same time, each successive draft revealed a greater awareness of the social problems of NEP. The final draft of the Code offered protection to women in de facto marriages, gave the housewife a right to property acquired with her husband's wages, extended alimony rights to the unemployed, and legalized adoption, all provisions designed to shield women and children from the negative effects of NEP. The jurists' response to the problems of *besprizornost'*, family instability, and women's vulnerability was perfectly crafted to remedy these social ills without betraying their commitment to the goal of free union. The draft attempted to "protect the weak and vulnerable," without diminishing, in Raevich's words, the full "freedom to contract and dissolve marriage."[54] The final version of the Code was a product of two groups: those who hoped to free marriage of all constraints and those who sought to protect women. By offering protection to women while promoting the option of free union, the recognition of de facto marriage appeared the ideal compromise. The 1925 draft of the new Family Code, presented for nationwide debate, reflected the confidence of both groups that it was possible to solve social problems without resurrecting traditional family bonds.

[53] Sharlet, "Stalinism and Soviet Legal Culture," p. 161.
[54] S. I. Raevich, "Brachnoe, semeinoe i opekunskoe pravo v usloviiakh NEPa," *Vlast' Sovetov*, p. 44.

6

Sexual freedom or social chaos: The debate on the 1926 Code

Aron Sol'ts: It seems to me that the draft suggested by the Commissariat of Justice is only a formal "step forward." It has nothing in common with the real steps forward we must take in the areas of culture, life, and development.

Nikolai Krylenko: So, Comrade Sol'ts wants what we now already have. All these countless *babi* with children, wives suing communists, and communists running from their wives . . . in one word, all those who protest to him about the current situation. Are they really protesting against the draft? What does Comrade Sol'ts want to change? The draft, which is not yet in effect, or the current law?

Sol'ts: The draft and the current law!

Krylenko: How do you want to change it? Tell us, Comrade Sol'ts, do you want to provide a legal basis for only the first marriage, to establish the right to enter marriage only once? Is that what you want? Is this so, or not so?

Sol'ts: Not so.

Krylenko: No, it is so. If we are to call ourselves Marxists, we must affirm that we cannot struggle with a definite phenomenon of life by punitive norms.

Sol'ts: I didn't suggest this.

Krylenko: Then tell us concretely, what are you suggesting?[1]

By October 1925, the final draft of the new Family Code was affirmed by Sovnarkom (Council of People's Commissars) and submitted to the Central Executive Committee (VTsIK) for ratification. Jurists had taken two years to agree on an acceptable draft, discarding at least three previous versions in an attempt to meet various needs and interests. Yet the final draft, introduced to the 434 delegates to the VTsIK, continued to provoke de-

[1] Ia. Brandenburgskii, A. Sol'ts, N. Krylenko, S. Prushitskii, *Sem'ia i novyi byt: spory o proekte novogo kodeksa zakonov o sem'e i brake* (Moscow, Leningrad, 1926): 21–23.

bate.[2] After several days of heated discussion, the delegates could not even agree whether to put it to a vote. The radical proponents of the Code were eager to vote. Dmitri Kurskii, an old Bolshevik who had helped set up the people's courts in 1918 and currently served as People's Commissar of Justice, pointed out that there had been ample discussion in the regional and district executive committees of the soviets and in the press.[3] But the conservative delegates insisted on additional discussion: The district (*uezd* and *volost'*) soviets, women's organizations, and the local newspapers had not yet discussed it. Both Mikhail Kalinin, a Politburo member and president of the VTsIK, and David Riazanov, Party member and director of the Marx-Engels Institute, proposed to remand the Code to the local level in the hope that its more radical provisions would be tempered by the conservatism of the peasantry. Kalinin cloaked his aim in an appeal to democracy: "Our main task lies in drawing the workers and peasants to participate in the legislative process."[4] Iury Larin, the Party member who had initiated the revisions of the Family Code in 1923 and an advocate of the final draft, sharply responded to its conservative critics: "If we make a decision on the Code solely on the basis of a majority vote in the villages, in the *skhod*, then we are taking the leadership of our country away from the Party, away from the vanguard, and turning it over to the most backward, long-bearded village elders, to whom Comrade Riazanov seems to belong."[5]

Many delegates to the 1925 VTsIK shared Kalinin's reservations. Of the main speakers, approximately 60 percent opposed the Code on moral grounds; and of this group, 35 percent identified their interests specifically with the peasantry. Only 20 percent of the speakers supported the draft without reservations,

[2] According to the *Stenograficheskii otchet zasedaniia 2 sessii Vserossiiskogo Tsentral'nogo Ispolnitel'nogo Komiteta 12 sozyva. 20 oktiabria 1925 goda* (Moscow, 1925): 540, the TsIK of the RSFSR contained 300 members and 134 candidate members. Of its members, 26% did not belong to the Party; and of the non-Party members, 23% were factory workers and 53% were peasants.

[3] "Stenograficheskii Otchet 2 Sessii Vserossiiskogo Tsentral'nogo Ispolnitel'nogo Komiteta 12 Sozyva. 20 oktiabria 1925 goda," in *Sbornik statei i materialov po brachnomu i semeinomu pravu* (Moscow, 1926): 188. Hereafter cited respectively as *1925 VTsIK* and *Sbornik*.

[4] Ibid., p. 191.   [5] Ibid., p. 192.

and these were mainly the jurists who had helped to author it.[6]
Both Kalinin and Larin shared the opinion that the population,
and the peasantry in particular, was not ready to accept the
Code. Such was Kalinin's hope and Larin's fear.

After considerable debate, the VTsIK decided to remand the
Code for further discussion. Between October 1925 and November 1926, when it was discussed again and finally ratified by the
VTsIK, the Code was widely debated in the press and local
organizations. Peasants, workers, jurists, Party organizers, sociologists, women, and young people met in the towns and in the
country, in factories, schools, and six thousand village meetings,
to debate the very meaning and purpose of marriage. In the
words of Kurskii: "Reports, disputes and articles on marriage
and family law have become a universal phenomenon."[7] Peasants and women boldly testified about their experiences; snide
jokes and sexual banter competed with scholarly legal polemics
on the meaning of marriage. The discussion was open and
forthright, marked by little ideological obeisance. The participants in the debate did not see themselves as members of self-
constituted groups, advocating clearly delineated positions.
Although the Commissariats of Justice, Land, and Internal Affairs, and Sovnarkom took positions on certain provisions of the
Code, it was not unusual for members of the same Commissariat
to advocate opposing positions in accordance with their personal
opinions.

The draft Code's proposal to provide the same legal rights to
people living together in de facto unions as to those in registered
marriages provoked the greatest controversy. De facto marriage
was happily hailed by some as the wave of the socialist future, a
hopeful portent of a new age when contractual formalities
would disappear and people would form social ties free from the
constraints of poverty and "bourgeois hypocrisy." Iakov Brandenburgskii, the long-time Party member, dean of the juridical
faculty of Moscow University, and an active proponent of the
new Code, expressed this view at a Zhenotdel meeting in Febru-

---

[6] These percentages were arrived at by tabulating the number of
speakers and their positions according to *1925 VTsIK*.

[7] D. I. Kurskii, "Predislovie," in Ia. Brandenburgskii, A. Sol'ts, N. Krylenko, S. Prushitskii, *Sem'ia i novyi byt: spory o proekte novogo kodeksa
zakonov o sem'e i brake*, p. 3.

ary 1926. He proudly told the assembled organizers that "the many cases of de facto marriage reveal a new, revolutionary form of life in the towns and in the country. These relations, developing in the heart of the working masses, have now found a careful and timely reflection in the law." Brandenburgskii optimistically predicted, "We should know where we are going, and we are going toward marriage without registration – this is a fact."[8]

Yet others argued that de facto marriage was not a sign of the socialist future, but rather of the chaos, disruption, and dislocation of a war-ravaged society. Ivan Stepanov, Party member and editor of *Izvestiia* and *Leningradskaia Pravda*, described Soviet social life in bitter terms: "We thought we could create institutions through which the development of harmonious, beautiful, and communist forms of marriage would be possible. But what has happened? Women remained chained to the ruined family hearth, and men, whistling gaily, walk out leaving women with the children."[9] The authors of the draft had hoped to craft a provision that would satisfy the libertarian critics of marriage as well as the defender's of women's interests, but instead, the recognition of de facto marriage incited an outpouring of opinions concerning the troubled status of women, marriage, and the family after almost a decade of Soviet rule.[10]

[8] Ia. N. Brandenburgskii, *Brak i sem'ia* (Moscow, 1926): 6, 23.
[9] I. Stepanov, "Problema Pola," in E. Iaroslavskii, *Voprosy zhizni i bor'by* (Moscow, Leningrad, 1924): 205.
[10] Some historians have viewed the 1926 Code as a positive move in the direction of sexual freedom, the liberation of women, and the transformation of the family. See Harold Berman, "Soviet Family Law in the Light of Russian History and Marxist Theory," *Yale Law Journal*, 56, no. 1 (1946): 25–57; Kent Geiger, *The Family in Soviet Russia* (Harvard University Press, Cambridge, Mass., 1968); John Hazard, *Law and Social Change in the USSR* (Carswell, Toronto, 1953); Alex Inkeles, *Social Change in Soviet Russia* (Harvard University Press, Cambridge, Mass., 1968); Nicholas Timasheff, *The Great Retreat* (E. P. Dutton, New York, 1946); Maurice Hindus, *House Without a Roof* (Doubleday, New York, 1961). According to this view, the changes in marriage and family law in 1936 represented a "sensational somersault," Hindus, p. 139. Under Stalin, "controversies over the role of women under socialism came to an end." See Gail Lapidus, *Women in Soviet Society. Equality, Development, and Social Change* (University of California Press, Berkeley, 1978): 94. Excep-

The politics of Left and Right

Throughout the year that the Code was being discussed, the leaders of the Party were engaged in a bitter struggle for power. The triumvirate of Stalin, Zinoviev, and Kamenev had successfully silenced Trotsky and the left opposition by January 1925, but with Trotsky gone, the unity of the triumvirate crumbled. The rift between Zinoviev and Kamenev, on the one hand, and Stalin on the other revived debate over policy toward agriculture and industrialization. Stalin, Bukharin, and the majority-wing of the Party defended the continuation of NEP, arguing in favor of greater concessions to the peasantry and a gradual development of industry on the basis of an expanding peasant market. The Left, increasingly critical of a policy that promoted petty capitalism in the countryside, advocated a quicker tempo of industrialization based on the increased extraction and appropriation of peasant surplus. The debate intensified throughout the year as Zinoviev and Kamenev reconciled with Trotsky to create a new, united opposition.

Even though a large majority of delegates to the 1925 and 1926 VTsIKs were Party members, the debate over the draft Code was not defined by the struggle for power going on at the upper levels of the Party. Neither the left opposition nor the majority wing of the Party held a defined position on the new Code. Yet references to the debate over agriculture surfaced repeatedly in the discussion of the impact of the Family Code on the peasantry. Several opponents of the draft, contending that frequent divorce, alimony, and de facto marriage were economically harmful to the *dvor*, invoked the ideas of Bukharin and the ideology of NEP in their critique of family policy.

Kalinin, for example, known for his "pro *muzhik*" (pro peasant) position on agrarian policy," voiced the opinion that the

tions to this view are provided by Beatrice Farnsworth, "Bolshevik Alternatives and the Soviet Family: The 1926 Marriage Law Debate," in D. Atkinson, A. Dallin, G. Lapidus, eds., *Women in Russia* (Sussex, 1978); and John Quigley, "The 1926 Soviet Family Code: Retreat from Free Love," *Soviet Union*, 6, pt. 2 (1979): 166–74. In a careful legal analysis, Quigley argues that the Code represented a temporary retreat from the socialist position on the family and that "the dominant thinking behind the 1926 Code was conservative." (p. 173.)

Code was "too bold."[11] Aleksei S. Kiselev, an Old Bolshevik, member of the Presidium of the Central Control Commission, and deputy commissar of the Workers and Peasants Inspectorate, also opposed the draft, claiming that it slighted the needs of the peasantry. In a perfect expression of Bukharin's approach to industrialization, Kiselev explained that the peasantry was the essential basis for the development of a socialist economy: "If we do not create a firm foundation for the family, if we do not create firm relationships between family members and firm guidelines in regard to the division of property, then we will weaken and shatter the economic base of our economy." Kiselev argued that the *dvor* was crucial to economic development, and while "we should not lag behind the peasant, we must consider his life and his economy."[12]

Shakhnazarov, a jurist and member of the Society for the Study of Soviet Law, noted that the state could not afford to ignore the interests of the middle peasants "and conduct an experiment with them." "In 1918 . . . a rifle was the best weapon of the revolution," he said, referring to the policy of forced grain requisitioning during the civil war. Yet "under today's conditions we build the economy on the *smychka* (alliance) with the peasants." He opposed the draft in the belief that its property provisions would lead to the weakening and eventual ruin of the peasant household.[13]

The proponents of the Code, expressing the Left's view of the peasantry's petty-bourgeois tendencies, retorted that family law should not reflect the interests of the most backward sector in Soviet society. Larin, who criticized the Party's agricultural policy for favoring the *kulak* (wealthier peasant),[14] claimed that Kalinin's suggestion to extend debate "under the slogan, 'Face to

---

[11] Isaac Deutscher, *Stalin. A Political Biography* (London, 1929): 299; 1925 VTsIK, p. 190.

[12] *III sessiia Vserossiiskogo Tsentral'nogo Ispolnitel'nogo Komiteta 12 sozyva. Stenograficheskii otchet* (Moscow, 1926): 687. Hereafter cited as *1926 VTsIK.*

[13] "Diskussiia po Povodu Proekta Kodeksa Zakonov o Brake, Sem'e i Opeke," *Rabochii sud,* 3 (1926): 231–242; *Leningradskaia pravda,* December 12, 1925: 6.

[14] E. H. Carr, *Socialism in One Country,* Vol. 1 (Macmillan, New York, 1958): 263, 270n. Isaac Deutscher, *The Prophet Unarmed* (Oxford University Press, London, 1959): 303n, notes that Larin's attitude toward the left opposition was ambiguous.

the Countryside,'" was an effort to alter the Code "in accordance with whatever suits the *kulak*."[15] Nikolai Krylenko, the senior deputy public procurator and a strong supporter of the draft, insisted that the purpose of family law was not to strengthen the peasant household. The needs of the "leading class" of the population, the working class, should determine state policy. Although peasants constituted the majority of the population and the *dvor* was a central economic unit, "It in no way follows that we should provide a legal norm in accordance with the interests of many millions of peasants." Pandering to the peasantry would only lead society backward, away from socialism. Krylenko offered a contemptuous parody of the peasant view of marriage as "a laboring union of a man and a woman, concluded for the free mutual support of the peasant household on the basis of a defined division of labor, and for the satisfaction of the sexual interests of the *khoziain* himself."[16] Although spoken half in jest, Krylenko's message was clear: Peasant social attitudes were hardly compatible with socialist ideals.

Evgeny Preobrazhenskii, the noted Party economist and left-wing spokesman for a more rapid approach to industrialization, supported the Code and shared Krylenko's disdain for concessions to the peasantry. "We cannot place our socialist legislation on par with the average peasant *dvor*," he said bluntly. Preobrazhenskii argued that Soviet family law was not responsible for the breakdown of the peasant household and the increasing number of *razdely* (household divisions). He argued that the large patriarchal household was inevitably fated to disappear. The process had begun before World War I when the laws on marriage and divorce were extremely strict. The present high rate of *razdel* was due, in part, to a higher "cultural level in the countryside." Preobrazhenskii acknowledged that *razdel* was not always economically feasible, but he welcomed the process as "evidence of a significant leap forward by peasant youth in cultural relations."[17] Krylenko agreed with Preobrazhenskii's view

[15] *1925 VTsIK*, p. 192. According to Carr, *Socialism in One Country*, Vol. 1, p. 237, Kalinin and Larin had locked horns earlier, in the 1924 VTsIK, over the question of class differentiation in the countryside.

[16] *Sem'ia, opeka, brak. Sbornik materialov k proektam semeinogo kodeksa USSR i RSFSR* (Khar'kov, 1926): 135.

[17] *1926 VTsIK*, pp. 677–680.

of *razdel,* claiming that the large number of *razdely* did not indicate economic ruin, but rather "the definite, natural process of disintegration of the former large family." The process of division, he believed, was inevitable and impossible to arrest by legislation. He staunchly proclaimed, "it is necessary with all decisiveness to end the reactionary utopia of preserving the peasant family."[18]

Preobrazhenskii understood the problems posed by the uneven economic development of his country, but he considered it a grave mistake to draft Soviet law to suit the peasants. "It is completely clear that the towns are in favor of this Code," he observed, "we cannot turn back just because the middle peasant cannot immediately adapt." Noting the huge gap between life in the countryside and the towns, Preobrazhenskii further asserted, "We cannot have two legislations, one for the countryside, the other for the town." Family policy must be designed to favor the towns and the "more progressive element."[19]

Aron Sol'ts, a member of the Party, the Supreme Court, and the Presidium of the Central Control Commission, directly addressed the political differences over the Code in a speech to the judges and jurists of the Leningrad provincial court. He attacked the polemical style popular among Party members, the tendency to identify every position with a class interest. "This is a *kulak* deviation, this is a *bedniak* deviation, this is a Philistine deviation," he mimicked. Sol'ts himself opposed the draft. He argued that the entire population, including the middle peasants, had to be drawn into the building of socialism. He strongly appealed for the continued cooperation of the NEP period, and he sharply attacked Krylenko for dismissing various sections of the population as petty-bourgeois. "We write laws not for communists, but for the entire country," he proclaimed. "It is impossible to build socialism with only one socialist hand."[20]

18 Ibid., pp. 560–562.
19 Ibid., pp. 679–680. The peasants were not pleased by Preobrazhenskii's words. One peasant delegate to the 1926 VTsIK sharply responded, "We have over 100 million peasants and we cannot dismiss them as Preobrazhenskii wants to do" (p. 690).
20 "Perelom v Diskussii o Brake," *Rabochii sud,* 4 (1926): 258–260. Sol'ts took a similarly nonantagonistic position on the Criminal Code, arguing against a class-based system of justice. See Carr, *Socialism in One Country,* Vol. II, pp. 439–440.

Krylenko, Preobrazhenskii, and other advocates of the new Code argued that the Party firmly lead the peasants toward socialism by overcoming their attachment to older social forms and customs. Sol'ts, Kalinin, and other opponents, on the other hand, held that the Party must consider the peasants' interests, for they constituted a majority of the population. The proponents of the Code believed in moving quickly toward socialism; the opponents, at a slower, more gradual pace. Both sides recognized that the peasantry, with their primitive mode of production, stubborn household interests, and strong patriarchal values, posed problems for the transition to socialism. They differed, however, on the best way to transform the economic and social life of the village. In this way, the debate over the Code paralleled the larger debates over industrial and agrarian policy.

Yet despite these parallels, many of the most active participants in the debate over the Code aligned themselves with neither the Left nor the Right in the larger political struggle within the Party. Krylenko, Brandenburgskii, and Kurskii, three of the draft's most ardent supporters, never sided with the left opposition. Similarly, many vocal opponents of the Code, such as Sol'ts, Kiselev, and Kalinin, did not later support Bukharin's right opposition. The case of Alexander G. Beloborodov, commissar of the NKVD in 1923, demonstrates how family issues and larger political positions of the Left and the Right did not neatly coincide. Beloborodov, expelled from the Party in 1927 for membership in the left opposition, expressed many reservations about the draft code in 1926. Although he favored a more rapid approach to industrialization, he took a more cautious approach to radical change on the social front.

As the country as a whole debated the draft Code, four main groups, defined by a common position on specific issues, emerged: the peasants, the protectionists, the progressive jurists, and the women's interest group.[21] The peasants advanced the clearest position: They were resolutely opposed to the new Code. They opposed the provision on alimony as detrimental to the *dvor;* they opposed simplification of the divorce procedure

[21] I have chosen these terms for the sake of clarity and convenience. They did not appear in the debate. I have avoided the terms "left" and "right" which are often confusing when applied to issues concerning women and the family, settling instead on "progressive" and

and legal recognition of de facto marriage. They argued that the government should adopt measures to strengthen traditional registered marriage, thereby discouraging "moral dissolution." Their greatest fear was economic: If demands for alimony or child support could not be met by the responsible member of the *dvor* (i.e., the husband or father), the entire household would be made to pay.

Although not particularly sympathetic to peasant patriarchalism, the protectionists shared certain elements of the peasant position, opposing the recognition of de facto marriage on economic and moral grounds. This group of prominent Party officials, jurists, sociologists, and health workers amplified many of the earlier objections jurists had voiced to the new drafts of the Family Code. They invoked the Marxist model of base and superstructure to argue that the draft Code was too advanced for the economic and social conditions of the country. Recognition of de facto marriage would undermine registered marriage; promiscuity and women's suffering would increase. De facto marriage represented a disintegration of the social fabric, to be countered with strong legal and governmental measures. The millions of *besprizorniki* needed strong, stable homes, which could only be created by strict statutes on marriage and divorce. The role of law in society was to set firm norms for people to follow.

The progressive jurists were perhaps the most complex group. They favored the new Code and the recognition of de facto marriage, although various members differed in their reasoning. Some took the libertarian position, hailing de facto marriage as part of a new socialist future; others were more cautious. All were deeply concerned about the plight of women in de facto marriages and advocated its recognition for three reasons: First, they hoped to provide some means of support for the abandoned de facto spouse; second, they viewed the registration of marriage as a mere technicality, fated to disappear with the advance of socialism; and third, they argued that it was "bourgeois hypocrisy" not to recognize de facto marriage. Contrary to

"protectionist." The positions taken by these groups will clarify their designations. Male and female peasants differed sharply on many provisions of the Code. The peasant group refers mainly to men who promoted the interests of the household.

the protectionists, the progressive jurists conceived the law as a reflection of social reality rather than a set of prescriptive norms.

The women's interest group was perhaps the least coherent group. Its members shared one common attribute: a sensitive and often highly personal awareness of the problems and difficulties of women. The group numbered among its members leading Party activists such as Vera Lebedeva, the head of the Department for the Protection of Maternity and Infancy (OMM), as well as many peasant and working-class women. The peasants and workers, who were largely uneducated, did not participate in the intellectual and juridical arguments, but they nonetheless defended the practical interests of women. They sharply rebuked the male peasant speakers who depicted women as cunning and greedy creatures. Yet they were not feminists: Women's liberation from traditional family roles was a remote issue to them. Underlying their passionate descriptions of women's plight was the belief that a woman needed the protection of a strong, stable marriage to raise a family. Women, they argued, needed to be liberated from the social effects of the new sexual freedom of men.

De facto marriage

The differences in the values these four groups attached to marriage and family life were most clearly revealed by the heated discussion of de facto marriage, for this provision, more than any other, directly challenged the basic, traditional conception of marriage. The peasants had the most straightforward position. They favored the clear, unambiguous registration of marriage and resolutely refused to recognize de facto relations. In their village meetings, they adopted the following resolutions: "Only registered marriage should be considered as legal marriage," and "With the aim of the earliest and most exact establishment of paternity, recognition of marriage registration is a necessity."[22] One peasant delegate to the 1926 VTsIK said of the draft, "The village does not need this. The village demands

[22] I. Dombrovskii, "Novyi Kodeks Zakonov o Brake, Sem'e i Opeke i Derevniia," *Ezhenedel'nik sovetskoi iustitsii*, 48 (1926): 1531.

standard laws that are stable. The village demands that wives and brides register. We do not want a situation where today they are tied to one and tomorrow to another, and the court recognizes all this as marriage."[23] Another peasant delegate asked simply, "How can we have unregistered marriage in our area? Ninety-five percent of the population there is illiterate and in the majority of cases they live under conditions of a subsistence economy and extended households. You preach here that every union should be considered marriage. But this is possible only for a small group of conscious citizens – for those like Comrade Krylenko."[24]

The peasants were deeply concerned that de facto marriage would undermine the economic unity of the household. The property of the *dvor* was held jointly, and the peasants feared that social instability would lead to the impoverishment or breakup of the *dvor*. The peasants of Arkhangelsk, in a resolution Kurskii deemed "extraordinarily characteristic," expressed the need to limit *razdel* in the interests of the household. Other village resolutions presented similar demands, including the need to limit divorce and the household's responsibility for alimony. One resolution specifically noted that a woman in an unregistered marriage should not have the right to *razdel*.[25] Marinenko, a peasant delegate to the 1925 VTsIK who described himself as "from the dark country, from a far and lonely province," stated his objections very simply: "In my province this plan does not please us. It will bring ruin to the family."[26] Another peasant launched a tirade against spongers, parasites, and conniving females. He argued that the recognition of de facto marriage would lead to endless legal confusion and inequities. Women would use the law to take advantage of men. Amid the laughter of the other delegates, he explained, "You go to a club a few times, help a woman find her way through a political question, and the next thing you know, you're in court."[27]

Many peasants believed that de facto marriage would lead to nothing less than social and moral chaos. The resolution from the peasants of Arkhangelsk declared that de facto marriage would foster "debauchery and other liberties in the village."[28]

---

[23] *1926 VTsIK*, p. 621. [24] Ibid., p. 648. [25] Ibid., pp. 563–564.
[26] *1925 VTsIK*, p. 156. [27] Ibid., p. 132. [28] *1926 VTsIK*, p. 563.

Volkov, a peasant delegate to the 1926 VTsIK, derided the notion that de facto marriage was a positive phenomenon. "The countryside does not want the chaos we have in the towns," he stated firmly. "What will happen if 85 percent of the population – the peasantry – will be occupied by those same things which you are occupied in the towns? We will drown in this chaos."[29] Many peasants expressed a deep mistrust of urban life and emphasized the need for strict morality, strong family bonds, and a clear definition of marriage.

The protectionists also opposed the recognition of de facto marriage, although they did not share the peasants' conservatism. This group, composed of well-known figures such as P. A. Krasikov, an Old Bolshevik and current procurator of the USSR Supreme Court, N. A. Semashko, the commissar of health, David Riazanov, Aron Sol'ts, and others in important judicial and Party positions, believed that the family would eventually wither away. Unlike the peasants, they looked forward to a socialist society. But they argued from a self-consciously Marxist position that the new Code did not fit the economic realities of the country. Krasikov contended that the family still served the crucial function of distributing the wealth among its members: the young and the old, men and women, the able-bodied and the disabled. Marriage and the family had an "extraordinarily important meaning" as long as society lacked "full socialization of the means of production and consumption." In light of "the insufficient development of social and productive relations," a change in the laws on marriage and the family would do more harm than good.[30]

Sol'ts charged that the Code was founded on the "idealistic principles" of sexual liberty and freedom from state interference. But these principles could only be realized in the communist society of the future. Sol'ts grimly observed, "We are destroying the family without assuming its material responsibilities."[31] A. M. Vasil'ev-Iuzhin, the deputy chairman of the

[29] Ibid., p. 689.
[30] P. Krasikov, "V Chem Sushchnost' Semeinykh Brachnykh Form," *Rabochii sud*, 1 (1926): 5–6.
[31] A. Sol'ts, "O Revoliutsionnoi Zakonnosti," *Pravda*, January 24, 1925, p. 4.

Supreme Court, also deemed the draft "premature." He accused Krylenko of being an "incomparable utopian," "an idealist" who believed "boundlessly in the strength of the laws he drafted, even though they do not have a strong material base." "I am an old Marxist and a revolutionary," Vasil'ev-Iuzhin announced. "As an old Marxist, I am accustomed to consider phenomena in terms of their development and movement. Everything we want now is not yet possible."[32]

Another protectionist, I. Kondurushkin, pointed out numerous practical problems. Recognition of de facto marriage would prompt endless disputes between partners that the courts would have to resolve. The new Code was incompatible with the needs of a peasantry still involved in petty-commodity production. And the government could not yet care for all the needy. Kondurushkin said frankly, "The collapse of the family at the present moment means this: an increase in the number of *besprizorniki*, a growth in criminality and even infanticide, and the triumph of church marriage in the countryside." Kondurushkin summed up succinctly: "The new Code wants to outstrip economics and history."[33]

Given the backwardness of productive relations, the protectionists emphasized the important social role of the marriage contract. Krasikov argued that marriage was primarily a social, not a private affair, and that its basis needed to be strengthened and publicized.[34] Registration, as Sol'ts pointed out, was the primary means of publicly affirming a marriage. "It is necessary to distinguish marriage from sexual intercourse," he noted.[35] Kondurushkin fiercely condemned the "anarchist" view that marriage was a purely personal affair. "Sooner or later," he pre-

---

[32] A. M. Vasil'ev-Iuzhin, "Eshche o Sem'e, Brake i Novom Semeino-Brachnom Kodekse," in *Sem'ia, opeka, brak. Sbornik materialov k proektam semeinogo kodeksa USSR i RSFSR*, p. 144.

[33] I. Kondurushkin, "Diskussiia o Brake," *Rabochii sud*, 2 (1926): 102–103.

[34] *1925 VTsIK*, p. 129; *1926 VTsIK*, p. 587.

[35] *Leningradskaia pravda*, January 19, 1926, p. 4. Raigorodskii, a member of the Collegium of Advocates, also contended that registration would bring clarity to sexual relations. See "Diskussiia po Povodu Proekta Kodeksa Zakonov o Brake, Sem'e i Opeke," p. 236.

dicted grimly, "you will run for social sanctions when you appeal to court."[36] And Riazanov angrily dismissed the new Code as "petty-bourgeois, Philistine, and anarchistic." Amid the jeers and applause of the other delegates, he loudly decreed, "Not every pairing is a marriage." "Old man!" hooted someone from the audience. "You need to be rejuvenated," yelled another. "Not every old man is bad," Riazanov retorted calmly. "And not every member of the intelligentsia is an intelligent person." The draft, in Riazanov's seasoned opinion, was nothing more than "left phraseology."[37]

The protectionists argued that the plan was not only premature, but that it actually harmed women's interests. In a scathing critique of the new morality, published in 1923, Ivan Stepanov, the editor of *Leningradskaia Pravda* and *Izvestiia,* argued that the breakdown of traditional marriage had resulted in even more oppressive conditions for women. The main problem lay in the government's inability to establish childcare centers and other communal facilities that would relieve women of their traditional burdens. Stepanov had nothing but contempt for the men who abandoned pregnant women and then glorified the new form of marriage. He insisted that the recognition of de facto marriage only encouraged male irresponsibility. Although the old law could not prevent men from abandoning their children, at least "earlier custom demanded that the father bear his burden in the upbringing of the child. New custom does not demand this." Stepanov concluded, "We made a revolution in such a manner that it benefited only men. Women have remained in a tragic position."[38]

As a member of the Central Control Commission, Sol'ts was especially knowledgeable about the problems of abandoned women. The wives of Party members constantly beseeched him to take action against their former husbands for nonpayment of alimony and child support. In Sol'ts's view, the draft misled women by encouraging them to believe that their interests could be protected. "I think we would help a woman more," he explained, "if we would say to her: 'The law protects you only in certain circumstances in the current economic situation. We are

[36] Kondurushkin, "Diskussiia o Brake," p. 103.
[37] *1926 VTsIK,* p. 641–642.
[38] Stepanov, "Problema Pola," pp. 205–207.

not able to protect you more fully.'" Sol'ts did not oppose sexual freedom in principle, but he argued that as long as the state could not offer women full protection, it had to encourage stable marriage. Alimony was a poor solution to the problems created by social instability.[39]

Osman Deren-Aierlyi, a 1925 VTsIK delegate, agreed with Sol'ts, fearing that men would use the new law to persuade women that marriage was unnecessary. People would refuse to register their marriages if the law recognized de facto relations. A massive court apparatus would then be needed to handle the influx of new disputes. "If we go in this direction," Deren-Aierlyi proclaimed, "all Russia will be transformed into one continuous all-national marriage!"[40]

The progressive jurists defended the recognition of de facto marriage against each and every one of these points. Kurskii drily replied to Deren-Aierlyi that he did not plan to organize group marriage at his advanced age.[41] Of all the progressive jurists, Kurskii had the most conservative approach to de facto marriage. He stated: "This Code is a means by which we can fight against male promiscuity. Why? Because in the former Code there was no factual protection for de facto marriage and here we have protected it. We speak to those comrades who have shirked and abandoned their responsibilities to women and children and say, 'You will answer for this.'"[42] Kurskii saw the Code as a means of defining de facto relations, not undermining registered marriage. He implicitly assumed that de facto marriage was a consequence of social instability, not a sign of future communist relations. He hoped the new Code would force the partners, especially men, to assume the same responsibilities as spouses in a registered marriage. Kurskii sought to bring de facto relations closer to the traditional conception of registered marriage, not the reverse.

[39] A. Sol'ts, "Vvedenie v Diskussiiu o Brake i Sem'e," *Rabochii sud*, 5 (1926): 349–360. For similar positions see also Kondurushkin, and N. A. Semashko, *Novyi byt i polovoi vopros* (Moscow, Leningrad, 1926): 21.

[40] *1925 VTsIK*, p. 154.

[41] Ibid., p. 184.

[42] Kurskii as quoted by Brandenburgskii in "Brak i ego Pravovye Posledstviia," in *Sbornik*, p. 30.

Many participants in the debate took a similar position. A. Vinokurov, a member of the Supreme Court of the USSR, argued that recognition of de facto marriage would help women. To claim, as the traditionalists did, that a sufficient material base did not exist only absolved men of responsibility. Unlike Kurskii, Vinokurov doubted that recognition of de facto marriage could eliminate promiscuity, for the divorce procedure made it possible "to register today and divorce tomorrow." If the traditionalists wanted to curb promiscuity, they had to prohibit divorce; a measure Vinokurov spurned as typical of "the priests' point of view."[43] The jurist Ryndziunskii rejected the traditionalist implication that women should bear the main responsibility for enforcing a stricter sexual morality. Women, "regardless of the threats and prohibitions of the law," were in no position to force men to register. The refusal to recognize de facto marriage hurt women the most.[44]

While Ryndziunskii, Kurskii, and Vinokurov emphasized that recognition of de facto marriage would protect needy women, several jurists took a more radical position, advancing the same libertarian arguments that initially provoked revision of the 1918 Code. Brandenburgskii insisted that de facto marriage was the result of "the new, revolutionary life," and that it was only "juridical fetishism not to include it under the law." It was as legally oppressive to perpetuate a distinction between registered and unregistered marriage as between legitimate and illegitimate children. He scorned the "bourgeois hypocrisy" that termed a registered union "marriage," regardless of the behavior of the spouses, but denied legal support to those who lived together without registration. He accused the protectionists of bourgeois prejudice: "There is no qualitative difference between the approach of our critics, who believe that only registered marriage should entail material responsibilities, and bourgeois civilized thought that teaches that the difference between marriage and cohabitation is a defined ceremony that bestows the protection of the law, and earlier, the protection of the church." In Brandenburgskii's estimation, cohabitation was in no way different from registered marriage. "We consider it necessary to

[43] *1926 VTsIK,* p. 663.
[44] G. Ryndziunskii, "K Popytke Iuridicheskogo Opredeleniia Sushchnosti Braka," *Rabochii sud,* 1 (1926): 22.

preserve registered marriage," he wrote, "but we categorically refuse to look at registration as a prior condition without which there can be no marriage. Registration is necessary, but only as registration of an already defined fact." In other words, marriage was a social fact; registration was merely a legal act.[45]

Brandenburgskii argued against the protectionist position that more women would force men to register if that was the sole form of legal protection. "This is not real life," he said. Law could not create the conditions for stable marriage. A product of consciousness and culture, stable marriage could not be legislated into existence. Yet Brandenburgskii wavered: Was stable marriage even a desirable goal? In the 1925 VTsIK he proclaimed, "We should not aspire to a highly stable family and look at marriage from that angle. Strengthening marriage and the family – making divorce more difficult – is not new, it is old: It is the same as bourgeois law."[46]

Brandenburgskii's arguments revealed a deep uncertainty about de facto marriage. Was it identical to stable, registered marriage, denied legal status by the bourgeois hypocrisy of the state? Or was it less stable than registered marriage, a product of social disintegration, signaling women's need for greater legal protection? Or did it represent a freer, more advanced form of relations between men and women? Depending on his reasoning, Brandenburgskii saw de facto marriage as the same, worse, or better than registered marriage. At various times, he consciously or unconsciously supported all these views. The contradictions perfectly mirrored the headlong collision between the socialist-libertarian tradition and the conditions of the time.

Krylenko was the most consistent representative of the libertarian perspective. Unlike the protectionists, who viewed marriage as a social institution, Krylenko considered it a strictly personal choice. "If you want – register. If you don't want – don't register," he announced. Krylenko noted that the 1918 Code defined "real marriage" by registration in ZAGS. "What is real?" he queried. "De facto marriage is not real in a juridical

45 Ia. Brandenburgskii, "K Diskussii o Proekte Brachnogo i Semeinogo Kodeksa," *Ezhenedel'nik sovetskoi iustitsii*, 46 (1925): 1414; and "Brak i ego Pravovye Posledstviia," in *Sbornik*, pp. 19, 37, 32.
46 Brandenburgskii, "Brak i ego Pravovie Posledstvy," p. 37; *Brak i sem'ia*, p. 25; and *1925 VTsIK*, p. 146.

sense, but it is in terms of life." It was ridiculous to argue, as the critics of the Code did, that marriage ought to be blessed by Soviet power rather than the church.[47] He welcomed the eventual disappearance of registration: "We cannot defend compulsory registration in communist society. If we preserve it now, it is as a means to something else, not because it has some intrinsic value." At present, registration was a legal means of self-protection for women, an unfortunate necessity in the turbulent transition to a communist society.[48]

Both Preobrazhenskii and the jurist F. Vol'fson shared Krylenko's libertarian views. Vol'fson argued that Soviet law differed from bourgeois law precisely in that it did not seek to protect, preserve, or stabilize the family. "This task is impractical and pointless," Vol'fson claimed. The purpose of the Code was to protect women in the transition period, "not to defend the family and marriage."[49] Preobrazhenskii argued that if Soviet society was to advance toward socialism, "We must struggle for things that do not yet exist." He insultingly observed that the opponents of the Code were mainly men, who "in every case smell of the Domostroi," the reactionary family law of the tsarist period.[50]

The women's interest group was less concerned with the technicalities of the law than with stating their strongly held views of Soviet social life. It shared the protectionists' concern for family disintegration and the high divorce rate, but differed on the question of recognizing de facto marriage. Vera Lebedeva, the head of OMM, proudly declared herself "on the extreme right" in opposing the draft.[51] The Zhenotdel officially favored it. Yet most women in the debate did not address themselves to the

---

[47] N. Krylenko, "Proekt o Brake i Sem'e," in *Sbornik*, p. 62.

[48] Ibid. Rostovskii stressed this view in his popular handbook, *Sovetskii zakon o brake i sem'e* (Moscow, 1926): 12, urging women to register solely for this reason. "When a marriage is registered, paternity is proven," he counseled. "Registration makes it easier for the mother to prove who is her husband and who is the father of her child, and because of this reason, frankly speaking, registration is useful."

[49] F. Vol'fson, "K Peresmotru Semeinogo Kodeksa," *Proletarskii sud*, 10–11 (1925): 5, 4.

[50] *1926 VTsIK*, pp. 675, 677.

[51] Vera Lebedeva, "Itogi i Perspektivy Okhrany Materinstva i Mladenchestva," in *Trudy III Vsesoiuznogo s"ezda po okhrane materinstva i mladenchestva* (Moscow, 1926): 30.

specific provisions of the draft. Of the seven women speakers in the 1925 VTsIK, only one clearly favored recognition of de facto marriage; the remainder confined their comments to the need for stricter norms of sexual behavior. Of the ten women speakers in the 1926 VTsIK, four favored the recognition of de facto marriage, two were opposed, and four did not mention the issue. More than half, however, focused on social instability and the problems women experienced in collecting alimony.[52]

One of the VTsIK delegates who favored ratification of the new Code suggested that the recognition of de facto marriage was an excellent means of protecting women at a time when the state could not.[53] Another delegate favored recognition but doubted that the law alone could resolve the problems of social life. She argued that the country needed children's homes, "not court procedures."[54] And a woman worker in a spirits factory wrote, "I think it is necessary to increase the number of childcare institutions so that women can stop fearing divorce and running after alimony."[55]

Many women spoke out against the recognition of de facto marriage and the simplified divorce procedure. Given the state's inability to shoulder the burden of child rearing, they feared divorce and regarded the recognition of de facto marriage as a direct threat to their own economic security. Ten women factory workers wrote a letter suggesting that only two types of women should have a right to child support: the legal ex-wife and the woman living openly with a man who did not have another family. Any woman who knowingly got involved with a married man did not deserve support. Women who had sexual relations with many men did not deserve even a "scrap of bread."[56] One woman worker in a sawmill factory wrote, "I think that women who have relations with several individuals should not be awarded alimony. If she does not know who the father of her child is, let her bring it up herself." And she added, "Such women are no better than street prostitutes, and alimony would only corrupt them even more.[57]

[52] See *1925 VTsIK* and *1926 VTsIK*.
[53] *1926 VTsIK*, p. 593.
[54] Ibid., p. 605.
[55] "Chto Predlagaiut Rabotnitsy," *Rabotnitsa*, 15 (1926): 16.
[56] "Chto Predlagaiut Rabotnitsy," *Rabotnitsa*, 13 (1926): 14.
[57] "Chto Predlagaiut Rabotnitsy," *Rabotnitsa*, 15 (1925): 16.

Women's positions in the debate demonstrated that all women did not have the same economic and legal interests. The interests of single and married women frequently diverged as a result of their different relationships to the male wage earner. While recognition of de facto marriage benefited the single woman, it directly threatened the wife. Yet even women who supported the recognition of de facto marriage did not embrace it as a new, emancipatory form of marriage. Given the difficulties that women experienced as single mothers, their practical experience told them that de facto marriage only emancipated the man.

What is marriage?

Many participants in the debate worried that the new Family Code did not define de facto marriage. In the event of a dispute between parties, the courts had no criteria by which to judge whether a marriage in fact existed. Krasikov pointedly asked, "If we have registered and unregistered marriage, then who will decide what is marriage?"[58] A draft of the Code advanced by the NKVD had defined marriage as "an unrestricted term of voluntary cohabitation, based on a free contract between a man and a woman," but the definition had been roundly criticized by Krylenko and others. Both Sovnarkom and the Zhenotdel also opposed this definition. The Zhenotdel opposed any definition, fearing it would be used to exclude some women from the protection of the law. Sovnarkom wanted to replace the words "unrestricted term" with a fixed minimum of time.[59] E. Rosenberg, a jurist, explored the question in depth. He wrote that if the draft rejected registration as the sole means of defining marriage, then a new definition had to be created. Neither the presence of love, sex, a common household, nor pregnancy alone provided adequate proof of "marriage." Moreover, Rosenberg feared that the recognition of de facto marriage would lead to "the disappearance of the very institution of marriage."[60]

[58] *1925 VTsIK*, p. 124.
[59] Ibid., p. 114.
[60] E. Rosenburg, "Proekt Kodeksa Zakonov o Brake, Sem'e i Opeke," *Ezhenedel'nik sovetskoi iustitsii*, 48 (1925): 1485. Krasikov shared this worry, adding that if registration lost its significance in the eyes of

As jurists and Party officials vied to provide a definition independent of the act of registration, "marriage" proved itself an ever more elusive concept. Several jurists considered the task of definition hopeless from the onset. Vinokurov, a member of the Supreme Court, argued that it was impossible to enumerate the essential characteristics of marriage, for people "combined in the most freakish variety." Only the courts could decide, on a case by case basis, if marriage existed.[61] The jurist Ryndziunskii argued that marriage was not a juridical act but "a phenomenon of life," and neither marriage nor life was subject to a precise legal definition.[62] Larin, referring obliquely to the terrible housing shortage in the cities, remarked with amusement that if a common residence was accepted as a criterion for marriage, "a significant part of the population must be considered to be chaste virgins," even though they were married.[63] And Vol'fson argued that a definition would only complicate the court process and lead to "purely metaphysical arguments about what is or is not marriage."[64]

Yet jurists and Party officials, undaunted by Vol'fson's counsel, offered a wild array of definitions for inclusion in the draft Code. Sural'skii, a member of the Collegium of Advocates, held that marriage was based on three elements: physical union, a joint household, and "a sacred or spiritual promise"[65] – an oddly old-fashioned definition for a Soviet jurist. Sol'ts, not surprisingly, insisted that registration had to be a feature of marriage,[66] while Nakhimson, the chairman of the Leningrad provincial court emphasized duration, stability, and recognition by a

the people, it might lead to a resurgence of Church marriage. See *1925 VTsIK*, p. 125.

[61] A. Vinokurov, "Idti v Khvoste ili Rukovodit'?," *Rabochii sud*, 17–18 (1926): 1046. F. Kompalov, a jurist in the Leningrad provincial court with extensive practical experience, also felt that the courts should determine the issue of de facto marriage on a case-by-case basis. See F. Kompalov, "Po Povodu Brachnogo i Semeinogo Kodeksa," *Rabochii sud*, 2 (1926): 106.

[62] G. Ryndziunskii, "K Popytke Iuridicheskogo Opredeleniia Sushchnosti Braka," p. 20.

[63] *1926 VTsIK*, p. 578.

[64] F. Vol'fson, "K Peresmotru Semeinogo Kodeksa," p. 5.

[65] "Diskussiia po Povodu Proekta Kodeksa Zakonov o Brake, Sem'e i Opeke," p. 235.

[66] *1926 VTsIK*, p. 610.

third party.[67] Beloborodov naturally supported the definition of the NKVD, which Ryndziunskii promptly branded "the best proof of the sterility of a juridical definition of marriage."[68] Vasil'ev-Iuzhin claimed that the birth of a child was the most important feature of marriage.[69] Krylenko, appalled at the idea that every sexual union resulting in pregnancy would be considered marriage, deemed Vasil'ev-Iuzhin's idea "nonsense."[70] Vinokurov did not hesitate to inform Vasil'ev-Iuzhin, his deputy chairman on the Supreme Court, that his definition lacked "an understanding of marriage as a social relation between a man and a woman," and was thus distinctly non-Marxist.[71] Brandenburgskii, surveying the field of flying formulas, despaired of ever reaching a workable and acceptable definition.[72]

The jurists, however, did finally arrive at a compromise, based on a proposal offered by Brandenburgskii himself. Incorporating the most commonly cited features of marriage, the definition of de facto marriage in the new Code included a common household, the joint upbringing of children, and the expression of marital relations before a third party.[73] Although this definition approximated the features of traditional marriage fairly closely, the debate revealed a range of opinion stretching from Sural'skii's "sacred element" to Vasil'ev-Iuzhin's generous equation of every pregnancy with marriage. Although the jurists ultimately adopted fairly conservative criteria for de facto marriage, the debate demonstrated the diversity of juridical opinion on the role and meaning of marriage in Soviet society.

---

[67] "Diskussiia po Povodu Proekta Kodeksa Zakonov o Brake, Sem'e i Opeke," p. 240.

[68] A. Beloborodov, "Nashi Raznoglasiia o Brachnom Kodekse," *Rabochii sud*, 1 (1926): 4; G. Ryndziunskii, "K Popytke Iuridicheskogo Opredeleniia Sushchnosti Braka," p. 19.

[69] M. Vasil'ev-Iuzhin, "Ob Osnovnykh Poniatiiakh v Novom Proekte Semeino-Brachnogo Kodeksa," *Pravda*, November 12, 1926, p. 2.

[70] As cited by Vasil'ev-Iuzhin. Ibid.

[71] A. Vinokurov, "Idti v Khvoste ili Rukovodit'?," p. 1045.

[72] Ia. Brandenburgskii, A. Sol'ts, N. Krylenko, S. Prushitskii, *Sem'ia i novyi byt: spory o proekte kodeksa zakonov o sem'e i brake*, p. 15.

[73] Ia. Brandenburgskii, "Chto Dala Nam Diskussiia o Brake i Sem'e," *Proletarskii sud*, 4–5 (1926): 5.

Divorce, alimony, and joint property

If the issue of de facto marriage and its definition rivetted the academic attentions of the jurists, the issues of alimony and property commanded the passionate interests of the debate's nonacademic participants. Peasants and women both held strong, albeit clashing, opinions on the economic facts of marriage.

The peasants took a dim view of divorce for both social and economic reasons. The very concept of divorce was alien to them for it jeopardized the existence of the *dvor* as the basic productive unit. Volkov, a peasant delegate to the 1926 VTsIK from Ivanovo-Vosnesensk province, explained that his wife had recently written to him about a neighbor whose husband had suddenly decided to seek a divorce. "Excuse me," Volkov exclaimed with perplexed indignation, "but something should bind him so that he cannot simply say that he does not want to live with his wife."[74] The peasants worried that the entire *dvor* would be held responsible for paying either the alimony or child support owed by one of its members. "Why should we all be made to pay?" cried almost every peasant who spoke before the VTsIK.

A. T. Kartyshev, one of the peasant delegates, stated plainly, "We should not be responsible for the sins of others. Brothers, sisters, relatives, and parents should not be responsible for sons or other relations." He insisted that the VTsIK must put an end to those situations where the peasant was forced to sell his last mare to pay for the support of his son's child.[75] Blinov, a peasant from Tambov province, adamantly agreed, "It is impossible for the peasant *dvor* to sell their horse or cow."[76] The poorer households simply could not afford to pay alimony. Korytin, a peasant from Smolensk province, argued that divorce should not be permitted without a compelling reason. Perhaps divorce had little significance in the towns, Korytin noted with disapproval, but to the peasant it was extremely important. "Rarely do a man and wife live alone," he said; "They live with a whole family and thus all suffer in the case of divorce. Why should my brother suffer if I divorce my wife and the court orders me to pay?"[77]

[74] *1926 VTsIK*, p. 690.   [75] *1925 VTsIK*, p. 133.
[76] *1926 VTsIK*, p. 659.   [77] *1925 VTsIK*, p. 167.

The economic indivisibility of the *dvor* was a considerable obstacle to the solution of the alimony problem. The peasants stressed that the court should secure payment only from the defendant's share, but this presented two problems. First, it was difficult, if not impossible, to isolate the defendant's share. Second, his share frequently proved insufficient to meet the needs of the woman or child. Two peasant delegates to the VTsIK showed a keen understanding of the property laws in the draft Code and the Land Code when they slyly suggested that the *dvor* be subject to the same laws as the urban family. The peasant woman who entered her husband's *dvor* after marriage should not be entitled to a full share of the household's property. Rather, her claim, like that of the housewife, should be limited to property acquired in the course of marriage. Kostenko, a peasant from the North Caucasus, brashly suggested the elimination of the section of the Land Code that entitled women to full property rights in the *dvor*.[78]

The protectionists sympathized with the peasants' complaints, although they did not support any diminution of women's rights. They argued from a Marxist perspective that divorce was an insupportable practice in both the countryside and the towns. Free union was fine, one delegate to the 1926 VTsIK from Tambov province argued, as long as children were not involved. He put the problem bluntly: "The woman says 'Here, dear comrade, you spent the night with me and as a result, I have "Ya-ya." Please support him. And he says to her, 'Get lost.'" Women could not collect alimony because men moved around to avoid the bailiff.[79] And even if the man paid his share, the typical award could not possibly support a child.[80] Sol'ts argued that alimony could not protect women. The economic questions of marriage could not be resolved through court orders. "The court passes sentence," Sol'ts noted wryly, "but at the same time, the defendant has the right to change his wife every week." "Don't have five wives," Sol'ts declared, "this is what must be said!"[81] The protec-

---

[78] *1926 VTsIK*, pp. 658, 682.   [79] Ibid., p. 660.

[80] "Perelom Diskussii o Brake," *Rabochii sud*, 4 (1926): 261.

[81] Ia. Brandenburgskii, A. Sol'ts, N. Krylenko, S. Prushitskii, *Sem'ia i novyi byt: spory o proekte novogo kodeksa zakonov o sem'e i brake*, pp. 19, 18; A. Sol'ts, "Vvedenie v Diskussiiu o Brake i Sem'e," pp. 354, 351; *Sem'ia, opeka, brak. Sbornik materialov k proektam semeinogo kodeksa USSR*

tionists argued that Soviet family policy encouraged sexual behavior that the economies of family and state could not accommodate. Alimony and child support cases were flooding the courts. Measures were needed to stabilize social relations and preserve the family.

Krylenko argued that men should be forced to pay alimony. Sympathy for their problems was nothing but a "petty-bourgeois" reaction, and Sol'ts was "the ideologue" of the petty-bourgeoisie.[82] Members of the Presidium of the Leningrad provincial court overwhelmingly favored the draft, claiming that alimony cases were not flooding the courts. One judge noted that alimony served as a "bridle" on male sexuality. Moreover, many judges noted that the draft was simply a written expression of current court practice. Since 1922, the courts had recognized joint property and awarded alimony to partners in de facto marriages.[83]

Brandenburgskii sought to address the problem of alimony by limiting and defining the terms of support.[84] On the one hand, he thought it disgraceful that a housewife married for fifteen years could be left with nothing after a divorce. But on the other hand, if a man remarried, and started a new family, how long should he be obligated to support his ex-wife?[85] Since the new Code expanded its coverage to include the unemployed spouse as well as the needy and disabled, Brandenburgskii feared that the law might be used as a refuge for those who did not want to work. A peasant speaker offered an example of a woman who married a man, feigned illness, divorced him, and planned to

---

i RSFSR p. 150. See also the argument of Krasikov in "V Chem Sushchnost' Semeinykh Brachnykh Form," pp. 5–8.

[82] Ia. Brandenburgskii, A. Sol'ts, N. Krylenko, S. Prushitskii, *Sem'ia i novyi byt: spory o proekte novogo kodeksa zakonov o sem'e i brake*, p. 24.

[83] "Zasedanie Presidiuma Leningradskogo Gubsuda," *Rabochii sud*, 1 (1926): 23–30; "Diskussiia po Povodu Proekta Kodeksa Zakonov o Brake, Sem'e i Opeke," p. 232.

[84] The Workers and Peasants Inspectorate suggested that a disabled spouse receive support for one year from the end of the marriage. Brandenburgskii proposed a six-month time limit for the support of an unemployed ex-spouse. "Divorced spouses do not constitute a family," he said. See Brandenburgskii, "Brak i ego Pravovye Posledstviia," in *Sbornik*, pp. 28–29.

[85] Ibid., p. 25; Brandenburgskii, *Brak i sem'ia*, p. 12.

live off his alimony for the rest of her life. "We must burn out these spongers with a red hot poker," the peasant declared.[86] The final version of the Code acknowledged such sentiment by defining and limiting the alimony term.

Although the progressive jurists agreed on the need to limit the alimony term, they had little sympathy with the peasants' complaints. Krylenko, engaging a peasant delegate to the 1925 VTsIK in a dialogue noteworthy only for its mutual lack of comprehension, insisted several times that the law would hold only the defendant responsible for alimony.[87] Impatient with the peasants' concerns, Krylenko later wrote that the essential peasant demand was to abolish alimony altogether, a point of view he would not tolerate.[88]

Kurskii took a more sympathetic view of peasant problems, but he shifted the legal responsibility for alimony and the *dvor* from the Family Code to the Land Code. "Of course, the important thing is that the demands of dividing property are painful for the *dvor,* but I think that the question of alimony in peasant life should not be considered here, but in the land laws."[89] Kurskii correctly pointed out that the Land Code, not the Family Code, had jurisdiction over alimony and child support in the countryside. In an effort to balance the needs of the woman and the child against the economic viability of the *dvor,* the Commissariats of Land and Justice decreed that if the individual property of the father was insufficient to care for the child, then a collection was to be made from the entire *dvor.*[90]

The draft code altered the land laws in only one respect. The recognition of de facto marriage entitled the unregistered peasant wife to collect alimony. The child support provisions were identical in both the 1918 Code and the draft, and the joint property provision of the draft was preceded and superceded by the property provisions of the Land Code. Thus in many respects, the discussion was, as Brandenburgskii pointed out, juridically superfluous. Yet the peasants seized the opportunity to express their general dissatisfaction with the notion of divorce.

[86] *1925 VTsIK,* p. 131.   [87] Ibid., p. 167.
[88] Krylenko, "Proekt o Brake i Sem'e," in *Sbornik,* p. 68.
[89] *1925 VTsIK,* p. 187.
[90] Ia. Brandenburgskii, "K Predstoiashchei Sessii VTsIK: Krestianskii Dvor i Alimenty," *Ezhenedel'nik sovetskoi iustitsii,* 38 (1926): 938.

In the blunt words of one peasant delegate, "It doesn't matter who is responsible. We must change this!"[91]

The women's interest group was resolutely opposed to the peasants on the question of alimony. Women peasants often differed with their men, insisting on a woman's right to collect alimony and child support after divorce, and displaying a surprising lack of sympathy for the economic interests of the patriarchal household. Panarina, a peasant delegate from Voronezh province, angrily demanded, "I hear now from the peasant delegates that we must not ruin our households or take alimony from the household's property. But what will the woman peasant be left with then? Why should the child suffer?" She adamantly declared that women must receive part of the common property, "even if we must divide the cow."[92]

The women's interest group was especially sensitive to the problems of divorce and alimony. Lebedeva, the head of OMM, opposed the draft precisely because she believed it would increase the number of divorces and abandoned women. Casting a common female complaint in Marxist language, she explained, "The level of the wage payment and the entire organization of our social relations of production do not engender family units that can endure the burden of two, three or four wives." Frequent divorce undermined the interests of women "because under the current material conditions, a man cannot support three wives."[93]

Working-class and peasant women did not need a formal education in Marxist political economy to grasp this point. Several women discussed the problems of divorce, alimony, and child support in precise budgetary terms. Offering their own modest family budgets as examples, they told the jurists that the average male wage could support no more than one family.[94] If a man married many times – as many did – it was even more difficult for women to collect adequate child support. One delegate to the VTsIK remarked, "We know of cases in which boys 18 to 20 years old have registered 15 times, and in 10 of these marriages

---

[91] *1925 VTsIK*, p. 134.   [92] *1926 VTsIK*, pp. 683–684.

[93] Vera Lebedeva, "Itogi i Perspectivy Okhrany Materinstva i Mladenchestva," in *Trudy III Vsesoiuznogo s"ezda po okhrane materinstva i mladenchestva* (Moscow, 1926): 30.

[94] "Chto Predlagaiut Rabotnitsy," *Rabotnitsa*, 15 (1926): 16.

there were consequences. What can the court take from him? Nothing."[95] A woman from a rural area wrote, "In the towns and in the country it is possible to find no small number of families abandoned by husbands. Although they sometimes pay child support, it is not enough to live on, and often they simply stop paying. This affects children most painfully of all. . . . In some cases, women are responsible for these tragedies, but mainly it is men."[96]

In view of the high level of female unemployment, the low level of wages in general, the concentration of women in low-paying jobs, the lack of adequate daycare, and the patriarchal structure of rural life, women passionately opposed frequent divorce and stressed that men should take more responsibility for their sexual behavior. Pasynkova, a delegate to the VTsIK, spoke for many women in her angry condemnation of male irresponsibility. "Some men have 20 wives," she said "they live with one for a week, another for two, and leave each one with a child. Indeed this should not be allowed!" Denouncing men's lack of commitment to marriage, she noted with sarcasm: "Men always say that women are guilty, they swear they have nothing in common with their wives. This is all ridiculous: Is it really possible to marry so many times and never have anything in common? They themselves don't want to live together."[97]

A delegate to the VTsIK who worked in a textile factory deplored the disintegration of family life she saw around her. She said, "A girl marries, a year or so passes – her husband abandons her, she goes to another, more children result." "What kind of life is this?" she asked her fellow delegates. She called attention to a widespread phenomenon wreaking havoc with working-class marriages. As men took advantage of the opportunities for social mobility created by the Revolution, some began to regard their wives as backward and uneducated. "When you are working in a factory, you note a very unpleasant picture," she said, "As long as a guy doesn't participate in political work, he works and respects his wife as he should. But just a little promotion and already something stands between them.

[95] *1926 VTsIK*, pp. 613–614.
[96] "Mysli Krest'ianka," *Krest'ianka*, 6 (1926): 7.
[97] *1925 VTsIK*, p. 136.

He begins to stay away from his family and his wife, already she doesn't please him."[98]

Gnipova, another delegate to the VTsIK, agreed. She said that she could understand a man who married for a short time and then divorced his wife because the two had nothing in common. But, she added angrily, "I can't forgive a man who lives with a woman for twenty years, has five kids, and then decides his wife no longer pleases him. Why did she please him before, but now she doesn't? Shame on you, comrade men." Gnipova accused men of using women, benefiting from their labor, and then discarding them as they grew older and less attractive. "He doesn't understand why she is ugly now," Gnipova lectured, "It's because she is worn out on his behalf." Gnipova castigated those men who betrayed their wives and justified their actions in terms of "love." "This isn't love," she said firmly, "this is swinishness." Gnipova pointed out that men took advantage of the easy divorce law to abandon their wives and families. She mimicked the popular male mentality: "Here is freedom. I feel free. Give me a divorce."[99]

The women delegates expressed special bitterness toward men who left their marriages because they no longer had anything in common with their wives. They distrusted the new "commonality" men found so readily in younger, less-burdened women. These women and thousands like them valued a different commonality in marriage: one based on a shared economy, a working partnership, and a mutual commitment to children. A commonality based on personal inclination and sexual attraction was threatening to women who had labored all their lives in the narrow confines of home or factory, who had children to feed and care for, and who were, to some degree, economically dependent on their husbands.

None of the women in the debate argued that women should imitate male sexual behavior. On the contrary, many insisted on the need for a more serious, responsible approach to sex and marriage. Gnipova criticized women for contributing to their own sexual exploitation. "You permitted this yourselves, comrade women. . . . We value ourselves too cheaply." "One man

---

[98] Ibid., p. 142.   [99] Ibid., p. 169.

should not have four women," she argued, "But should wait two months for one. The question is, how can we avoid being exchanged like gypsies?" Gnipova pleaded for an end to male promiscuity so that "our children will not suffer and our households will not be ruined."[100]

Ruined households and suffering children were recurrent themes in the discussion over the draft Code. An older peasant delegate from Siberia named Shurupova described the consequences of divorce in her speech to the VTsIK. "There is no danger for the man," she declared, "for he meets another and will live with her. But for the woman it is horribly difficult to live under such conditions. All she gets is poverty, and poverty gets you nowhere." She noted that the country desperately needed children's homes, but added, "If the state took responsibility for this now it would fail." In the absence of adequate state resources, Shurupova put the blame on men. "Our side makes mistakes," she said, "but all the same, the majority of the guilty ones are men." Shurupova argued that a man must support his children no matter how many ex-wives he had. She flatly told the male delegates, "If you love tobogganing, then you have to pull your sled uphill."[101]

Women sought to preserve the family insofar as it represented the very real personal bonds between parents and children. The "withering away" of the family did not represent an abstract restructuring of gender relations, but the ever-present possibility that they would be unable to feed their children. Women's opposition to divorce and free union was based on their desperate need for full access to their husbands' wages. One working-class wife noted with grim honesty, "Women, in the majority of cases, are more backward, less skilled, and therefore less independent than men. . . . To marry, to bear children, to be enslaved by the kitchen, and then to be thrown aside by your husband – this is very painful for women. This is why I am against easy divorce."[102] Another woman, working in the Zhenotdel in a rural area, read an article of Alexandra Kollontai's in her local paper, and expressed similar disapproval. She wrote, "It seems to me that her [Kollontai's] view is directed toward the destruc-

[100] Ibid.   [101] Ibid., pp. 138–139.
[102] "Chto Predlagaiut Rabotnitsy," *Rabotnitsa*, 15 (1926): 16.

tion of the family. She proposes 'free love' and 'free union.' Her opinion is that the spiritual life of a person, insofar as it is vast and complex, cannot be satisfied by union with one, but that a person needs several 'partners.' . . . In our opinion, in the countryside, this is simply called debauchery." She wrote, "We need to struggle for the preservation of the family. Alimony is necessary as long as the state cannot take all children under its protection."[103]

Many women spoke directly against free union, insisting that a limit be placed on the number of divorces possible under the law. One textile worker said, "My request from the other women workers is to pass a decree ending serial marriages."[104] A cleaning woman in Moscow wrote a letter expressing the same sentiment: "We must restrict divorce because it damages the state and the mother."[105] Other women went even further, demanding that people who had extramarital affairs be punished. A group of ten housewives argued that the government should "strengthen the punishment for husbands who got involved with other women, and also establish punishment for these women."[106]

These women fiercely defended a strict sexual morality and were willing to enforce it by repressive measures against both men and women. Rejecting several of the more progressive features of Soviet family law, they sought to limit divorce, establish punitive measures for extramarital relations, and limit men's responsibility for children born out of wedlock. Ironically, they sought to reestablish many features of the patriarchal system of tsarist law.

Women's sexual conservatism was a direct result of the gap between law and life. Their financial positions were so precarious that they could ill afford the personal freedom inherent in Soviet divorce law. Their own family incomes, shakily balanced on the thin line separating subsistence from ruin, could not withstand the loss of the male wage. Under these circumstances, the suppression of female sexuality outside of marriage served not only male interests, but the economic interests of the entire

[103] "Mysli Krest'ianka," *Krest'ianka*, 6 (1926): 7.
[104] *1925 VTsIK*, p. 143.
[105] "Chto Predlagaiut Rabotnitsy," *Rabotnitsa*, 13 (1926): 14.
[106] "Chto Predlagaiut Rabotnitsy," *Rabotnitsa*, 15 (1926): 16.

family. Women's sexual conservatism served as a strategy to preserve the family as an economic unit.

Paternity

Like alimony, the issue of collective versus single paternity also provoked both material and moral concerns. The various groups held a curious mixture of views on this issue. Kostenko and Kartyshev, peasant delegates to the 1925 VTsIK, sought to minimize the liability of any one household and therefore argued that all the men who had been sexually involved with a woman should be made to pay. Men should bear the consequences of their actions, Kostenko said; collective paternity would serve as a deterrent against male promiscuity. Making no secret of his sympathy for the well-to-do peasant, Kartyshev feared that the courts would recognize the richest man even if he was not the responsible party.[107] One woman delegate argued that collective paternity would better serve the interests of the child. "Joint support is a better guarantee that the woman will receive some sort of support."[108] The Zhenotdel and others, male and female, argued the opposite: it would be easier to collect child support from one man rather than several.

Iakhontov, a jurist who supported the draft, strongly favored single paternity. He argued that mothers could more easily collect their payments, and expressed dismay that some people opposed recognition of de facto marriage while supporting collective paternity: "I am surprised at those comrades who talk about strengthening the family and support joint paternity. How can a normal relationship between mother and child develop when the court awards paternity to five men, stating that the mother has had simultaneous relations with all five? This will hardly strengthen the family."[109] Iakhontov considered collective paternity to be more progressive than single paternity, but argued that it could only work when the cultural and moral level of the population was advanced. The country, he concluded, was not ready for this provision.

[107] *1925 VTsIK*, p. 132.
[108] Ibid., p. 142. [109] Ibid., p. 159.

The role of law

The notion that the country was culturally too backward to accept certain aspects of the law was shared by many of the jurists, especially those in the protectionist group. They argued that the law must be used to guide the population toward socialism. Krasikov, the staunchest proponent of this view, claimed that the law should "bring the population along definite channels and provide clear norms."[110] Krasikov argued that as long as the state could not assume the role of the family, Soviet law, like bourgeois law, had to be "a compulsory device." "It is not a dissertation, not advice, not a pious well-intentioned wish," he sternly admonished, "it is a rule, a constraint, a directive subject to fulfillment."[111]

The jurists in the protectionist group suspected that without clear direction, the people would either fall into promiscuous patterns of behavior or return to the reactionary leadership of the church. They distrusted spontaneity as a reliable source of revolutionary change. Krasikov pointed out, that in 1917, many people were not ready to abolish church marriage, but "this did not mean that we should not lead them."[112] He noted too that although the population displayed spontaneous tendencies toward de facto marriage, this was not necessarily a positive development.

The progressive jurists, on the other hand, took the position that law could not fundamentally transform the reality of peoples' lives. Vol'fson directly contradicted Krasikov's normative view of law with his libertarian assertion that the purpose of family law was "not to instruct citizens in good behavior." If people opted to live in de facto marriages the law could not deter them. Vol'fson wrote, "The mistake of the proponents of 'normative' marriage lies in a peculiar juridical fetishism, in the belief that this or that definition of law can change life."[113] Underlying this approach, however, was the agreeable belief that the

[110] Ibid., p. 126.
[111] *1926 VTsIK*, p. 587. See also comments of Raigorodskii in *Leningradskaia pravda*, December 12, 1925, p. 6.
[112] *1925 VTsIK*, p. 126.
[113] F. Vol'fson, "K Peresmotru Semeinogo Kodeksa," pp. 5–6. See also

new forms of existence were positive indications of the advance toward socialist society. Brandenburgskii sanguinely predicted, "Undoubtedly we are moving toward an end to state interference in people's social lives. . . . It is ridiculous to say that the forms can strengthen marriage or give it greater continuity. Not even the bourgeois countries have accomplished this."[114] Thus Brandenburgskii's view of law had two components. First, the law could not create stable marriage even if this were a desirable goal. Law was essentially a superstructural form that evolved from the basic conditions of life. And second, these new forms of life were desirable, for they pointed to the dwindling role of the family, the law, and the state.

Brandenburgskii and the progressive jurists put forward the libertarian idea of law. New Soviet citizens were spontaneously moving toward freer forms of social relations, and it was the duty of the law to reflect this positive trend. Krasikov, on the other hand, representing the protectionists, had little faith in the spontaneous movement of the masses toward socialism. Law needed to establish prescriptive norms that would take into account, and ultimately remedy, the backward nature of Soviet social and economic life.[115]

"A new revolutionary life" or "A ruined family hearth?"

The new Code on Marriage, the Family, and Guardianship was finally ratified by the VTsIK in November 1926 and passed into law in January 1927. In a last ditch effort to block its passage, Riazanov moved to exclude recognition of de facto marriage

A. M. Kollontai, "Brak i Byt," *Rabochii sud*, 5 (1926): 368; and comments of Iakovchenko in "Perelom v Diskussii o Brake," p. 261.

[114] Brandenburgskii, "Brak i ego Pravovye Posledstviia," in *Sbornik*, p. 21.

[115] Peter Maggs and Olympiad Ioffe describe these differences more fully in their discussion of legal nihilism and normativism in *Soviet Law in Theory and Practice* (Oceana, London, New York, 1983): 34–39. Legal normativism was officially recognized as the only acceptable doctrine of law in 1938. It was most fully articulated by Vyshinskii, the prosecutor of the Moscow trials.

from the final version, but the delegates voted him down. The final Code differed from the draft in some minor details, but the most important provisions of the draft – the recognition of de facto marriage, the establishment of joint property, and the simplified divorce procedure were all preserved. Unlike the draft, the final version stated that registration of marriage was in the interests of the state and society, and it offered a clear definition of de facto marriage based on cohabitation, a joint household, mutual upbringing of children, and third-party recognition of the marriage. In place of the unlimited term of alimony established by the 1918 Code and subsequent drafts, it limited alimony for the disabled to one year, and for the needy or unemployed, to six months. It slightly expanded the rights and obligations of support to include not only needy brothers and sisters, and children and parents, but grandparents and grandchildren as well. Thus the final version of the Code reflected many of the concerns expressed by delegates about firm marriage norms, women's special needs, and limits on alimony, although it largely ignored peasant objections to divorce, alimony, and child support.

The ratified Code revealed the contrast between the libertarian vision of social relations and the material reality of life, incorporating in its provisions both the vision and the reality. The provisions on divorce and de facto marriage, for example, epitomized the uneasy balance between social freedom and its painful consequences. On the one hand, the socialist-libertarian tradition insisted that all impediments to divorce be removed; on the other hand, material reality demanded that the law remedy the plight of abandoned women and children. Even the progressive jurists, active proponents of the socialist-libertarian tradition, expressed this conflict within their own diverse and vacillating perspectives on de facto marriage. Whether they saw it as a sign of the revolutionary future or of social breakdown, their arguments to recognize de facto marriage contained both perspectives, unconscious of the contradiction.

The Soviet heirs to the libertarian vision were confronted with the state's inability to assume a major role in social welfare. Until the state was prepared to make contraception, children's homes, and employment available to women, any attempt to free them from their dependence on the traditional family was doomed to failure. Equality under the law was not enough. Ironically, the legal efforts to undermine the coercive bonds of "bourgeois marriage" intensified women's difficulties and placed them in an even more vulnerable position. The women's group argued convincingly that freedom of divorce for a woman without any means of support only benefited men. The paradox was tragic: Increased sexual and social freedom not only favored the man, but made the woman's burden harder to bear.

Alexandra Kollontai was the only leading figure who actively promoted the idea that the state should assume the burden of child care immediately. She proposed the creation of a general fund, through a tax of 2 rubles per person, to be used to establish nurseries, children's homes, and support for single mothers. Kollontai argued that alimony protected only those women whose husbands were rich enough to support them. "How can a peasant guarantee his wife alimony if for six months of the year he lives on bread and *kvass* (sour milk)?" she asked, "Or a worker whose salary barely suffices to support himself?" Displaying a brand of personal politics, Kollontai sharply confronted the men in her audience: "One can scarcely find a single one of you, who reaching age 30, has not had three de facto wives already. Which one will you support, Comrades Brandenburgskii and Krylenko?" Kollontai believed that alimony was demeaning to women and that all relationships, including casual sexual ties, should receive the same legal protection.[116]

Her proposal was widely discussed and just as widely criticized. Brandenburgskii, in a speech to the Zhenotdel, cogently replied that the state would need at least 120 million rubles a year to place all the needy children in state institutions. If the state taxed all adult males, the levy per person would be almost equal to the amount of the current income tax. "Therefore," Brandenburgskii reasoned, "beginning with an innocent figure of 2 rubles a year per person, we end by doubling taxes." Brandenburgskii added that "this would be the most unpopular tax we could establish" among the peasantry. "The proposed plan is a good one," he concluded, "but for the time being, it is unacceptable."[117]

Yet peasant opposition to a tax increase was only part of the

[116] Kollontai, "Brak i byt," pp. 364–377.
[117] Brandenburgskii, *Brak i sem'ia*, p. 18. See also Baskakova, peasant delegate to the *1926 VTsIK*, p. 632.

problem. The peasants regarded the fundamental premises of the Code as intrusive and threatening. All the major provisions of the Code – alimony, divorce, and domicile provisions – assumed individualized, independent social relations based on a modern, industrial economy. Reflecting the historic ascendancy of town over country, the Code presupposed family relations based on wage labor. The Code simply could not be justly enforced in the countryside.

The peasants were not opposed, on principle, to the intervention of the state in social affairs. One delegate to the VTsIK, from Tula province, suggested that if the responsible party in the *dvor* was unable to pay child support or alimony, the state should make up the difference. A peasant woman from the Urals wrote, "It is not necessary to award support to a mother of a child born from a union with a married man. The child in such cases should be placed in a children's home."[118] If the state wanted to support extramarital relations, children born out of wedlock, and sexual "freedom," and did not insist that the household bear the consequences, the peasants did not object. Yet as long as the state could not "make up the difference," both the peasants and the women's group had no recourse but to defend the traditional family.

The progressive jurists quickly grew impatient with such views. Brandenburgskii said that the peasant woman from the Urals advanced a "monstrous argument": "This is the old position that exists in bourgeois law," he noted dismissively.[119] Krylenko, in a fit of irritation with the peasants, burst out, "We have heard suggestions that tempt one to shrug one's shoulders. These suggestions establish limits on divorce, continuing and compulsory marriage in the name of the *dvor*, compulsory marriage as law, and do not take de facto marriage into account. This just shows the character of people's thinking."[120]

The progressive jurists were, to a certain extent, blinded by their own ideals. They hastened to applaud "new, revolutionary forms of life" when, in fact, social reality was far more complex. They were impatient with the "backward" ideas of women and peasants, although ironically, these groups unconsciously advanced a message any Marxist should have understood: Until

[118] Brandenburgskii, *Brak i sem'ia*, p. 15.
[119] Ibid.
[120] *1925 VTsIK*, p. 173.

the state could assume a greater role in social welfare, until agricultural relations were based on wage labor, neither peasants nor women were prepared to accept the material consequences of greater social freedom.

The protectionists recognized the unhappy consequences of freedom; they sympathized with the complaints of women and peasants. But they had no alternate program to the draft Code. As Marxists, they realized that Russia was too backward to implement the draft Code, yet they denied the logical outcome of their own position: namely, the decision to adopt laws that did correspond to social reality. Peasant customary law conformed to social reality in the countryside, reflecting and reinforcing centuries of patriarchal relations. And it was no coincidence that many of the suggestions made by working women and peasants recalled the more repressive features of prerevolutionary family law. Yet as socialists, the protectionists clearly found these alternatives unacceptable.

Progressive jurists such as Krylenko hammered on this weak point in the protectionist critique. Krylenko insightfully noted that while the protectionists spoke out against the draft, they actually objected to the 1918 Family Code. In a powerful challenge to the draft's opponents, Krylenko demanded, "Would it please you to establish a difference between the legitimate and the illegitimate child? Would it please you to establish a difference in the rights of these children to support? . . . Would it please you to limit the right to divorce? To forbid divorce?" Krylenko accurately observed that the protectionists criticized frequent divorce and the problems of alimony and child support, but their critique applied as surely to the 1918 Code as to the draft.[121]

The protectionists offered the most realistic assessment of social relations in the 1920s. They saw that sexual freedom without proper material guarantees was a disaster for women and children. But they were caught in an inescapable bind: Their analysis as Marxists contradicted their programmatic needs as

[121] N. V. Krylenko, *Proekt kodeksa o brake i sem'e. Doklad prochitannyi v otdele rabotnits TsK VKP (B). 12 Ianvaria 1926* (Moscow, 1926): 99, 13. See also Ia. Brandenburgskii, A. Sol'ts, N. Krylenko, S. Prushitskii, *Sem'ia i novyi byt: spory o proekte novogo kodeksa zakonov o sem'e i brake*, pp. 21–23.

Party leaders. Trapped by two unsatisfactory choices, the protectionists were incapable of offering an alternative program. They could propose laws that reflected the social relations of a backward peasantry and a small, impoverished working class. Or, they could adopt laws that embodied the social ideals of the Revolution. The first choice was unacceptable in a socialist country, and the second only exacerbated the already painful difficulties of social life. Yet the protectionists did not stand alone. All the participants in the debate faced the same dilemma. They faced it with different degrees of consciousness, but all were caught within the tragic contradiction of trying to build socialism in an underdeveloped country.

7

Controlling reproduction: Women
versus the state

The primary means of regulating the birthrate within the family was
artificially induced miscarriage or abortion.

> *Soviet demographers A. G. Vishnevskii*
> *and A. G. Volkhov commenting on the*
> *1920s and early 1930s*[1]

In the spring of 1920, when abortion was still prohibited in the
Soviet Union, Nikolai Semashko, the commissar of health, was
deluged by letters concerning the frightening popularity of the
practice. One worker from a factory staffed largely by young
women wrote, "Within the past six months, among 100 to 150
young people under age 25, I have seen 15 to 20 percent of
them making abortions without a doctor's help. They simply use
household products: They drink bleach and other poisonous
mixtures."[2] The letters, from Party members as well as workers,
indicated that the law against abortion did little to deter women
who wanted to terminate their pregnancies.

The practice of abortion had been widespread in Russia prior
to the Revolution despite the strict legal prohibition against it.[3]

[1] A. G. Vishnevskii, A. G. Volkhov, *Vosproizvodstvo naseleniia SSSR* (Moscow, 1983): 173.

[2] N. Semashko, "Eshche o Bol'nom Voprose," *Kommunistka*, 3–4 (1920): 19, 20.

[3] Laura Engelstein, "Abortion and the Civic Order: The Legal and Medical Debates," in Barbara Clements, Barbara Engel, Christine Worobec, eds., *Russia's Women. Accommodation, Resistance, Transformation* (University of California Press, Berkeley, 1991): 191, writes that physicians at the Pirogov Society Congress in 1910 believed that abortion, common in all social classes, had reached "epidemic proportions." See also pp. 192, 195.

The Criminal Code of 1885 defined abortion as a "premeditated act" of murder. It prescribed stiff punishment for both those who performed and those who underwent the procedure. After 1905, many doctors and jurists urged reform of the abortion laws; prominent professional organizations recommended legalization. Yet despite criticism of the existing legislation, only a few advanced the feminist argument that women had the right to make their own reproductive choices.[4]

The October Revolution and subsequent civil war did little to halt the practice of underground abortion. In fact, famine, hardship, and economic ruin spurred increasing numbers of women to seek illegal abortions. In 1920 Semashko argued that abortion was justifiable "only in the most extreme, most exceptional desperate situations," but he recognized that criminalization did little to change the circumstances that drove women to abortion. Urging better care for pregnant women and mothers as part of "the struggle against abortion," he also recommended that the operation be performed legally by doctors in hospitals "under conditions where it will do the least damage" to women.[5]

Several months later, in November 1920, the Commissariats of Health and Justice (NKZdrav and NKIu) legalized abortion. Their decree stated:

For the past ten years the number of women having abortions has been growing in our country and around the world. The legislation of all countries struggles against this evil by punishing women who opt for abortion and the doctors who perform it. This method of struggle has no positive results. It drives the operation underground and makes women the victims of greedy and often ignorant abortionists who profit from this secrecy.

Acknowledging that repression was useless, the decree permitted women free abortions in hospitals, but only by doctors; *babki* (peasant midwives) or midwives would face criminal sanctions and be deprived of their right to practice. The decree explained that "the moral survivals" and "painful economic conditions of the present" made abortion necessary. It offered women a safe,

[4] Ibid., pp. 188, 189, 193. Some female physicians and feminists like M. I. Pokrovskaia did argue this position; see pp. 200, 194.
[5] Semashko, p. 21.

legal, and financially just alternative to the back alleys of the past.[6]

With the decree, the Soviet Union became the first country in the world to give women a legal, cost-free opportunity to terminate pregnancy. Yet despite the enormous freedom the decree granted women, it never recognized abortion as a woman's right. The decree clearly stated that abortion was "an evil" and that legalization must be linked to "agitation against abortion among the masses of working women."[7] Semashko felt the need to stress that abortion was not a matter of individual right, for it had the potential to depress the birthrate and hurt the interests of society and the state.[8] Officials in the Commissariats of Health and Justice believed that once women had access to sufficient food, housing, child care, and medical services, they would have no further need for abortion.

The decree, strongly shaped by prevailing patriarchal notions of motherhood, showed little awareness of the limits children placed on women's ability, even under the most prosperous conditions, to enter public life. Official ideology recommended maternity clinics, creches, and daycare centers as the chief solution to the conflict between work and motherhood. One researcher on abortion, expressing the prevailing official view, wrote, "We hope that in the future, with the increase in the material wealth of our Union, in the standard of living, and in the cultural level of the working people, that women will lose their fear of maternity. Pregnancy will become a joy and not a sorrow, and abortion as a mass phenomenon will no longer have a role in our Union."[9] The idea that women had a basic right to control their own fertility received little consideration as such. Even Alexandra Kollontai, a powerful champion of women's liberation, believed that motherhood was "not a private matter." She argued that the need for abortion would disappear once child care

[6] Ia. A. Perel', ed., *Okhrana zhenshchiny-materi v ugolovnom zakone* (Moscow, Leningrad, 1932): 32. A. B. Gens, *Abort v derevne* (Moscow, 1926): 12–13.

[7] Gens, p. 13.

[8] Semashko, p. 21.

[9] L. E. Shiflinger, "Iskusstvennyi Abort," *Ginekologiia i akusherstvo*, 1 (1927): 68.

was available and women understood "that *childbirth is a social obligation.*"[10]

The discussions over abortion in the early 1920s, like those before the Revolution, were not framed in terms of individual rights. The concept of women's reproductive rights was minimally developed, the notion of fetal rights even less so. One legal expert questioned when the fetus became a juridical personality, noting that the peasants believed that membership rights in the *dvor* began at conception. Some judges expressed the view that abortion was tantamount to murder, but only when the woman was in an advanced stage of pregnancy. In one case, an unemployed woman worker with four small children was abandoned by her husband in the eighth month of pregnancy. She begged a midwife to perform an abortion and the baby died. A judge convicted both the midwife and the mother of murder, but the Supreme Court later reduced the midwife's sentence and exonerated the mother. Under Soviet law, the fetus was not considered a person entitled to rights. A woman who had an abortion at any stage in her pregnancy was exempt from prosecution.[11]

In sum, prevailing opinion on abortion rested on three basic tenets: first, that poverty drove women to seek abortion, and that better material circumstances would thus obviate the need for it; second, that the decision to bear a child was not personal but social; third, that society's reproductive needs ultimately took primacy over an individual woman's desires. The libertarian tendencies so evident in discussions over marriage and divorce never extended to the issue of maternity.

Contraception

Material and institutional support for mothers, not contraception, was the alternative officials most frequently proposed to abortion. In the 1920s and 1930s the issue of contraception was markedly absent from almost all the juridical, theoretical, and

[10] Alix Holt, ed., *The Selected Writings of Alexandra Kollontai* (Norton, New York, London, 1977): 145, 149.

[11] G. Meren, "Iskusstvennoe Izgnanie Ploda – Ubiistvo?" *Proletarskii sud*, 22 (1926): 1353–1355.

programmatic discussions of women's liberation. Neither jurists, who vigorously promoted women's emancipation through law, nor women Party leaders such as Inessa Armand and Nadezhda Krupskaia discussed birth control at any length. Kollontai's extensive writing on women, maternity, and sexuality contained few references to contraception.[12]

Yet despite the leadership's resounding silence, the idea and the practice of contraception were not foreign to Soviet women. Although basic birth control devices such as condoms and diaphragms were unavailable to the vast majority, Soviet demographers estimate that a significant share of women in the 1920s were practicing some form of contraception, most commonly coitus interruptus.[13] Doctors' reports indicate that women were desperate to find a safe, painless, and reliable means of limiting birth.

The most vocal supporters of contraception, not surprisingly, were those officials who came into frequent and intimate contact with women. Vera Lebedeva, for example, the head of the Department for the Protection of Motherhood and Infancy (OMM) under the Commissariat of Health made a lone appeal for reproductive freedom when she affirmed "the rationalization of sexuality, where a person wants to be a master just as in other areas."[14] By the late 1920s, doctors constituted an organized, knowledgeable group that favored contraception. Medical journals were filled with pleas for contraception to reduce the widespread reliance on abortion. The Kiev Conference of Midwives and Gynecologists in 1927 declared that contraception was "a vital, moral measure in the present time," which should be incorporated in the practice of midwifery. Some doctors considered contraception an evil, but, as one writer noted, it was a lesser evil than abortion.[15] Doctors and OMM officials became

---

[12] On contraception see, Holt, pp. 118, 212; Barbara Clements, *Bol-shevik Feminist. The Life of Aleksandra Kollontai* (Indiana University Press, Bloomington, 1979): 58–59; Janet Evans, "The Communist Party of the Soviet Union and the Women's Question: The Case of the 1936 Decree 'In Defense of Mother and Child'," *Journal of Contemporary History*, 16 (1981): 768.

[13] Vishnevskii, Volkov, p. 174.

[14] See Lebedeva's introduction to A. B. Gens, *Abort v derevne*, p. 7.

[15] M. F. Levi, "Itogi Legalizatsii Aborta v SSSR Skvoz' Prizmu Bur-zhuaznoi Nauku," *Ginekologiia i akusherstvo*, 2 (1932): 162.

increasingly aware of the desperate need for contraception as they encountered the crippling consequences of repeated abortions. By the midtwenties, OMM officially proclaimed that birth control information should be dispensed in all *konsultatsiias* and gynecological stations as "an essential means" of struggle against the increase in abortion.[16]

Yet it was women themselves, often illiterate, provincial, and in the estimation of the Party, "politically backward," who far outstripped the Party and state officials in their understanding of the relationship between reproductive control and liberation. Representatives of Zhenotdel, the women's section of the Party, in the rural villages reported that "women thirst for lectures on abortion and contraception."[17] The head of a Briansk hospital for railroad workers and their families noted that abortion patients begged the doctors for help. "Give us the means to prevent pregnancy and we will stop showing up in the hospital," they pleaded.[18]

The contraceptive techniques that women understood and practiced were not especially effective. They tended to rely on traditional folk practices like coitus interruptus, douching, and barrier methods. When all else failed, they resorted to abortion, legal and otherwise. A survey published in 1930 of 1,087 peasant women in a *kolkhoz* (collective farm) covering 21 villages in Smolensk *okrug* (district) revealed that almost half used some form of birth control. The most popular methods were coitus interruptus (472 women), and douching (22). Only one woman's partner used a condom. Barrier methods were also not popular: One woman used a cervical cap (*kolpachok*), and four used small balls to block the cervix (*globuly*). Despite the traditional peasant emphasis on large families, more than one of every four women admitted to a legal or illegal abortion, making abortion the second most popular form of birth control after coitus interruptus.[19]

[16] S. S. Iakubson, "Puti Okhrany Materinstva i Mladenchestva," *Sovetskaia vrachebnaia gazeta*, 21 (1933): 1016.

[17] Gens, p. 45.

[18] N. M. Emel'ianov, "K Voprosu o Roste Iskusstvennogo Aborta i Padenii Rozhdaemosti," *Ginekologiia i akusherstvo*, 5 (1927): 430.

[19] B. Ressin, "Opyt Obsledovaniia Polovoi Sfery Zhenshchin v Kolkhoze," *Ginekologiia i akusherstvo*, 3 (1930): 346, 344.

Of 200 women in a Saratov abortion ward, 40 percent claimed some knowledge of contraception and about one in five women actually practiced it. Douching with water, vinegar, or chemical solutions was the most popular method, followed by coitus interruptus. Women also injected iodine, applied alum and powdered quinine, and used balls or glycerin-soaked tampons to block the cervix. One woman even used a mushroom![20] In a Briansk hospital serving railroad workers and their families, most women either knew of or practiced coitus interruptus. A smaller number used small balls (*shariki*), or water or vinegar douches. Many explained that crowded living conditions made it almost impossible to use anything but coitus interruptus. When an entire family shared a small hut, room, or curtained-off corner with no indoor plumbing, it was not easy to douche after intercourse. Almost every woman who had an abortion asked the doctors for something to prevent future pregnancies.[21] Only one study of 788 spinners and weavers in Moscow province in 1926 concluded that the women did not use any form of contraception.[22]

Although the data on contraception are limited, it appears that a significant number of rural and urban women were aware of contraception, eager for information, and practicing coitus interruptus for want of a better method. Condoms and diaphragms, simple to produce and use, were almost impossible to get in the 1920s and 1930s, because of the rubber shortage. Tanya Matthews, a Russian emigré to Britain, recalled her doctor's comments on contraception in 1933: "Things are difficult now," he explained. "There are pills, but they do more harm than good. Best thing is rubber, but it is as hard to find as a pair of galoshes. We have no preventatives of any kind now."[23] Under these circumstances, abortion played a critical role in enabling women to limit fertility. According to one Soviet demographer, even in a major city like Leningrad at the end of the 1920s,

[20] Shiflinger, p. 66.   [21] Emel'ianov, p. 430.

[22] G. A. Ianovitskii, "Rezul'taty Ginekologicheskogo Obsledovaniia Rabotnits Tekstil'noi Fabriki im. Oktiabr'skoi Revoliutsii," *Ginekologiia i akusherstvo*, 3 (1929): 331. Ianovitskii's conclusions about women textile workers are at odds with other studies. It is not clear why he found that no women used contraception.

[23] Tanya Matthews, *Russian Child and Russian Wife* (London, 1949): 103–104.

abortion, not contraception, played the primary role in limiting births.[24]

Obtaining a legal abortion

The 1920 decree made the hitherto hidden needs of women visible. Crowds of women overwhelmed Soviet medical facilities with their demands for abortion. Initially, several provincial departments of OMM tried to eliminate applicants by granting abortion for medical reasons only.[25] In January 1924, the Commissariat of Health attempted to impose some order on local officials. Each provincial OMM was instructed to establish a commission composed of a doctor and representatives from OMM and the Zhenotdel to decide who would receive an abortion. The commissions were expressly instructed to explain the health risks of abortion and its negative impact on society to every woman they interviewed.

Given the inadequate resources of the hospitals and the huge demand for abortion, the commissions were given very specific criteria. They were to give first priority to women with medical problems. Second priority went to healthy women with social insurance (*zastrakhovannye*). White-collar and blue-collar workers and their families were covered by insurance, but students, servants, handicraft workers, the free professions (writers, artists, etc.), peasants, and the unregistered unemployed were not. Among the insured, single, unemployed women registered with the Labor Exchange got first priority, followed in order of preference by single, working women with at least one child, married women workers with three or more children, working-class housewives with three or more children, and all remaining women who were insured. Uninsured women were to be admitted after the insured, in the same order listed above. Peasant women were considered on an equal basis with working-class housewives.[26]

[24] V. V. Paevskii, *Voprosy demograficheskoi i meditsinskoi statistiki* (Moscow, 1970): 340, quoted in Vishnevskii and Volkov, p. 174.

[25] I. Gromov, "Pravo Ne Byt' Mater'iu," *Sud idet!*, 2 (1924): 108.

[26] Perel', p. 33; Gens, p. 14, 16. The state system of insurance covered only 10–12 percent of the population. In 1926, the Commissariat of

The criteria were formulated according to a hierarchy based on class position and social vulnerability. Workers received preference over every other social group, and the unmarried and the unemployed received top priority. The list indicated which women the state considered most worthy of abortion, privileging wage labor and social need. Peasant women were classified with working-class housewives because both performed unpaid work within the household. The unmarried and the unemployed, both socially needy groups, had the strongest right to abortion, followed by working-class women with large families. The married woman with one or two children had a lesser claim to make on the state's limited medical resources. In this sense the priority lists corresponded perfectly to official thinking on abortion in the early 1920s: In the eyes of the state, unemployment, illegitimacy, and poverty drove women to abortion. The Commissariat of Health allocated its services accordingly.

In order to be eligible for an abortion, a woman had to face a formidable bureaucracy. She needed to compile documents attesting to her pregnancy, her place of work, her residence, and her marital status. The unemployed needed confirmation of their status from the Labor Exchange. A number of women tried to bypass the bureaucracy by requesting doctors to perform abortion for a fee, and many doctors complied. In the early 1920s, there was considerable confusion over the legality of these "private" abortions. The 1920 decree did not permit doctors to perform abortion outside of a registered hospital, but the Criminal Code of 1922 prohibited abortion only under "unsuitable conditions," leaving the "suitability" of a room, home, or office open to interpretation. In 1923, the Moscow Department of Health prosecuted a number of doctors who were performing abortions in their homes, but many health officials believed that in view of the high demand for abortion, the long waiting lists, and the limited number of hospital spaces, doctors should be permitted to perform abortion any place that was sanitary.[27] In January 1924, however, the Commissariat of Health specifically

Health tried to set up a system of voluntary maternity insurance for women who were not covered by the state. See "Zakonoproekt O Vzaimnom Strakhovanii Materinstva," *Rabochii sud*, 11 (1926): 765.

[27] L. Vengerov, "Nakazuemost' Iskusstvennogo Aborta po Ugolovnomu Kodeksu," *Proletarskii sud*, 2–3 (1923): 9–10.

ruled that "suitable" conditions meant the hospital only.[28] Thus, doctors could continue to perform private abortions for a fee, but only in state medical facilities. Yet the confusion lingered, and the 1926 Criminal Code did little to dispel it: By substituting the word "unsanitary" for "unsuitable" it continued to leave prosecution to the discretion of the courts.[29]

Once a woman received permission for abortion, the operation itself was relatively safe. Women rarely died from a hospital abortion. In Moscow, an abortion was safer than giving birth: A woman's chances of dying from infection after childbirth were between 60 and 120 times higher than after an abortion.[30] Between 15 and 30 percent of women did, however, experience potentially serious complications, including bleeding, inflammation, fever, and greater risk of future miscarriage.[31] Poverty, malnutrition, and lack of medical attention left the female population in generally poor health. Unchecked venereal diseases, untreated vaginal infections, and repeated legal and illegal abortions multiplied the risks of the operation.[32]

The operation itself, although safe, was excruciatingly painful. It lasted between five and ten minutes and was performed without anesthetic. Doctors used the method of dilation and curettage, inserting an instrument through the cervix and scraping the walls of the uterus. A young woman with three children and two previous abortions was so frightened of another hospi-

---

[28] Perel', p. 33.

[29] A. Leibovich, "Nekotorye Stat'i Novogo Ugolovnogo Kodeksa, Kasaiushchiesia Sudebno-meditsinskoi ekspertizy," *Proletarskii sud*, 8 (1927): 681–682.

[30] Levi, p. 159; A. S. Madzhuginskii, "O Smertnosti Posle Operatsii Iskusstvennogo Aborta," *Ginekologiia i akusherstvo*, 3 (1933): 60–61. Madzhuginskii notes that out of 175,000 abortions performed in a gynecological clinic in Moscow, there were only 9 deaths, or roughly 1 death for every 20,000 abortions, p. 60.

[31] Ia. I. Rusin, "O Pozdnem Samoproizvol'nom Aborte," *Ginekologiia i akusherstvo*, 4–5 (1930): 565; M. Mironov, "Obzory, Retsenzii i Referaty," *Vrachebnoe delo*, 10 (1927): 773; "VIII Vsesoiuznyi S"ezd Akusherov i Ginekologov v Kieve, 21–26 Maia, 1928," *Ginekologiia i akusherstvo*, 4 (1928): 474, 483. Hereafter cited as "VIII S"ezd."

[32] On women's gynecological health, see the case studies of Ressin and Ianovitskii. A. S. Madzhuginskii, "Dannye Patronazhnogo Izucheniia Vliianiia Iskusstvennogo Vykidysha na Zdorov'e Zhenshchiny," *Ginekologiia i akusherstvo*, 4–5 (1930): 509.

tal abortion that she went to a midwife when she became pregnant again. Ending up in a hospital with a severe hemorrhage, she told the attending physician that she went to the midwife because "I was afraid of the pain. I could not bear it again. I had already undergone some very painful abortions and I always remembered this terrible pain with horror." Another woman described her experience in the same way. "I had borne the pain of birth easily," she remembered. "But the pain from the abortion was much greater. . . . For two weeks (prior to her third abortion) I could not sleep or eat. The thought never left my mind that it was my lot to bear such terrible torture."[33] Tanya Matthews offered a chilling account of her first abortion, performed in a hospital by her own doctor for a fee. Sitting in the waiting room, she watched the doors of the operating room open every fifteen minutes as the women were wheeled out on stretchers. "Their faces looked like greenish white masks with beads of perspiration on their foreheads." Then her turn came:

The doctor said, "Well, get on the table. . . . Be a good girl and don't scream. Nobody screams here." My legs were tied. . . . I heard the voice of Peter Ilyich giving orders to the assistants. . . . The nurse stood at my side holding my hands. . . . Acute, piercing pain stabbed me. I screamed without realizing it. "Quiet! Quiet!" I heard the severe voice of Peter Ilyich. "You hinder my work. Take a deep breath. . . . It will soon be over," he commanded, not interrupting his work. I felt the horrible scratching movements of some instrument inside me. My limbs became weak and moist with cold, sticky sweat. I clenched my teeth, counting minutes which seemed like eternity.

After the operation was over, Matthews weakly asked the doctor, "Why didn't you tell me you would do it without anesthetic?" He coolly replied, "We are saving ether for more important operations. Abortion is nothing; women stand it easily. Now that you know, it's a good lesson to you, too."[34] Some doctors, reluctant to perform abortion at all, may have seen the pain as a positive deterrent to women who "sought to escape pregnancy."[35]

[33] P. I. Kolosho, "Opyt Primeneniia Mestnoi Anestezii pri Iskusstvennom Aborte," *Sovetskii vrachebnyi zhurnal*, 8 (1926): 569.

[34] Matthews, p. 104.

[35] This judgmental phrase appears in a number of doctors' reports. See for example, Gens's compilation of questionnaires sent to doctors in *Abort v derevne* and "VIII S"ezd," p. 485. Levi, p. 154, notes that the 1920 decree was greeted with hostility by doctors. Two

Who received legal abortions?

According to official ideology and the 1920 decree, women sought abortion out of desperation: The impoverished, the unemployed, and the unmarried would be most heavily represented among the women in the abortion wards. In the words of one legal expert, "Life itself shows that abortion is practiced by working women only in exceptional cases due to extreme poverty, illness, or genetic defects."[36] This expert, however, could not have been more wrong. By the late 1920s, statistical data showed that the profile of the "typical" abortion patient was very different from what the officials in the Commissariats of Justice and Health might have predicted in 1920. But if the majority of women were neither poverty-stricken, unemployed, nor unmarried, who were they?

The overwhelming majority of women who received legal abortions lived in the cities. Most abortions were performed in Moscow and Leningrad. In 1926, doctors performed a total of 102,709 hospital abortions in all of Russia. Although Moscow and Leningrad combined held only 3.5% of the female population, they accounted for 39% of Russia's abortions. The number of abortions dropped as one moved from the urban to the rural areas. Doctors performed 30% of all abortions in the provincial (*guberniia*) and district (*okrug*) towns, 16% in the smaller towns. Only 15% of the nation's abortions were performed in the rural areas, although 83% of the nation's women lived there.[37] In other words, almost 85% of Russia's women lived in the countryside, but 85% of the abortions occurred in the towns.

Because of a general scarcity of health care services in the countryside, most rural women did not even have the option of

months before abortion was prohibited, one doctor suggested to his colleagues that an injection of local anesthetic would decrease women's suffering enormously. See Kolosho, pp. 569–573. Abortion is still performed in the Soviet Union today without anesthetic.

[36] I. Gromov, p. 107.

[37] The following sociological profiles of abortion patients are based primarily on the data in *Aborty v 1926 g.* (Moscow, 1926). This source provides information on where the abortions were performed, but not on the residency of women who received them. See p. 8. *Narodnoe khoziaistvo* (Moscow, Leningrad, 1932): 2, 21.

legal abortion in the early 1920s. There were few hospitals before the Revolution, and by 1921 many of these had ceased to function. Those that remained lacked beds, linens, medicine, and even basic instruments. Rural medical personnel did little to inform peasant women about their right to abortion, although some performed abortions on individual request. Lebedeva wrote, "It seemed dangerous and simply impermissible to open the doors of the district hospitals for abortions when there were still no beds." The health authorities feared that the demand for abortion would "swamp the weak regional health care network."[38]

Women in the towns had greater access to abortion than their rural counterparts, but they also had a greater desire to limit fertility. A study conducted between 1929 and 1933 showed that the fertility of women migrants dropped substantially after four years of city living. The fertility of long-term city residents was even lower.[39] Living outside the large, extended household – so essential to economic prosperity in the countryside – urban women had less incentive to bear children. The transition to wage labor, the elimination of the family as the basic unit of production, cramped quarters, and the lack of necessary consumer goods all encouraged women to reduce family size. Abortion was thus not only more available in the cities, but much more appealing to urban women.

The social composition of the women who received abortions reflected the urban base of the phenomenon. Only 10% of the women who received abortions in 1926 were peasants. The vast majority were either married to or working as *sluzhashchie* (white-collar employees) (37%) or workers (33%). The unemployed constituted the next largest group (12%), while students and the free professions combined accounted for less than 4%. An additional 4% were composed of independent, nonagricultural *khoziaiki* (petty entrepreneurs). Thus fully 86% of the women who received abortions had made the transition to the world of

[38] Gens, p. 5.
[39] Ellen Jones, Fred Grupp, *Modernization, Value Change, and Fertility in the Soviet Union* (Cambridge University Press, Cambridge, 1987): 85–86. There were 280 births per 1,000 rural women aged 16–44 in the four years prior to migration, and 216 in the four years after.

Table 10. *Abortions and the urban female population, 1926*

Social composition	Having abortions		Urban female population	
	Number	Percent	Number	Percent
Sluzhashchie	30,240	35	652,692	30
Workers	27,605	32	511,532	23
Unemployed	10,635	12	234,054	11
Indep. khoziaiki	3,883	4	152,665	7
Free professions	349	.4	7,838	.4
Other	14,189	16	617,348	28
Total	86,901	99.4	2,176,129	99.4

Note: All categories include women employed in given occupation and wives of men in given occupation.
Source: Compiled from statistics in *Aborty v 1926 g.*, pp. 14, 15, 32, 33, 50, 51. Valentina B. Zhiromskaia, "Sotsial'naia Struktura Gorodskogo Naseleniia RSFSR v Vosstanovitel'nyi Period (1921–1925)," Kandidatskaia dissertatsiia, Institut Istorii SSSR (Moscow, 1982): 216.

wage labor and were either studying, working for wages, or married to wage workers.

The social composition of women receiving abortions in the towns roughly mirrored the composition of the larger urban female population[40] (see Table 10). The percentage of women workers in the abortion wards was markedly higher than their percentage in the urban population, which may reflect either the special preference the commissions awarded to working-class women or the stronger incentives among workers to reduce family size. *Sluzhashchie*, too, had a greater presence in the wards than in the town population. The percentage of women in the free professions was exactly the same, and independent *khoziaiki*

[40] Table 10 is derived from two separate sources in which the categories for social composition were not identical. Categories for the town population as a whole, such as state wards, declassé, etc., that did not appear in social composition data for the abortion wards were simply changed to "other," accounting for the large size of this category.

were somewhat underrepresented in the wards. Although the abortion commissions gave priority to unemployed women – and women suffered greatly from unemployment in the 1920s – it is striking that the unemployed did not feature prominently among women receiving abortions in the towns. Apparently the unemployed had no more reason to seek abortion than women with steady incomes. Although state officials believed that extreme need motivated women to seek abortion, the social composition of the women in the wards suggests that women were motivated less by desperation (as experienced by the unemployed) than by other factors shared by urban women of all social classes.

Although women were represented in roughly the same proportions in the urban abortion wards as in the larger female urban population, abortion was much more prevalent among certain social groups. Yet because many of these groups were only a tiny percentage of the female population, these differences were not reflected in the composition of the women in the wards. Table 11 shows the number and rate (abortions per 1,000 women) of abortions for women of different social groups in Moscow in 1926.

The groups with the highest rates of abortion were the women in the free professions (93 abortions per 1,000 women), the wives of the unemployed (85.5), female agricultural *khoziaiki* (74.4), the wives of agricultural *khoziaiki* (62.2), and women workers (58.9). Yet with the exception of women workers, these groups were a small percentage of the female population of Moscow and accounted for only a tiny percentage (7.5%) of the abortions performed there. Thus although women in certain groups were more likely to resort to abortion, the social composition of the women in the wards was fairly representative of Moscow's female population. Women workers, for example, accounted for 10.7% of Moscow's female population and 14.3% of the abortions performed.

There was no apparent correlation between a women's status as a housewife or a wage earner and her propensity to resort to abortion (see Table 12). In 1926, Moscow's female population was evenly divided between wage-earning women and housewives. The abortion rate was almost identical between the two (wage earners, 42.8 abortions per 1,000; housewives, 45.2.) Moreover,

Table 11. *Abortions among women aged 14–44 in Moscow, 1926*

Occupation	Number of women in Moscow	Percent of fem. pop. of Moscow	Number of abortions in 1926	Percent of all abortions in 1926	Abortion rate[a]
Workers	65,717	10.7	3,872	14.3	58.9
Wives of "	94,246	15.3	4,372	16.2	46.4
Sluzhashchie	141,730	23.0	5,197	19.2	36.7
Wives of "	135,120	22.0	5,886	21.8	43.6
Agr. khoziaiki	3,992	.6	297	1.1	74.4
Wives of "	1,640	.3	102	.4	62.2
Other khoziaiki	17,997	3.0	320	1.2	17.8
Wives of "	40,139	6.5	838	3.1	20.9
Unemployed	57,649	9.4	1,838	6.8	31.9
Wives of "	16,859	2.7	1,442	5.3	85.5
Students	–	–	844	3.1	–
Wives of "	–	–	303	1.1	–
Free professions	2,032	.3	189	.7	93.0
Wives of "	1,759	.3	59	.2	33.5
Unknown	24,613	4.0	860	3.2	34.9
Wives of "	11,177	1.8	600	2.2	53.7
TOTAL	614,670	99.9	27,019	99.9	

[a]Per 1,000 women.
Source: M. Gernet, "Povtornye i Mnogokratnye Aborty," *Statisticheskoe obozrenie,* 12 (1928): 113.

Table 12. *Abortions among housewives and wage earners*
in Moscow, 1926

	Number of women	Percent of fem. pop.	Number of abortions	Percent of all abortions	Abortions per 1,000 women
Wage earners	313,730	51.0	13,417	50.0	42.8
Housewives	300,940	49.0	13,602	50.0	45.2

Source: Excerpted from Table 11.

the women in the abortion wards were equally divided between wage earners and housewives. Here too, the composition of the wards mirrored that of the larger population.

The early expectations of officials also proved a poor predictor of the marital status of the women in the wards. While the commissions gave priority to single women, the majority of women in the wards (69%) were not escaping the stigma of illegitimacy, but were ensconced, for better or for worse, in registered marriages[41] (see Table 13). The wards in Moscow and Leningrad contained the largest percentage of unmarried women (18%), and in the rural areas, only 13% were unmarried.

The overwhelming majority of women (78%) who received abortions were already mothers (see Table 14). In the rural areas, the percentage of childless women (14%) was even smaller than nationwide (16%), and the percentage of women with big families larger. The abortion wards in Moscow and Leningrad held the highest percentage of childless women (20%). Women with

[41] The data in *Aborty v 1926* did not divide women into "single" or "married" but into "registered marriage" or "unregistered marriage." In the 1920s, this latter category included a variety of relationships ranging from long-term, stable unions to short-term sexual relationships. It can, however, be interpreted as a nonmarried or single state. V. Khalfin, "Istreblenie Ploda (Abort) v Moskve i Moskovskoi Gubernii," *Problemy prestupnosti*, Vypusk 2 (Gosudarstvennoe Izdatel'stvo, 1927): 195–196 concludes that women in registered marriages also prevailed in the wards of Moscow and Moscow province (78.3%) over those in de facto marriages (17.4%). He also pointed out the common misperception that women in de facto relationships were more likely to have abortions.

Table 13. *Marital status of abortion patients by location, 1926*

Marital status	Moscow and Leningrad		Guberniia and okrug towns		Other towns		Rural areas		Total	
	Number	Percent	Number	Percent	Number	Percent	Number	Percent	Number	Percent
De facto marriage	7,094	18	2,984	10	1,553	9	2,043	13	13,674	13
Married	30,996	78	18,017	59	10,844	66	10,722	68	70,579	69
Unknown	1,756	4	9,483	31	4,042	25	3,038	19	18,319	18
Total	39,846	100	30,484	100	16,439	100	15,803	100	102,572	100

Source: Aborty v 1926 g., pp. 14, 32, 50, 68.

Table 14. *Family size of women having abortions, 1926*

Number of children	Moscow and Leningrad		Guberniia and okrug towns		Other towns		Rural areas		Total	
	Number	Percent	Number	Percent	Number	Percent	Number	Percent	Number	Percent
None	7,967	20	4,393	14	2,004	12	2,235	14	16,599	16
1	12,988	33	8,925	29	4,498	27	2,686	17	29,097	28
2	9,019	23	6,918	23	3,857	23	3,138	20	22,932	22
3	4,855	12	3,604	12	2,190	13	2,658	17	13,307	13
4	2,221	6	1,921	6	1,234	8	1,858	12	7,234	7
5 or more	1,758	4	1,996	7	1,273	8	2,457	16	7,484	7
Unknown	1,038	3	2,859	9	1,383	8	771	5	6,051	6
Total	39,846	101	30,616	100	16,439	99	15,803	101	102,704	99

Source: Aborty v 1926 g., pp. 18, 36, 54, 72.

small families (one or two children) constituted the largest group of women who received abortions in the towns (56–50%). In the rural wards, however, women with three or more children predominated (45%). Over half the women (56%) receiving abortions in Moscow and Leningrad had one or two children, while only about one-fifth had three or more. In the countryside, the figures were reversed: only 37% of women had one or two children, while 45% had three or more. In Moscow and Leningrad, only 4% had five or more children, while in the rural areas, this group was four times as large. Thus urban women opted for abortion most frequently after one or two children; rural women, after three children or more. Yet urban or rural, abortion was being used primarily by mothers. Furthermore, the differences in the family sizes of urban and rural abortion patients are consonant with the differences in urban and rural fertility. This suggests that both urban and rural women were using abortion to limit the size of their families; they simply differed as to what constituted an acceptable size.

The largest group of women who received abortions (58%) were between the ages of 20 and 29, the next largest group (31%), 30 to 39. Only a tiny fraction of women were under 17 (less than 1%), and only 3% were 18 to 19 (see Table 15). Not surprisingly, women were clustered in the ages 20 to 40, a time when most women had married and begun to have children. As one moved from the urban to the rural areas, the percentage of older women receiving abortions increased. The over-40 group was more than twice as large in the rural areas (9%) as in Moscow and Leningrad (4%). The 30- to 39-year old women constituted 30% of the women in Moscow and Leningrad, 38% in the countryside. Women who got abortions in the countryside tended to have larger families, and thus opted for abortion at a later age in their childbearing years. A slightly larger percentage of women in the youngest age group received abortions in the rural areas, but this group was so small that the differences were insignificant.

The women who flooded the abortion wards in the 1920s confounded the initial expectations of the abortion commissions and the state. Although officials from the Commissariats of Health and Justice believed that extreme need drove women to seek abortions – and consequently structured the commissions'

Table 15. *Age of women receiving abortions, 1926*

Age	Moscow and Leningrad		Guberniia and okrug towns		Other towns		Rural areas		Total	
	Number	Percent	Number	Percent	Number	Percent	Number	Percent	Number	Percent
17 & under	119	.3	112	.4	73	.4	79	.5	383	.4
18–19	1,157	3	969	3	498	3	470	3	3,094	3
20–29	24,782	62	18,065	59	9,089	55	7,695	49	59,631	58
30–39	12,028	30	8,191	27	5,250	32	6,067	38	31,536	31
40 & older	1,399	4	1,219	4	811	5	1,358	9	4,787	5
Unknown	361	1	2,110	7	718	4	134	.8	3,323	3
Total	39,846	100.3	30,666	100.4	16,439	99.4	15,803	100.3	102,754	100.4

Source: Aborty v 1926, pp. 18, 36, 54, 72.

criteria accordingly – the typical abortion patient was neither unmarried nor unemployed. She was not a young maid in trouble, a woman involved in casual sex, or even a partner in an unregistered marriage. On the contrary, she was in her twenties or early thirties, married, and usually the mother of at least one child. Her chances of being a housewife or a wage earner were equal, and she was either employed as or married to a worker or *sluzhashchii* with insurance. The social composition of the women in the wards was a representative cross section of urban society itself.

Why did women have abortions?

Women had a variety of reasons for seeking abortion, but the questionnaires distributed by the commissions listed only six possibilities (see Table 16). Poverty was the single most important reason for abortion, cited by about half of all women in the abortion wards in both the towns and the countryside.[42] One researcher noted that women tended to exaggerate their material desperation in the hope that the commissions would be more likely to approve their request,[43] yet given the conditions of life in the 1920s, this was not an implausible motive. Babies required food, clothing, diapers, and living space, all of which were in short supply. Safe and healthy substitutes for breast milk did not exist, and nursing tied a woman down for at least eight to nine months. Diapers were not available and even cloth was scarce. Tanya Matthews described her "sacrifice" of a worn "prerevolutionary bedsheet" to make diapers for her newborn.[44] For families crowded close in tiny rooms or apartments, the presence of a wailing, fretful infant could make a scarcely bearable situation intolerable. Almost half of the women who sought abortions in 1924 lived with a family of four or more people in one room.[45] And conditions became even worse during the First Five Year Plan. In 1932, the government allocated 4.6 square meters of

[42] Emel'ianov's case study of women in Briansk supports these national figures.
[43] Khalfin, p. 201.   [44] Matthews, p. 194.
[45] V. Z. Drobizhev, *U istokov Sovetskoi demografii* (Mysl', Moscow, 1987): 81.

Table 16. *Motivations of women receiving abortions by location, 1926*

	Moscow and Leningrad		Guberniia and okrug towns		Other towns		Rural areas		Total	
Poverty	19,071	48%	15,178	50%	7,559	46%	7,713	49%	49,521	48%
Illness	4,910	12	4,090	13	3,554	22	2,973	19	15,527	15
Conceal preg.	215	.5	216	.7	272	2	645	4	1,348	1
Still nursing	2,693	7	2,751	9	940	6	807	5	7,191	7
Do not want an-other child	6,236	16	2,524	8	1,874	11	2,023	13	12,657	12
Unknown	6,721	17	5,857	19	2,240	14	1,642	10	16,460	16
Total	39,846	100.5	30,616	99.7	16,439	101	15,803	100	102,704	99

Source: *Aborty v 1926*, pp. 14, 32, 50, 68.

living space per person in the towns – scarcely enough space to lie down in. Houses lacked running water, toilets, baths, stoves; many were cold, dank, fetid, and in a chronic state of disrepair.[46]

The death rate for children remained extremely high even as activists and medical personnel battled successfully to reduce it. A study in the mid-1920s of 541 Moscow spinners and weavers showed that fully 70% had lost a child, mainly to hunger and poor living conditions. The loss of a child was a common experience shared by urban and rural women alike. One peasant women told a doctor, "The conditions of life are so difficult. There is no chance to bring up the children we already have."[47] The streets of the cities, the railroad stations, and the markets swarmed with abandoned children – the *besprizorniki* – who were desperate for food and shelter. Childcare institutions, serving only a fraction of the population, were overcrowded, understaffed, and poorly provisioned well into the 1930s.

In one study, 2,207 rural doctors reported that poverty and material vulnerability motivated well over half (62%) the women who sought abortion. In their visits to doctors, women spoke of the famine of 1921–1922, the poor harvest of 1924, too little land, unemployment, the difficulties in feeding a child, the loss of their huts to fire, the desire "not to propagate beggary," and even not having enough cloth to wrap up the baby. About half of this group were women with large families who simply could not care for another child. One peasant woman told a doctor with black humor, "The educated women stopped giving birth long ago. Only we, silly women, continued to bear children."[48]

Despite the pressure women may have felt to cite poverty, a strikingly large percentage simply told the commissions that they did not want to have a child. For women in Moscow and Leningrad, it was the second most important reason cited. A

---

[46] William Chase, *Workers, Society, and the Soviet State. Labor and Life in Moscow, 1918–1929* (University of Illinois Press, Urbana, Chicago, 1987): 183–192; Neibakh, "Zhilishchnoe i Kommunal'noe Khoziaistvo vo Vtoroi Piatiletke," *Sovetskaia vrachebnaia gazeta*, 15–16 (1932): 947.

[47] Ianovitskii, p. 332; Gens, p. 23.

[48] This information is based on Gens's questionnaires to 2,207 rural doctors. See Gens, pp. 22–25, 31–36.

catchall reason, it covered a variety of possibilities. Numerous researchers observed that family instability, short-term unions, and a pervasive "fear of tomorrow" left many women reluctant to bear children. Although most abortion patients were married, the prevalence of divorce and the difficulties of collecting alimony and child support must have adversely affected women's view of motherhood.[49] For peasant women, the growing number of *razdely* (family divisions) produced smaller families, which in turn, increased the woman's work. Her contribution was more essential than ever in a small, poorly equipped household, and she had little time for bearing and rearing a child. Many peasant women commented on how difficult it was to work while pregnant or caring for a baby.[50]

There were positive as well as negative motives for abortion. When Tanya Matthews went to get an abortion in 1933, her doctor said, "What's wrong with your husband? Didn't he marry you to produce children for him?" "It's an old-fashioned view, Peter Ilyich," she replied, "We have studies and careers to think about. Life is very hard as it is, without children."[51] The Revolution brought new opportunities; mass literacy campaigns and the activities of the Zhenotdel expanded women's horizons and choices. One doctor noted that women who went to work or became involved in political activities showed a new "impatience for children." The "new, revolutionary life" transformed women's expectations and thus their attitudes toward childbearing.[52]

Illness (cited by 15% overall) was the second most important reason women cited for abortion. Women in the small towns and rural areas were more likely to cite illness than in Moscow and Leningrad, because of the difficulty they had in getting medical attention. Women's health was shockingly poor by modern standards, especially in the rural areas. They suffered from a wide number of chronic infections, complications from previous

---

49 Gens, p. 8; P. P. Kazanskii, "4,450 Sluchaev Nepolnykh Vykidyshei," *Ginekologiia i akusherstvo*, 6 (1927): 517; Emel'ianov, p. 430; M. Kaplun, "Brachnost' Naseleniia RSFSR," *Statisticheskoe obozrenie* (1929): 95–97.

50 Gens, p. 23.   51 Matthews, p. 103.

52 Both Jones and Grupp, and Vishnevskii and Volkov argue that factors such as urbanization, women's employment, and increased literacy encouraged women to reduce family size. See pp. 70–121, and 173–176, respectively.

births, venereal diseases, fibroids, and other untreated illnesses. Often women had to care for a sick husband or family member, leaving little time for a new baby.[53]

Urban and rural women had roughly the same motives for abortion with one significant exception. The desire to hide an illegitimate pregnancy figured much more prominently among the motives of women in the countryside than in the towns. In Moscow and Leningrad, women who wanted "to conceal pregnancy" constituted but a tiny fraction of the abortion patients (.5%), but as one moved from town to country, the share of this group steadily expanded eightfold to 4%. Rural doctors reported that an even larger percent (fully 20%) of the women who came to them seeking abortions fell into this category.[54]

In the countryside, the great shame of illegitimacy could both ruin a girl's chances of marriage and provoke her father to throw her out of the *dvor*. Unmarried, pregnant peasant women spoke of their "conscience before the people" and sought abortion due to "fear, shame, parents, and public opinion." Many of these women reflected the social changes in village life wrought by the Revolution and the long years of war. Widows took up with soldiers temporarily billeted in their villages. Young people showed less sexual restraint. One rural doctor noted that although sexual morality had changed, attitudes toward illegitimacy remained the same, forcing many women to opt for abortion.[55]

In the towns, the smaller presence of women motivated by the wish to conceal pregnancy suggests that urban women found illegitimacy less compelling than other reasons for abortion. In the transition from country to city, migrants may have relaxed their harsh attitudes toward illegitimacy. Urban women, freed from the constraints of the patriarchal household, may have found it easier to bear and raise children out of wedlock.

Much of the information above suggests that women used abortion to limit family size rather than as a stopgap solution to an accidental or out-of-wedlock pregnancy. The point is rein-

[53] Gens, p. 24.
[54] Ibid. Many of these women never traveled to the commissions, accounting for the great discrepancy between the figure cited in Table 7 and the reports of the rural doctors. See section on illegal abortion below.
[55] Ibid., pp. 24–25, 35–36.

forced by evidence that women resorted to abortion repeatedly. Almost half of those who received abortions in Moscow and Leningrad had had at least one previous abortion. Over 50% had one, 25% had two, and about 20% had three or more. In the provincial towns and the rural areas fewer women had previous abortions (about one-third and one-quarter of the women, respectively), a reflection of higher fertility patterns as well as the limited availability of abortion. Here too, the repeat patients had fewer prior abortions.[56]

In both cities and rural areas, the more pregnancies an abortion patient had, the more likely she was to have had a previous abortion (see Table 17). In the abortion wards in Moscow and Leningrad, 22% of all women with two pregnancies had a prior abortion. Yet among the women with five pregnancies, fully 71% had had a previous abortion. The figures were somewhat smaller in the rural areas, but the percentage of women with prior abortions still continued to increase with the number of pregnancies. Not only did a woman's likelihood of having had an abortion increase with the number of pregnancies she had, but her number of abortions increased with the number of pregnancies (see Table 17). The abortion rate (abortions per 100 pregnancies) among each group rose steadily with each new pregnancy. In Moscow and Leningrad, the percentage of pregnancies resulting in abortion rose from 11% in the first group, to 18% in the second, to 22% in the third. In the rural areas, the percentage increased from 6% in the first and second groups to 8% in the third. Thus abortion, for many women, was more than a one-time solution to an accidental pregnancy. As women moved through their reproductive life cycles, they relied on abortion, again and again, to help limit the size of their families. In the words of two Soviet demographers, after 1920, "Abortion quickly entered the mass practice of the family."[57]

Illegal abortion

Even after abortion was legalized, thousands of women still turned to *babki*, midwives, hairdressers, nurses, and a variety of

[56] *Aborty v 1926 g.*, p. 9; M. Gernet, "Povtornye i Mnogokratnye Aborty," *Statisticheskoe obozrenie*, 12 (1928): 111.
[57] Vishnevskii, Volkov, p. 173.

self-administered home remedies to terminate their pregnancies. Their reasons varied widely: Some sought to avoid the pain of the hospital procedure; others could not travel to the abortion commissions and the hospitals; some were rejected by the commissions; some wanted to keep pregnancy a secret; and many simply trusted the practices of the *babka* and midwife over those of the modern doctor.

The *babka* played a crucial role in birth and abortion in the village. Many peasant women who had never been in a hospital or even been examined by a doctor had borne numerous children with the help of the *babka*. When they sought an abortion, the *babka* was the first person they turned to, naturally and with confidence. *Babki* performed abortions in a number of ways: They used knitting needles, spindles, wire, crochet hooks, shoe buttoners, goose feathers, carrots, and plant roots to induce miscarriage; they brewed teas from saffron, camomile, aloe, and ergot. And they counseled women on a variety of self-administered remedies, including the age-old practices of heavy lifting, hot baths, and mustard plasters, as well as doses of quinine, bleach, and the chemical corrosive, sublimate.[58] It is impossible to gauge how safe or effective these remedies were because only a small fraction of their recipients were treated in the hospitals. Doctors saw only the botched work of the "ignorant" *babki* and midwives; they had no conception of their successes.

The activities of the *babki* were shrouded in silence. Not only were their practices illegal, but their clients often needed to keep pregnancy a secret. The *babki* and the women they served were bound together in a pact of silence that often remained unbroken unto death. Numerous observers noted that women refused to disclose the details of their abortions or the names of the *babki* even on their deathbeds, steadfastly maintaining that a fall or heavy lifting had caused the miscarriage.[59]

Some evidence suggests that folk remedies were not as ineffective or as dangerous as doctors so heatedly proclaimed. One woman, entering a hospital with a hemorrhage, admitted she had self-induced abortion by inserting a goose feather into her cervix. Yet she noted that she had successfully induced eleven

[58] Ressin, p. 344; Gens, p. 30.
[59] Gens, pp. 27, 17; V. L. Karpova, "K Voprosu ob Abortakh i Aktivnom Vmeshatel'stve pri Infitsirovannom Vykidyshe na Sele," *Vrachebnoe delo*, 1 (1930): 28, 30.

Table 17. *Prior abortions and pregnancies among women receiving abortions, 1926*

	Moscow and Leningrad			Rural areas		
	Number	Percent	Abortion rate[a]	Number	Percent	Abortion rate
Group 1			11%			6%
2nd Pregnancy						
0 Abortions	5,412	78		1,617	89	
1 Abortion	1,514	22		204	11	
Total	6,926			1,821		
Group 2			18%			6%
3rd Pregnancy						
0 Abortions	3,729	54		1,779	83	
1 Abortion	2,712	39		345	16	
2 Abortions	501	7		27	1	
Total	6,942			2,151		

Group 3				
4th Pregnancy				
0 Abortions	2,348	41	1,569	74
1 Abortion	2,071	36	469	22
2 Abortions	1,117	19	92	4
3 Abortions	219	4	4	.2
Total	5,755		2,134	
Group 4				
5th or more preg.				
0 Abortions	4,097	29	4,391	60
1 Abortion	3,387	24	1,719	24
2 Abortions	2,992	21	736	10
3 Abortions	1,811	13	260	4
4 Abortions	963	7	122	2
5 Abortions	1,019	7	69	1
Total	14,269		7,297	

a Abortions per 100 pregnancies.

Source: *Aborty v 1926 g.*, pp. 10–11.

previous abortions with this method.[60] A railroad mechanic's wife in Krasnoiarsk had performed abortions for years. She instructed her husband to make her a tapered metal tube, which she boiled before each operation. She inserted the tube into the cervix, and using a rubber balloon, blew a small amount of air into the uterus. She had safely used this method on herself and other women numerous times.[61] Although this woman was probably not typical, her story suggests that there were women who practiced abortion safely, and earned the trust and allegiance of the women in their communities.

The frequency of illegal abortion is measurable only by the numbers of women who ended up in the hospital. The successes and failures who never entered a hospital constituted the "dark" or unknown figure of illegal abortion. Yet not all women who entered the hospitals with incomplete abortions were the victims of illegal abortion. Some were suffering from spontaneous or accident-induced miscarriages. Doctors and researchers varied widely in their estimations of what percentage of women suffering from these "incomplete abortions" were actually victims of illegal abortion. Estimates ranged from 10% to 95%. Some argued that it was impossible to determine if a hemorrhage was spontaneous, self-induced, accidental, or deliberately induced by someone else. Others maintained that the vast majority of women who entered the hospital with bleeding accompanied by infection and high fever were undoubtedly the recipients of illegal abortions.[62] Women themselves confused the issue still further by refusing to admit to illegal abortion.

The following data are based on women who entered the hospitals with incomplete abortions. Unfortunately, it is impossible to tell precisely what percentage were deliberate (illegal) abortions (self-induced or performed by someone else), what percentage spontaneous or accident-induced miscarriages. Yet since

[60] Karpova, pp. 27–28.

[61] V. V. Khvorov, "K Kazuistike Abortmakherstva," *Vrachebnaia gazeta*, 15 (1930): 1149.

[62] Magid, p. 104, cites Gens with the high figure of 95%. A. A. Verbenko, S. E. Il'in, V. N. Chusova, T. N. Al'shevskaia, *Aborty i protivozachatochnye sredstva* (Meditsina, 1968): 10, claim 92% of the women who entered the hospitals in Moscow in 1924 with incomplete abortions were the victims of illegal practices; Madzhuginskii, p. 48, believed 33%; and Rusin, p. 568, only 10%.

it is likely that illegal abortion constituted a significant fraction of the incomplete abortions (and since this is the only sociological data we have on women receiving illegal abortions), incomplete abortion is used here as a rough index of illegal abortion.

In the early 1920s, the numbers of women hospitalized with incomplete abortions were extremely high. In the rural hospitals, the number of women with incomplete abortions actually outstripped the number receiving legal abortions. Moreover, between 1922 and 1924, the number of incomplete abortions increased each year. Thus despite the legalization of abortion, illegal abortion was still widely practiced, especially in the countryside. The ratio of incomplete to legal abortions dropped by the later twenties, but the presence of illegal abortion remained quite significant.[63]

By 1926, 14% of the women in the abortion wards – 17,201 women out of 119,910 – were being treated for the consequences of an incomplete abortion. The number of women treated for incomplete abortion was almost the same in Moscow and Leningrad as in the rural areas. Yet because rural hospitals performed far fewer abortions, women suffering from incomplete abortions occupied twice as many beds (23%) in the rural wards than in Moscow and Leningrad (12%) (see Table 18). The percentage of women in the wards being treated for incomplete abortions was highest in the provinces of the Central Industrial Region (CIR) surrounding Moscow: Ivanovo-Vosnesensk (40%), Riazan (35%), Nizhegorod (30%), and Kostroma (25%). In almost half of the nation's provinces, one of every five beds allocated for legal abortion was filled with a woman being treated for an abortion begun outside the hospital. In the rural areas, one study showed clear evidence of the great predominance of illegal abortion. In 1930, among 1,249 women in a large *kolkhoz* in the Smolensk area, fully half had suffered an illegal abortion, either self-administered or performed by *babki*.[64]

Women continued to go underground for many reasons. Some health officials suggested that women turned to illegal abortion because they were rejected by the commissions. In sev-

[63] Between 1922 and 1924, rural doctors performed 40,828 legal abortions and treated 41,684 women for complications resulting from illegal abortions. Gens, p. 27.
[64] *Aborty v 1926 g.*, pp. 6–7; Ressin, p. 344.

Table 18. *Legal and incomplete abortions by location, 1926*

Type of abortion	Moscow and Leningrad	*Guberniia* and *okrug* towns	Other towns	Rural areas	Total
Legal	39,851	30,616	16,439	15,803	102,709
Incomplete	5,219	3,744	3,474	4,764	17,201
Percentage of all incomplete abortions nationwide	30%	22%	20%	28%	100%
Percentage of women in the wards with incomplete abortions	12%	11%	17%	23%	14%

Source: *Aborty v 1926 g.* (Moscow, 1929): 8.

eral urbanized provinces, high rates of both incomplete abortion and rejection by the commissions suggest a vicious circle: Women who suffered the effects of botched illegal abortions occupied beds in the abortion wards, thereby reducing the places available for women requesting legal abortions, and forcing, in turn, more women to get illegal abortions. Abortion wards in the provinces of Riazan, Kostroma, Vladimir, and Ivanovo-Vosnesensk, where the commissions rejected a high percentage of applicants, all held high percentages of women suffering from abortions begun outside the hospital. Yet with the exception of Vladimir and a few other provinces, the number of women being treated for incomplete abortions well exceeded the numbers turned away by the commissions. In Ivanovo-Vosnesensk, for example, 2,863 women were treated for incomplete abortions, but only 665 had been turned down by the commissions. Nationwide, 17,201 women were treated for incomplete abortions, but only 6,102 women were refused by the commissions.[65] Thus rejection by the commissions – or the

[65] *Aborty v 1926 g.*, p. 8.

inability of medical facilities to meet the demand – was clearly not the only reason women went underground.

Many rural women who needed abortions never even applied to the commissions. A trip to the commission, followed by a trip to the hospital, was nearly impossible. Roads were impassable for a large part of the year. Even if a household owned a horse, it could rarely spare the animal, and a woman might have to walk thirty to forty miles to get to a hospital. Many hospitals in rural areas did not even perform abortions. Moreover, the commissions required proof of pregnancy, marital status, family size, and workplace. Even if a woman could procure the necessary documents from a doctor and the local soviet, the paperwork and her subsequent absence exposed the purpose of her journey to the entire village. Over 1,900 doctors reported that rural women begged them to perform abortions privately without permission from the commissions. In the words of one doctor, "If a hospital refuses a maid or a widow, they immediately turn to the *babki*."[66] As a result of the lack of available hospitals, the difficulties of applying to the commissions, and the tradition of relying on the *babka*, illegal abortion was widespread in the countryside. Peasants constituted 18% of the women in the wards being treated for incomplete abortion, but only 10% of the women receiving legal abortions.

There were other differences between the women who received legal abortions and the women who were treated for abortions begun outside the hospital, but these were not especially significant. The overwhelming number of women in both groups were married (about 85%). The unemployed, favored by the abortion commissions, accounted for far fewer of the incomplete abortion patients (5%) than the legal abortion patients (12%). More women with incomplete abortions were childless, perhaps because the commissions favored women with children or because the unwed sought to avoid the publicity of the commissions. But in other respects, the social composition of the two groups was similar. The great majority of women treated for incomplete abortions, like their "legal" counterparts, were already mothers. The largest group (46%) had small families of one or two children.[67]

[66] Gens, p. 15, 20, 38–46.
[67] *Aborty v 1926 g.*, p. 20, 38, 56, 74, and 24, 42, 60, 78.

Thus overall, women with incomplete abortions tended to be somewhat older and have fewer children than the women who received legal abortions. Peasants figured more prominently in their ranks and the rural hospitals treated a larger percentage. Yet the respective profiles of the two groups were remarkably similar. Like the women who received legal abortions, workers and *sluzhashchie* accounted for the largest group of women treated for incomplete abortion, and they tended to be mothers, aged 20 to 29, with small families.

Data on women with incomplete abortions provides a rare look at the shadowy and secretive world of underground abortion. If women who ended up in the hospitals with incomplete abortions were roughly representative of women who went underground, the sociological profiles show that women who suffered illegal abortions did not differ significantly from those with legal abortions. And most important, both groups were, by and large, indistinguishable from the millions of married mothers whose choices about reproduction ultimately determined Russia's birthrate.

Abortion and the birthrate

By the late 1920s, doctors and researchers had become deeply concerned about women's reliance on abortion. They made frequent references to the falling birthrate, the thousands who suffered complications after the operation, the labor time lost during recuperation, and the debilitating impact of abortion on women's health. A doctor reporting to the Scientific Association of Doctors in Simferopol in 1927 concluded that in the Crimea, the large number of abortions "stands as a great antisocial factor and poses a threat to the steady growth of the population." At the First All-Ukrainian Congress of Midwives and Gynecologists that same year, a doctor from Starobel'sk announced that the ratio of abortions to births had shot up from 40 abortions per 100 births in 1924, to 84 per 100 in 1925, and surpassed the number of births at 107 per 100 in 1926.[68] Vera Lebedeva felt the need to counter these dire forecasts by pointing out that abortion had not significantly affected the birthrate. Yet she

[68] "Nauchnaia zhizn'," *Vrachebnoe delo*, 14–15, 16 (1927): 1107, 1196–1197.

noted that in Moscow there were 65 abortions per 100 births in 1926, and the numbers were growing. By 1928, a Moscow doctor at the Eighth Congress of Midwives and Gynecologists noted that the number of abortions had surpassed the number of births. He warned, "We must pay attention to the menacing predominance of abortions over births among contemporary young women and the inevitable consequences: a decrease in the birthrate and the labor capability of women. Abortion, in the final analysis, places a heavy burden on the state because it reduces women's contribution to production." One delegate from the North Caucasus commented that there were four times as many abortions as births in his area, and another, from the Ukraine, referred to "an epidemic of abortions."[69]

By the late 1920s, the number of abortions had surpassed the number of births in a number of cities. In Briansk, there were 35 legal and known illegal abortions per 100 births in 1924; 46 in 1925, 166 in 1926, and 244 in 1927. The number of abortions by 1927 was 2.5 times the number of births.[70] In Leningrad, there was almost a sixfold increase in the rate of abortion between 1924 and 1928 from 5.5 to 31.5 abortions per 1,000 people. The ratio of abortions to births went from 21 abortions per 100 births in 1924 to 138 in 1928.[71] In Moscow in 1921, there were 19 abortions per 100 births; there were 21 in 1922, 19 in 1923, 19 in 1924, 31 in 1925, 55 in 1926, 87 in 1927, 130 in 1928, and 160 in 1929. By 1934, the number of abortions per births had jumped to 271, although it fell somewhat in 1935 to 221. Thus by 1928, Moscow's abortions had surpassed its births, and by the 1930s, there were twice as many abortions as births annually.[72] If the number of illegal abortions were added, the effect on the figures would have been more striking still. And while the increase in abortion was greatest in the big cities, the nationwide figures were also significant. In Russia in 1926, doctors performed 121,978 legal abortions. By 1935, this figure had jumped to 1,500,000. In 1926, there were 1.3 abortions for every 1,000 people, in 1935, 13.1, a more than tenfold increase.[73]

---

[69] "VIII S"ezd," pp. 474–475, 478, 482, 485.
[70] Emel'ianov, p. 425.   [71] Vishnevskii, Volkov, p. 174.
[72] Frank Lorimer, *The Population of the Soviet Union: History and Prospects* (League of Nations, Geneva, 1946): 127; Levi, p. 156.
[73] *Aborty v 1926*, p. 6; the estimate on abortions in 1935 is derived from statistics supplied by E. A. Sadvokasova, *Sotsial'no-gigienicheskie aspek-*

And as the number of abortions rose, the crude birthrate fell. Between 1927 and 1935 it dropped from 45 births per 1,000 people in 1927, to 43.7 in 1928, 41.4 in 1929, 39.2 in 1930, 36.9 in 1931, 34.6 in 1932, 32.4 in 1933, 30.1 in 1934, and 30.1 in 1935. Although many factors contributed to the fall in the crude birthrate, it is striking that the decline, beginning in 1928, coincided with the astounding increase in abortion. By the late 1920s, in Briansk, Moscow, Leningrad, parts of the Ukraine, the North Caucasus, and other areas, the number of abortions exceeded the number of births, and continued to rise. In the words of Soviet demographers, abortion had become "the primary means of regulating the birthrate within the family."[74]

Although we know little about the women who received abortions in the early thirties, figures on abortion and the birth rate suggest that the millions of peasant women who came to the cities and entered the workforce in this period had powerful motivations for limiting family size. Between 1932 and 1934, 2,834,300 women settled in the towns,[75] and thus increased their opportunities to receive legal abortion. Collectivization, industrialization, and urbanization were accompanied by a sharp increase in legal, and most likely, illegal abortions as well. Women entered the workforce in record numbers. Plant managers strongly discouraged pregnant women from applying for jobs in order to escape the costs of the generous Soviet maternity leave provisions. Abuses were legion: Women applicants were often subjected to pregnancy tests and ordered to have abortions or seek work elsewhere. And of course women sought abortions on their own. A study of women receiving abortions in the early 1930s showed that fewer were motivated by poverty, more by the wish "not to have a child."[76] Famine in the countryside, rationing in

ty regulirovaniia razmerov sem'i (Meditsina, 1969): 30, on abortion in 1937–1938. Sadvokasova notes that there were 500,000 abortions between 1937 and 1938, and a threefold drop in 1937, the year after the decree. For number of births in 1926 see L. Lubnyi-Gertsyk, "Estestvennoe Dvizhenie Naseleniia SSSR za 1926," *Statisticheskoe obozrenie*, 8 (1928): 86. Statistics for 1935 figured using 1933 population figure from *Handbook of the Soviet Union* (American-Russian Chamber of Commerce, New York, 1936): 3.

[74] Lorimer, p. 134; Vishnevskii, Volkov, p. 173.
[75] *Zhenshchina v SSSR* (Moscow, 1936): 63.
[76] D. Khutorskaia, M. Krasil'nikov, "Bor'ba s Podpol'nymi Abortami," *Sotsialisticheskaia zakonnost'*, 4 (1936): 21, 22.

the cities, and the forced dispossession of millions of peasants all contributed to the sharp drop in the birthrate. Legalized abortion was not the cause of this fall – it was simply one of several methods women used to keep from bearing children.

In June 1936, amid a great rush of propaganda, the Soviet Central Executive Committee (TsIK) and Sovnarkom issued a decree outlawing abortion. Those who performed the operation were liable to a minimum of two years in prison, and even the women who received abortions were subject to high fines after the first offense. The new law offered incentives for childbearing by providing stipends for new mothers, large bonuses for women with many children, and longer maternity leaves for white-collar women. It also increased the number of maternity clinics, childcare institutions, and milk kitchens. In addition to its pronatalist measures, it made divorce harder to get and stiffened criminal penalties for men who refused to pay alimony or child support. The prohibition against abortion was the centerpiece of a larger campaign to promote "family responsibility."[77]

Officials never discussed publicly the real reasons for prohibiting abortion. Touting new advances in the standard of living and the joys of motherhood, they insisted that women no longer needed abortion. They stressed the temporary nature of the earlier legalization and proclaimed that every woman could now realize her right to be a mother. Yet the official justification for the prohibition made little sense. If the standard of living was so high that women no longer needed to resort to abortion, why bother criminalizing it?

Evidence strongly suggests that the prohibition was motivated by a deep concern over the falling birthrate coupled with a dawning awareness of the deeper meaning of the statistics on abortion. The statistical organs' own data on abortion patients had long belied official assumptions. The creators of the 1920 decree believed that once poverty was eliminated, women would have no further need for abortion. The criteria of the commis-

---

[77] *Proekt postanovleniia TsIK i SNK SSR o zapreshchenii abortov, uvelechenii material'noi pomoshchi rozhenitsam, ustanovlenii gosudarstvennoi pomoshchi mnogosemeinym, rasshirenii seti rodil'nykh domov, detskikh iaslei, detskikh sadov, usilenii ugolovnogo nakazaniia za neplatezh alimentov, i o nekotorykh izmeneniiakh v zakonodatel'stve o razvodakh* (1936); G. A. Baksht, "K Voprosu o Zapreshchenii Abortov," *Sovetskii vrachebnyi zhurnal*, 12 (1936): 884.

sions – favoring the most materially and socially vulnerable – implicitly reflected this belief. Yet the majority of women who sought both legal and illegal abortions in the 1920s were not the unemployed, the unmarried, or the very young, but relatively secure, married mothers, in the prime of their childbearing years. In short, they were neither the neediest, the most vulnerable, nor the most marginal. Primarily urban wage earners or the wives of wage earners, these women were responding not only to poverty and material deprivation, but to the new opportunities opened up by the revolution: education, employment, and political work in a wider world.

In 1934, S. G. Strumilin, working with the organs on budgetary statistics, completed an immense research project on the birthrate and the infant death rate. He collected data on 10,000 women for the span of their married lives going back to 1914. Strumilin's conclusions had a profound impact at the highest levels of the government, for they challenged many of the assumptions supporting the state's view of abortion. First, Strumilin noted that the marriage rate had risen steadily between 1914 and 1933. Although this should have produced an increase of 2.5 million mothers and at least 750,000 births, in fact, the birthrate had fallen. Second, Strumilin showed that as families ascended the social scale from peasant to unskilled worker to skilled industrial worker, marital fertility dropped. Moreover, women who combined wage work with child rearing and household labor had even lower fertility than average. Third, he predicted that if economic targets were met, and if more than 5 million women entered the labor force in the near future, births in the towns could be expected to decrease by 400,000, a drop in the birthrate of almost 10%. By 1935, the women born during World War I would enter their childbearing years. A small cohort to begin with (because of the drop in the birthrate during the war), even greater reductions in the birthrate could be expected when these women entered the workforce.[78] Strumilin's research showed that improved material conditions and upward mobility would decrease the birthrate.

[78] Strumilin's study is cited by Sadvokasova, pp. 28–29. Strumilin looked at the percentage of married women, aged 16 to 49, between 1914 and 1933, in determining the rise in the marriage rate.

The figures on marriage, the birthrate, abortion, and the sociology of abortion patients combined to produce an unmistakable message: First, the birthrate was falling and would continue to do so in the future; and second, Russia's mothers were relying on abortion repeatedly through their reproductive lives to limit the size of their families.

Officials assumed that the fall in the birthrate could be arrested by criminalizing abortion. This assumption was a sharp reversal of the state's earlier view, which held that criminalization could do little to change the difficult social conditions that impelled women to seek abortion. Yet by 1936, officials had abandoned the notion that repression was useless. They now embraced the stark thinking of the jurist who proclaimed, "It makes sense to apply more repressive measures."[79]

The 1936 law confused women's method for limiting marital fertility (legal abortion) with their motivations. The state believed that by depriving women of the method of limiting fertility, it would also eliminate their motivation for doing so. Statistics soon proved this belief completely erroneous. Criminalization destroyed the option of legal abortion for hundreds of thousands of women, but it never succeeded in convincing women to return to the childbearing practices of the patriarchal peasant family. Ultimately, the state failed to raise the birthrate substantially. The prohibition produced an immediate increase, but it lasted only a few years. By 1938 the birthrate began to drop again and by 1940 it had returned to its level of 1935, before the prohibition on abortion.[80]

Despite the prohibition, the incidence of abortion remained high. In Moscow, there were 9.7 abortions per 1,000 people in

[79] "Obsuzhdaet Zakonoproekt," *Sotsialisticheskaia iustitsiia*, 17 (1936): 2–4; "Rabotniki Iustitsiia Aktivno Uchastvuite Obsuzhdenii Zakonoproekt," *Sotsialisticheskaia iustitsiia*, 18 (1936): 1–4; A. Gertsenzon, A. Lapshina, "Zakon o Zapreshchenii Aborta," *Sotsialisticheskaia zakonnost'*, 10 (1936): 31; D. A. Glebov, "Zakonoproekt TsIK i SNK Soiuza SSR ot 25 Maia 1936," *Sovetskii vrachebnyi zhurnal*, 11 (1936): 802–803; O. P. Nogina, "Zadachi Okhrany Materinstva i Mladenchestva," *Sovetskii vrachebnyi zhurnal*, 5 (1936): 321–325; "V Zashchitu Materi i Rebenka," *Sotsialisticheskaia zakonnost'*, 7 (1936): 17–20.

[80] Ansley Coale, Barbara Anderson, Erna Harm, *Human Fertility in Russia since the Nineteenth Century* (Princeton University Press, Princeton, N.J., 1975): 16.

1925, 15.8 in 1926, and 12 in 1939.[81] In the Russian towns, there were 6.1 in 1926, 9.6 in 1938, and 10.8 in 1939. And in the countryside, .3 in 1926, and 1.3 in 1939.[82] Thus by 1939, despite the prohibition, the incidence of abortion was higher than in 1926 during the period of legalization. Many of the abortions performed after 1936 were "clean-up" work doctors did on women who entered the hospitals hemorrhaging from illegal abortions. One demographer estimates that after 1936, only 10% of all abortions performed in hospitals were legal abortions performed for medical reasons. The remaining 90% were abortions begun outside the hospital: 30% illegal abortions and 60%, spontaneous miscarriages.[83] Yet any woman entering a hospital after 1936 would have been deeply reluctant to admit to an illegal abortion, and it is likely that the percentage of illegal abortions treated in the hospitals was much higher. After 1936, doctors saw an enormous increase in the numbers of women suffering from infections, peritonitis, perforation, hemorrhage, chronic inflammation, sepsis, infertility, and other complications. The death rate from illegal abortion soared. A study in the 1960s of 1,000 menopausal women revealed the frightening prevalence of illegal abortion after the 1936 decree. The fecund years of many of these women coincided with the period of prohibition. Of the fertile women, only one-third had borne children but never had an abortion. About 5% had ended every pregnancy in abortion, and over 60% had borne children and had abortions. Among women who had had abortions, 28% had one, 23% had two, and 49% had three or more. On average, a fertile woman had about five pregnancies with three ending in abortion.[84]

Repression, in the long run, proved useless in either raising the birthrate or eliminating abortion. Illegal abortion never disappeared, even in the period of legalization, and many women undoubtedly returned to the underground practices of willing

[81] A. Gertsenzon, N. Lapshina, "Zakon o zapreshchenie aborta," *Sotsialisticheskaia zakonnost'*, 10 (1936): 29; Sadvokasova, p. 30.

[82] On abortions in 1925 and 1926, see *Aborty v 1926*, p. 8; on population in towns and countryside in 1926, see Lubnyi-Gertsyk, p. 86; and Sadvokasova, p. 30, on abortion rate in 1938 and 1939.

[83] Sadvokasova, p. 31, 32.

[84] Verbenko et al., pp. 12–13.

doctors, midwives, and *babki*. Evidence strongly suggests that the decline in the birthrate in 1938 signaled women's success in expanding the networks for illegal abortion.[85] In the absence of reliable contraception, women continued to use abortion, albeit illegal, as a primary method of birth control. And they suffered, they sickened, and they died as a consequence.

[85] Elizabeth Waters, "From the Old Family to the New: Work, Marriage and Motherhood in Urban Soviet Russia, 1917–1931," Doctoral Dissertation, University of Birmingham (Birmingham, 1985): 306; also her chapter, "Regulating Fertility." Waters writes that the 1938 drop in the birthrate signaled women's success in "reconstructing" the illegal abortion networks, but evidence in this chapter shows that these networks had never fully disappeared. Vishnevskii, Volkov, p. 174.

8

Recasting the vision: The resurrection of the family

> What I eat and drink, how I sleep and dress is my private affair, and my private affair also is my intercourse with a person of the opposite sex.[1]
>
> *August Bebel, 1879*

> It is necessary to put an end to the anarchist view of marriage and childbirth as an exclusively private affair.[2]
>
> *P. A. Krasikov, Deputy Chairman of the Supreme Court, 1936*

The prohibition on abortion in June 1936 was accompanied by a campaign to discredit and destroy the libertarian ideas that shaped social policy throughout the 1920s. After the ratification of the 1926 Family Code, the problems posed by divorce, alimony, family instability, and *besprizornost'* continued to mount. The process of forced collectivization created fresh streams of homeless, starving children, and rapid industrialization subjected the family to new and terrible strains. As women poured into the wage labor force at the end of the first Five Year Plan, the press drew increasing attention to a new phenomenon of "unsupervised and neglected" children (*beznadzornost'*). By 1935, the state had begun to crack down heavily on juvenile crime and the children of the streets. In 1936, jurists repudiated many of their earlier ideas, and in a clear ideological shift, demanded the strengthening and stabilization of the family. Couching the new policies in a populist appeal for social order, the Party aban-

[1] August Bebel, *Women under Socialism* (New York, 1910): 467.
[2] "Rabotniki Iustitsii Aktivno Uchastvuite v Obsuzhdenii Zakono-proekta," *Sotsialisticheskaia iustitsiia*, 18 (1936): p. 3. Hereafter cited as *SIu.*

296

doned its earlier vision of social relations in favor of a new reliance on mass repression. The "withering-away" doctrine, once central to the socialist understanding of the family, law, and the state, was anathemized.

Alimony and divorce

The new Code on Marriage, the Family, and Guardianship became law in January 1927. Proponents of the new Code had argued that the law should reflect life, but within a year it was strikingly apparent that life also reflected the law. The new Code had an immediate impact on the divorce rate throughout the country. The number of divorces, already very great, increased between 1926 and 1927 in the European part of the USSR, from 1.6 to 2.7 per 1,000 people. The rural areas showed an increase in the divorce rate from 1.4 to 2.0, and in the towns, the rate doubled from 2.9 to 5.8.[3] In the towns of the Central Industrial region, which included Moscow, the divorce rate more than doubled (3.0 to 7.2), and in the towns of the Leningrad region (*oblast,*) it almost tripled (3.3 to 9.0). In Moscow, the numbers jumped from 6.1 to 9.3; in Tver from 4.8 to 7.6, Iaroslavl, 4.0 to 7.8, and Leningrad, 3.6 to 9.8. And towns that had had lower divorce rates showed even greater increases: from 1.9 to 6.2 in Saratov, 1.9 to 6.3 in Samara, 1.9 to 4.6 in Ivanovo-Vosnesensk, and 1.8 to 7.8 in Voronezh. In Leningrad there were 265 divorces per 1,000 marriages in 1926 and 657 in 1927. In Moscow, the numbers jumped from 477 to 741. Thus by 1927, two-thirds of all marriages ended in divorce in Leningrad, and in Moscow, three-quarters.[4] The divorce rate continued to rise in Moscow, reaching 10.1 in 1929, with almost four-fifths of all marriages ending in divorce (see Table 19).

In 1927, about 20% of all men and 17% of women entering

[3] S. N. Prokopovich, *Narodnoe khoziaistvo SSSR*, Vol. 1 (Izdatel'stvo imeni Chekhova, New York, 1952): 74.

[4] *Estestvennoe dvizhenie naseleniia RSFSR za 1926 god* (Moscow, 1928): LIV; M. Kaplun, "Brachnost' naseleniia RSFSR," *Statisticheskoe obozrenie* (1929): 95–97. S. Ia. Vol'fson, *Sotsiologiia braka i sem'i* (Minsk, 1929): 410, notes that the divorce rate showed similar increases in Belorussia and the other republics.

Table 19. *Marriage and divorce in Leningrad and Moscow,*
1918–1929 (per 1,000 population)

	Moscow			Leningrad		
	Marriage	Divorce	Divorces/ 100 Marriages	Marriage	Divorce	Divorces/ 100 Marriages
1918	7.5	2.1	28	14.4	–	–
1919	17.4	3.4	19	19.5	–	–
1920	19.1	3.7	19	27.7	1.9	7
1921	16.9	5.1	30	20.9	2.4	11
1922	15.3	3.5	23	14.9	2.3	15
1923	16.1	3.8	24	14.9	3.4	23
1924	14.9	4.5	30	12.4	3.2	26
1925	13.6	5.6	41	13.2	3.1	23
1926	12.7	6.0	47	13.6	3.6	26
1927	12.6	9.3	74	15.0	9.8	65
1928	12.7	9.6	76	16.5	–	
1929	12.9	10.1	78	16.2	–	

Source: S. N. Prokopovich, *Narodnoe khoziaistvo SSSR*, Vol. 1 (Izdatel'stvo Imeni Chekhova, New York, 1952): 66, 75.

marriage in the towns had already been divorced. In the countryside, the figures were slightly lower but still considerable – 11% of men and 9% of women. The sociologist S. Ia. Vol'fson termed the situation "sexual anarchy," noting that many men took advantage of the new Code to marry one woman after another in a dizzying merry-go-round of serial relations.[5] By the end of 1927, the phenomenon was widespread enough to prompt the Supreme Court to rule that any man who registered a marriage for the sole purpose of sexual relations and then divorced was liable to criminal prosecution.[6]

The increase in divorce and the confusion in social relations was captured in a popular joke told in Moscow in the mid-1930s:

A man comes to court and is asked to pay alimony (one-third of his income) to his ex-wife.
"I can't, I'm already paying that to another ex-wife," he said.

[5] Kaplun, p. 91; Vol'fson, *Sotsiologiia braka i sem'i*, p. 380.
[6] "Raz"iasnenie Plenuma Verkhovnogo Suda RSFSR," *Ezhenedel'nik sovetskoi iustitsii*, 12 (1928): 383. Hereafter cited as *ESIu*.

"Well, you must pay a second 'third'," said the judge.

"I can't, I'm already paying that too," the man replied.

"Well, then you must pay a third 'third'."

"I can't, I'm paying that too."

"What do you mean," asked the judge, "You are paying all your wages to former wives? Then what are you living on?"

"I'm living on the alimony my wife is getting from five other men," the man replied.[7]

In reality, however, the redistribution of wealth was not nearly so effective or amusing. The new Family Code provided a simplified divorce procedure but the difficulties faced by divorced women remained essentially the same. Although women were filtering back into the workforce throughout the 1920s, in most branches of industry the percentage of women workers barely exceeded prewar levels. The number of creches and daycare centers was still pitifully small. In 1926–1927 there were only 1,629 preschools serving 85,349 children. If seasonal and rural facilities were included in these numbers the state still only served about 150,000 children out of a population of 10 million. Vol'fson explained, "This means that the state still carries only the most insignificant percent of the burden of caring for preschool children. The remainder falls to the family."[8]

Moreover, although certain provisions of the new Code offered additional protection to women, others exacerbated women's problems. Transferring divorce from the courts to ZAGS simplified the procedure and lightened the courts' caseloads, but it simultaneously extended and complicated the process of suing for alimony or child support. Under the 1918 Code, the judge set the monetary award immediately after he heard the divorce case. But beginning in 1927, either spouse could register a divorce in ZAGS without the consent or even the knowledge of the partner. If no notation was made concerning support, the needy spouse, most often the woman, was forced to file a separate suit. The new Code thus introduced a time lag, which many women could ill afford, between the divorce and the award. The procedure was particularly disadvantageous to women who were uneducated, unaware of their rights, or ignorant of court and administrative procedures.[9]

[7] Ella Winter, *Red Virtue* (New York, 1933): 145.

[8] Vol'fson, *Sotsiologiia braka i sem'i*, pp. 386, 389.

[9] N. S. Dad'iants, *Iski ob alimentakh* (Moscow, 1927): 9.

The new Code also limited the term of support, permitting only one year of alimony to a disabled spouse, and six months to the unemployed. This provision affected support awards set before 1926 as well: If a man had already paid alimony for more than six months or a year, a judge had the power to cancel his future payments.[10] Two commentators critically observed that this retroactive provision "neglects the phenomenon of our contemporary unstable life: women who remain in a desperate position." They noted, "The woman, in the course of a long married life, helped her husband by her 'worries' to create his good 'position.' But thanks to married life she has earned many disabilities (frequent abortions, many illnesses, syphilis, and so on). What sort of position is this woman in? Are her interests protected by the new Code? Of course not."[11]

Yet despite the time limits on alimony, the new Code prompted many women, especially those in de facto marriages, to bring suit for support after divorce or abandonment. Studies showed an increase of about one-third in the number of support suits. In the Siberian region (*krai*) in 1926, there were 17,815 cases involving support, representing 9% of all civil cases. In the first six months of 1927, there were 11,579 cases or 10% of civil cases. Projecting the number of cases over the entire year, there would have been more than 23,000 support suits in 1927: a 30% increase over 1926. The study showed that of 179 cases brought to people's court in the district (*okrug*) of Novosibirsk, an area that covered two towns and three villages, the overwhelming majority (79%) concerned child support. Of the remainder, 10% consisted of elderly parents suing their adult children for support. Only 7% involved alimony.

Most of the plaintiffs in the towns and the villages of Novosibirsk *okrug* were women. In the towns, 75% of the plaintiffs were either unemployed workers, housewives, or invalids, a surprisingly high percentage in light of the limited number of suits for personal support. In the countryside, 75% of the plaintiffs were *bedniachki* (poor peasants), and 7% were *batrachki* (landless laborers). The plaintiffs, primarily women, were clearly in finan-

---

[10] Ibid., p. 5; L. I. Fishman, "Po Povodu Novogo Kodeksa Zakonov o Brake," *Pravo i zhizn'*, 3 (1927): 7–8.

[11] S. S. Bronstein, S. S. Konstantinovskaia, "Imushchestvennie Vzaimootnosheniia Mezhdu Suprugami," *Pravo i zhizn'*, 6–7 (1927): 72.

cially desperate straits. The defendants were slightly better off. In the towns, almost half (45%) were white-collar workers (*sluzhashchie*), about one-quarter were blue-collar workers, and one-fifth, craftsmen (*kustarniki*). Only a tiny fraction were unemployed. In the countryside, 25% of the defendants were *bedniaks* and about 40% were *seredniaks* (middle peasants). Very few prosperous peasants were involved in support suits. In both the urban and rural cases, the men tended to be just above their female partners on the social scale. The class discrepancies were not large enough, however, to resolve the financial problems the defendants faced in paying alimony or child support, for even *sluzhashchie* and *seredniaks* had trouble making monthly payments.

The study also highlighted the problems created by the transfer of divorce from the courts to ZAGS. Most suits took longer than a month to resolve and some dragged on for six months or more. Alimony and support suits were supposed to be resolved quickly so that a woman without income would be able to support herself and her children, but the courts were slow and the lag time between the divorce and the award was significant.[12]

Child support awards throughout the country were small, especially in the countryside. In Viatka province, for example, the plaintiffs were mostly peasants, and the district (*uezd*) court awarded about 4 rubles or less a month. As in the Siberian *krai*, the cases took longer than they should. One case dragged on so long that the plaintiff finally wrote, "I have become reconciled to my position." There were other problems as well. Judges frequently did not specify the amount of the award, but automatically decreed: "Collect from the defendant a living wage according to the rates of the statistical bureau." They failed to investigate the financial backgrounds of the contending parties and made no effort to locate fathers in paternity suits.[13] Both the Siberian and the Viatka studies charged that alimony and support cases were undermined by red tape, poor preparation, needless delays, and "formalistic" rulings.

[12] *Obzor praktiki narodnykh i okruzhnykh sudov Sibirskogo kraia po primeneniiu kodeksa zakonov o brake, sem'e i opeke* (1928): 1–5.

[13] Krinkin, "Dela alimentnye," *ESIu*, 49–50 (1928): 1245–1246; G. Uvarov, "O Passivnosti Suda v Razreshenii Alimentnykh Del," *Rabochii sud*, 17–18 (1929): 1165.

The main obstacle to collecting alimony, however, was not the cumbersome court process, but the defendant's refusal to pay. The Viatka study showed that more than 90% of men refused to pay voluntarily.[14] The procedure for collecting alimony from a reluctant defendant was fairly simple, although corruption, bumbling, and popular ignorance of the law often led to endless complications and delays. If the spouses agreed in ZAGS to an alimony or child support award, and the man then refused to pay, the woman could get a court order to collect. In the absence of a support agreement, she could file suit. In either case, a bailiff, provided with a list of debtors, was empowered to collect the money.[15] But in actuality, the bailiffs, overloaded with alimony cases, were slow to search for missing or delinquent defendants. Men changed their jobs and addresses in an effort to avoid payment. One fellow changed his job so often within two years that he had to get a new passport: There was no more room to stamp his place of employment.[16] Bailiffs sometimes sent women to their ex-husbands' workplaces to collect their money. Unsure about their rights and unaccustomed to dealing with bureaucracies, women were easily put off by employers or bookkeepers, who were known to "misplace" court orders and to "forget" to deduct the awards from defendants' salaries. In some cases, the bailiff only sent a routine summons ordering a defendant to pay and took no further action on the case. Some bailiffs simply mailed the court order to the defendant's workplace, an action that usually produced no results.[17] In any case, thousands of women anxiously awaited awards that never came.

Moreover, punitive measures were rarely applied to men who refused to pay child support. Although the Criminal Code established that "malicious" refusal to pay was punishable by six months in prison or a fine of up to 300 rubles, the Supreme Court ruled in 1927 that nonpayment of alimony or child support could only be considered "malicious" if the defendant had

---

[14] Krinkin, "Dela Alimentnye," p. 1246.

[15] Dad'iants, *Iski ob alimentakh*, pp. 9, 21.

[16] P. Liublinskii, "Uklonenie ot Platezha Alimentov (st. 158)," *Sotsialisticheskaia zakonnost'*, 10 (1936): 36. Hereafter cited as *SZ*.

[17] N. Zaks, "Zamechaniia po Prakticheskoi Rabote," *Proletarskii sud*, 2 (1926): 5; "O Posobnikakh Zlostnym Neplatel'shchikam Alimentov," *Pravda* (May 28, 1936): 2.

the means to pay but refused.[18] Given the very real difficulties workers and peasants had in meeting their payments, women had limited legal recourse.

As a result of the delays and difficulties impeding the payment of alimony and child support, the VTsIK and SNK decreed in 1928 that people who were responsible for support had to inform the bailiff and their employers of any change in address, employment, or earnings. Failure to report these changes was a criminal offense. Several months later, the Commissariat of Internal Affairs (NKVD) sent a circular to its *krai, oblast'*, and provincial departments demanding closer attention to divorces and support arrangements involving children. The local organs were instructed to transfer automatically to the courts all cases in which support was contested. The NKVD instructed the local ZAGS to inform parents of their financial responsibilities to their children and to ensure that child support was clearly established where warranted.[19] These instructions, an early administrative attempt to emphasize family responsibility, were the direct result of the problems created by transferring divorce from the courts to the ZAGS.

Problems persisted – indeed intensified – into the early 1930s. Although men continued to flout the court orders, convictions for nonpayment actually dropped between 1932 and 1934. And even when convictions were obtained, sentences were light. Most men received sentences of compulsory labor, usually for a term of six months, to be served in their own place of work. In practice, this amounted to little more than a fine. A significant percentage received "probational compulsory labor," a virtual synonym for acquittal.[20]

The case of Anna Nikitina, a 28-year-old factory worker typified the situation. In 1934, after her husband Nikitin disappeared, Anna supported two young children and her elderly

[18] "Raz"iasnenie Plenuma Verkhovnogo Suda RSFSR," *ESIu*, 8 (1927): 240; V. V. Sokolov, *Prava zhenshchiny po sovetskim zakonam* (Moscow, 1928): 63.

[19] "V Sovnarkome RSFSR," *ESIu*, 18 (1928): 555; "Ofitsial'naia Chast'," *ESIu*, 33 (1928): 923. Brandenburgskii strongly supported the idea of forcing a person who owed alimony to register a change of residence or salary. See his "Zhizn' Pred"iavliaet Svoi Trebovaniia," *ESIu*, 28 (1928): 666.

[20] Liublinskii, pp. 32, 34.

mother on her earnings of 150 to 200 rubles a month. When social workers finally located Nikitin, Anna brought suit. The court ordered him to pay 38 rubles a month, and Nikitin quickly moved to the countryside. The bailiff sent a court order to his new residence only to discover that he had moved again, this time to a nearby state farm (*sovkhoz*.) The bailiff then sent a new order to the *sovkhoz* director, but without success: Anna still received no money. Within the next six months, the court authorities sent a series of orders and inquiries to the director and the procurators at the *raion* (district) and *oblast'* levels. As a result of this paper barrage, Anna received 266 rubles, which cancelled Nikitin's debt of the past nine months. Anna then returned to court and successfully petitioned the judge to raise her award to 70 rubles a month. Once again, Nikitin stopped payment, prompting a new flurry of court orders. Meanwhile, Anna's children were going hungry. Finally, after the *sovkhoz* director was threatened with a suit, Nikitin reluctantly sent another lump-sum payment that bore no relation to the new amount ordered by the judge. Another summons to the *oblast'* procurator elicited the response that Nikitin's residence was now unknown, although documents revealed that he continued to work and live at the *sovkhoz*. A suit was then filed against the *sovkhoz* director. Fully two years after she first appeared in court, Anna awaited trial of both her husband and his employer. Her children were still suffering the loss of income.[21]

Nikitin's success in circumventing the judge's rulings, his collusion with his employer, the court's ineffectiveness, Anna's frustration, and the children's misery reflected a pattern repeated in thousands of cases each year. In 1934, 200,000 cases of alimony passed through the people's courts.[22] The problems enforcing the awards engendered a growing discontent among women and court employees alike.

The persistence of Besprizornost'

The seemingly intractable problem of *besprizornost'* had forced a steady retreat from the policy of state child rearing, culminating

[21] Ibid., pp. 37–38.   [22] Ibid., p. 32.

in the 1926 decree that legalized adoption. The decree provided some relief for the overcrowded children's homes, but it did not put an end to *besprizornost'*. Even as the economy recovered its prewar strength, homeless and neglected children continued to haunt the streets. As the social links between *besprizornost'*, single mothers, divorce, and male irresponsibility emerged more clearly, state agencies placed an ever greater emphasis on family responsibility. More than any other social factor, *besprizornost'* was responsible for the shift.

In 1927 there were approximately 190,000 children in state institutions, and between 95,000 and 125,000 on the streets.[23] Orphans from poor or landless peasant families, *batrak* children who worked as herders in the summer, children of large, impoverished families and of single mothers, neglected children, runaways from the children's homes, could all be found on the streets.[24] The Fifth All-Russian Congress of the Department of People's Education (ONO) noted that the current sources of homelessness and juvenile crime were no longer famine and hunger, but "the breakup of the old life and the continuing absence of any stable form of new life."[25] The horrors of famine gradually yielded to the less dramatic consequences of poverty and family disintegration as the main sources of *besprizornost'*.

The All-Union Meeting on *Besprizornost'*, held in April 1927, affirmed that *besprizornost'* still had a "mass character" because of "economic and life conditions." The meeting's final resolutions reflected the prevailing policy toward the *besprizorniki*, stressing the need for preventive measures, including "strengthening the responsibility of parents for the care of their children"; clearing

[23] For the lower estimate, see TsGAOR fond 5207, op.1, delo 336, pp. 41, 46. A higher estimate is cited in TsGAOR fond 5207, op. 1. delo 392, p. 18 and "Orientirovochnyi Trekhletnii Plan Bor'by s Detskoi Besprizornost'iu," in *Sbornik deistvuiushchikh uzakonenii i resporiazhenii pravitel'stva Soiuza SSR i pravitel'stva RSFSR, postanovlenii Detkomissii pri VTsIK i vedomstvennykh rasporiazhenii* (Moscow, 1929): 28. Hereafter cited as *Sbornik 1929*.

[24] Fond 5207, op. 1, delo 326, p. 45; I. Daniushevskii, "Kak Preduprezhdat' Detskuiu Besprizornosti," in S. S. Tizanov, M. S. Epshtein, eds., *Gosudarstvo i obshchestvennost' v bor'be s detskoi besprizornost'iu* (Moscow, Leningrad, 1927): 10.

[25] "O Bor'be s Detskoi Besprizornost'iu," in Tizanov, Epshtein, eds., p. 40.

the streets of *besprizorniki;* and preparing them to work by establishing workshops and job training programs in the children's homes.[26] The emphasis on prevention revealed a heightened awareness of the ties between *besprizornost'* and family disintegration, as well as a stronger commitment to preserving the family unit.

In June 1927, the VTsIK and SNK launched an ambitious three-year plan aimed at the final eradication of *besprizornost'.* Following the resolutions passed at the All-Union Meeting on *Besprizornost'* two months earlier, the plan stressed job training, the transfer of teenage inmates to productive work, increased help for single mothers, and jobs for unemployed teenagers. The plan provided 80 rubles a year to every workshop that employed a teenager; it increased the number of children of preschool age to be sent to paid foster care; and it set up dormitories for single mothers. It instructed local executive committees to work out additional economic incentives to encourage adoptions by peasants.

The plan aggressively sought to reduce the number of children in state institutions. It set a goal of 68,000 children, mainly teenagers, to be sent out of the homes between 1927 and 1929: 22,000 would go to peasant families, 25,000 to factories and workshops, and 21,000 to their parents, who would receive financial assistance. The plan established several measures to help single mothers preserve their families, including temporary government aid. Stressing paid foster care and family assistance, the plan revealed the implicit official assumption that the family could care for children more effectively than the state.[27]

According to local reports, the plan successfully reduced the number of children on the streets. The numbers dropped from an estimated 125,000 to less than 10,000 by October 1928. Yet a letter from the Detkomissiia noted that local officials tended to

[26] "O Metodakh Bor'by s Detskoi Besprizornost'iu," in *Sbornik 1929,* p. 40; Z. Sh. Karamysheva, "Pedagogicheskie Problemy Sotsial'no-Pravovoi Okhrany Nesovershennoletnykh v RSFSR, 1917–1932," Candidate of Pedagogical Science, Nauchno-Issledovatel'skii Institut Obshei Pedagogiki Akademii Pedagogicheskikh Nauk SSSR (Moscow, 1976): 45.

[27] "O Plane Bor'by s Detskoi Besprizornost'iu," in *Sbornik 1929,* pp. 20–25. *Sistimaticheskoe sobranie zakonov RSFSR,* I, (Moscow, 1929): 635–638.

exaggerate the decreases, claiming unlikely reductions from 1,500 to 720 street children in Kursk province, 2,000 to 450 in Orlov, and 12,000 to 4,000 in the North Caucasus.[28] Although reliable figures are not available, the estimates indicated huge transfers, involving thousands of children, from the streets to the children's homes, and from the homes to workplaces, families, and foster care. Given the persistence of juvenile unemployment in the late 1920s and the limits on the number of teenagers that could have been absorbed by factories or cooperatives, most of the *besprizorniki* must have been sent to peasant families or returned to impoverished relatives.

As the center stepped up the pressure to get children off the streets, the covert war between the central authorities and the localities intensified. In April 1928, the Central Committee of the Party strictly instructed the local central committees to clear the streets of *besprizorniki* and to ensure that the children did not return to their old haunts. Yet in 1930, according to information from the Detkomissiia, the children's homes were still "in an extraordinarily difficult position," because local officials continued to interpret the instructions from the center as license to close the homes. They moved homes into unfit buildings, from one town to another, and from towns to rural areas. The Detkomissiia noted that many homes were in unsanitary places, and the allocations for feeding, teaching, and caring for the children were "totally insufficient."[29]

The policy of peasant adoption proved a poor substitute for well-funded children's homes. There were numerous complaints: that the families exploited the children and did not permit them to attend school; that the state provided no follow-up supervision; and that the sums provided for the children's upkeep were too small.[30] Children adopted by prosperous peasant households in search of additional labor were "exploited in the most unscrupulous manner." Some children ran away and be-

[28] TsGAOR, fond 5207, op. 1, delo 392, pp. 18–21.

[29] "Postanovlenie VKP (b)," and "Po Dokladu Detkomissii pri VTsIK i NKProsa RSFSR o Khode Raboty po Bor'be s Detskoi Besprizornost'iu," in *Sbornik deistvuiushchikh uzakonenii i rasporiazhenii pravitel'stva SSSR i pravitel'stva RSFSR, postanovlenii Detkomissii pri VTsIK i vedomstvennykh rasporiazhenii* (Moscow, 1932): 5–6. Hereafter cited as *Sbornik 1932*.

[30] TsGAOR, fond 5207, op. 1, delo 392, pp. 32–37.

came *batraks;* others wandered into the towns. One court member noted that a number of angry and victimized *besprizorniki* in his district had brought suit for compensation for their labor in the *dvor.* The court recognized the validity of their claims but was forced to adhere to the 1926 adoption decree that had denied adoptees the right to wages or *vydel* (movable property). In light of these cases, the court member urged the government to rescind the law on adoption.[31]

Yet the critics of peasant adoption had little effect on the direction of policy. With the revival of the economy, officials began promoting adoption by urban dwellers. Invalids, workers, *sluzhashchie,* pensioners, craftsmen, cooperative members, *artely,* and even students were encouraged to take children from the homes. Urban residents were guaranteed a lump sum of 50 to 100 rubles, monthly payments of 8 to 15 rubles, a 10 percent rebate on rent, and other tax privileges to help defray the costs of raising a child. The children were not to be sent out to work before the age of twelve.[32] The rules governing urban adoption (or patronage, as it was called) closely followed the earlier model developed for peasant adoption. Families or individuals in need of extra income were urged to apply, and every effort was made to provide them strong monetary incentives.

Throughout the late twenties, policy clearly favored the family as an inexpensive alternative to state care. In contrast to the 1926 Family Code, which sought to narrow the circle of family responsibility, Brandenburgskii proposed at the November 1928 VTsIK that legal responsibility for children be extended to stepparents if the natural parents died or were unable to provide adequate care. Given the large number of divorces and remarriages, his proposal would affect a significant number of families. He also moved that if a child's parents or guardian died and left an inheritance, the beneficiary be compelled to support the remaining children. In both motions, the VTsIK sought to diminish the responsibility of the state by broadening the definition of "family" and its obligations.[33]

---

[31] Statsenko, "Peredacha Vospitannikov Detskikh Domov v Krest' ianskie Sem'i," *ESIu,* 31 (1929): 732.

[32] M. Popov, *Detskaia besprizornost' i patronirovanie* (Izdanie Oblastnoi Detkomissii Ivanovskoi Promyshlennoi Oblasti, 1929): 17–20.

[33] *III sessiia Vserossiiskogo Tsentral'nogo Ispolnitel'nogo Komiteta, XIII sozyva. Biulleten' No. 17* (1928): 1–2. For a case involving stepparents

Earlier arguments had championed the superiority of the state over the family in raising children, but now every effort was made to encourage parents to keep their children from becoming wards of the state. A circular from the Commissariats of Health and Justice in 1927 explained that mothers who abandoned their children should not necessarily be deprived of parental rights insofar as the children's homes were already severely overcrowded. Governmental aid to needy mothers was deemed preferable to putting infants and children in state homes, which were plagued by high death rates. If a mother was unable to provide care, the baby should be placed with a foster family, who would be aided for its effort. The circular demanded that the criminal penalties for abandoning a child be increased, and that parents pay for children who were placed in state facilities. It noted that the courts should join the struggle against *besprizornost'* by actively searching for fathers who refused to pay alimony and child support. The Commissariat of Health directed its Department of Maternity and Infancy (OMM) to organize a large number of juridical consulting offices to inform women of their legal rights. In May 1927, the Supreme Court decreed that parents who abandoned their children near the children's homes were subject to criminal prosecution; and in May 1930, similar sanctions were threatened against parents who abandoned their children in OMM clinics after taking them there for treatment.[34]

Employing a mixture of inducements and threats, officials made every effort to reduce the financial burden of the state, to compel parents to support their children, and to preserve family ties. Although the emphasis fell largely on short-term, preventative measures, paternal and family responsibility were beginning to emerge as important issues. Yet thus far the measures were all administrative in nature: practical in orientation, they developed directly from concrete needs to lessen overcrowding in the children's homes, to reduce the infant death rate, and to solve the problem of *besprizornost'*. They were not accompanied by a mass ideological campaign to resurrect traditional family bonds. Social workers, judges, and other officials were involved in daily

and children, see E. Kazanskii, "K Novym Izmeneniiam Kodeksa Zakonov o Brake, Sem'e i Opeke," *ESIu*, 35 (1928): 954.

[34] Ia. A. Perel', ed., *Okhrana zhenshchiny-materi v ugolovnom zakone* (Moscow, Leningrad, 1932): 18, 19–20.

efforts to patch up the family, but they still shared an official commitment to its eventual "withering away." Their position was neatly articulated by the sociologist S. Ia. Vol'fson in a major work published in 1929. Vol'fson wrote that the state was currently forced to use the family as "an auxiliary social formation," even as it was divesting the family of its social functions. The state was thus caught in a "position of compromise" due to "the need to use this social cell."[35]

Women and wage labor

In 1928, the Party leadership embarked on a massive effort to collectivize agriculture and industrialize the economy. Within the next ten years, the country underwent a wrenching transformation as millions of peasant men and women flooded the cities and new industrial centers to enter the wage labor force. Between 1928 and 1937, 6.6 million women entered the workforce in industry and service.[36] The social relations that had characterized NEP changed dramatically and irreversibly.

Initially, however, the drive for industrialization had little effect on women's share and position in the workforce. The first Five Year Plan (FYP) was launched in 1927 – 1928, and although it opened new prospects for men immediately, it offered fewer opportunities to women. Up to 1930, women still constituted roughly the same portion (28%) of the labor force as in 1923. Their share of factory jobs actually fell between 1929 and 1930. The drop reflected the plan's overwhelming emphasis on developing heavy industry, where women were poorly represented.[37] In the metal industry, for example, women had by 1931 not yet recouped the share of the labor force they held in 1920.[38] Throughout the better part of the first FYP, women remained segregated in the traditional female industries: Their share of jobs in electrical stations, mining and fuel, metallurgy, and ma-

---

[35] Vol'fson, *Sotsiologiia braka i sem'i*, pp. 444, 445, 379, 376, 443.
[36] P. M. Chirkov, *Reshenie zhenskogo voprosa v SSSR (1917–1937)* (Izdatel'stvo "Mysl'", Moscow, 1978): 124–125.
[37] B. Marsheva, "Zhenskii trud v 1931 godu," *Voprosy truda,* 1 (1931): 31, 32, 33.
[38] G. Serebrennikov, "Zhenskii Trud v SSSR za 15 Let," *Voprosy truda,* 11–12 (1932): 60.

chine production held steady below 8% at the beginning of 1930. They continued to dominate industries such as textiles, sewing, clothing, rubber, and matches.[39] One strong advocate for women's employment noted with disappointment that despite the growing need for skilled and unskilled labor in 1929, women were moving into the labor force "at a snail's pace."[40]

Several economists voiced concern that the first FYP worked to the disadvantage of women. One worried that the emphasis on heavy industry would undermine women's share in production. Critical of the plan's priorities, she argued that "the stable position of women's labor is possible only under a general storming ascent of *all* our industry."[41] Other economists noted with apprehension that Gosplan's (state planning commission) formula to link wages to productivity would have a negative impact on women, who were concentrated in the more backward, less productive sectors. Another proposed that the surplus generated by increased investments and productivity in heavy industry be distributed fairly among all workers, not just the highly skilled in priority industries.[42]

These radical critiques of the favored pattern of industrialization had little effect on planning. And in any case, they were soon rendered superfluous by the mass influx of women into every industry in the fall of 1930. This "turning point" in policy was not the result of the Party's concern for women's interests, but rather, the growing and insistent need for new sources of labor.[43] As reserves of urban male workers were depleted, the Party turned to the wives and daughter of workers, an untapped source of labor that could meet the shortage without placing additional strains on housing and the food supply. In October 1930, the TsIK announced "the complete elimination of unem-

---

[39] Marsheva, "Zhenskii trud v 1931 godu," p. 33; I. Berlin, Ia. Mebel', "Strukturnye Sdvigi v Naselenii i Proletariate," *Voprosy truda*, 11–12 (1932): 21.

[40] Marsheva, "Zhenskii trud v 1931 godu," p. 32.

[41] B. Marsheva, "Problema Zhenskogo Truda v Sovremennykh Usloviiakh," *Voprosy truda*, 2 (1929): 40.

[42] F. Vinnik, "O Planirovanii Zarabotnoi Platy," *Voprosy truda*, 1 (1929): 49–50; F. Bulkin, "Leningradskie Soiuzy i Zarabotnaia Plata v Piatiletke," *Trud*, No. 240, 1928.

[43] Solomon Schwarz notes that a "turning point" occurred in fall 1930, see *Labor in the Soviet Union* (Praeger, New York, 1951): 66.

ployment in the Soviet Union."[44] By the end of 1931, women's share of industrial jobs showed its first appreciable increase since 1923, as 422,900 new women entered industry, almost three times the number of the two previous years combined.[45]

Moreover, for the first time since the civil war, women began entering male-dominated industries in significant numbers. Women's share of heavy industry, which had declined steadily between 1923 and 1930, now showed an increase. In the eighteen months between January 1930 and July 1931, the percentage of women holding jobs in heavy industry leaped suddenly from 22% to 42%. And while women's share of both heavy and light industry expanded, their growth in the former was more rapid, from 14% to 24%, but only 51% to 58% in the latter.[46] Women made unprecedented gains in the male-dominated sectors of construction, railroads, mining, metallurgy, and machine production.

The inroads women made in 1930–1931 continued through the second Five Year Plan, which relied heavily on female labor. In the first half of 1932, more than half of the new workers were women. They made up 44% of the country's new construction workers and fully 80% of the new industrial workers.[47] Between 1932 and 1937, 4,047,000 new workers entered the labor force; 3,350,000 (82%) of them were women.[48] By 1932, women had become one of the most important sources of labor in the drive to industrialize.

The increasing reliance on women had a significant impact on the composition of the labor force. In 1930, 28% of workers in large-scale industry were women, in 1937, 42%. In the large industrial centers, women composed an even greater fraction of the labor force: In Leningrad, 49% of all workers in large-scale industry were women. By 1937, there were 9,357,000 women in all branches of the economy (35%). Women composed 40% of

[44] *Rabochii klass – vedushchaia sila v stroitel'stve sotsialisticheskogo obshchestva, 1927–1937 gg.*, Vol. 3 (Izdatel'stvo Nauka, Moscow, 1984): 224.
[45] B. Khasik, "Vovlechenie Zhenshchin v Tsenzovoi Promyshlennost' SSSR v 1931," *Voprosy truda*, 2 (1932): 47.
[46] Serebrennikov, pp. 63, 63; Khasik, p. 48.
[47] Serebrennikov, p. 64.
[48] Schwarz, p. 72.

the workers in industry, 21% in construction, 34% in commerce, 72% in health services, and 57% in education.[49] Thus by the end of the second FYP women were heavily represented in every branch of industry, including those previously dominated by men. Their numbers were split almost equally between light and heavy industry: Of 9.4 million women employed by the national economy, almost half (4.3 million) worked in heavy industry, construction, and transport.[50]

The entrance of women into the labor force also had a substantial effect on the family. Initially, the new women workers came mainly (64%) from the towns: the unemployed, and the wives, sisters, and daughters of workers. As they entered the workforce, the birthrate dropped and family size decreased from 4.26 in 1927 to 3.8 in 1935. The combination of smaller families and the increase in the number of female wageworkers decreased dependency ratios within the family: from 2.46 dependents for every provider in 1927 to 1.59 by 1935.[51] The dependency on men that had crippled women's chances for independence in the NEP years largely vanished. The statistics seemed to indicate the dawning of a new era for women. For the first time since 1920, the promise of women's liberation appeared to have a solid material foundation.

Party leaders and planners began again to give serious attention to the socialization of household labor. Child care and socialized dining, deferred in the 1920s, became pressing necessities. In December 1931, the Central Committee dusted off Lenin's old fulminations against housework and took on "the task of transforming forms of individual consumption to social feeding."[52] One economist enthusiastically predicted that the second FYP would "achieve 100% socialization of the basic aspects of daily life."[53] The number of childcare facilities expanded rapidly: creches for infants increased twentyfold be-

---

[49] *Sovetskie zhenshchiny i profsoiuzy* (Proizdat, Moscow, 1984): 50; Schwarz, p. 72.

[50] *Sovetskie zhenshchiny i profsoiuzy*, p. 50.

[51] Schwarz, p. 145.

[52] Central Committee decree quoted by V. Val'ter, "Obshchestvennoe Pitanie – Vazhneishee Zveno v Bor'be za Profinplan," *Voprosy truda*, 11–12 (1931): 85.

[53] Serebrennikov, p. 67.

tween 1928 and 1934 from 257,000 to 5,143,400, and daycare
centers increased by a factor of 12, going from 2,132 centers in
1927–1928 to 25,700 in 1934–1935, serving 1,181,255 children.[54] Childcare facilities were hastily organized in factories,
kolkhozes, sovkhozes, cooperatives, and homes.

The expansion of the childcare network was directly tied to
the need to involve women in production. When SNK targeted
women as a critical source of untapped labor in December 1930,
it directed Gosplan to develop a proposal to meet the daycare
needs of working women as well as those expected to enter the
labor force for the first time. Four months later, in April 1931,
SNK approved Gosplan's proposal, adding that space was to be
set aside in all newly constructed houses for creches and daycare. The Commissariats of Enlightenment and Health were instructed to organize parents into voluntary daycare cooperatives
at home and at work. *Sovkhozes* and *kolkhozes* were ordered to set
up creches. A circular from the Commissariat of Health noted
that child care in the towns should be geared to shift work in
order to "aid the active participation of women workers in production, social life, and study." In the countryside, seasonal, permanent, and movable field creches were organized. A decree of
the All-Union Soviet of Housing Cooperatives in April 1931
noted the need to create creches, children's centers, communal
laundries, and dining rooms in cooperative houses. It specified
that 20% of the kitchens in cooperative houses be set aside for
communal dining rooms. Housing cooperatives were instructed
to set up sixteen-hour-a-day childcare centers, to hire personnel,
and to staff kitchens to prepare food for their residents. The
cost of staffing daycare and dining facilities would be met by
deductions of 10% from each person's rent payment and by long
term loans from the Commissariat of Labor. Housewives were
encouraged to enroll in special courses to prepare them for
wage work in communal kitchens, daycare centers, and laundries.[55]

For a brief moment, it appeared as if the social vision of the
1920s had finally come to life, revived by an enormous transfu-
sion of state spending for social services. The unemployment of

[54] *Zhenshchina v SSSR* (Moscow, 1936): 124, 127.
[55] Ia. Perel, A. A. Liubimova, eds., *Okhrana materinstva i mladenchestva*
(Moscow, Leningrad, 1932): 24, 25, 27, 31–32.

NEP, so crippling to women in its economic and social effects, disappeared. The material conditions for the "withering away" of the family and the liberation of women appeared ever more favorable. One women activist earnestly wrote, "In order to involve these millions of new women workers in socialist construction, it is necessary to reconstruct life on a socialist basis, freeing women from housework and the responsibility for children."[56] Her comments reflected the new climate of the times.

Town planners enthusiastically sketched new towns and living centers. One proposal designed single-occupancy, movable living units resembling giant capsules, to be used by the "liberated" members of former families. Frederick Starr notes that in the huge new industrial towns "communalization by necessity was already in practice," largely because of a lack of facilities. In his estimation, utopian planners "were quite reasonable in concluding that the family had indeed become an institution of the past," given the rapid increase in female employment, the decreasing fertility of urban women, and the centrifugal pressures of labor mobility on family life. Planners argued that the socialization of housework was more economical and efficient: The costs would be offset by the new, increased productivity of women.[57]

Krupskaia spoke of the need to "help people live humanly." Keeping women's needs at the forefront, she cautioned that the economy was only one area in which socialism would be built. She stressed the need to create "the material conditions for collective life" and "for the liberation of women from household slavery."[58] Stalin broadcast the benefits of collectivization in an appeal to women, and countless rural activists picked up his words. By destroying the patriarchal household as the primary unit of production, collectivization offered a radical restructuring of rural life that would free women from centuries of oppression. Mechanization, increased productivity, individual

---

[56] Ibid., p. 11.
[57] S. Frederick Starr, "Visionary Town Planning during the Cultural Revolution," in Sheila Fitzpatrick, ed., *Cultural Revolution in Russia, 1928–1931* (Indiana University Press, Bloomington, 1984): 208, 231, 232.
[58] N. K. Krupskaia, *O bytovykh voprosakh. Sbornik statei* (Moscow, Leningrad, 1930): 3–6.

wages or credits, and the socialization of household labor created a new material basis for women's liberation in the countryside. At last, the rural and urban family would "wither away."

Yet the new enthusiasm for women's liberation sparked by the
radical transformation of the economy was short-lived. Although unemployment disappeared, the number of daycare facilities increased, and opportunities for education and job training expanded, the promise of female independence was never
fulfilled. The strategies for accumulation that shaped the first
and second FYPs left women nearly as dependent on the family
unit in 1937 as they had been a decade earlier. Dependency
ratios decreased with women's entrance into the workforce, but
actual dependency on the family unit did not. Between 1928 and
1932, real wages fell by a shocking 49%. As a result, real income
per capita did not increase as more members of the family went
to work, but actually decreased to 51% of the 1928 level.[59] In
other words, two workers were now employed for the cost of
one. Two incomes were now necessary where one had once sufficed. If the male "family wage" had reinforced the family unit
by ensuring women's dependence on men, the precipitous fall in
wages had a similar effect: Individuals relied on the pooled contributions of family members to ensure a decent standard of
living. The family, as E. O. Kabo had critically noted in 1924,
continued to serve the crucial functions of income distribution
and consumption equalization.

The situation improved little during the second FYP. The
level of real wages dropped each year between 1928 and 1931,
stabilized between 1932 and 1933, registered a slight gain in
1933, dropped again in 1934 and 1935, and remained stable
through 1937. Solomon Schwarz argues that living standards
could not have dropped much further after 1931 without "a
complete disintegration of economic life." In 1937, the real
earnings of workers were still far below the level of 1928.[60]

Women's entrance into the labor force may have had less to do
with new opportunities than with a desperate need to offset the
falling income of the family. Planners may have consciously engi-

[59] Naum Jasny, *Soviet Industrialization, 1928–1952* (University of Chicago Press, Chicago, 1961): 447.
[60] Schwarz, pp. 160–163.

neered a drop in real wages to mobilize reserves of female labor in the urban family.[61] Although more work needs to be done on the relationship between wages and the recruitment of female labor, one point is clear. Wage policy did not encourage the "withering away" of the family, but rather relied on the family unit as an effective means of labor exploitation. In a period openly defined by the intensification of accumulation within every industry and every factory, it was the institution of the family that enabled the state to realize the surplus from the labor of two workers for the price of one.

Enforcing social order

The entrance of millions of women into the workforce marked a turning point not only in labor policy, but in social policy as well. The upheavals of the first and second FYPs created massive social disorder throughout the country. Huge numbers of peasants were violently uprooted from their villages and sent to forced labor camps. Starving, homeless children, reeling from the brutalities of collectivization and famine, flooded the cities. Between 1932 and 1934, 29,903,000 people arrived in Soviet towns as 23,947,000 departed.[62] Waves of people rolled in and receded, placing unprecedented demands on housing and other social services. Beneath the slogans of planned socialist construction lay a bustling Dickensian netherworld of drunkenness, crime, and speculation that thrived amid the wretched, overcrowded housing, broken families, and poverty in the cities and towns.

The mass exit of mothers from the home left millions of children without supervision during the hours after school. Living in crowded, squalid communal apartments, children escaped to the streets where they mingled with the *besprizorniki*, who quickly initiated them into the arts of petty crime. The phenomenon of *beznadzornost'* began to receive greater attention as militia men,

[61] Schwarz implies that this was the case, arguing that planners were conscious of the effect of the fall in real wages on women's desire to enter the labor force. See p. 66.

[62] *Narodnoe khoziaistvo SSSR* (Moscow, Leningrad, 1932): 401, 405.

judges, educators, and social workers encountered the consequences of poverty and neglect.

The children rounded up from the streets by the authorities
told personal tales of broken families, drunken fathers, divorce,
and immiseration. They described neighborhoods where the
line between the working class and the criminal world was
blurred. Mothers sent their children out to beg; older thieves
trained street children to pick pockets.[63] "Home" was freq: ·ntly
"a hearth of drunkenness and dissolution,"[64] a crowded co. er
of a room shared by many people. One 13-year-old, arrested
numerous times for theft, brazenly explained, "My father works
as a janitor. Where? I don't know. He is never home and I mostly
hang out on the streets and in the bazaar. I don't study or work.
I rob apartments." Another 13-year-old arrested for mugging
said, "My mother is an invalid. She lives on a pension. I am a
thief and I am simply accustomed to this way of life." A young
teenager said, "I haven't lived with my father for about two
months because he married someone else. After the death of my
mother, life was very hard and I decided to leave the house. I live
where I can and steal in order to eat." Yet another 13-year-old
explained, "I am forced to steal because my brother Pavel threw
me out of the house and I have nowhere to live and no other way
to exist."[65]

Children arrested by the militia in Moscow in 1931, for example, represented this mix of the orphaned and the neglected.
Between January and July, the militia rounded up 4,654 children, and sent them to four receiving stations in Moscow *oblast*.
The children were split almost equally between *besprizorniki* and
beznadzorniki. The vast majority were boys, between 10 and 14
years of age. About half came from working-class families, and
approximately one-third from the peasantry. Over half (55%)
were runaways from the children's homes. Most of the children
had been on the streets for only a short time: about 40% for less
than a month, and a quarter, for less than six months. About
30% had been on the streets for more than a year. More than a
third of the children said they lived on the streets because they

[63] M. Vinogradov, "Aktual'nost' Zakona 7 Aprelia," *SIu*, 19 (1935): 11.
[64] V. Tadevosian, "God Zakona 7 Aprelia 1935 g.," *SZ*, 4 (1936): 9.
[65] Strelkov, "Praktika Narsuda Vostochnoi Sibiri po Delam o Prestupleniiakh Nesovershennoletnikh," *SIu*, 26 (1935): 8, 9.

were unhappy in the children's homes; slightly more than a quarter cited troubled family circumstances.[66]

According to another study, 59% of teenagers convicted for crimes for the first time lived with their families. Of those with a history of criminal activity, 44% lived with their families, while 47% were *besprizorniki*. In Kiev, the statistics were similar: 59% of teenagers arrested had at least one parent; 41% were orphans. Here, more than half came from peasant backgrounds.[67]

The phenomenon of *beznadzornost'* was recognized as early as 1927 when the Commissariat of Enlightenment (NKPros) adopted measures against unsupervised children and street hooligans. Targeting the workers' districts, factory settlements, and rural areas as the greatest problem sites, the commissariat urged social organizations to develop after-school activities for children and discussion groups on child rearing for parents. But ever-harsher measures were enacted against street children, *besprizorniki* and *beznadzorniki*, through the early 1930s. In 1931, the militia, ordered to keep the streets of the cities clear, rounded children up in huge dragnets and dispatched them to receiving stations and the local Commissions on the Affairs of Minors (Komones.) Two large sweeps of Moscow that summer briefly cleared the streets, but the children soon filtered back. The receiving stations, converted into temporary quarters for children awaiting placement in children's home, were terribly overcrowded. The homes already held more children than they could possibly support. They logically refused to accept any more. In the Danilovskii monastery, converted to a receiving station, 300 children were living in an area of 300 square meters. The children slept, side by side, on a damp, muddy floor. A social worker at the monastery admitted, "It is a prison regime. There is no political or educational work and no job training." According to the Moscow Department of People's Education (MONO), there were 240 receiving stations in the *oblast'*, holding 17,274 children. Officials were stymied in their efforts to find permanent lodging for them. The children's homes were in disrepair, lacking dishes, tables, stools, benches, and beds. In the

---

[66] TsGAOR, fond 5207, op. 1, delo 487.

[67] B. Utevskii, "Nesovershennoletnie i Molodye Retsidivisty," *SIu*, 20 (1935): 3; Starovoitov, "Oblastnaia Prokuratura Kievshchiny v Bor'be s Detskoi Besprizornost'iu i Prestupnost'iu," *SZ*, 4 (1936): 11.

Lenin home, children slept two and three to a bed and ate five to ten from one bowl. In another home, half the children had no shoes. The sanitary conditions in many of the homes were deplorable.[68]

After the sweeps of Moscow in the summer of 1931, MONO officials, desperate to relieve overcrowding in the receiving stations, sent about 1,000 children to the Commissariat of Justice. In an eerie portent of the future, the criminal justice system assumed the work that the social service agencies could not handle. By the end of September, a report from the Moscow Soviet noted that there were approximately 2,000 children on the streets. In October, another sweep showed that number to be too small: It netted 2,811 children, 400 of whom were sent to the Commissariat of Justice to be prosecuted for criminal activities. About half of the children rounded up by the militia were between 8 and 16 years old; about one-third, 16 or older. Many had arrived from Siberia and the Ukraine, refugees from collectivization and forced resettlement. A social worker in the Danilevskii monastery noted with sharp bureaucratic impatience, "We must have a daily purge of the streets of Moscow. We must take children who steal and who continually pass through the Commissions away from their parents. This is necessary if we are to eliminate the hooligans and ruffians who demoralize the children's homes. And in order to do all this, we must have a receiving station that works continuously."[69]

In February 1933, the Moscow Executive Committee and Soviet instructed the militia not to permit any child vendors, beggars, acrobats, singers, or shoe shiners on the streets, around the markets, or in the railroad stations. Such children were to be promptly rounded up and dispatched to the proper agencies. The militia was to enforce "correct social order" in the streets and other public places. Public fighting, loitering, and aimless wandering, especially in the vicinity of the railroad stations, markets, movies, and clubs, was strictly forbidden. Adults who used children to beg or sell goods were liable to a fine of 100 rubles or thirty days of compulsory labor.[70]

Although the militia easily rounded the children up, the same

[68] TsGAOR, fond 5207, op. 1, delo 487.   [69] Ibid.
[70] TsGAOR, fond 5207, op. 1, delo 547.

old obstacles to housing and caring for them remained. The Commission on Juvenile Crime (Komones) had nowhere to send the children and no way to enforce order. In March 1935, a special meeting was held with representatives from Komones, the Commissariat of Enlightenment, the Komsomol, and the courts. The significance of the meeting was underscored by the prominence of its chairman, A. Ia. Vyshinskii, the newly appointed procurator-general of the USSR (and after Genrikh Iagoda, the head of the NKVD, the only major legal official with All-Union credentials.)[71] Faishevskii, the head of Moscow Komones, offered a gloomy report. The commissions were overloaded with cases and unable to cope effectively with juvenile crime and recidivism. Komones continued to act as a "revolving door" for *besprizorniki* and juvenile offenders. The *raion* Komones, operating with no more than two or three employees, were badly understaffed. The problems of the 1920s – understaffing, a shortage of funds, weak links with other social and juridical organizations, and limits on child placements – remained unresolved.

Faishevskii complained that Komones had no "material base to fight crime." Despite a steady barrage of letters from the local commissions to the children's homes, efforts to place children often proved futile. Moreover, the children's homes were loathe to accept children with parents. Places in the corrective facilities run by the NKVD were limited. Recent statistics from Komones showed the use of the same ineffective methods applied through the 1920s. Only 4% of juvenile offenders were placed in children's homes. The vast majority simply received a warning or a talk.[72] Streetwise teenagers knew that the commissions did not have the power to enforce punishment more exacting than a lecture on morality, and they behaved accordingly. The bottom line, in Faishevskii's view, was that there was no place to send the young people who passed through Komones.[73]

[71] See Eugene Huskey, *Russian Lawyers and the Soviet State. The Origins and Development of the Soviet Bar* (Princeton University Press, Princeton, N.J., 1986): 185 on Vyshinskii's rise. Arkady Vaksberg, *Stalin's Prosecutor. The Life of Andrei Vyshinsky* (Grove Weidenfeld, New York, 1991): 62–71.

[72] V., "Soveshchanie po Bor'be s Detskoi Prestupnost'iu," *Za sotsialisticheskuiu zakonnost'*, 4 (1935): 42.

[73] V. K. "O Detskoi Prestupnosti," *SIu*, 13 (1935): 11–12.

Vyshinskii agreed with Faishevskii. He spoke harshly against the lax behavior of the militia, the absence of special institutions for difficult children, and adults who used children for criminal purposes. He noted that Komones was unable to cope with "the noted growth of juvenile crime." In his view, both Komones and the legislation on juvenile crime were outdated. Announcing a plan to create a special branch of the All-Union Procuracy devoted to juvenile crime, Vyshinskii argued that Komones be eliminated and replaced by the courts, the militia, and the procuracy.[74] Vyshinskii's suggestion ran directly counter to the juridical beliefs of the 1920s and early 1930s pioneered by Pashukanis and his adherents. Whereas jurists had previously sought to limit the role of the courts and the law in social life, the dissolution of Komones would have the opposite effect: strengthening the courts and the procuracy by extending their jurisdiction.

In April 1935, Vyshinskii's push to broaden the jurisdiction of the courts over juvenile crime achieved partial success. In a new law, SNK granted the courts sweeping new powers: All children above the age of 12 who committed theft, violence, bodily harm, mutilation, attempted murder, or murder were removed from the jurisdiction of Komones and transferred to criminal court to be tried as adults. If found guilty, they were to be sentenced to adult penalties.[75] Anyone who organized children for the purposes of prostitution, beggary, or speculation was liable to a prison term of no less than five years. One commentator noted approvingly that the new law would "destroy the chain of irresponsibility and lack of supervision surrounding teenage criminals."[76]

The April law immediately resulted in a tidal wave of arrests and trials. Huge numbers of teenagers were arrested, mainly for

[74] V., "Soveshchanie po Bor'be s Detskoi Prestupnost'iu," p. 42.

[75] *Sbornik deistvuiushchikh uzakonenii i rasporiazhenii partii i pravitel'stva, postanovlenii detkomissii VTsIK i vedomstvennykh rasporiazhenii po likvidatsii detskoi besprizornosti i beznadzornosti*, Vypusk IV (Moscow, 1936): 102. Hereafter cited as *Sbornik 1936*. See also, John Hazard, "The Child under Soviet Law," *University of Chicago Law Review*, 5, no. 3 (1938): 424–445.

[76] Orlov, "Bor'ba s Prestupnost'iu Nesovershennoletnikh," *SIu*, 26 (1935): 6.

petty theft, and sentenced to prison. Most were between the ages of 12 and 15. F. M. Nakhimson, the head of the Leningrad provincial court, noted that 70% of the teenagers arrested in six *oblasts* after the April law were younger than 15.[77] In East Siberian *krai*, about half were under 15; in Leningrad *oblast*, the number was near 60%. Most of the teenagers were arrested for theft or hooliganism rather than more serious crimes like murder or rape. In Kiev, 78% were arrested for theft, 14% for hooliganism, and 8% for rape and more serious crimes. In Leningrad *oblast'*, 85% were convicted for theft, and in East Siberian *krai*, 70% for theft and 25% for hooliganism.[78]

In the Siberian town of Tomsk, typical arrests included a 13-year-old boy from a working-class family whose father was ill and unable to work. While the boy was temporarily living on the street, he met two runaways from a labor colony and the three began to steal. Another 13-year-old was arrested for picking the pocket of an elderly man. A 12-year-old whose father was a stevedore and mother a street sweeper was arrested for stealing produce from an *artel* of the blind.[79] In one tragic case, an impoverished woman worker, abandoned by her husband without support, sent her 11-year-old son to steal firewood and dig up leftover potatoes in a nearby *kolkhoz* field. Although the case was eventually dismissed, she was initially prosecuted for theft.[80] In most cases, the children came from broken families, living on the bare margins of survival. They were arrested for petty crimes against property.

One month later, in May 1935, Vyshinskii's triumph was complete. His recommendations at the meeting on juvenile crime two months earlier were implemented in full. Sovnarkom and the Central Committee abolished Komones and transferred re-

---

[77] "V Gosudarstvennom Institute Ugolovnoi Politiki," *SIu*, 31 (1935): 18.

[78] Strelkov, "Praktika Narsudov Vostochnoi Sibiri Po Delam o Prestupleniiakh Nesovershennoletnikh," p. 8; Orlov, "Bor'ba s Prestupnost'iu Nesovershennoletnikh," p. 6; Starovoitov, "Oblastnaia Prokuratura Kievshchiny v Bor'be s Detskoi Besprizornost'iu i Prestupnost'iu," p. 11.

[79] Kazachkov, "Kak v Tomske Sumeli Izvratit' Postanovlenie Pravitel'stva 7 Aprelia 1935 g.," *SIu*, 29 (1935): 8.

[80] V. O. "V Bor'be za Likvidatsiiu Beznadzornosti i Besprizornosti Detei," *SIu*, 27 (1935): 9.

sponsibility for all juvenile crime to the procuracy and the
courts. Their decree charged that *besprizornost'* was not the result
of poverty, but rather, "the poor work of the local Soviet, Party,
professional, and Komsomol organizations." It claimed that the
majority of children's homes were poorly organized, that there
was insufficient attention to the "criminal element" among children, that street children were not dispatched quickly enough to
homes, and that parents were sanctioning juvenile hooliganism,
thievery, debauchery, and vagrancy. The children's homes were
once again instructed to send all children over the age of 14 to
technical schools, factories, *sovkhozes, kolkhozes,* or machine tractor stations. The heads of these enterprises were directed to
accept "unconditionally" all children and to provide them with
wages and housing. The chairman of the town or village Soviet
was given direct responsibility for the orphans in his district; he
would be personally liable for any children that remained on the
streets. The militia was told to respond strictly to street hooliganism, public fighting, or any interference with passersby. Children's homes, no matter how overcrowded, no longer had the
right to deny needy children admittance. Parents were made
liable for 200 ruble fines and damages for juvenile hooliganism
or mischief committed by their children.[81] If parents failed to
supervise their children, the state had the right to remove the
child and place him or her in a children's home at parental
expense. All republic, regional, and local procurators were instructed to appoint special procurators for juvenile cases.[82]

Jurists and criminologists now targeted family disintegration
as the primary source of juvenile crime. Claiming that crime was
no longer motivated by poverty or social conditions, officials
sought to make parents responsible for their children's behavior
by establishing repressive measures to enforce responsibility.
V. Tadevosian, the USSR deputy procurator for juvenile affairs,
righteously announced that in the Soviet Union, "where life has
become better and gayer, where the material and cultural level
of the workers is raised to new heights – in such a country there
is no basis and cannot be a basis for *besprizornost'* and crime."
"Material need and poverty are no longer the basic reasons for

[81] *Sbornik 1936*, pp. 7–11.
[82] V. Tadevosian, "Voprosy Protsessa po Delam Nesovershennoletnikh," *SZ*, 10 (1936): 19.

crime," he declared.[83] Another criminologist admonished sternly, "One of the basic reasons for juvenile crime – *besprizornost'*
and *beznadzornost'* – is the lack of responsibility among parents
and guardians for the upbringing of their children . . . and frequently, the direct instigation of children by adults to thievery,
beggary, and dissolution." Parents were hauled into court along
with their children and sentenced to prison. One drunken father was sentenced to five years for abandoning his son and
ignoring the boy's petty thievery. In another case, in which a
Party member's son was caught stealing, the court promptly informed his cell of his "indifferent attitude toward his child."[84]

Tadevosian linked women's entrance into the labor force with
beznadzornost' and called for the constant supervision of teenagers in organized after-school activities. "Hanging around in
the streets," in his view, was one of the major causes of juvenile
crime. Citing a study of juvenile offenders in Moscow and
Leningrad, he argued that 90% "spent time in an unorganized
way," loitering in courtyards, markets, and the streets.[85] Nakhimson, citing the same study, reiterated that juvenile crime
was not the result of poverty.[86] Ia. Berman, chairman of the
Supreme Court, wrote a lead article in *Sotsialisticheskaia iustitsiia*
castigating the courts for ignoring parental irresponsibility and
the needs of children. He linked the neglect of children to the
courts' loose attitude toward alimony cases, claiming that fully 80
percent of court awards were never paid. Berman called for
increased penalties for parental negligence and more vigorous
prosecution of adults who involved children in crime. He omi-
nously declared, "The threat of repression, the threat of punishment and its proper application should be strong supplementary weapons in the Party's struggle for the elimination of the
survivals of the old capitalist society."[87]

Leading jurists denounced Komones and its parent organiza-

[83] V. Tadevosian, "God Zakona 7 Aprelia 1935 g.," p. 7; Tadevosian,
"Prestupnaia Sreda i Pravonarusheniia Nesovershennoletnikh," *SIu*,
31 (1935): 11.
[84] V. G. "V Bor'be za Likvidatsiiu Beznadzornosti i Besprizornosti Detei," p. 9.
[85] Tadevosian, "Prestupnaia Sreda i Pravonarusheniia Nesovershennoletnikh," pp. 9–10.
[86] "V Gosudarstvennom Institute Ugolovnoi Politiki," p. 18.
[87] Ia. Berman, "Sud na Okhrane Detei," *SIu*, 23 (1935): 1–2.

tion, the Commissariat of Enlightenment, for their "liberal, jelly-like attitude toward juvenile crime," for their "putrid view that children must not be punished." Tadevosian strictly instructed the courts about their new role in trying juvenile cases. The pedagogical methods of Komones, he explained, were based on "the hypocritical principles of the liberal bourgeoisie."[88] Komones's work with juveniles was "useless," "an endless study of social life and toothless admonitions to children and parents." Under no conditions were the people's courts to repeat the mistakes of Komones by sentencing juveniles to "pedagogical measures." They were to obey the April law and sentence the children as adults.[89]

Despite Tadevosian's harsh injunction to replace pedagogy with punishment, judges frequently balked at sentencing minors as adults. Schooled in the progressive pedagogical climate of the 1920s, many wondered, "How can we punish children?" Consequently, they often sentenced juvenile offenders to short or probational terms. Tadevosian took an especially harsh line toward these "liberal opportunist 'defenders' of children," charging that they "discredited the courts and revived the practices of Komones."[90]

Yet the judges were hampered in their mandate to carry out the April law not only by their humane "Komones-like" reservations, but by many of the same problems that had stymied Komones in the first place. Short of sending children to prison, the April law did little to expand the judges' options. Judges frequently remanded juvenile offenders to parents who worked full time, lived in communal apartments, and were clearly unable to keep their children off the streets.[91] There were simply not enough children's homes, labor colonies, reform schools, and corrective institutions to fill the need. The *kollektors*, designed as temporary waystations for teenagers after sentencing, quickly became prisons. And while the May law stated that par-

---

[88] Tadevosian, "Voprosy Protsessa po Delam Nesovershennoletnikh," pp. 19–21.

[89] V. Tadevosian, "Bor'ba s Prestupleniiami Nesovershennoletnikh," *SZ*, 11 (1935): 4.

[90] Tadevosian, "Bor'ba s Prestupleniiami Nesovershennoletnikh," p. 6; Mashkovskaia, "O Metodakh Bor'by s Detskoi Prestupnost'iu," *SZ*, 4 (1936): 15.

[91] Mashkovskaia, pp. 15, 16.

ents should pay for their children's internment in a state facility, the vast majority of parents of juvenile offenders simply could not afford the 250 rubles per month it cost to maintain a child in such a facility.[92] In some areas, judges sentenced up to half of juvenile offenders to "probational deprivation of freedom," a sentence that had no consequences whatsoever.[93]

The April and May laws marked the final leg of a long retreat from socialized upbringing, yet they also represented a qualitatively new approach to *besprizornost'* and juvenile crime. Frustrated by Komones's revolving door, fearful of the new, potentially explosive mix of *besprizornost'* and *beznadzornost'*, and impatient with the financial drain imposed by the children's homes, the Party had by 1935 finally discovered an inexpensive institution with a seemingly limitless capacity for homeless children and juvenile delinquents: prison camps. In a sharp break with the pedagogical and rehabilitative ideals of the revolution, the Party designated the family, along with the militia, the courts, and the procuracy, to enforce social order on the streets. Far from withering away, the family was becoming an indispensable unit in the state's control of its citizenry.

The crackdown on men

The growing use of repression against *besprizornost'*, juvenile crime, and parental irresponsibility, was linked to a strong campaign on the issue of alimony. Newspapers and journals publicly shamed men who took advantage of women, Party officials called for stricter penalties for nonpayment of alimony, and jurists exposed court procedures as overly bureaucratic, formalistic, and detrimental to the interests of women and children. In an extraordinary burst of attention to the alimony problem, researchers undertook several detailed studies of the people's courts, demonstrating in no uncertain terms that women's complaints throughout the 1920s and early 1930s were amply justified.[94]

---

[92] Bezrukova, "Bor'ba s Detskoi Prestupnost'iu v Leningrade," *SZ*, 4 (1936): 14, 15.
[93] V. Tadevosian, "God zakona 7 Aprelia 1935 g.," *SZ*, 4 (1936): 10.
[94] See for example, Ingel', "Praktika Orekhovo-Zuevskogo Narsuda po Alimentnym Delam," *SIu*, 32 (1935): 12–13. Alimony made up a sig-

In Zapadnyi *oblast'*, the courts heard 11,485 cases of alimony in 1935, roughly 20 percent of all civil cases. About 65 percent (7,465) of the alimony cases involved suits for child support. Almost one-third of these were filed by mothers returning to court because their husbands refused to pay. In more than one-quarter of the alimony cases, the study found that the judges made awards based on superficial knowledge of the financial standing of the defendant and the plaintiff. Many awards were too small to support a child, and worse, cases took a long time to be processed: More than half took a month or more, while some dragged on for almost a year. After the judge rendered a decision, the waiting period continued as the judge transferred the order to the bailiff.[95]

Another study, undertaken by the representatives of OMM, showed that the court orders were frequently lost by accountants in workplaces or even stolen by the defendants. In the factory Red Profintern, the finance department was unable to determine how many of its workers were subject to salary deductions for alimony. They rarely had the ex-wives' correct addresses and frequently withheld less than the full sum from the defendants' wages.[96] A study of the Moscow courts in 1933 noted that prosecutors considered alimony cases too "petty" to merit attention and were often guilty of "bureaucratic heartlessness." Here too about one-quarter of the court decisions were never carried out, clerks at the workplace lost the lists, and few sanctions were enacted against nonpayment.[97]

The problems women faced in the mid-thirties were quite similar to those of a decade earlier. Yet by 1935, jurists attached a new "political significance" to alimony. The study on Zapadnyi *oblast'* harshly concluded: "The shocking attitudes of the people's courts must be quickly eliminated. Once more it is necessary to warn the courts that every manifestation of bureaucratism and

nificant fraction of the cases considered by the local courts. In 1935 in Orekhova-Zuevskii *raion*, for example, an area with many women textile workers, there were 5,000 alimony cases constituting fully one-third of all cases considered by the people's courts that year.

95 Gromov, "Sudebnaia Praktika po Alimentnym Delam Trebuet Reshitel'noi Perestroiki," *SIu*, 12 (1936): 8.

96 Ibid.

97 L. Otmar-Shtein, "Bol'she Aktivnosti i Energii v Bor'be za Interesy Detei," *SIu*, 9 (1935): 12–13.

red tape, lack of attention to the interests of mothers and children . . . will be decisively stopped and considered proof of a lack of discipline and undervaluation of the political significance of alimony cases." The Moscow study recommended that workplace accountants who delayed or interfered with the correct and speedy deduction of alimony be criminally liable.[98]

Beginning in 1934, pressures mounted on the courts to eliminate red tape and to prosecute nonpayers. In May, the All-Union Procurator sent angry letters to the local procurators charging that their approach to alimony cases was characterized by "inappropriate indulgence and spinelessness."[99] A year later, in June 1935, the Commissariat of Justice sent out a circular urging prosecutors to review alimony cases carefully. It solemnly warned, "A liberal policy toward people who do not pay alimony and indulgence toward them by the workers of justice is completely insupportable."[100]

Hostility toward men who refused to pay alimony was increasingly expressed in public. *Sotsialisticheskaia iustitsiia* published the name of a Party secretary in Sverdlovsk *oblast'* who had abandoned his wife and three children in 1933 and then ignored the court order to support them. The journal condemned his "heartless bureaucratic attitude toward children."[101] Numerous other articles denounced men in important positions by name for similar offenses.[102] One writer urged that men who used and abandoned women, treated them with contempt, or subjected them to public humiliation be tried for "sexual hooliganism." In a radically feminist redefinition of criminal behavior, he argued that men who showed "contempt for the personhood of women" be criminally liable. Male promiscuity, in his view, was a form of "sexual hooliganism" because it denied women their

---

[98] Gromov, p. 8. Otmar-Shtein, p. 12.

[99] S. Fainblit, "Dela Alimentnye," *Za sotsialisticheskuiu zakonnost'*, 12 (1934): 36. See also N. Lagovier, "Prokurorskii Nadzor po Alimentnym Delam," *SZ*, 5 (1936).

[100] "Tsyrkuliary NKIu," *SIu*, 20 (1935): 25.

[101] "Signaly s Mect," *SIu*, 32 (1935): 17.

[102] Livshits, "Rebenok – v Tsentre Vnimaniia Sovetskoi Obshchestvennosti," *SIu*, 24 (1935): 8; I. Rostovskii, "Na Bor'bu s Narushiteliami Prav Materi i Rebenka, s Dezorganizatorami Sem'i," *SIu*, 26 (1936): 16; "20 Mesiachnaia Volokita," *Pravda* (January 8, 1935): 4; "V Zashchity Prav Materi i Rebenka," *SIu*, 12 (1935):16.

"human dignity" by treating them solely as "bed partners."
"Means of compulsion" were available for men who did not respond to cultural persuasion and education.[103]

Although there is no evidence that this proposal was ever
considered seriously, a Commissariat of Justice committee,
headed by Krylenko, developed and presented a plan to SNK to
increase the punishment for nonpayment of alimony from six
months of compulsory labor to a year in prison, to mark the
alimony obligation in the defendant's passport, and to hold the
administration at the defendant's workplace answerable for nonpayment.[104] In a debate over the plan at the Institute of Criminal Policy, F. E. Niurina, the Deputy Procurator of the RSFSR,
supported the suggested changes, arguing that "the current
legislation is extraordinarily convenient for individuals who
maliciously refuse to pay alimony." She noted that there were
more than 200,000 court cases of nonpayment in 1934 alone.
Vyshinskii, ever the enthusiastic proponent of punitive solutions, added that only "threats of severe punishment" could
change social behavior. "We must strike the shirkers on their
hides," he declared. "We must show that Soviet power is not
fooling around." Other jurists disagreed, arguing that it was
pointless to raise the penalty from compulsory labor to a prison
term, because an imprisoned father could do very little to support his wife and children. Others suggested revoking the provision in the 1926 Family Code that permitted divorce without
mutual consent. One jurist observed that the most effective measure against the nonpayment of alimony was to limit the number
of times an individual could divorce.[105] Several suggestions were
reminiscent of the proposals made by women and peasants in
the debates of 1925–1926.[106]

The Supreme Court, influenced by the increasingly repressive
climate, ruled in July 1935 that parents who maliciously neglected their children should be sentenced to prison.[107] In
March 1936, the Presidium of the Supreme Court sent a letter to

[103] K. Pletnikov, "Na Zashchitu Zhenshchiny ot Izdevatel'stva," *SZ*, 11
(1935): 29–30.
[104] Livshits, "Rebenok – v Tsentre Vnimaniia Sovetskoi Obshchestvennosti," p. 8.
[105] "Izmenenie Zakonov ob Alimentakh," *SIu*, 29 (1935): 20.
[106] See Chapter 6 on the debate over the 1926 Code.
[107] "Postanovlenie Prezidiuma Verkhsuda RSFSR ot 11 iiulia 1935 g. o
Mere Nakazaniia po ch. 2, st. 158 UK v Sviazi s Delom po Obvi-

the courts demanding that they compile quarterly reports reviewing the status of all alimony cases and the competence of the judges and bailiffs. It requested the NKVD to ensure that ZAGS sent its paternity declarations and information on contested divorces to the courts. The NKVD was charged with finding those men who did not pay alimony and bringing them to court. The courts were told to take a second look at all alimony and paternity cases in which the mother was denied an award. Workplaces were to review systematically court orders to guarantee that the proper sum was being deducted from the defendant's wages.[108]

The June 1936 law

The campaign against male irresponsibility culminated several months later in an explosion of profamily propaganda surrounding a draft of a new law. It was designed to increase the penalties for nonpayment of alimony, make divorce more difficult, prohibit abortion, and expand the number of childcare facilities. Published on the front page of *Pravda* on May 26 and widely distributed in pamphlet form, the new legislation promised to "struggle with a frivolous attitude toward the family and family responsibility."[109]

The proposed law prohibited abortion unless the woman's health was endangered. Doctors who performed the operation could be sentenced to two years in prison, nonmedical abortionists to more than three years. Anyone who forced a woman to get an abortion was subject to two years in prison. Women themselves were liable to social censure for the first offense, and to a 300 ruble fine for the second. The new law also granted an increase in the insurance stipend for birth, and doubled the monthly payment to employed mothers of infants from 5 to 10 rubles a month. It provided similar supports for uninsured working mothers, and it granted almost four months of preg-

neniiu Kashtanova i dr.," *SIu*, 23 (1935): 6–7; "Rech' Zam. Prokurora Respubliki T. Niurinoi," same issue, pp. 2–5.

[108] "Sudebnaia Praktika," *SIu*, 19 (1936): 23.

[109] *Proekt Postanovleniia TsIK i SNK Soiuza SSR o zapreshchenii abortov, uvelichenii material'noi pomoshchi rozhenitsam, ustanovlenii gosudarstvennoi pomoshchi mnogosemeinym, rasshirenii seti rodil'nykh domov, detskikh iaslei, detskikh sadov, usilenii ugolovnogo nakazaniia za neplatezh alimentov i o nekotorykh izmeneniiakh v zakonodatel'stve o razvodakh* (1936).

nancy leave to *sluzhashchie* as well as workers. It established criminal penalties for employers who refused to hire a pregnant
woman or lowered her pay, and it allowed a pregnant woman to
perform less strenuous work at her former salary level. To every
mother with seven children or more, it granted 2,000 rubles for
five years for every child born thereafter. Mothers with eleven
children were to receive 5,000 rubles per additional child for
one year and 3,000 rubles for the next four years. The draft
further expanded the number of maternity clinics, daycare centers, creches, and milk kitchens.

In addition to its pronatalist measures, the draft ended the
ubiquitous practice of postcard divorce, requiring both spouses
to appear in ZAGS and have the divorce noted in their passports.
It increased the cost of divorce to 50 rubles for the first divorce,
150 rubles for the second, and 300 rubles for the third. It set
minimum levels of child support at one-third of the defendant's
salary for one child, 50 percent for two children, and 60 percent
for three or more. It also increased the penalty for nonpayment
to up to two years in prison.

Unlike the debates over the 1926 Code, discussion of the draft
lasted less than a month and was carefully orchestrated from
above. The "discussion," punctuated by paeans of praise for the
Party for permitting open debate, contrasted sharply with the
debate in 1925–1926, which was marked by an absence of self-
congratulation and an abundance of sharp, spirited exchange.
Krylenko, for example, righteously intoned, "Only a government deeply believing in unity with the people and the rectitude
and correctness of the measures it suggests could allow itself this
route of direct involvement of the masses in legislative work."
His comments were typical of the many who prefaced every
declaration with elaborate praise for Stalin and the Party.[110]

The actual "debate" among jurists and Party leaders was
stilted and confined to carefully worded pronouncements in favor of the proposed law. The people who had distinguished
themselves by their openness, passion, and wit in the 1920s, now
fearfully hastened to repeat formulaic phrases that came from
above. They constructed contorted explanations of the differences between the "bourgeois" and "socialist" prohibition of

[110] *Na shirokoe obsuzhdenie trudiashchikhsia* (Moscow, 1936): 4. See other
articles in this collection for similar comments.

abortion. An early article by Lenin opposing Malthus was unearthed to provide the necessary quotations. The jurist A. Lisitsyn explained that abortion was no longer needed in the Soviet Union because conditions were so propitious for raising children. Tadevosian, too, noted socialism's great economic advances over capitalism and wondered with false incredulity, "Is it possible to suggest that workers could refuse to have children? There is no basis for such a suggestion."[111]

Officials lectured on the joys of children, parental and patriotic pride, upward mobility, and the happiness of the worker-mother. The rocketing rate of abortion and the plummeting birthrate received scarcely a mention. In a rare reference to the birthrate, Sol'ts noted, "Our life becomes more gay, more happy, rich and satisfactory. But the appetite, as they say, comes with the meal. Our demands grow from day to day. We need new fighters – they built this life. We need people." Sol'ts explained to Soviet women that motherhood, "a great and honorable duty," was not only their "private affair, but an affair of great social significance." In a shameful retreat from his earlier sensitivity to women's hardships, he praised "the great happiness of maternity" and insisted that women deserved strict punishment for abortion.[112]

Krylenko observed that the abortion law had two purposes: "to protect the health" of women and "to safeguard the rearing of a strong and healthy younger generation." Reprovingly, he told women, "The basic mistake in every case is made by those women who consider 'freedom of abortion' as one of their civil rights." And Krasikov, deputy chairman of the Supreme Court, scaled the pinnacle of hypocrisy with his suggestion that poverty and cramped housing could no longer justify abortion because the maternity stipends and daycare centers allotted by the new law could rightfully be viewed as salary increases and an extension of housing space. Deputy Procurator Niurina spoke of Stakhanovite work in the area of motherhood; Vyshinskii, Berman, Vinokurov, and other jurists expressed similar opinions.[113]

[111] "Obsuzhdaet Zakonoproekt," *SIu*, 17 (1936): 2, 3.
[112] Ibid., p. 4.
[113] See the discussion among jurists in "Rabotniki Iustitsii! Aktivno Uchastvuite v Obsuzhdenii Zakonoproekta," *SIu*, 18 (1936): 1–4 for views similar to Krylenko's.

Tadevosian was among the few jurists who took issue with the new law. Although he publicly opposed abortion, he spoke out against making it a criminal offense, arguing that educational measures against abortion were sufficient. More important, he claimed that the state should not "compel a woman to bear children by 'force.'" Abortion could only be curtailed by increasing the standard of living and the availability of child care. He alone honestly acknowledged that the housing shortage limited women's ability to have large families. As deputy procurator of juvenile affairs, Tadevosian was acutely aware that unwanted and neglected children abounded and that forbidding abortion would only swell their numbers.[114]

Discussion of the new law was slightly freer among workers, peasants, housewives, students, and other groups holding less important social positions. Although their contribution had little or no impact on the ultimate adoption of the legislation, many critical letters were printed in *Pravda* alongside the more propagandistic pieces favoring the legislation. Predictably, a good number of letters extolled the happiness of large families. The workers from Trekhgornia textile factory, for example, sent a letter describing the discussions over the proposed law on the shop floor. Their letter, fairly typical in its cozy, joking tone, read: "Comrades hurried to congratulate the carpenter Semechkin, the father of eight children. But he is not alone. Vorobeva had seven children. And there are many in the factory who have five or six. They say, 'Don't worry, we're still catching up.'"[115] Many women testified to the horrors of abortion and the personal joys of motherhood. They wrote how abortion had ruined their health, how happy they were to have refused abortion, how terrible life was before the Revolution, and how wonderful it was to raise children in Soviet society.[116]

Yet women also debated whether it was possible to be the mother of a large family and still contribute to social and politi-

[114] Ibid., pp. 2, 3.
[115] "Trekhgorka Golosuet," *Pravda* (May 27, 1936): 2.
[116] See for example, "Ia Mat' Chetyrekh Detei," "Odobriaiu Zapreshchenie Abortov," "Kak Ia Stala Invalidom," "I Za I Protiv," *Pravda* (May 27, 1936): 2; "Istoriia Abortov," "Predlozheniia Kalininskikh Tkachikh" (May 28, 1936): 2; "Berite Primer s Menia," (May 29, 1936): 4; "Govorit Sovetskaia Mat'" (May 30, 1936): 4; "Otvet Nine Ershovoi" (May 31, 1936): 3.

cal life. Although a few letters argued that it was possible to do both, others contended that abortion was necessary if women were to study, work, and take an equal place in society with men. Many women described the painful conflicts between work and motherhood in highly familiar, modern terms.[117] One young woman wrote that students needed the right to abortion: "Only those who do not know the condition of student life can declare that it is possible to combine maternity and studies in the institute without problems. It is especially impossible when husband and wife live at different ends of town in different dormitories."[118] Twenty-one students from the Moscow Energy Institute wrote that "women lose their full freedom" if forced to give birth against their will.[119] Women workers suggested that abortion should be available to women with large families, limited incomes, or crowded apartments. Another letter proposed that single women have access to abortion because a child might limit their chances to marry and build productive lives. And one young woman boldly essayed that when the country had laundries, daycare, ready-made children's clothes, and decent shoes, then "it will be possible to think about larger families."[120] Taken together, the letters suggested that there was considerable support for legal abortion for women with large families, students, single women, poor women, women in crowded apartments, and women with important posts; in short for almost any Soviet woman who found herself with an unwanted pregnancy.

Although many women disagreed with the prohibition of abortion, they strongly supported the more stringent measures on divorce and alimony and the expansion of childcare facilities. The women of Trekhgornia textile factory suggested that men who refused to pay alimony "should be forced to dig canals and build houses"; alimony payment would be deducted from their

[117] See *Pravda*, "Zhenshchina-Obshchestvennitsa" (June 5, 1936): 4; "Mnenie Znatnoi Traktoristki" (June 7, 1936): 3; "Neskol'ko Predlozhenii k Zakonoproektu o Zapreshchenii Abortov" (June 16, 1936): 4.
[118] "Studentke-Materi Nuzhny L'goty" *Pravda* (June 6, 1936): 4.
[119] "Chto Tolkaet Zhenshchinu na Abort" *Pravda* (June 1, 1936): 4.
[120] See *Pravda*, "Uchityvat' Ne Tol'ko Zdorov'e no i Semeinoe Polozhenie" (June 4, 1936): 3; "Ogranichit' Prava Aborta," "Kak Obespechit' Vzyskanie Alimentov" (June 1, 1936): 4; "Chto Meshaet Obzavestis' Sem'ei" (June 30, 1936): 4.

wages for compulsory labor. Two women technicians wrote, "The father who does not want to fulfill his paternal responsibilities is a destroyer of the family." Other letters suggested that the fees for divorce should be even higher than those proposed, and that divorce should be returned from ZAGS to the courts.[121] Women approved the idea of strengthening the family if it meant increasing the responsibility of men toward their wives and children.

In a park in Red Presnaia in Moscow, a district with a long history of working-class militancy, a woman worker in a public discussion of the 1936 law, yelled out, "Destroy all the men and everything will be in order."[122] The state drew upon this deep fount of bitterness to justify the resurrection of the family. The 1936 law offered women a tacit bargain: It broadened both state and male responsibility for the family, but in exchange it demanded that women assume the double burden of work and motherhood. The idea that the state would assume the functions of the family was abandoned. The new bargain was possible precisely because of women's painful experiences – in the 1920s and in the new Soviet industrial revolution – with the disintegration of the family. Although it satisfied certain social needs, it also marked the beginning of the state's abdication of social responsibility and the double burden that Soviet women bear today. Ultimately, this bargain, which has comfortably accommodated both men and the state, has left women with the lion's share of responsibility for work, shopping, housework, and child care.

[121] See *Pravda*, "Trekhogorka Golosuet," and "Polnoe Zapreshchenie Aborta – Nepravil'no" (May 27, 1936): 2; "O Posobnikakh Zlostnym Neplatel'shchikam Alimentov" (May 28, 1936): 2; "Kak Dolzhen Proiskhodit' Razvod" (June 8, 1936): 3.
[122] Livshits, "Rebenok – V Tsentre Vnimaniia Sovetskoi Obshchestvennosti," p. 8.

Conclusion
Stalin's oxymorons:
Socialist state, law, and family

> We should not aspire to a highly stable family and look at marriage
> from that angle. Strengthening marriage and the family – making di-
> vorce more difficult – is not new, it is old: it is the same as bourgeois
> law.[1]
>
> *Iakov Brandenburgskii, arguing before*
> *the VTsIK in 1925*

> These "theories" were reflected also in denial of the socialist charac-
> ter of Soviet law, in attempts to portray Soviet law as bourgeois law – as
> law resting on the same bourgeois principles and expressing the same
> social relationships inherent in the bourgeois order. These persons trod
> the well worn path of Trotskyite–Bukharinist perversions. . .
>
> *Andrei Ia. Vyshinskii, 1948*[2]

In the two decades between 1917 and 1936, the official Soviet
view of the family underwent a complete reversal. Beginning
with a fierce, libertarian commitment to individual freedom and
"the withering away" of the family, the period ended with a
policy based on a repressive strengthening of the family unit.
Similar shifts occurred in the ideology of the state and the law as
the Party systematically eliminated the libertarian currents in
Bolshevik thought. A legal understanding of crime based on
social causation and rehabilitation yielded to a new emphasis on
personal culpability and punishment. Open intellectual exchange gave way to fearful caution, honest debate to a stiff,
brittle mockery of discussion. By 1936, newspapers trumpeted

---

[1] *Stenograficheskii otchet zasedaniia 2 sessii Vserossiiskogo Tsentral'nogo Ispolnitel'nogo Komiteta, 12 sozyva. 20 oktiabria 1925 goda* (Moscow, 1925):
146.
[2] Andrei Y. Vyshinsky. *The Law of the Soviet State* (Macmillan, New York,
1948): 53.

support for a strong socialist family, elaborate legal codes, and a powerful state. The concepts of socialist family, law, and state, more reminiscent of Constantine Pobedonostsev than Marx, had become the new holy trinity of the Party.

The shifts in ideology occurred unevenly and often in a contradictory fashion. The abolition of the Zhenotdel in 1930 eliminated an important center of ideas and activities promoting women's interests. Weakened by a lack of support and funding through the 1920s, the Zhenotdel had already lost much of its power by the end of the decade.[3] Yet despite its weakness, the organization had planned and made possible such meetings as the 1927 Women's Congress, which brought hundreds of working-class and peasant women together to criticize men, the Party, and the state, to explore the sources of their oppression, and to discuss their ideas for change. Richard Stites notes that the abolition of the Zhenotdel marked "the end of the Proletarian Women's Movement."[4]

At precisely the same time that the Zhenotdel was disbanded, however, the first five-year plan revived early ideas of women's emancipation and the "withering away" of the family. Many Party activists, prompted by women's entrance into the workforce, enthusiastically took up the causes of daycare, socialized dining, and women's liberation from household responsibilities. In the legal arena, a group of jurists led by Krylenko, drafted a new "minimalist" criminal code in 1930 designed to undercut the foundations of law. The draft contained no sanctions against juvenile crime, and strongly emphasized social motives for criminal behavior and "socially oriented preventative and readaptive measures" in lieu of punishment.[5]

Stalin's speech to the Sixteenth Party Congress in 1930 typified the contradictory combination of retreat and revolutionary revival. Still adhering to the eventual "withering away" of the state, he articulated a new dialectic of state power. "We are for

---

[3] Richard Stites, *The Women's Liberation Movement in Russia. Feminism, Nihilism, and Bolshevism, 1860–1930* (Princeton University Press, Princeton, N.J., 1978); Carol Eubanks Hayden, "The Zhenotdel and the Bolshevik Party," *Russian History*, 3, II (1976).

[4] Stites, p. 344.

[5] John Hazard, "The Abortive Codes of the Pashukanis School," in F. J. M. Feldbrugge, *Codification in the Communist World* (A. W. Sijthoff, Leiden, 1975): 160.

the withering away of the state. And we are also for the strengthening of the dictatorship of the proletariat. . . . The highest development of state power with the aim of preparing for the withering away of state power – here is the Marxist formula. Is this a 'contradiction?' Yes it is a 'contradiction.'"[6]

Yet by the end of the first five-year plan, policy began to veer sharply away from the "withering-away" doctrine. In 1932, Vyshinskii published a call for firm, centralized control of the judiciary and a new stability of law. In stark opposition to Pashukanis and his followers, he argued that law would achieve its fullest expression under socialism, not under capitalism as the commodity exchange school had maintained.[7] In 1933, the establishment of the All-Union Procuracy provided a strong centralized power base for Vyshinskii and his ideas. The plurality of legal opinions and journals disappeared. Vyshinskii viciously attacked Pashukanis at the Seventeenth Party congress in 1934 for "legal nihilism."[8] Vyshinskii's appointment as Procurator General in March 1935 constituted a clear triumph over Krylenko, the Russian commissar of justice and a proponent of the "withering-away" doctrine in law.[9]

[6] I. V. Stalin as quoted in *Sovetskoe gosudarstvo*, 9–10 (1930) on frontispiece of volume.

[7] A. Vyshinskii, "Revoliutsionnaia Zakonnost' i Nashi Zadachi," *Pravda*, (June 28, 1932): 2. On Vyshinskii's article as a turning point, see Eugene Huskey, *Russian Lawyers and the Soviet State. The Origins and Development of the Soviet Bar, 1917–1939* (Princeton University Press, Princeton, N.J., 1986): 180, and "From Legal Nihilism to Pravovoe Gosudarstvo: Soviet Legal Development, 1917–1990," forthcoming in volume edited by Donald Barry. Legal historians differ as to when the Party officially abandoned the withering-away doctrine in favor of strong socialist law. Huskey pinpoints Vyshinskii's article and Sovnarkom's accompanying decree as signals for the turn, Hazard cites Stalin's 1930 speech to the Sixteenth Party Congress, and Peter Solomon points to Stalin's secret directive in May 1933 halting deportation of the *kulaks* and chastizing local officials for excesses. See Hazard, p. 166; Peter Solomon, "Local Political Power and Soviet Criminal Justice, 1922–1941," *Soviet Studies*, 37, no. 3 (1985): 313.

[8] Robert Sharlet, "Pashukanis and the Withering-Away of Law in the USSR," in Fitzpatrick, ed., *Cultural Revolution in Russia, 1928–1931* (Indiana University Press, Bloomington, 1984); and his "Stalinism and Soviet Legal Culture," in Robert Tucker, ed., *Stalinism. Essays in Historical Interpretation* (Norton, New York, 1977).

[9] Huskey, *Russian Lawyers and the Soviet State*, p. 185.

By the spring of 1935, the shift in policy toward law and the family was inscribed in new laws designed to use the family to counter juvenile crime. Vyshinskii succeeded in destroying and impugning Komones, the Commission on the Affairs of Minors , the Procuracy gained vast new powers over juvenile crime, and the Party spearheaded a campaign to enforce alimony and child support awards. Jurists, once highly sensitive to the social causes of *besprizornost'*, abortion, and juvenile crime, now justified repression with the facile, even cynical claim that conditions had improved.

By 1938, Vyshinskii branded the legal theories of the 1920s as "exceedingly crude perversions," produced "by a group of pseudo Marxists who have spared no effort to litter our juridical literature with pseudo-scientific rubbish." He called Pashukanis "a spy and a wrecker" and claimed that Stuchka and other jurists "trod the well-worn path of Trotskyist-Bukharinist perversions."[10] Pashukanis and Krylenko were both arrested and shot in 1937. Alexander Goikhbarg, the idealistic author of the 1918 Family Code, and Aron Sol'ts, an active participant in the VTsIK debates in 1925 and 1926 who was also a high ranking member of the Central Control Commission and the Procuracy, were both committed to mental institutions. Many other participants in the debate over the Family Code, like Alexander Beloborodov, Aleksei Kiselev, and Pyotr Krasikov were murdered in prison between 1936 and 1939. Countless other jurists and activists disappeared into the camps.

By 1944, the reversal in family law was complete: the Family Edict of that year repudiated the remaining traces of the legislation of the 1920s by withdrawing recognition of de facto marriage, banning paternity suits, reintroducing the category of illegitimacy, and transferring divorce back to the courts. In Peter Juviler's words, the Family Edict sought to promote family stability "by sparing a man and his legal family the financial and emotional shocks that might arise from paternity and support suits."[11] The twenty year conflict between the legal wife and mistress over the income of the male wage earner was finally

[10] Vyshinskii, *The Law of the Soviet State*, pp. 38, 53.
[11] Peter Juviler, Henry Morton, *Soviet Policy Making. Studies of Communism in Transition* (Pall Mall, London, 1967): 33.

resolved in favor of the family. The most revolutionary provisions of the 1918 and 1926 Codes were all eradicated.

The roots of the reversal in family law go back to the 1920s. The legacy of Russian underdevelopment, the lack of state resources, the weight of a backward peasant economy, society, and traditions, the wartime devastation of the industrial base, unemployment, famine, and poverty all seriously undermined the early socialist vision. The *besprizorniki* played a crucial role in forcing the state, decree by decree, to abandon collective child rearing. Many of the suggestions offered by women and peasants in the 1920s – to limit divorce, enforce responsibility for alimony, and stop male promiscuity – were eventually taken up in Stalinist law and family policy. The harsh rhetoric of family responsibility undoubtedly found an appreciative audience.

Yet the state pursued its own agenda through the 1936 law, which was not necessarily shared by the Soviet population. Tadevosian admitted after World War II that "High fertility of the Soviet family was one of the socialist state's basic purposes in publishing the decree of June 27, 1936 on the banning of abortion."[12] Although women supported certain sections of the law, there is no evidence that Soviet women, living in overcrowded, makeshift rooms, juggling work and family, strained by the effort to outfit and feed their children, supported the prohibition on abortion. The pronatalist emphasis of the law, extolling families of seven or eight children, mocked social conditions and added immeasurably to the heavy burden of work and motherhood that women already bore.

Moreover, economic and social statistics suggest that repressive measures against irresponsible husbands and fathers were not the most effective way to protect women and children. Although men were undoubtedly irresponsible in their behavior toward their former wives and children, it did not follow that a worker's wages could support two families. Men could be forced to pay, but the sum was usually deducted at the expense of a second wife and family. Repression had limited social value in circumstances in which limited income, rather than personal culpability, determined the fate of families. Men undoubtedly

[12] Quoted in ibid., p. 32.

exacerbated women's suffering, but the individual male wage earner did not hold the key to women's liberation.

Finally, although material conditions played a crucial role in undermining the vision of the twenties, they were not ultimately responsible for its demise. One jurist wrote in 1939, "The insistence on the 'withering away' of the family was overturned by life itself."[13] Yet this was not entirely true. The juridical commitment to free union and the "withering away" of the family was sustained despite the adversities of NEP. Officials in the Commissariats of Land and Justice maintained a strong dedication to women's liberation in the countryside despite powerful peasant opposition. Jurists continued to push for the socialization of housework despite the lack of state resources. The ideological reversal of the 1930s was essentially political, not economic or material in nature, bearing all the marks of Stalinist policy in other areas. The 1936 law had roots in the popular and official critiques of the 1920s, but its means and ends constituted a sharp break with earlier patterns of thought, indeed with a centuries-long tradition of revolutionary ideas and practices.

Stalinist policy toward the family was a grotesque hybrid: Rooted in the original socialist vision, starved in the depleted soil of poverty, and ultimately deformed by the state's increasing reliance on repression. Yet the lineaments of the original vision could still be discerned in the hybrid of 1936. Unlike Nazi family policy, for example, Stalinist ideology never held that women's place was in the home. Despite the emphasis on a strong, stable family, the Party continued to encourage women to enter the workforce, and, moreover, continued to couch its appeals in the older rhetoric of women's liberation. Officials pursued aggressive policies aimed at training, promoting, and educating women, all of which were antithetical to fascism. And despite the new glorification of family, law, and state, Stalinist jurists never entirely disavowed the legislation of 1918 and 1926. They rejected its fundamental aim, namely to promote the "withering away" of the family, and they sanctioned the destruction of its authors, but they continued to claim a continuity between the legislation of the 1920s, 1930s, and 1940s. They still proudly

[13] M. Reikhel', "Voprosy Semeinogo Prava i Proekt Grazhdanskogo Kodeksa SSSR," *Problemy sotsialisticheskogo prava*, 2 (1939): 83.

maintained that socialism freed "tens of millions of working mothers for participation in production and social life."[14]

The tragedy of the reversal in ideology was not simply that it destroyed the possibility of a new revolutionary social order, although millions had suffered and died for precisely this. The tragedy was that the Party continued to present itself as the true heir to the original socialist vision. Cloaking its single-minded focus on production in the empty rhetoric of women's emancipation, it abandoned its promise to socialize household labor and to foster freer, more equal relations between men and women. And the greatest tragedy is that subsequent generations of Soviet women, cut off from the thinkers, the ideas, and the experiments generated by their own Revolution, learned to call this "socialism" and to call this "liberation."

[14] Reikhel, pp. 85, 84; S. Vol'fson, "Sem'ia v Sotsialisticheskom Gosudarstve," *Problemy sotsialisticheskogo prava*, 6 (1939): 39, 43; G. A., "Sem'ia i Brak v SSSR i v Kapitalisticheskikh Stranakh," *Sovetskaia iustitsiia*, 2 (1937): 29–33.

Index

abortion, 136, 168, 254, 255–64,
265, 266, 267, 268, 270, 273,
275, 277, 278, 279–81, 284–9,
290–9, 294, 295, 296, 331, 333–
5, 340, 341
  Decree of 1920 on, 255–7, 261,
  265, 291
  and doctors, 254, 260, 261, 262–3,
  264, 277–9, 281, 287–9, 331
  effects of birthrate on, 266, 288–
  95
  eligibility for, 261–3
  illegal, 254, 259, 280–8, 293–5
  and illegitimacy, 279
  and infection, 263, 284, 294
  medical procedure during, 263–4
  motivations for, 275–80
  prerevolutionary, 254–5
  profile of patients receiving, 265–
  75
  prohibition of, 291–5, 331–6, 341,
  342
  role of *babki* and midwives in, 255,
  257, 258, 264, 280–1, 284, 285,
  287, 288, 289, 295, 331
Abukomov decision (1922), 155,
194–6
adoption, 50, 52, 70, 73–4, 76, 97–
100, 193, 197, 205, 208, 210,
213, 308
alimony, 51–3, 56, 103, 109, 133–5,
145, 151, 157, 161, 162, 171,
173–6, 183, 184, 187, 188, 191–
5, 197, 204–8, 210–13, 218,
222, 223, 225, 228, 229, 233,
237–41, 245, 246, 250, 251, 252,
278, 291, 296–303, 304, 309,
327–32, 335, 336, 340, 341

awards, 138–42, 157, 161–2, 173–
6, 233, 298–9, 301–3, 328–9
  and Family Code of 1918, 51, 52,
  56
  and Family Code of 1926, 213, 300
  and 1936 decree, 291, 331–2,
  335–6
  and peasants, 139–40, 145, 151,
  157, 161–2, 173–6, 183, 194,
  197–8, 222–3, 237–41, 250–1
  problems with, 192–3, 301–4,
  328–31, 341–2
  procedures regarding, 299
  sociology of, 135–9, 300–4
  statistics on, 133–5, 300–1, 328
All-Russian Central Executive Committee (VTsIK), 1, 49, 55, 56,
65, 66, 75, 92, 98, 104, 152, 186,
203, 204, 211, 214, 215, 224,
225, 226, 229, 231, 233, 237,
238, 240, 241, 242–4, 246, 248,
297, 303, 306, 308, 337, 340
  VTsIK meeting of 1923, 203–4
  VTsIK meeting of 1925, 215, 225,
  231, 233, 240, 246
  VTsIK meeting of 1926, 224, 226,
  229, 233, 237, 238
All-Russian Congress of the Department of Peoples Education, 305
All-Russian Congress of the Department for the Social and Legal
Protection of Minors (1924), 80
All-Russian Congress for the Protection of Childhood (1919), 61–5
All-Union Congress of Women
Workers and Peasants (1927),
113, 115, 118, 124–6, 128, 131,
144, 177–9, 182, 184, 338

Soviet and East European Studies